A History of
Russian-Soviet Music

A HISTORY OF
RUSSIAN-SOVIET
MUSIC

By JAMES BAKST

ILLUSTRATED

GREENWOOD PRESS, PUBLISHERS
WESTPORT, CONNECTICUT

Library of Congress Cataloging in Publication Data

Bakst, James.
    A history of Russian-Soviet music.

    Reprint of the 1966 ed. published by Dodd,
Mead, New York.
    Bibliography: p.
    Includes index.
    1. Music--Russia--History and criticism.
2. Music--Russian Republic--History and criticism.
I. Title.
[ML300.B28 1977]   780'.947   76-55406
ISBN 0-8371-9422-9

Acknowledgment is made to *The Polish Institute of Arts and Sciences in America, Inc.* for permission to reprint the author's article *Music and Soviet Realism* which originally appeared in *The Polish Review,* Vol. vii, No. 1, Winter 1962, pp. 67–74.

Originally published in 1966 by Dodd, Mead & Company, New York

Reprinted with the permission of Dodd, Mead & Company

Reprinted in 1977 by Greenwood Press, Inc.

Library of Congress Catalog Card Number 76-55406

ISBN 0-8371-9422-9

Printed in the United States of America

Preface

Russian music (symphony, opera, and ballet) is an art of world-wide importance. Outside Russia, however, the historical, cultural, and esthetic aspects of Russian music have not been sufficiently explored. While there is hardly an area or style (medieval, renaissance, baroque, classical, romantic, and modern) in Western music which has not been studied thoroughly, the evolution of Russian music is little known in the Western world.

In the United States there is a growing interest in Russian culture and art. This book is designed for those who love music and want to know more about Russian music; it examines Russian music chronologically beginning with the founding of the Russian state in the ninth century and culminating with the present age of Soviet realism. Part One of the book deals with Russian music up to 1917; Part Two treats music in the Soviet period. The historical stages, the composers, and the musical styles characteristic of Russian music are clearly and carefully elaborated.

The author presents a picture of the development of Russian music from the historical and artistic points of view. The main emphasis is on Russian music beginning with Glinka and ending with the contemporary field. The discussion is based on the growth of social and artistic consciousness in nineteenth-century Russia and the influence of this awareness on the music of Russian composers, including Mussorgsky, Borodin, Rimsky-Korsakov, and Tchaikovsky.

The first chapter deals with musical culture in the Grand Duchy of Kiev, the City of Novgorod, and the Tsardom of Muscovy during the formation of a strong national state. The second chapter is devoted to the eighteenth century, in which Russian culture, spurred on by Peter the Great's reforms, was brought closer to the realm of Western influence. The vast problems involved in the development of a Russian musical art, in an autocratically governed country characterized by serfdom, are clarified. The close of the eighteenth century witnessed the beginning of liberal ideas in Russia which, in spite of the suppression of the revolutionary Decembrists in 1825, influenced Russian cultural and artistic life in the nineteenth century.

Many different trends were displayed during the nineteenth century. Russian music was influenced by Russian literature, folklore, and art. The author reveals the influence of the variety of social and cultural trends on the characterizations inherent in the music of Glinka and his successors. The development of Russian music in the nineteenth century does not lend itself to mechanical divisions. The processes underlying the evolution of Russian musical forms were influenced by Russian social and political conditions and were variously reflected by Russian composers. Rimsky-Korsakov, for example, composed the opera *The Golden Cockerel* in the same year that Scriabin composed the *Poem of Ecstasy*. These two compositions are musically and esthetically dissimilar but remain accurate reflections of the social and political conditions of the period.

The second main division of the book deals with Soviet music. The Soviets seek to demonstrate to the world the achievements of Russian composers of the past and the aims of contemporary Soviet composers. The chapters on the Marxist-Leninist philosophy of art and on Soviet Realism in music will acquaint the reader with the nature and objectives of Communist ideology in music. The discussion of Soviet music is based on what Soviet music critics and composers have said about Russian-Soviet music and on the author's evaluation.

Because this book is designed for the general student and reader, the author has avoided technical musical terminology, which is usually reserved for professional musicians, and has confined himself to simple musical details and explanations which can be appreciated by the reader.

Contents

PART TWO

Illustrations

Part One

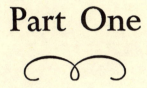

CHAPTER 1

Musical Culture in Ancient and Medieval Russia

Musical Culture in the Grand Duchy of Kiev

THE SLAV and Finnish tribes inhabiting the region between Lake Ladoga and the Dnieper's upper waters paid tribute to Northmen (Variags) from Rus, a region probably located in Sweden. In 859, the tribes freed themselves from the Northmen and then three years later, unable to settle their quarrels, invited the Northmen to come and rule over them. Three brothers, Ruric, Sineus, and Truvor, princes of Rus, accepted the invitation and founded, in 864, the Russian state with the City of Novgorod as its chief city. This is the story told by Nestor (1056–1114), one of the earliest Russian chroniclers and a monk of the Pechersky Cloister of Kiev.

According to Nestor, the City of Kiev was founded by three brothers named Kiy, Shcheck, and Khoriv. After their deaths, the Variags, Askold and Dir, followers of Rurik, seized Kiev. In 882, Rurik's successor, Oleg, conquered Kiev and made it the chief city of what became the Grand Duchy of Kiev.

The Grand Duchy of Kiev was formed from the consolidation of various eastern Slavic tribes, who united against the attacks of militant neighboring peoples, and attained its greatest power during the first half of the eleventh century. Its territory extended from the Black Sea to the Baltic Sea and from the upper Volga region to the Danube. It was a feudal state with a heterogeneous population. Although the various tribes were not firmly united, the new state formed the nucleus of the political and cultural development of the Russian people.

Under Prince Svyatoslav, who reigned from 964 to 972, the Grand

3

Duchy of Kiev became one of the most important states in medieval Europe. Kiev was visited by merchants and diplomatic guests from various countries. Painters, architects, and medieval scholars came there and were welcomed by the prince and the nobility.

The family of Prince Vladimir (956–1015) intermarried with leading European ruling families. Contacts between Kiev princes and Byzantine emperors were of great importance to the Grand Duchy, especially when the Greek orthodox church became, during 988 and 989, the official church of the Grand Duchy. Newly built churches and monasteries became centers of learning. The written language was not solely the privileged possession of the Russian clergy, however. Book knowledge was popular among the upper classes of the population. Russian chronicles record that Prince Yaroslav the Wise, who reigned from 1019 to 1054, was devoted to books and constantly read them. According to the chronicles, Yaroslav "assembled writers with whom he translated Greek books into the Slavic language so that believers would enjoy the divine teaching." Yaroslav's grandson, Vladimir Monomakh, who reigned from 1113 to 1125, was an outstanding writer who composed several important works.

The Kiev princes encouraged architecture and painting. Palaces and churches were symbols of the power and glory of the state. Inlaid pictures and frescoes, depicting religious and secular subjects, were popular. The most famous example of architecture in Kiev is the Cathedral of St. Sophia, which was built in the eleventh century.

Music was important in the daily life of Russian families. It was played during ceremonies, receptions, festivities, and hunts. It was a popular pastime in the homes of the Kiev nobility. Although the church did not approve of secular music, Russian aristocrats cultivated musical entertainments and supported singers and instrumental players. Some members of the nobility composed music in a style similar to that of Western troubadours.

The princely court in Kiev employed Russian and foreign musicians. The foreign musicians brought their own musical repertoire and manner of playing. The Russian chronicler describes the musical entertainment at a ceremonial reception by Prince Svyatoslav Yaroslavich: "Some emit *gusli* sounds; some sing organ sounds; others make *zamra* squeaks, and everyone enjoys himself, as it is customary, before the prince." [1]

Music was important at state functions. Military music was played at the departure of troops and during battles. Ancient Russian chronicles and poetic works mention trumpets and various percussion instruments. The church, which usually condemned all instruments connected with pagan customs and secular entertainments, recognized the trumpet. An ancient church precept states: "Just as a trumpet assembles warriors, during prayer it assembles heavenly angels, while *gusli* and *sopeli* assemble shameless devils."

The Christian Byzantine culture did not eradicate ancient pagan customs and representations. The masses and even the nobility retained many survivals from pagan times including traditional funeral feasts and lamentations. Ancient Russian chronicles contain the texts of lamentations used in princely families, which abound with metaphors and forms of popular versification. For example, an inconsolable widow is compared to a turtledove; the death of a friend is compared to the sunset.

The idea of national consciousness emerging in the Grand Duchy of Kiev was reflected in heroic and glorifying songs. A victorious outcome of a military expedition and the heroic deeds of warriors were described in songs, which were popular with the prince's troops, among whom military honor, courage, and devotion to duty were prized above everything. The authors of these songs were highly respected by the prince and his entourage as men possessing wisdom and keen insight.

Music in the Grand Duchy of Kiev was also developed by the "buffoons" or *skomorokhs*. The *skomorokh* was a skillful and resourceful artist, popular in all sections of medieval Russian society. He participated in every national festivity, and his presence was required at family celebrations. He is mentioned in Russian folk songs, proverbs, and adages. The word *skomorokh* is probably of Arabic origin, denoting laughter or ridicule.

The ancient Russian *bylinas* (epic songs) mention the *skomorokhs* at Prince Vladimir's banquet in Kiev where they occupied a place of honor at the table. They are represented on frescoes in the Cathedral of St. Sophia in Kiev and illuminated Russian manuscripts.

The orthodox church was not favorably disposed towards the *skomorokhs* and often issued condemnations and interdictions of them. The priests warned their congregations against the sinful plays of these buffoons which attracted the common people and left the churches empty. Church literature often identified a *skomorokh* with the devil, and their performances were likened to the temptations of Satan.

The *skomorokhs* were musicians, actors, dancers, animal trainers, acrobats, and magicians. They were creators of epic songs and tales. The Russian word which described a *skomorokh* was *umeltz*, that is, a versatile person. Their garb consisted of a short coat and narrow trousers.

The *skomorokhs'* art was national in character and can be traced to Slavic antiquity when they performed important functions in pagan rites and plays. They disguised themselves with masks, which were supposed to possess magic powers, and through the centuries became the symbols of buffoonery.

Many *skomorokhs* traveled around the country and were always welcomed by the people. They added the art of magic and miracle making to their work as musicians, actors, and entertainers. Despite their popularity, they did not have social rights and the protection of the law. Those who attached themselves to the household of a prince, however, were similar to Western minstrels and enjoyed the patron's protection.

Church singing was highly developed in the Grand Duchy of Kiev. The Russian princes invited Byzantine architects to build churches and musicians to contribute their art.

Russian church music was vocal, without instrumental accompaniment. The Byzantine monophonic style of music was of two types: one was an expressive narrative psalmody based on speech intonations; the other, usually used in hymns, was melodic and emotional.

The forms of Byzantine church singing were perfected in the eighth century and systematized in the *Octoechos* of the Greek church, compiled by St. John of Damascus. It is a liturgical book containing the stanzas and canons of the liturgy in the order of their tones and includes compositions of St. John and Byzantine composers.

During the Middle Ages, Russian church composers developed a style of "sign singing." The signs were inscriptions with specific meanings, written above the words of the text. Each syllable had a corresponding musical sign, which indicated a definite tone, a group of tones, or a short tune. The signs indicated the pitch, duration, dynamics, and expressive aspects of a performance.

In addition to sign singing, there existed in the Grand Duchy of Kiev *kondakarny* singing, heard with laudatory hymns or *kondaks*. It was characterized by melodic embellishments, chromaticisms, the modulating transition of modes, and virtuosity of performance. It was written down with specific signs which have not been deciphered.

Kondakarny singing was not popular among the masses of the Russian people. Its refined style was practiced by the educated segments of society in the eleventh and twelfth centuries. It appealed to an audience with a well-developed cultural background and flourished during the prosperous era of the Grand Duchy.

Kiev exercised a strong influence on the development of Russian national consciousness in the medieval period. For many centuries, the arts which developed there served as models in Russian states and principalities. In the second half of the eleventh century, the power of the Grand Duchy began to decline. The Grand Duke found it difficult to maintain his authority and the unity of the feudal principalities. The princes asserted their political independence and became involved in disputes for leadership.

As a result of these dissensions, the Grand Duke was powerless to repel sudden invasions by nomadic tribes in southern Russia. The Pechenyegs and the Polovtsy raided and devastated Russian principalities. The author of the Russian epic, *The Lay of Igor's Host,* wrote: "The struggle against the vile invaders ceased because a brother said to his brother 'this is mine and that is also mine.' And, while the princes regarded petty things as great things, vile people from every direction were victorious on Russian soil."

Kiev was divided into many independent principalities. Eventually there were formed three independent, but linguistically and culturally related, eastern Slavic nationalities. By the end of the thirteenth century, Great Russia emerged, including the northern regions of Vladimir, Rostov, and Novgorod. The southwestern regions formed Little Russia, and toward the end of the seventeenth century, the eastern regions constituted Belorussia, or White Russia.

Despite these divisions, the national sentiments which originated in the Grand Duchy of Kiev were kept alive in the consciousness of the people. The memories of Kiev's grandeur, of the wealth and courage of its princes, of princely entertainments, and of Russian military prowess lived in the minds of the masses. The result was the emergence of an heroic epos characterized by a feeling of pride in Russian nationalism. These epic songs, stories, and legends were called, in Russian nineteenth-century literature, *bylinas*. The word *bylina* is derived from the word *byl* (was), and it indicates the realistic, rather than the fairy tale, character of the heroic epos. Among the people, the performer of the bylinas was called *starina* or *starinka* (old man).

The imagery of the *bylinas,* encompassing the stories and events accumulated over several centuries, can be associated with historical persons and events. Dobrinya, for example, an uncle of Prince Vladimir, became the Dobrinya Nikitich of Russian folklore; Ilya Muromets is reminiscent of Prince Oleg; the fabulous snake Tugarin which ejects fire from its mouth is identified with the Polovetsian Khan Tugor. Many *bylinas* are stories about Prince Vladimir, known in folklore as "The Dear Bright Sun," and his heroic bodyguard.

The *bylinas* were preserved in northeastern Russia, which became the center of unification and the bulwark of the struggle against the invading Tatars from the east. Through the centuries, the individual characteristics of persons and events described in the epic songs were obscured. The heroes of the *bylinas* became stereotypes of persons possessing courage, resourcefulness, modesty, love of truth, pride, and independence. The narrative is characterized by smoothness and solemnity. The *bylinas* are performed as a combination of singing and narration with elements of recitatives, rests, retardations, and repetitions of short tunes. The rhythmical variations of a tune enable the performer to diversify and accentuate aspects of the text. This style is presently being practiced in the northern regions of Russia.

The isolation of various Russian regions resulted in the evolution of specific local characteristics in church singing. The church tunes and melodies, although based on similar sign elements, were diversified. The various singing styles were called *raspevy*. Cities such as Vladimir, Rostov, Yaroslavl, Novgorod, and Pskov and monasteries and churches had their own *raspevy*. From the musical point of view, the *raspevy* were significant because they introduced original elements of intonation into traditional music.

Another interesting development was the emergence of spiritual songs cultivated by the *kaliki perekhozhiye*,[2] the blind wandering singers or pilgrims who traveled to Constantinople, Jerusalem, and other centers of Christianity. The wandering *kalika* was a characteristic figure in ancient Russia, and the image of the *starishcha–kalitishcha* is common in the Kiev *bylinas*. Not only did travel to holy places acquaint Russians with foreign countries, but it also influenced the subject matter of the *bylinas,* too often characterized by fantasy and superstition. The music of the spiritual songs is as varied as the poetic text. They often reflect the influence of Russian dramatic lyric songs, of sign melodies, of various intonational characteristics, and of *bylina* recitatives.

Musical Culture in the City of Novgorod

The City of Novgorod played an important role in preserving and developing the cultural traditions of the Grand Duchy of Kiev. Novgorod was, next to Kiev, the most important city in ancient Russia. The princes of Kiev often occupied the throne in Novgorod, and, in troublesome times, took refuge there.

The inhabitants of Novgorod had their own church (St. Michael's) in Kiev. Novgorod architecture imitated the architecture of Kiev. The main cathedral in Novgorod was an architectural copy of the St. Sophia Cathedral in Kiev and was also dedicated to St. Sophia. Novgorod church dignitaries were educated in Kiev monasteries and were experts in Greek and ancient Slavic writings.

When Kiev's power declined in the twelfth century, Novgorod's influence grew. Novgorod merchants sailed the Baltic and North Seas, the Atlantic Ocean and the Mediterranean Sea toward Italy and other eastern countries. The economic wealth of the city produced a political administration different from that of other Russian principalities. Novgorod became an oligarchic republic ruled by merchants and *boyars* (noblemen). Legislative and military decisions were vested in a *Veche,* a popular assembly whose members belonged to the merchant and landowning sections of society. The *Veche* elected the ruling administration. Because of its geographic position, Novgorod suffered less than other Russian cities during Tatar invasions. Although the Tatars came close to Novgorod and damaged it, they could not completely subdue it.

During the Mongol (Tatar) domination (1238–1462), Novgorod was the only Russian city in which literature and the arts flourished.

Because of its close ties to Kiev, Novgorod preserved the purity of ancient Russian civilization. Manuscripts of church music in Novgorod contain the earliest examples of Russian sign singing.

The comfortable and prosperous life of the Novgorotsy fostered household music-making. The mercantile activities in the city, which brought crowds of foreign guests and visitors from other Russian cities, encouraged public festivities and celebrations. Singing and playing invariably accompanied these activities.

The most important participant in Novgorod festivities was the *skomorokh,* or puppeteer. The traditions of *skomorokh* art were finally formulated in Novgorod and it became genuinely popular. The Novgorod *skomorokhs* developed the Russian puppet show. The puppet characters, although slightly changed through the centuries, have survived to the present time in the masks of *Petroushka.*

The art of *gusli* playing was also developed in Novgorod. In addition to the *gusli,* the *skomorokhs* used the *gudok,* a string instrument played with a bow; and the *domra,* an instrument resembling the tambour.

The Novgorod *skomorokhs* enjoyed legal rights, and lived in special sections of the city. The parents transmitted their art to their children.

The Novgorod *skomorokh* was a respected person and his image was perpetuated in epic poetry. The popular *skomorokh,* Sadko, played the *gusli* and accumulated great wealth. The *bylina* about Sadko and the power of his music-making recalls the Greek myth about Orpheus. Another hero of Novgorod *bylinas,* Vasili Buslayev, was also a famous *gusli* player.

Both Sadko and Vasili Buslayev were historical personalities. Buslayev lived in the middle of the twelfth century and was a *posadnik,* that is, a vice-regent of the Novgorod prince; Sadko, a wealthy merchant who lived at the same time, is mentioned by the ancient Russian chronicler for building a stone church at his own expense. These two heroes are popular representations of heroic Novgorod personalities.

The Novgorod *bylinas* were different from those of Kiev because they described the popular life and customs of the city, the daring and initiative of merchants and the rivalries of various municipal groups, rather than military deeds and victories and the defense of the country against foreign invaders. A certain fairy tale element emerges in the *bylinas* about Sadko with the deification of rivers and seas, important in Novgorod's mercantile life.

The Novgorod *skomorokhs* developed the short-story *bylina,* which was based on humorous situations in family life. These *bylinas,* called *peregudkas,* had a vivid musical style, which included short, lively tunes with clear, precise rhythms resembling comic dance songs.

In addition to an elaborate architectural style, Novgorod developed an original style of painting. The greatest Russian painter of the Middle Ages, Andrei Rublev, was educated in Novgorod where he learned the art of icon painting. Novgorod painters were invited by the Tatar khans of the Golden Horde to paint for the Tatar nobility.

The Novgorod school of church singing produced prominent composers, performers, and theoreticians who attained recognition in all parts of Russia. The sacred plays in Novgorod churches were similar to the *sacre rappresentazioni* in Italy.

One musical art, which was unique in Novgorod, was the art of bell ringing. Church bells were first used in Novgorod where the technique of bell casting was highly developed. Church services and ceremonies were accompanied by elaborate bell ringing. Churches and monasteries had their own styles. A bell was used to call the Novgorotsy to the *Veche.* The great *Veche* Bell was a symbol of the freedom and independence of the Free City of Novgorod. When the Moscow tsar, Ivan the Third, conquered Novgorod (1475–1478), his first act was to carry away the *Veche* Bell. With the silencing of this landmark, the freedom of Novgorod and the sole hope for a parliamentary democratic system in Russia came to an end. The cultural accomplishments of the city were adopted by Moscow which thenceforth became the center of Russian political and cultural life.

Musical Culture in the Tsardom of Muscovy

In the fourteenth century, the Moscow princes began to unify and consolidate the separate feudal principalities of Russia. By the end of the fifteenth century, the territory of the Moscow State extended from Novgorod to the Ural Mountains and from Ryazan to the Arctic Sea.

In 1380, Prince Dmitri Donskoy defeated the Tatars on Kulikovo Field. This victory fostered the growth of Russian national consciousness in the patriotic literature of the period. A poem, *Zadonshchina,* called for national unity. One hundred years later, Ivan the Third broke the Tatar domination. The rise of national consciousness was reflected in historical songs, which glorified state events, such as the military victories over the Tatars, Poles, and Lithuanians.

Historical songs were popular during the reign of Ivan the Terrible (1533–1584). The power of the Moscow state was at its height, and the songs described the successes of the tsar, replacing the *bylinas,* which ended their development in the seventeenth century. Historical songs were different from *bylinas* because they contained less fantasy and poetic invention and more vitality, dramatic representation, and realistic description.

Moscow soon became the political and cultural center of Russia. Building activity changed the appearance of the city. The Kremlin wall was built in the fifteenth century. Architects from Novgorod, Pskov, Rostov, Suzdal, and even Italy came to Moscow. Cathedrals and palaces were built in the Kremlin. Among them were the Uspensky (Assumption) Cathedral, designed by the Bolognese architect, Aristotle Fioraventi, from 1475 to 1479; the Granovitaya Palata, designed by the Italian architects Marco Ruffo and Pietro Solari, from 1487 to 1491; the Arkhangelsky (Archangel) Cathedral, designed by Aloisio Novy, from 1505 to 1509 and the Blagoveshchensky (Annunciation) Cathedral erected by the Pskov builders from 1484 to 1489. The Bell Tower of Ivan the Great, in Lombardo-Byzantine style, was erected between 1508 and 1515. The belfry and the chapel were added by Boris Godunov in 1600. When Ivan the Terrible conquered Kazan, the last Tatar stronghold on the Volga, the victory was commemorated by the Pokrovsky Cathedral (Cathedral of Vasili Blazhenny) in Red Square. It was begun in 1554 and completed in 1679.

Moscow tsars cultivated church singing. Ivan the Terrible invited famous masters of the art to Moscow. Church tunes were collected in a book called *Obikhod* (Everyday Practice). A special *Stoglavy Council,*[3] called by tsar Ivan the Fourth in 1551, promulgated rules concerning icon painting and church singing.

After the Turkish occupation of Constantinople in 1453, Moscow was regarded as the "Third Rome." In 1472, Ivan the Third married Sophia, daughter of the last Byzantine emperor, Constantine Palaeologus, and assumed the title of "Tsar of all Russia." Ivan's grandson, Ivan the Fourth, added the Byzantine title of "autocrat" and became "The Autocrat (*Samoderzhets*) of all Russia."

The tsar's court demanded appropriate artistic activities. Ivan the Third (or his son Vasili Ivanovich) established a chorus of thirty to thirty-five singers, who accompanied the tsar on his travels. In the eighteenth century, the chorus was reorganized into the court chorus.⁴ The tsars employed groups of *skomorokhs,* and Ivan the Terrible particularly admired their art. The Italian organist, John Salvatore, came to Moscow during the reign of Ivan the Third. In 1586, Queen Elizabeth sent a gilded clavichord to Tsarina Irene, wife of Tsar Fyodor Ivanovich. According to the royal ambassador, "the tsarina marvelled at the loud musical tone, and crowds, by the thousands, clustered near the palace to hear the wonderful music." ⁵ Organ music was popular in the Moscow court during the seventeenth century.

By the sixteenth century, excessive expression began to characterize church singing. A sixteenth-century pamphlet entitled *Beseda Sergiya i Germana* (A Discussion of Sergei and Herman) describes church singing practices in the following words: "They bellow like bulls, kick with their feet, shake the hands, and nod the heads like people who are possessed." ⁶

The forms of church sign singing reached their greatest development during the fifteenth and sixteenth centuries. Similar to the richly ornamental architecture and flowery literature of the period, church music was characterized by a wealth of melodic ornamentation independent of the text. This ornamentation, called *razvody* (tunes), became fixed and was indicated by special signs which, by the sixteenth century, numbered a few hundred.

There also was a special type of religious gala singing called *demestvennoye,* characterized by intricate melodies, a variety of modes, and a profusion of ornamentation. Such singing was not subject to the rules of the *Octoechos* and represented a variety of secular, rather than church, music, using a special variety of musical signs.

Polyphonic (many-voiced) church music evolved in the middle of the sixteenth century. This polyphony was called *strochny* (line or part) singing. The polyphony was usually two-part or three-part. A four-part polyphony appeared in the middle of the seventeenth century. It was crude and primitive, often characterized by an acerbity of harmony. In three-part polyphony, the sign melody was written as a middle voice with simple melodies added above and below.

As the Moscow state grew politically and economically, cultural changes were brought about. Sign singing no longer satisfied the demands of the times and eventually yielded to new artistic forms.

During the seventeenth century, the Moscow state expanded its territory and became a powerful multinational feudal state. The peasantry was reduced to serfdom and the tsar relied on the support of a landowning nobility.

The period of 1598 to 1613 was filled with peasant revolts. The Moscow government was helpless to suppress popular discontent as well as strife and jealousy among the nobility. The weakened state was invaded by Poland and then Sweden.

The "Times of Troubles" ended with the rise of the Romanov dynasty. The Romanov tsars restored the power of the nobility and the serfdom of the peasantry. During the second half of the seventeenth century, the suppressed dissatisfaction of the masses erupted in the Volga region, the Ukraine, and central Russia. The most serious uprising was led by Stepan Razin. In 1670–1671, Razin headed the impoverished Cossacks, and his revolt spread from the Don to the Volga.

The dissolution of social customs and the decline of old traditions were reflected in Russian popular songs, the character, form, poetic expression, and subject matter of which showed the people's discontent and the glorification of popular leaders. A cycle of 'Razin' songs describes his various exploits and efforts to redress popular grievances; and in them, Razin's image has been romanticized and idealized. The songs are dramatically narrated descriptive Russian ballads.

There also were "songs of freemen," which romantically described the free, untrammeled aspects of life in the region of the steppes. These songs were created by runaway peasants who had escaped from the oppression of serfdom and had become Cossacks. Lyrical songs described the oppressive customs of Russian family life and the enslavement of personality and reflected the dissolution of the patriarchal traditions of Russian family life. Many songs describe a young girl's farewell to her family before marriage and her separation from loved ones. The melodic style of these songs is very expressive. An example can be found in Russian "drawling songs." The melodies are continuous, smooth, unconstrained, and are ruled only by the rhythmical elements of words and the singer's breathing. Many of the melodies are variations of a melodic intoned motive.

The main characteristic of the lyrical drawling song is polyphony.

When sung by a chorus, the singers add contrapuntal variations (*podgolosky*), which seem to have branched out of and then merged with the main melody, yielding a unison or an octave. The art of the *podgolosky* has its special rules and customs. The lyrical drawling songs and the *podgolosky* are noted for their individuality and musical creativity. The importance of these songs was noted by Gogol in *Dead Souls*,[7] by Nekrasov in *Who Lives Well in Russia?*,[8] and by Turgenev who described the emotion of the songs in *The Singers*, a story in *A Huntsman's Diary*.[9]

Satirical songs ridiculing religious and secular authorities, laziness, hypocrisy, mercenariness, and licentiousness were also popular in the seventeenth century. These songs reflected the emergence of attitudes among the Russian masses critical of the intellectual stagnation which dominated their life. Along with religious themes in writing and painting, there developed more secular interests in daily life and science.

These developments influenced Russian church music. Religious texts of church music were adapted to contemporary spellings and pronunciations. Choral polyphonic music based on colorful harmonic relationships gradually supplanted the monodic music which had dominated church music for nearly five hundred years. When the Ukraine united with the Moscow state in 1654, the influence of Ukrainian church music containing polyphonic elements absorbed from Polish Catholic music became strong in Russian church music. Ukrainian church musicians introduced Russian church composers to *partesnoye* singing, that is, part singing in the Ukrainian choral style. Thus Russian church music broke with the medieval conceptions, which regarded music as the servant of religion. Music was recognized as an art with independent esthetic values. The introduction of *partesnoye* singing led to the development of the choral ecclesiastical (spiritual) concerto whose style was devoid of religious characteristics, but included dynamic effects and colorful harmonic contrasts. The form of the concerto consisted of choral parts (tutti) and vocal parts (ripieni).

In order to counteract the influence of secular music, the Russian church developed a nonreligious style of music called *kant*. During the second half of the seventeenth century, *kants* became popular in Moscow. The form of a *kant* was simple. It was a symmetrical and strophic choral composition whose form was A-A_1-B-A_2-B in a major or minor tonality. There were also Biblical *kants* called "psalms" which were based on Biblical Psalms.

The second half of the seventeenth century witnessed the decline of the art of the *skomorokhs* who were the heralds of popular discontent, and in 1649, they were banished from Moscow. At the same time, the court of Tsar Mikhail Fyodorovich became interested in music of the West, whose musicians, including flutists, clarinetists, trombonists, and many others, were invited to Moscow. Boyarin Matveyev, a relative of Tsar Alexei Mikhailovich, encouraged the establishment of a Moscow Court Theater in 1674. The presentations, written by Russian writers, were moral comedies, Biblical and historical works, and translated foreign plays. The theater, however, did not exist very long. A court group opposed Western "Latin" influences; and after the death of Tsar Alexei in 1676, the theater was closed.

The seventeenth century was important in preparing the ground for Peter the Great's reforms of Russian musical activities and education and for the development of Russian music in the eighteenth century.

CHAPTER 2

c~~~~o

Russian Musical Culture in the Eighteenth Century

THE BEGINNING of the eighteenth century was a turning point in Russian history. Peter the Great transformed medieval Russia into a powerful state with a strong central government capable of defending the country from its internal and external enemies. Peter's reforms introduced radical changes in the cultural life with the result that there was a rapid rise of nationalistic Russian culture. These reforms, however, affected only the upper strata of Russian society, while the life of the peasants, reduced to serfdom, became more difficult.

Eventually, backbreaking oppression of the peasantry resulted in an insurrection, led by Emelyan Pugachov (1773–1774), which was ruthlessly suppressed by Catherine the Great. The failure of this revolt did not break the national spirit. The dream of emancipation and freedom grew stronger among the oppressed, impoverished peasants and found a sympathetic response among liberal members of the Russian nobility. In 1790, Alexander Radishchev (1749–1802), a prominent liberal, published a book entitled *A Voyage from Petersburg to Moscow*, which condemned serfdom and feudal oppression. These, then, were the circumstances under which Russian art was developing.

Russian musical culture, throughout the eighteenth century, grew at a fast pace. Opera, piano compositions, and symphonic works, musical forms previously unknown in Russia, began to appear, introduced by foreign musicians who were settling there in great numbers. Russian musicians quickly assimilated the experiences and accomplishments of foreign composers. Many Russian composers went abroad to receive a musical education based on Western European

17

musical classicism. While studying Western European methods, Russian composers did not slavishly copy them, but rather created compositions whose musical language was Russian. The end of the eighteenth century witnessed a truly significant event: the formation of a national Russian school of composition.

The prerequisites for development of a Russian musical art were established during the reign of Peter the Great. During this period the trends of musical culture were clearly defined. Musical forms prevailing at the end of the seventeenth century, such as polyphonic vocal concertos, *kants,* and theatrical music, were continued into Peter's reign, but under different treatment. Musical customs and social attitudes toward music changed. The function of music in society became more important. Church music became less dependent upon religious influences and more of an adjunct to functions at the imperial court as Peter limited the power of the church in state politics.

The tsar and those surrounding him viewed music in terms of the simplest requirements of Russian life. Music existed in the form of military themes, and military brass bands played music for victory celebrations. Music was needed for dances, drinking songs, and Peter's "assemblies," which were compulsory gatherings of Russian nobility. Music was also important at Peter's uproarious amusements, which included staged comic weddings, masquerades, and the mockery of old religious customs.

This rather narrow utilization of music did not prevent Peter and his collaborators from appreciating the full measure of its function in life. Peter sent three noblemen, Tolstoy, Matveyev, and Kurakin, to study musical culture in Italy, France, and Holland. Describing musical celebrations in Venice, performance of oratorios in Rome, salon music in Paris, and the "collegium musicum" in Amsterdam, the Russian travelers stressed the connection between musical culture and social customs in Western Europe. They credited the well-developed city life in Paris and Venice to a flourishing musical culture. Peter recognized the importance of the social, secular, and humanistic aspects of music, and accordingly instituted reforms in Russian society and its musical life.

While stressing education in general, Peter devoted a great deal of attention to the popularization of music among the nobility. Secular music, currently condemned and banned by the church, was introduced by order of the tsar. Music became a requirement at court celebrations and "assemblies" in the homes of the Petersburg aristocracy, where an orchestra played various dances introduced from abroad, such as minuets, allemandes, gavottes, and sarabandes. An excellent description of these occasions was given by the poet Pushkin in *The Blackamoor of Peter the Great:*

Clouds of tobacco smoke filled the room dimly lighted by tallow candles. Nobles, ambassadors, foreign merchants, and shipmasters, crowded the room, moving in every direction, while a band played constantly. But this was not yet the actual dancing. The beginning of dancing was announced by a corpulent master of ceremonies. Through the entire length of the hall two rows were formed opposite one another, one of men, the other of women. While mournful music filled the air, men and women bowed and curtsied. This continued for half an hour, until the master of ceremonies ordered the musicians to play a minuet.

To acquaint the Petersburg population with contemporary music, Peter organized weekly concerts in which the music of Western European composers, such as Corelli, Vivaldi, and others, was performed. Attendance was made compulsory by the tsar.

In spite of this compulsion, the Russian nobility gradually became accustomed to domestic music-making as a means of spending leisure time. Prominent noblemen, such as Menshikov, Yaguzhinsky, Golovin, Stroganov, and Cherkassky, had their own instrumental groups, as did the Tsarina, Catherine. Their repertory consisted chiefly of dance music, minuets, polonaises, English dances, and amorous lyrical songs accompanied by the ensemble.

Clavichords were imported from abroad and children of the wealthy nobility were educated in music. As time went on, many noblemen began to teach their serfs music, inviting foreign musicians as teachers or sending serfs abroad to obtain a musical education, many of whom became prominent musicians and composers.

Open-air festivals, arranged by Peter to celebrate military victories or the conclusion of peace treaties, were carried out with instrumental music and singing. On these occasions it was customary to sing special greeting *kants* which glorified Peter, the country, and its military heroes. Some of these *kants* were marchlike in character, some were solemn, and others were sung in an elated mood.

The tradition of these welcoming *kants* deeply influenced Russian classical music, even in the nineteenth century. Elements of popular "honoring songs" and *kants,* especially chordal structure and solemn, marchlike rhythms, were carried over into the classical choral compositions which glorified the motherland and the heroic Russian people. A remarkable example of this tradition is the concluding chorus of praise, the *"Slavsya"* in Glinka's opera *A Life for the Tsar*.

In 1702 a *Kunst* (art) theater was established in Moscow by German traveling companies. This was the first professional musical theater in Russia open to the public. A special building to house it, called "The Comedy Temple," was erected in Red Square. Music was an extremely important feature; arias were assigned to actors and instrumental music accompanied marches and processions. Theatrical music acquired a festive, eulogistic, and propagandistic character in allegorical spectacles celebrating Peter's military victories. A group of band players headed by a conductor named Syenknech also arrived in Moscow. It probably played in the *Kunst* theater and at court functions.

Although this theater did not exist long, its contribution to Russian musical life was significant. It brought music to the entire city population, irrespective of social standing. Thus, the foundations of a professional theatrical art were established in Peter's time.

In 1733, Empress Anna, wanting to enhance the splendor and magnificence of the imperial court, invited an Italian operatic company, directed by the composer Francesco Araja, to Petersburg. In 1736, he presented, for the first time, an Italian opera entitled *The Power of Love and Hatred*. His *La Clemenza di Tito* was the first operatic work presented in Russian. From then on Italian, and later French, operas were regularly performed in the court theater.

In 1755, the court theater in Petersburg introduced Russian operas sung by Russian artists. The first Russian opera, based on a text by the poet Sumarokov, was composed by Araja. It was called *Cephalus and Procis*, a story taken from Greek mythology. During this period, all Russian operas were written on mythological and allegorical subjects which had nothing in common with Russian life and customs.

During the last quarter of the eighteenth century, ideas and thoughts reflecting dissatisfaction with prevailing social conditions, especially the oppression of peasants under serfdom, appeared in Russian literature and art. Theatrical productions ridiculed graft, injustice, governmental cupidity, and excessive admiration for foreign ideas. Russian audiences saw, on stage, a truthful portrayal of social reality. The plots, taken from the immediate environment, reflected, as far as possible in those times, the customs and procedures of daily Russian life. An important feature of this art was the independence and distinctive originality of creative artists who realized the tremendous appeal of national popular plays.

A group of national composers emerged including the following: Yevstigney Fomine (1761–1800), Dmitri Bortnyansky (1751–1825), Vasili Pashkevich (1742–1800), Danila Kashin (1760?–1841), Mikhail Matinsky (1750–1820), Ivan Khandoshkin (1740–1804), Maxim Berezovsky (1745–1777), Josef Kozlovsky (1757–1831), and Fyodor Dubyansky (1760–1796). Of these composers, Matinsky, Khandoshkin and Kashin were serfs.

The emergence of these composers was made possible by the historical and cultural development of Russia. A national democratic musical art was prepared by the earlier development of Russian music. This art, though based on old national musical forms, represented new aspects in ideological content and style. A Russian democratic art was germinating in direct contrast to court culture. Russian composers, writing music which was national, realistic, and accessible to the Russian public, consciously opposed the tastes of the court aristocracy.

The historical basis of national and social advance in music was paralleled in Russian literature. *The Brigadier* (1766) and *Nedorosl* (The Ignoramus) (1782) by Fonvisin were remarkable comedies; the patriotic poem "Rossiada" (1719) by Khersakov; *The False Demetrius* (1760–1770), a patriotic drama by Sumarokov; and *Rosslav* and *Vadim* (1760–1770), heroic tragedies by Knyazhnin were all evidence of the cultural significance of eighteenth-century Russian writers and poets. In the musical field, forms represented by operatic, vocal, and instrumental composition emerged during the eighteenth century and reached their greatest development in the nineteenth century.

The Folk Song in the City

Peasant folk songs were popular in the Russian city, but the manner of performance was different from that of the village where one group of people sang the song and another group added supporting voices in the manner of free improvisations harmonizing with the song. It was an original, free counterpoint which has survived through the centuries and is popular even now. A first singer called the *zapevalo,* that is, "he who starts the singing," was supported by the *podgolosky,* the supporting voices. The melody of the *podgolosok* was usually a variant of the original melody. The harmonies of these improvisational arrangements were not always based on triads or more complex chords such as seventh chords and their inversions. They were mostly consonances of two tones among which the interval of a fourth, also used as a consonance, has become a distinct musical intonation in Russian folk music.

The entries of supporting melodies do not form a regular or "correct" four-part singing. The supporting melody comes in when necessary, disappears, and reappears again. The same folk song never repeats its supporting melodies; they are always improvised. Through centuries of experience and practice, these choral songs evolved into a style of folk improvisation whose musical structures, despite the improvisational freedom, are comparatively as perfect and logical as accepted forms of classical music.

In cities, folk songs were performed in a different manner; there a solo was supported with chordal-harmonic accompaniment on various instruments such as the guitar, balalaika, harp, and clavichord, or the three-part voices of a *kant.* Popular collections, which contained folk songs arranged in this manner, were published in the eighteenth century and enjoyed wide circulation.

Performance of such arrangements of folk songs led to changes in the original peasant melodies. Harmonic accompaniments and chordal textures introduced new melodic turns which were characteristic of major and minor diatonic scales. Original peasant melodies were usually in the natural minor scale. Changes also appeared in the rhythmic aspects of folk songs. Intricate, uneven, metrical measures in folk songs were changed into even-numbered configurations. These two- and four-measured divisions changed the drawling structure of folk songs. A new type of folk song was produced, also popular, but with characteristics different from the old peasant songs. Between 1776 and 1795, an arranger named Vasili Trutovsky published *A Collection of Simple Russian Songs* in four books. Of Ukrainian descent, he was a singer and player on the psaltery, the Russian *gusli,* in the imperial court. He collected, arranged, and performed Russian and Ukrainian folk songs.

In 1790, Ivan Prach published *A Collection of Russian Folk Songs* arranged for voice with piano accompaniment. Prach was a Czech who settled in Russia, became a music teacher, and founded the first piano school in Russia. He made a number of piano arrangements of Russian songs and composed popular music.

These two collections of folk songs included dance songs, drawling songs (songs in the particular peasant style of intonation), *khorovodny* songs (melodies for singing and dancing in a ring), and round dances. The harmonizations of these folk songs were not based on traditional peasant polyphony with its supporting voices, but on chordal-harmonic accompaniments in the eighteenth-century classical tradition. In their collections, Trutovsky and Prach developed a new folk song style, which was cultivated in Russian cities during the second half of the eighteenth century. Their collections were very popular; and during the nineteenth century, they were the sources from which Russian composers drew popular musical themes for their compositions. Prach's text was also known abroad and from this collection Beethoven took the Russian folk songs which he incorporated into the "Rasoumofsky Quartets," opus 59.

The gathering and writing down of folk songs during the second half of the eighteenth century was not a casual occurrence. It coincided with the growing interest in fairy tales, proverbs, sayings, and the study of popular customs, beliefs, and rites. In the history of Russian music, the compilation of folk songs during the eighteenth century was of tremendous importance because they became the foundation of the Russian national school of music.

Lyric Songs

A wealthy nobleman and ardent music lover by the name of Grigori Teplov, compiled and published in 1759 a collection of songs entitled "Idleness in Busy Moments, or a Collection of Lyrics with Tones for Three Voices." The texts of the songs, written by the poets Sumarokov, Yelagin, and Dmitriev, were of an amorous nature, mostly the complaints of a lover separated from his beloved. The music of these songs reveals characteristics of popular dance rhythms of the period: minuets, gavottes, and sicilianes. It is probable that in some songs, words were fitted to a given melody. Some lyrics reveal the unmistakable influences of folk songs. Other songs are in the style of *kants* in which the upper two voices are close to each other, while the bass voice ranges in the low registers. The light, dance-like characteristics of the melodies, however, are different from the reserved regularity of *kant* tunes.

The songs in Teplov's collection occupy an intermediate position between the older chants and the emerging sentimental lyric songs, popular during the second half of the eighteenth century. Teplov's songs were usually performed as solos, duets, or with instrumental accompaniment. Teplov's collection became so popular that between 1770 and 1780, it was succeeded by similar collections compiled by anonymous authors. By the end of the eighteenth century, these songs were called "Russian Songs."

Two composers, Fyodor Dubyansky and Josef Kozlovsky, became known as outstanding creators of "Russian Songs." Dubyansky was a prominent violinist, but little is known of his life. Kozlovsky was a teacher and a very active musician at the end of the eighteenth and beginning of the nineteenth centuries. At one time he managed orchestras in imperial theaters and directed musical activities at court functions. He was a prolific, versatile composer of songs and incidental music to plays of Russian dramatists. He also composed many polonaises for court celebrations, one of which, set to the poet Derzhavin's words, "Let the Thunder of Victory Resound," became famous during the first half of the nineteenth century.

The "Russian Song" was the immediate forerunner of the nineteenth-century Russian romance. As time went on, the content of "Russian Songs" was gradually individualized. Personal feelings and emotions of man and woman were being expressed more clearly and more truthfully. The artificial conventions and affectations characteristic of earlier "Russian Songs" and of the art of the aristocratic salon yielded to sincerity of self-expression. Purely Russian melodic traits and turns, characteristic native musical intonations, became more prominent and popular.

During the last quarter of the eighteenth century, Russian music came under the influence of sentimentalism. The advocates of this artistic movement stressed the intimate, personal life of man. Susceptibility to tender, delicate feelings was regarded as the most valuable of human attributes. In order to reveal the "life of the heart" sentimentalist composers stressed languishing sadness and melancholy in their songs. The introspective tendency affecting Russian literature at the

close of the eighteenth century was a reaction against the social up-
heaval initiated by the French Revolution. French "Rescue Operas"
of the revolutionary period were presented in Petersburg and their exciting plots and tensions were not lost on Russian audiences. The
quiet, bucolic sentimentalism in the poetry of Karamzin and popular
novels was a psychological reaction against the revolutionary excesses
in France. The favored theme in Karamzin's poetry was the description of intimate aspects and delicate feelings of simple souls, an appreciation of nature, and a deeper understanding of the inner lyrical
world of man. The ideals of this "small world" were expressed by
Karamzin in his description of a happy man:

> One with little can be happy,
> Not chained in feelings, free in spirit . . .
> In soul as upright as in body
> He does not look for gifts beyond the ocean,
> Does not wait for ships at sea,
> Is not afraid of roaring winds.
> Under the sun his home he builds,
> And there he lives from day to day,
> His thoughts not running far away.
> He looks sincerely into his neighbor's eye,
> Tears of grief do not mar his food.
> He loves his work, enjoys his walks in fields,
> And rest in noonday sun.
> With hand and mind he neighbors helps,
> A pleasant friend is he,
> A faithful, happy husband,
> Father of happy little ones,
> Who in his boredom does not upon the muses call,
> And does not the charming graces soothe
> With poetry and prose.

Sentimentalism played an important role in the development of
Russian art.[1] The famous Russian literary critic Belinsky observed in
1840 that sentimentalism cleared away the last vestiges of rude tem-
pers prevailing during the pre-Petrine period, and that Russian society
realized at last that it possessed a heart and soul capable of indulging
and expressing tender emotions.

The introduction of psychological content in "Russian Songs" was
paralleled by modifications of musical form. Many songs of this period

followed the form of *kants*. Gradually the melody in "Russian Songs" was emancipated from the chordal texture of the accompaniment and became more expressive and independent. The instrumental accompaniment gained in complexity, creating a vivid musical representation of artistic imagery. A typical example is the song composed by Dubyansky to the words of the poet Dmitriev. The song's mood is the grief of separation from the beloved and sorrow over ruined happiness. In the poetical text, imagery borrowed from folk poetry is paralleled by imagery taken from salon atmosphere:

The bluish dove languishes, it languishes day and night, but, alas, lovely Chloya, my dearest friend will not wake up.

Activity of Foreign Musicians in Russia

Direct ties with Italian vocal culture were effected through the activities of Italian composers in Russia such as Francesco Araja (1736), Baldassare Galuppi (1776), Giuseppe Sarti (1784), and Domenico Cimarosa (1789). In addition, Russian composers Maxim Berezovsky, Dmitri Bortnyansky, and Yevstigney Fomine journeyed to Italy in order to complete their musical education.

Galuppi was active in Petersburg. In addition to presenting his operas, *Didone Abbandonata* and *Ifigenia in Tauride,* he often appeared as soloist at the imperial court playing his own sonatas, thereby becoming one of the first representatives of the new classical clavier style in Russia. He also influenced the development of Russian church music as conductor of the court chapel and teacher of Bortnyansky. As a result of Galuppi's activities, Russian church music first experienced Italian melodic and operatic influences.

The composer Paisiello's activity was not wholly limited to opera. As the most outstanding composer of *opera buffa,* he helped to popularize this form in Russia. In 1782, while living in Petersburg, he composed the opera *Barber of Seville*. Incisive comedy, mastery of ensembles, melodic wealth, and perfection of form made this work an excellent example of Italian *opera buffa* many years before Rossini. While living in Petersburg, Paisiello also composed harpsichord concertos, pieces for violin and harpsichord, divertimentos for wind instruments and compositions of an entertaining character, all of which exercised a strong influence on upcoming Russian composers.

Sarti was invited to the imperial court. While living in Petersburg, he composed operas, both *buffa* and *seria,* operas on French texts and one based on a Russian libretto "The Beginning of Oleg's Administration." He also composed choral compositions and contributed to research in acoustics, for which he was elected member of the Petersburg Academy of Science. Sarti's activities demonstrated the influence of Russian culture on an Italian composer.

At this time magnificent palaces and structures were being built in Petersburg, many of which were on the estates of fabulously wealthy Russian nobles. A whole army of foreign artists, sculptors, and architects worked on these projects. The costumes, dresses, and furniture were dazzling and overwhelming. This luxury was especially characteristic of the reign of Catherine the Great, when Russian autocracy reached unprecedented power and all court functions assumed propagandistic importance as the glorification and exaltation of imperial prestige and the idea of empire.

The ode flourished in poetry. In music, the pompous, triumphant style of court music was connected with the name of Sarti. His brilliant cantatas and oratorios suited the splendor and magnificence of imperial festivals, in which operas, ballets, concerts, masquerades, and fireworks followed one another. For these festivals, Sarti composed music whose sonorities were tremendously effective. In one of his cantatas, composed for an imperial function staged outdoors, Sarti had two choruses, two orchestras, a band of hunting horns, gunfire, and fireworks. The band of hunting horns was an interesting ensemble. The instruments were oversized hunting horns requiring a special stand for support while in use. The band was perfected by a Czech musician, Johannes Maresh, around 1750 and was originally established on the estate of Prince Naryshkin. Every player in the band played only one tone of definite pitch. The entire ensemble could play a chromatic scale of four and one-half octaves from a low A to a high E.

Sarti had excellent command of orchestral and choral writing. He created contrasts of sonorities whose magnificent effects and staggering power admirably suited the requirements of outdoor imperial functions.

Another foreign influence was a Spanish composer, Vicente Martin y Solar, who settled in Petersburg where he presented his own and Italian operas. He composed several operas on Russian librettos. Two librettos, *The Grief of the Hero Kosometovich* and *Fedul and His*

Children, were written by Empress Catherine. Another libretto, *The Village Holiday,* was written by V. Maikov. Martin's music, while revealing the influences of Russian melodies, was not outstanding. The conventional character of his music was probably due to the compulsion of composing music to order and the absurdity of Catherine's librettos.

Opera in Eighteenth-Century Russia

A public "Russian Theater" was established in Petersburg in 1756 and presented dramatic and operatic spectacles. This was the beginning of the Russian theater. Another theater of the same type was shortly established in Moscow. In addition, there were a number of theatrical enterprises managed by foreigners.

An important part in Russian musical-theatrical activities was performed by serf theaters and orchestras, in which specially trained serfs presented an extensive and varied repertory. Theaters existed on manorial estates in various parts of Russia and fostered the dissemination of theatrical musical culture in the most remote provinces of the country. Some serf artists became distinguished singers and musicians. One of these, Parasha Zhemchuzhnaya, the daughter of a village smith, became the wife of Count Sheremetyev.

The life of a serf artist was not easy. Many were educated and cultured individuals whose social position was to be a slave of the landlord. This servitude became the source of many tragedies among the most talented serf artists and musicians. It was not unusual to find an advertisement in a Russian newspaper:

For sale, a manor serf who plays the violin and knows how to write. Also for sale two English sows and a Danish stallion.[2]

Serf theaters existed in Russia until the abolition of serfdom in 1861.

The exact date of appearance of the first Russian composition for a musical theater is not known. In 1740, a composer, Kolychev, wrote a musical comedy based on Russian folk tales. At the same time, two prominent actors, Volkov and Dmitrievsky, composed a comic opera, *Tanyusha.* In 1772, Popov composed a comic opera, *Anyuta.*

The three most popular Russian operas composed during the second half of the eighteenth century were *The Miller-Magician, The Cheat,* and *The Matchmaker* by Sokolovsky; *The St. Petersburg*

Gostiny Dvor (Rows of Shops and Arcades) by Matinsky; and *The Misfortune from a Carriage* by Pashkevich. The existence, in these operas, of comic and satiric elements and successions of songs and arioso numbers interspersed with spoken dialogues without music, represented the birth of the Russian comic opera.

The plots of these comic operas were based on lives of peasants. They showed, as much as was permissible under prevailing conditions, the injustices and burdens of life under serfdom. In this respect, Russian comic opera was similar to advanced Russian literature, especially Russian literary comedy. But, while such a literary work as Radishchev's *Journey from Petersburg to Moscow* represented an open call against serfdom, Russian comic operas confined themselves to a description of the excesses of serfdom.

The music of early Russian operas grew from the foundations of Russian folk songs. These operas represented the greatest achievement of eighteenth-century Russian composers who made use of genuine folk melodies, or, as they were then called, "voices." The operatic music bore the stylistic imprint of "Russian Songs" and *kants,* that is, genres having the widest circulation in Russian cities. At the same time, Russian composers utilized the methods of musical expression developed by foreign operatic composers, recreating and subordinating these musical experiences to the requirements of Russian national art.

The libretto of the opera, *The Miller-Magician, the Cheat,* and *The Matchmaker,* was written by a well-known author, Ablesimov. In 1779, the opera was presented in Moscow and soon after in Petersburg. Ablesimov indicated in his text the specific folk melodies to be sung in particular numbers. Sokolovsky, a violinist in the Moscow theater, collected and arranged the melodies for the opera. In 1790, the opera's music was rearranged, probably with the collaboration of the composer Fomine. No biographical facts about Sokolovsky, the original composer of the music, exist. It is known only that at one time he was the conductor of the Moscow theater.

The plot of the opera is as follows:

The action takes place in a Russian village. Anyuta and Philemon are in love with each other, but they cannot marry because Anyuta's father, Ankudin, wants her to marry a peasant, while her mother, Fetinya, wants her to marry a nobleman.

Philemon asks Faddey the miller to help him in this situation.

Faddey, who has the reputation of a magician, agrees to be the match-maker. To Ankudin he represents Philemon as a peasant; to the mother he represents him as a nobleman. He succeeds in bringing the affair to a happy ending, explaining that Philemon is a petty nobleman without serfs, and is therefore a suitable groom for Anyuta from the point of view of her parents:

> "Himself a landowner, himself a peasant,
> Himself a serf, and himself a boyar."

The plot is a light domestic comedy. What is important is the staged presentation of characters of the Russian peasantry and the utilization of folk songs. The language of the actors contains genuine peasant speech and intonation.

The overture was probably written by Fomine. It is in sonata-allegro form. The main melody is a folk song called "The Young Married Woman" or "My Beloved Is Angry With Me." Several times in the overture, Fomine returns to this melody, thus retaining a folk song atmosphere. The second theme is a Ukrainian song, "Ho, Ho, the Green One," reminiscent of the popular American song, "The Children's Marching Song":

> This old man, he played one;
> He played knick-knack on his thumb.
> With the knick-knack paddy-wack,
> Give your dog a bone,
> This old man came rolling home.

The overture's gay rhythms immediately suggest to the audience that the operatic plot is based on peasant life. The acting characters are musically described in solo numbers—songs, verses, and arias. Most of the melodies are arrangements of genuine folk songs.

The main character of the opera is the miller. He is a smart, cunning Russian peasant known as a magician. From his very first words, however, it becomes evident that he neither believes in deviltry nor magic. In his song in the first act, "Who Can Live by Fraud," he tells the audience that witchcraft is only a means for clever people to make money. The tune is that of the famous Russian folk song, "Down the River Mother-Volga," sung in an eighteenth-century manner, the words describing the reckless revelry of traveling merchants. The melody's spirit enhances the characterization of the worldly miller advocating the knack of easy living.

Witty patter and tongue twisters are employed in various scenes. The libretto, describing peasant life and customs, and the music, based on folk songs, is an example of an early Russian opera. It was very popular during the first quarter of the nineteenth century and Pushkin referred to it in his writings.

St. Petersburg Gostiny Dvor is another example of an eighteenth-century national opera. It was also known under the title "As You Live, So Is Your Reputation." Mikhail Matinsky, a composer during the reign of Catherine the Great, wrote the libretto and the opera. A second edition of the opera was issued in 1792 and another composer, Vasili Pashkevich, collaborated in the new arrangement.

Matinsky was born in 1750. Information about his life is confusing and meager. He was a serf of Count Yaguzhinsky and educated in a special school for intellectuals who did not belong to the nobility. He had traveled abroad with Count Yaguzhinsky. For a short time, he lived in Italy. Given his freedom by the Count, Matinsky taught geometry and geography at the Smolny Institute for girls in Petersburg. He wrote the libretto for the opera, *The Pasha of Tunis*. In addition to composing music, he translated foreign scientific and artistic works.

Very little is known about Pashkevich. At first he played the violin in court theaters and then served as composer and conductor at the court of Catherine the Great. He composed three operas: *The Misfortune From a Carriage, The Miser,* and *Faveus.* He also wrote a few musical numbers for a play, *The First Government of Oleg.* Pashkevich also collaborated with the Spanish composer, Martin, in composing music for the opera, *Fedul and His Children,* the libretto having been written by Empress Catherine.

The plot of *St. Petersburg Gostiny Dvor* tells the story of the merchant Skvalygin and his wife Solomonida who decide to marry their daughter Khavronya to the scrivener Kryuchkodey. Skvalygin is a money-grabber who does not care how he acquires his funds. Kryuchkodey, hoping to receive a rich dowry from his future father-in-law, helps Skvalygin to commit illegal transactions, cheat creditors, and avoid paying his debts. Kryuchkodey and Skvalygin deceive their debtors Protorguyev, Razhivin, Peroboyev, and two inexperienced ladies, Schohepetkova and Krepishkina, who imprudently gave Skvalygin promissory notes and pledges. Thanks to the intervention of two honest and kindhearted people, Skvalygin's nephew, Khvalimov, and an army officer, Pryamikov, the swindlers are exposed. Kryuchkodey's engagement to Khavronya is broken off and both Skvalygin and Kryuchkodey beg for mercy. The opera concludes with a glorification of truth and justice.

The exposure of graft, embezzlement, swindling, and cheating was a true picture of the sordid conditions plaguing the lives of common people in eighteenth-century Russia. The opera is an excellent example of satiric comedy. The depraved and vicious streaks of merchants and magistrates during Catherine's reign are embodied in the characters Skvalygin and Kryuchkodey. Matinsky's literary talent enabled him to create a libretto of exceptional significance. As a realistic and accurate portrayal of merchant life, a truthful sketching of customs and merchant dialects of the period, *Gostiny Dvor* has no equal in Russian literature. The characters' names suggest particular foibles: Kryuchkodey—a crooked doer; Khavronya—a sow; Khvalimov—a praiseworthy person; Pryamikov—an upright man; and Solomonida —questionable female wisdom. Synonymy in Russian literature was prominent during the nineteenth century. Gogol, one of the greatest writers of the first half of the nineteenth century, was famous for synonymy in the names of heroes in his novel *Dead Souls* and in his comedy *The Government Inspector,* characterizations which became bywords in Russian life.

The satiric trend of the opera is unfolded in solo numbers. The arias of Skvalygin, Solomonida, and Kryuchkodey are musical descriptions satirizing the cupidity and callousness of Skvalygin, the mendacity and unscrupulousness of Kryuchkodey, and Solomonida's addiction to drinking. Kryuchkodey mourns the bad times: "What times are these when one is told not to take bribes?"

The music of this opera, unlike that of *The Miller,* was originally composed by Matinsky in the manner and feeling of folk song intonations, but with greater melodic variety. The popular choral scenes anticipate similar ceremonial choral ensembles in Glinka's *Ivan Susanin* and *Ruslan and Ludmilla,* the marriage ceremony in Dargomijsky's *Russalka* and Rimsky-Korsakov's *The Tsar's Bride,* all composed in the nineteenth century.

The Misfortune from a Carriage or *Coachmen before Departure* is a one-act opera by Fomine based on a libretto by N. A. Lvov (1788). Fomine, the son of a soldier in the artillery, was born in Petersburg in 1761. He received his musical education in the Petersburg Academy of Arts. Upon graduation, he went to Italy where he studied music in the academy in Bologna. He then returned to Russia as an Academician and worked as an operatic coach in court theaters. Around 1790, Fomine made his debut with an opera *Bolelsavovich, the Hero From Novgorod.* Fomine also composed a heroicomic opera-ballet, *The Americans* or *The Golden Apple,* based on a libretto by the famous Russian fabler, Krylov. The operas, *The Americans* and *Pasha From Tunis,* signaled the rising influence of romance and exoticism of faraway countries, characteristic of some Western European operas at that time, such as Mozart's *Abduction From the Seraglio,* Grétry's *The Cairo Caravan,* and Haydn's *The Apothecary.*

Fomine, who died in 1800, also composed a melodrama, *Orpheus,* and choral music to tragedies by the Russian dramatists Ozerov and Knyazhnin.

The Coachmen is written in the spirit of a popular peasant comedy. The plot is simple: To escape military service, Filka, an inveterate knave, attempts to recruit, as a substitute, Timothy, a young coachman; Filka is thwarted in his plot by the timely interference of other coachmen.

The music of the opera is notable for the integration of Italian *bel canto* with drawling qualities and the free improvisational roundelays of peasant choruses. It is the first and only example of the adaptation of peasant song idioms to professional music. Fomine did not adhere to natural modes prevalent in peasant melodies. Instead he favored major modes with digressions into parallel minor modes. The predominance of regular dominant-tonic cadences is the fruit of Fomine's Italian training and a concession to the influences of Russian city music. The musical texture is a free adaptation of Western polyphonic methods to Russian folk idioms.

Comic operas, based on stories from everyday life, were not the only operas. There were fairy tale operas, fantastic and decorative, and pastoral operas which described idyllic peasant life. These operas were all connected with the operatic style of the imperial court. The comic opera, however, based on situations taken from everyday life, occupied the most important position. Even foreign composers succumbed to its influences. In 1780, Raupach, a German composer, wrote an opera, *Kind Soldiers,* on a libretto by Kheraskov. In 1786, Stabinger, also a German composer, composed an opera, *Happy Tanya,* on a libretto by Gorchakov. In 1787, Bulain, a French composer, penned an opera, *Sbytenshchik* (The Man Who Went Astray) on a libretto by Knyazhnin. Finally, in 1799, Blima, a Czech composer, wrote *Ancient Yuletide* based on a libretto by Malinovsky.

Not all national popular operas exposed the sordid quality of social conditions. Some operas contained monologues in the spirit of Rousseau, whose ideas penetrated as far as Russia. For example, in the opera *Regeneration,* libretto and music by Matinsky (1777), a peasant girl sings:

> There are amusements in the city
> Only not for our morals:
> There simplicity polite
> Is all pretension, not the same;
> Plays, enjoyments, freedom,
> Are only found in the fields;
> Boredom, noise, and dissension there,
> Peace, contentment here, are natural with us.

In the opera, *The Village Holiday,* based on a libretto by Maikov, there is a description of the happy state of peasants living in serfdom:

> We lead a happy life,
> Working every hour;
> We spend our life in the field
> In happiness and joy;
> We labor with our hands,
> And consider it our duty
> To live with such work;
> Paying our quitrent,
> We lead a blissful life,
> Under the watchful eye of our landlord.

The influence of the court and nobility in operatic affairs remained very strong. Khrapovitzky, Empress Catherine's secretary and her collaborator in the writing of operatic librettos, wrote in his memoirs in 1790: "France perished because of excesses and vices; we must preserve morals."

Instrumental Music in the Eighteenth Century

Instrumental music by Russian composers dates from the eighteenth century. The ties of instrumental music to the demands of daily life were close and varied. Some instrumental forms developed in connection with court and manorial functions. Musical forms popular among Russians living in cities were dances and arrangements of folk songs and church melodies. The dances were mostly minuets, quadrilles, polonaises, and waltz rhythms, the latter, however, regarded as rather plebeian.

Chamber music was popular among exclusive society groups. Instrumental compositions, such as clavier sonatas, were composed by foreign musicians who were temporarily living or permanently settled in Russia. Although this music was Western in spirit and technique, the important thing to note is that it accustomed Russian composers to the emerging sonata style of the Mannheim and Viennese composers.

Like the development of the opera, the popularization of instrumental forms at first depended on court functions and the mode of life on manorial estates. Although the Russian nobility and middle classes were becoming accustomed to new dance forms, the influence of court functions in instrumental music continued until the end of the century.

Among the first to distinguish himself as a Russian composer of instrumental music was Kozlovsky, who became famous as a composer of festive brilliant polonaises for court functions. These polonaises, written for chorus and orchestra, were almost like cantatas. The treatment of a polonaise as a festive dance was characteristic of eighteenth-century court life. Kozlovsky's contemporaries felt a patriotic fervor in his polonaises as well as a heroic power, and they appreciated these works above official court music. The famous polonaise, "Let the thunder of victory resound, rejoice courageous Russ," evoked not only imagery of court celebrations, but visions of Russian military victories and the greatness of the Russian state as well. At the turn of the century, the tune of this polonaise, set to the words of the ode, "Be glorified by this, oh Catherine," became the unofficial national anthem. The tune has often been mentioned in Russian literature. The poet Pushkin mentions it in his novel *Dubrovsky,* in which the despotic landowner, Troyekurov, angrily paces back and forth whistling the tune, "Let the thunder of victory resound."

While Kozlovsky's polonaises represented the grand style, the art of great celebrations, numerous dance forms acquired the importance of household music. Collections of various dances composed by Russian composers were published and popularized in the homes of townspeople and the landed gentry. In some musical collections for household use, dances were interspersed with instrumental arrangements of popular tunes and drinking songs. Many Western-type dances were often changed in the Russian manner, the dances assuming the melodic turns of Russian songs.

Clavier "symphonies" were written by Russian composers for domestic consumption. These were not symphonies in the real sense of the term. They were compositions possessing a common rhythmic character of motion, scale passages, and elementary harmonic figurations.

Besides domestic dance music, arrangements of songs, clavier symphonies, and the ballet, as an independent musical production completely divorced from operatic presentation, were cultivated in the theater and were growing steadily in popularity and importance.

By the close of the eighteenth century, the clavichord and piano appeared in many Russian homes. A new musical literature for piano, violin and piano, and other chamber music combinations began to emerge. There were "Russian" piano sonatas, piano concertos, and variations for violin and piano. The variation form became very popular, and variations on popular tunes were written, not only by Russian composers, but foreign composers as well. Two composers, Khandoshkin and Gesler, were outstanding in the new instrumental form. Khandoshkin, a Russian, was a pianist and violinist who composed valuable examples of early Russian piano and violin music. Gesler, a German who spent a great part of his life in Russia, wrote piano music and was active in establishing the early Russian piano school in the beginning of the nineteenth century.

Khandoshkin's fame as a composer rests largely on his violin compositions. But his piano compositions also reveal his skill as a composer in contemporary piano style and as an arranger of Russian songs.

By far the most outstanding piano composer in the eighteenth century was Bortnyansky. At the time when popular piano compositions were chiefly in dance forms, Bortnyansky wrote serious sonatas, chamber music, and symphonies. In his technique of composition he approached the styles of the Italian and Viennese schools. His works were written mostly for court performances in Pavlovsk and Gatchina, suburbs of Petersburg to which the imperial court sojourned at various periods. In this connection, it should be recalled that the symphonies of Mannheim composers and many symphonies of Haydn were also composed for court functions, despite the fact that their content was outside the esthetic boundaries of court music.

Bortnyansky's instrumental music is usually chamber-like in dimension. His orchestral works are light and transparent in texture. His style reflects the influence of Johann Christian Bach, Haydn, and Mozart. It is a classical style with well-balanced designs, clear harmonic textures, and smooth melodic lines. Bortnyansky's music has a more personal feeling than that of other eighteenth-century Russian composers and is more European than Russian in character. He was the first Russian composer of "pure" instrumental music who embodied personal feelings, thoughts, and moods in classical forms. Unlike Russian operas, in which characterizations were achieved through folk songs, with scenes from the Russian environment predominating, Bortnyansky's musical themes were closer to the purity of Mozart's instrumental style than to Haydn's style, in which some of his musical ideas were based on popular folk materials. Bortnyansky's contribution was the creation of a Russian musical art based, not on folk song materials, but on the more complex foundations of independent instrumental forms. His music might appear less national and less Russian than that of his contemporaries, but it gradually led to the music of Glinka in the nineteenth century, and separate threads even penetrated the work of Tchaikovsky.

Compared to Bortnyansky, Khandoshkin represented a brilliant virtuoso concerto style. He stood apart, in the sense that he was less influenced by Western ideas. Khandoshkin's natural gifts were probably stronger and he was more daring in his methods. His violin style is very expressive and improvisational. The historical significance of these two composers is tremendous. Their arrangements of eighteenth-century dance music eventually culminated in Glinka's "Kamarinskaya" and "Valse Fantaisie." Russian musical classicism was born in the compositions of Bortnyansky and Khandoshkin.

During Stalin's regime, a marked nationalistic outlook developed. Soviet criticism analyzes eighteenth-century Russian music in terms of historical materialistic dialectics. It sees a revolutionary democratic character in the development of progressive thinking in eighteenth-century Russia. To this trend the imperial regime responded with greater reaction. The policies of the autocratic Russian government increased the latent revolutionary unrest in Russian society. Historically, it is true that Russian social conditions were different from *petit-bourgeois* conditions in Germany and large-scale bourgeois conditions in France. Liberal ideas in Russia assumed a popular and national character. The materialism and other social ideas of Radishchev differed from contemporary French materialism. For the same reason, Russia did not found a philosophical school of abstract activity similar to the philosophical school of German idealism represented by the philosopher Kant.

The development of Russian progressive musical esthetics overcame the ideological one-siddedness of Western European musical thinkers. Cultivated members of the Russian intelligentsia considered themselves to be the ideologists of the people. According to Communist thinking, the emancipation and ascendancy of the bourgeoisie in Western Europe created an outward show of freedom, while precautionary valves of liberalism lessened revolutionary pressure by separating European intelligentsia from the people.

According to contemporary Soviet criticism, the end of the eighteenth and the beginning of the nineteenth centuries saw Russian thinkers taking a close look at Western capitalism. Progressive Russians did not share the naïve faith in bourgeois society clouding the minds of many Western thinkers during the Enlightenment. Communists maintain that the mental blindness of these people led to disillusionment which, in turn, was followed by romantic contradictions. Russian thinkers, according to this argument, were neither blind nor disillusioned. Their belief was that capitalism, as a system, was inimical to humanity and should be fought, subdued, and conquered.

This fits the frame of Communist dialectics, but is not particularly realistic because European capitalism, at the end of the eighteenth century, was still an amorphous system. Whatever liberal ideas were entertained then by some members of Russian nobility, motivations were purely political, not economic. In evaluating the Soviet view, one should bear in mind that capitalism, in the modern sense, was nonexistent in eighteenth-century Russia. Western European capitalism was only beginning to emerge and it is very unlikely that progressive Russians even knew the meaning of industrial capitalism.

Radishchev's ideas combined a primitive materialism with ideas of a revolutionary peasant democracy. He was followed, during the first half of the nineteenth century, by Belinsky, Herzen, Chernishevsky, and Dobrolyubov. Their materialistic views combined with revolutionary struggle to reconstruct Russian society. The revolutionary energy of the Russian masses was so tremendous that, despite centuries of cultural and economic backwardness, this energy produced men having the courage to maintain unity of theory and practice as well as knowledge and action. During the years preceding the emancipation of the peasants (1840–1860), these men's views came closer to dialectical and historical materialism: Belinsky in his literary and art criticisms, Herzen in his memoirs *Byloye i Dumi* and in the newspaper *Kolokol* (The Bell), which he published in London, Chernishevsky in his famous dissertation *Esthetic Relations of Art to Reality,* and Dobrolyubov in his literary criticisms, one of which, *What Is Oblomovshchina?,* was a scathing condemnation of Russian society, the manorial system, and serfdom. Oblomov is the hero of Goncharov's novel of the same name. Dobrolyubov's criticisms were remarkable for the keen insight with which they traced and analyzed the degenerating "Oblomov" mentality, which was also found in the heroes of Pushkin and Lermontov's literature.

During the eighteenth century, as well as the first half of the nineteenth, Russian music, as an ideological political activity, fell far behind Russian philosophy and literature. But the impulses of revolutionary democratic development in progressive Russian thought, as a whole, were already evident in musical activity and esthetic ideas of art.

❦

CHAPTER 3

Russian Musical Culture
1800-1850

BEGINNING WITH the nineteenth century, the process of development of Russian music became more intense and diverse. Signs of a distinct national style began to appear, followed by the formation of a national musical school between 1830 and 1835.

The rapid development of Russian music was a particular manifestation in the growth of national trends fostered by social and political events taking place in Russia.

The beginning of the nineteenth century signified the end of the golden age of Catherine the Great's nobiliary empire. Serfdom, forming the economic basis of the Russian state, was straining under the impact of social and political onslaughts, which, in turn, led to contradictions and antagonisms within Russian society.

The nucleus of an intelligentsia, opposed to the autocratic regime which governed Russia, was formed among the Russian nobility. The attitude of this intelligentsia was influenced by French Revolutionary ideas. The Napoleonic wars of the first decade of the nineteenth century helped to disseminate liberal ideas throughout Russian society. Younger members of the Russian nobility, who took part in the wars and became acquainted with the accomplishments of European culture, absorbed progressive democratic ideas. Upon returning to Russia, these Westernized Russians were determined to change Russian social and political realities. This was the beginning of the nobiliary period of liberation and emancipation movements whose first active leaders were the Decembrists (1825) including Prince Schepin-Rostovsky, Rileyev, Prince Serge Trubetskoy, Prince Obolensky, and Chaadayev. Around 1840–1860, the leadership was taken over by Herzen. The objective of these revolutionaries was the abolition of serfdom and Tsarist autocracy, and the release of national forces for independent development and growth. In the light of social and political conditions in Russia, the development of national economic and cultural foundations became an urgent problem. An interest in the past and present history of the country was aroused. Patriotic feelings were quickly stimulated. Napoleon's invasion of Russia in 1812 gave powerful impetus to the growth of national consciousness and the development of a Russian national culture.[1] Patriotic feelings and national cultural aspirations in Russian society assumed various guises. The serf-owning nobility saw its patriotic duty in the preservation of the old social order and traditions.[2] New thoughts and foreign ideas were ridiculed. Instead, the times preceding Peter's reforms were presented as the ideal world of valor and virtue. Official poets extolled the autocratic Tsarist regime and the patriarchal unity of the Tsar and the people. The negation of everything new and non-Russian became an obsession. In 1806, Count Rostopchin, writer and statesman, published an article in which he tried to prove the advantages of the old-fashioned wooden plow for Russian agriculture. Admiral Shishkov, the minister of education in the government of Nicholas the First, fought for many years to preserve the church-slavonic foundations of the Russian language, and to prevent the introduction of popular speech idioms and foreign words, seeing in such innovations the moral decline of Russian society.

These varying trends in Russian society influenced the development of artistic culture. Russian art began to assimilate outstanding elements in Western culture, changing them to suit Russian realities. The bonds with French classic literature, prevailing during the eighteenth century, gave place to a sentimental, pathetic literature, and finally to romantic trends. The poet Zhukovsky introduced Russian readers to translations of German romantic poetry in which nebulous philosophical themes were interwoven with elegiac sensitivity and descriptions of nature were blended with mysterious visions and gloomy fantasy. The novels of Sir Walter Scott and the poetry of Byron exercised a tremendous influence on Russian literature at the beginning of the nineteenth century. The fervent appeal and social content of French romanticism, especially of Victor Hugo, met with a warm response from the Russian literary intelligentsia.

Translations of Western European literature were followed by the creation of a Russian romantic literature by Zhukovsky, Kozlov, Bestuzhev-Marlinsky, Zagoskin, and others. The works of these writers presented whimsical combinations of practical daily imagery with fantastic pictures, of exoticism and Russian reality, and of nobility and humanity combined with callous bloodthirstiness. The outstanding feature of early Russian romanticism was exaggeration of feelings, of spiritual drives and motivations, and of passions inevitably resulting in a fatal denouement and the emergence of a strong personality.

Despite exaggerations, melodrama, and profusion of decorative paraphernalia, Russian romanticism is significant for its wealth of artistic content, its truth and vitality of feeling, its humanity and its optimism. Russian literature, while absorbing Western romanticism, did not become an imitative art. Russian writers directed their attention to reality, daily life, folklore, and popular speech idioms. While creating pictures of Russian life, they utilized the imagery of folk poetry, combining the variety of national themes with the assimilated wealth of Western art. Thus, the Russian literary school was formed in the works of Batyushkov, Karamzin, Zhukovsky, Krylov, and Griboyedov, crowned by the works of Pushkin, the founder of contemporary Russian literature and language. The same trends characterized the school of Russian painters including Kirpensky, Tropinin, Venezianov, Orlovsky, and the national music of Glinka.

The main features of Russian artistic culture during the first third of the nineteenth century—its diversity, profound optimism, national characteristics, progressive aspirations, and lofty humanity, were reflected in Pushkin's works. The critic Belinsky wrote that "Pushkin was the perfect embodiment of his time." It is customary to refer to this cultural period as "The Pushkin Period." Many artistic works in literature, painting, and music were influenced by his poetry. His influence was significant in the development of vocal lyrics, romances, and operas—musical genres connected with poetry. The content and variety of vocal forms in music were determined by the influence of Pushkin's art.

The revolt of the Decembrists was the most important event in Russian history during the first half of the nineteenth century. The revolt profoundly influenced the revolutionary thinking of Russian intelligentsia. The autocratic regime of Tsar Nicholas could not stop the growth of liberal ideas in Russian society. Public life attracted larger segments of the population and the machinery of government was run by a large bureaucracy. A rich merchant class became influential in the cities. A new class of intellectuals, not belonging to the nobility, developed a strong and influential voice. Younger members of the nobility, indoctrinated with liberal ideas, openly voiced their opposition to serfdom, and were acutely responsive to pressing social and political problems.

The revolutions of 1830 and 1848 in Western Europe stimulated liberal ideas in Russian society, but, at the same time, hardened the Tsar's policies. As Herzen, one of Russia's greatest political writers and revolutionary leaders, wrote, "Tsar Nicholas wanted to kill everywhere and in everyone every vestige of independence, personality, fantasy, and will." The Tsar and his government were hostile to manifestations of Russian culture. Pushkin, Lermontov, and outstanding representatives of Russian society were the victims of this gloomy reign. The atmosphere of police terror, bigotry, and obscurantism almost paralyzed the activity of Russian creative artists such as Gogol and Glinka.

The Russian intelligentsia was interested in German philosophic thought, especially Hegel's philosophy and Fourier and Saint-Simon's ideas of utopian socialism. The trend of artistic culture was moving toward the imagery of daily reality, of prosaic subjects, little noticed, but containing significant social meaning. Literature turned towards naturalism, aiming to reveal the life of serfs in villages and ordinary people in cities. Similar realistic trends emerged in painting and in music. These were not objective representations, but rather personal critical expressions of attitudes toward life which changed the national character of Russian arts. The monarchical aspect of Russian nationalism retained its influence only among a small group of Russian nobility. The new popular nationalism, a critical representation of Russian reality in arts, was based on lifelike, realistic, and democratic concepts.

CHAPTER 4

⌒⌒

Vocal Music:
Alabiev, Varlamov, and Gurilev

ALABIEV, VARLAMOV, and Gurilev were composers of Russian vocal music during the first half of the nineteenth century. Their art songs, in which the melody and the accompaniment change or vary to express the meaning of the text, were called "romances." Unfolding a panorama of prevailing social, political, and cultural conditions, the "romances" revealed the liberal sentiments rising in some sections of Russian nobility and the democratic ideas of Russian intellectuals.

Alabiev

Alexander Alabiev was born in Moscow in 1787, where his father was an executive in the Department of Mines. Alabiev was educated in a boarding school attached to Moscow University. His musical education began in early childhood and he became a professional pianist. Upon graduation from school, he took a position in the Department of Mines.

During the Napoleonic invasion in 1812, Alabiev became an officer in a regiment of hussars. He participated in the Battle of Leipzig and was promoted for courage in the line of duty. His cultural contacts in Germany left an indelible impression on his musical ambitions. After he returned to Russia, Alabiev settled in Petersburg and studied composition. His first songs were published in 1820.

In Petersburg, Alabiev became acquainted with the poet Griboyedov and with liberal-minded intellectuals who later joined the Decembrist movement. He became interested in the theater, especially in vaude-

ville. He composed vocal solos, ensembles, and instrumental selections
for various spectacles. In 1822, he composed a comic opera, *The
Moonlit Night*.

In 1823, Alabiev left Petersburg for Moscow where he pursued the
life of a man-about-town. He continued his musical studies and composed romances, choruses, and incidental music for various theatrical
productions.

In 1825, Alabiev's life was jolted by an unfortunate incident. During a card game he assaulted one of the players, who died a few days
later. Alabiev was arrested and after a trial for assault and battery that
lasted almost three years, he was deprived of all civil rights and exiled
to Siberia.

During his Siberian exile, Alabiev composed songs, orchestral
works, and chamber compositions. Life in exile changed his outlook.
He became introspective and subdued. In 1832, Alabiev was given
permission to go to the Caucasus.

Alabiev's first compositions show the influence of German romanticism which he absorbed during the war years in Germany. Life in exile and then in the Caucasus enhanced his somber romantic characterizations. In the Caucasus, Alabiev became acquainted with M. A.
Maximovich, a collector of Ukrainian folklore. In 1834, Alabiev
arranged twenty-five Ukrainian songs for voice and piano. This was
the first independent collection of Ukrainian songs published in
Russia.

Although Alabiev was not granted full amnesty, he returned to
Moscow. He continued to compose romances and operas until he died
in 1851. His last operatic effort was music to Shakespeare's *Tempest*.

Among Alabiev's compositions, about one hundred and fifty are
romances based on texts of early nineteenth-century Russian poets
and writers including Delvig, Zhukovsky, Pushkin, Karamzin, Odoyevsky, Ogarev, Vyazemsky, Griboyedov, Kozlov, and Lazhechnikov.
Alabiev's music is contemplative, tranquil, and melancholy. His musical lyricism was influenced by the thoughts, ideas, and feelings of
Russian intellectuals of the first half of the nineteenth century. He set
to music romantic subjects and lyric poetry predominant in the Russian poetry of his time.

As a composer, Alabiev possessed the gift of penetrating the hopes
and desires of his contemporaries as well as the psychological refinements of Russian poetry. His melodies reflect his exile, solitude, wan-

derings, friendship, joyful abandon, patriotic themes of war and peace, social inequality, and thoughts on life and death.

Alabiev's romantic style was influenced by the music of Weber, Spohr, and especially by Schumann's songs. His romances are a typical Russian phenomenon engendered by Russian artistic culture in the eighteenth century. The art song was an essential aspect of musical life in Russian cities in the eighteenth century and the beginning of the nineteenth century.[1]

Alabiev's lyricism and human, emotional appeal influenced Russian art songs during the nineteenth century. Compared to Schubert's songs, Alabiev's romances are more colorful, but not as diverse. In Schubert's style are crystallized centuries of Western European romantic aspirations. The ramifications of Western European culture and its democratic orientation cannot be compared with the circumscribed field of aspirations before Russian intellectuals during Alabiev's life.

Alabiev's timid personality, suppressed by the police regime of Nicholas the First, cannot be compared to Schubert's frank stature. The limitations imposed on Russian intellectuals during the first half of the nineteenth century discouraged an art song style similar to Schubert's. All Alabiev could do was absorb the accumulation of motives, intonations, and folk songs in Russian cities, reinterpret them under the influence of Western European cultural ideas, and endow them with potentialities for future development by later Russian composers. Besides original melodic inventions, Alabiev's romances include intonations of peasant folklore. In the history of Russian music, Alabiev's romances prepared the peasant genres developed later by Dargomijsky and Mussorgsky.

Some romances composed by Alabiev around 1840 have a deep social and philosophical content which reflects the growing concern of Russian intellectuals with problems of serfdom and peasant life. There are, for example, the romances based on texts by Ogarev: [2] *The Hut, The Tavern,* and *The Village Watchman.* They describe the hopelessness and futility of peasant life and their ideational content anticipates similar vignettes in Turgenev's *The Hunter's Diary* and in Nekrasov's poetry.[3] The text of *The Pub* is as follows:

> Let us drink, Vanya,
> From cold and sorrow,
> People say the sea

Is knee-deep for drunkards
Yes, only knee-deep.

Anton has a daughter,
A young blue-eyed girl,
A nice girl,
Such a wonderful girl.

He is rich, Vanya,
He will reject you point-blank,
Brother, you will be disgraced
When he will show you the door.

Am I fit for her?
My dilapidated hovel,
And the rent I slave to pay,
And to feed my old mother,
To feed the old woman!

Let us drink from sorrow!
Oh, brother! The mug cannot
Make a pauper forget his grief,
Yes, forget his grief.

Varlamov

Alexander Varlamov was born in 1801. His father was a civil service employee of moderate financial means. Varlamov was enrolled as a choirboy in the Court Chapel where his music teacher was the composer Bortnyansky.

Varlamov graduated from the Chapel in 1819 and became a professional musician. He spent a few years in Holland, and upon returning to Russia, taught singing in the Chapel. Dissatisfied with his work, Varlamov went to Moscow where he worked in the office of Imperial Theaters.

Varlamov's first romances were published in 1833 and became very popular. He often appeared as a singer at concerts. He died in Petersburg in 1848.

As a song composer, Varlamov was less talented than Alabiev. He was not interested in the varieties of romantic impressions and philosophical meditations. His simple and sincere music reflected the emotional aspects and experiences of ordinary people. He preferred subjects which described elegiac meditations [4] or impetuous passions. In his romances, Varlamov often passes from a state of peaceful contemplation into one of violent revelry, from a state of excitement into one of passivity. Such contrasts give his romances a feeling of anxiety and agitation. His romances seem to reflect the dissatisfaction and discontent experienced by various sections of Russian society during the 1830's. Exaggerated feelings in the romances seem to express the desire of Russian intellectuals to avoid oppressive realities.

Many of Varlamov's romances, composed in the style of heartrending, sentimental gypsy songs, enjoyed tremendous popularity. Varlamov's attitude is reminiscent of the Byronesque romantic personality of the early nineteenth century, a type re-created in Lermontov's poetry and in his novel, *A Hero of Our Time.*

Varlamov's musical intonations were similar to intonations common in the everyday life of his time and they contain features of Russian songs, folk songs, and dance rhythms. One of his most famous songs in this genre is "The Red Sarafan," which became so popular that it has often been accepted as an authentic Russian folk song. The lyrics were written by a little-known writer, Tzyganov. They are in the form of a dialogue between a mother and her daughter. The mother tells her daughter that one's young years are short and shall never return. She advises her daughter to take advantage of the brief span of youth and enjoy life. The daughter expresses similar sentiments and tells her mother not to toil hard since the span of life is short.

Varlamov was one of the outstanding Russian composers of musical "Schubertianism," not as an imitation of Schubert's musical style, but as a sociomusical trend.[5]

Gurilev

Alexander Gurilev was born in Moscow in 1802. He was the son of a serf on the estate of Count Orlov. Gurilev studied music with his father, who had been a composition student of the Italian composer, Sarti. Later, Gurilev studied piano with John Field. After the death of Count Orlov, the Gurilev family was emancipated.

During the 1830's, Gurilev taught piano in Moscow and published romances and piano compositions, including mazurkas, waltzes, and variations. During the early 1850's, he became emotionally disturbed and died in 1856.

Gurilev's romances are characterized by a sincere lyricism reminiscent of Varlamov's style. They reveal an exciting naïveté and spontaneity, rather than an individuality of expression.[6] Gurilev was attracted to peaceful, meditative images. His melody and harmony are more graceful and refined than Varlamov's. Gurilev was influenced by the sentimentality of early nineteenth-century Russian music and poetry. Many of his romances are typical musical genres, which were popular in everyday Russian life.

Gurilev's romances were often performed by gypsy choruses. His popularity, like Varlamov's, was due to his ability to express himself in musical intonations which reflected Russian reality and the emotional experiences of ordinary people.[7]

CHAPTER 5

Glinka

MIKHAIL GLINKA was the first Russian composer to summarize, in his music, the results of the historical development of Russian music. Glinka was the originator of the Russian national musical school. He was a daring innovator who infused new vigor into national music and established the boundaries between the past and future of Russian music. Glinka was the founder of the Russian school of classical music which contributed, during the second half of the nineteenth century, many compositions to the musical treasury of the world. His music reflects many facets of Russian reality—heroism, simple genres, lyricism, fantasy, comedy, and drama. He had a profound understanding of Russian national psychology and aspirations.

Glinka intuitively understood the intonational characteristics of peasant songs whose melodic, rhythmic, and tonal patterns he recreated in his music. His compositions contain musical intonations of contemporary city genres and some aspects of ancient Russian church music, in which Glinka discovered the influence of Russian folk songs.

Glinka believed that if one desired to understand the spiritual values of Russian national culture, he must study the Russian cultural heritage as an expression of the historical development of the thoughts, feelings, and aspirations of the Russian people. Glinka differed from his forerunners, who never thought of the Russian people as a spiritual entity and confined themselves mainly to the recreation of musical forms and intonations prevalent in their own environment.

Glinka's musical style is a synthesis of Western musical devices and forms, including the vocal polyphony of the sixteenth and seventeenth centuries; the polyphony of Bach and Handel; the tragic pathos of

Gluck's operas; the classicism of Haydn, Mozart, and Beethoven; the impetuous romanticism of Berlioz and the romantic lyricism of Chopin. Glinka adapted these ingredients to his objectives while retaining, at the same time, his musical originality and individuality.

Even in the music of foreign countries, Glinka was able to discover features similar to Russian national music. In his mature years, he traveled to Spain hoping that Spanish tunes would supply him with materials for composition because, as he said: "They resemble somewhat Russian tunes." He also pointed out the resemblance between Russian and oriental folk songs. "There is no doubt," wrote Glinka, "that our plaintive Russian song is a child of the north, and perhaps transmitted to us by the inhabitants of the east." In his declining years, Glinka sought to derive the laws of Russian national harmony from the polyphony of Palestrina and Lassus, hoping that the results of his research "would be applied to Russian church music."

Glinka's musical creativity coincided with the development of Western musical romanticism. His musical imagination was romantic and he often mentioned his "unrestrained fantasy." Novelty and variety of impressions were vital necessities for Glinka. In his youth, he was often excited by geographic descriptions and stories. In later years, Glinka expressed a desire to travel to different countries. A thirst for new impressions was characteristic of Glinka's life and musical creativity. His compositions reveal a variety of local and national colors, of descriptive episodes. He was inspired by the monotonous Russian steppes, the plaintive Russian songs, the balmy Italian nights, the impassioned rhythms of Spanish dances, the romantic legends of medieval knighthood, and the simple peasant genres in a Russian village.

Glinka never succumbed to excessive emotions or unrestrained imagination. Vague, uncertain music repelled him. His own compositions were clear and logically constructed. He studied counterpoint in order to control his creative imagination. He stated that in composing music his "unrestrained fantasy" required a literary text or program. Glinka's remark indicates his desire to develop creative ideas on the basis of real, objective facts.

Using classical musical designs and programmatic representations, Glinka avoided exaggerated romantic subjectivism. Clarity and logic of stylistic elements combined with intense feeling and refined expressive means enabled Glinka to achieve a synthesis of classical and romantic artistic principles.

Glinka's creative method was realism, not as a sentimental representation of imagery or types, but as a disclosure of the inner meaning of generalized imagery and types. The simplicity of his music and the sincerity of his emotional expression relate his music to Pushkin's poetry. These qualities make Glinka the greatest Russian classical composer.

Glinka loved economy of expression and musical means. His compositions do not contain tedious musical passages, often found in romantic compositions of his time. Glinka's sense of the proportion of musical forms determines the characteristic clarity and balance of their component parts. He had perfect mastery of all types of musical construction, from simple sectional patterns to the most complex sonata form. Musical form, in Glinka's style, does not have structural meaning. It has an esthetic significance derived from the indissoluble unity of expressive musical means and artistic imagery, a unity which Glinka successfully attained in small forms as well as large symphonic conceptions.

Glinka gave meticulous attention to every musical detail, especially to melodic aspects. Avoiding vertical successions of harmony, he achieved a freedom of melodic movement in four-part writing. Glinka's harmony is the result of polymelody which is a free melodic interweave. These melodic patterns are not independent polyphonic voices, but offshoots of the main melody. Polymelody is characteristic of Russian folk songs in which the main melody is sometimes supported by free improvisational melodic interweaves. Polymelody characterizes Glinka's variations in which changing harmonic figurations surround the basic melody.

Glinka's harmony is clear and simple. When he wants to obtain special color effects, he resorts to unusual harmonic successions. As a rule, Glinka adheres to logical and consistent patterns of diatonic harmony. Whenever chromatic elements occur, they are passing and do not interfere with the stability of the diatonic foundation. Glinka did not care to deviate from the main tonality; he preferred to stay in it for a long time. Modulations, when they occur in his music, however, may be either sudden or gradual.

In instrumentation, Glinka adhered to the classical principle of balancing instrumental groups and timbres. His orchestrations are light and transparent. He avoids cumbersome instrumental stratifications. The brilliance and virtuosity of Glinka's orchestrations are due to differentiation of timbres and his ability to reveal qualities of individual instruments, especially in solo passages.

Glinka regarded the balancing of tone gradations as the main condition of good orchestration. He was opposed to exaggerated dynamics and artificially contrived effects. He summarized his ideas about the orchestra in the statement: "The beauty of a musical thought brings out the beauty of an orchestra."

Glinka's musical thinking relates him more closely to the great masters of the classical period than to those of the romantic period. The healthy and sober objectivity of Glinka's music, based on a positive and optimistic approach to Russian national reality, became the essential characteristic of composers of the Russian national musical school who carried on his artistic and esthetic principles.

Glinka was born on June 1, 1804, in the village of Novospasskoye, the hereditary estate of his father in the government of Smolensk. Glinka was a gentle, inquisitive and impressionable boy. He loved nature and village life. In her recollections of her brother, his sister Ludmila Shestakova writes:

My brother understood and loved passionately the Russian people. He knew how to talk to peasants. The villagers understood, obeyed, and respected him. In his childhood he often listened to their opinions. Whenever he returned to the village for the Summer, or even in Winter, he would assemble peasants and manor serfs, give them presents, and organize festivities with refreshments, dances, swings, and other amusements.[1]

Glinka was attracted to music at an early age. He often listened to his uncle's orchestra of serf musicians and he soon developed a passion for music. He loved Russian folk songs and he wrote in his later years: "Perhaps the songs which I heard in my childhood were the first reason why I began to develop mostly Russian national music."

Fascinated by the orchestra, Glinka learned to play the flute and violin. At the age of eleven, he began to take piano lessons. He studied languages, history, literature, and drawing. He was enraptured by geography books which awakened an interest in foreign countries and a desire to travel, which persisted throughout his life. In his mature years, Glinka was a very cultured person. He spoke eight languages, including Persian, Spanish, and Italian.

In 1817, Glinka was enrolled in a boarding school for noblemen's children in Petersburg. He became acquainted with the progressive social ideas which eventually brought on the Decembrists' uprising. Among Glinka's tutors was Küchelbecker, a friend of Pushkin and a member of the secret revolutionary society. Although Glinka never joined the secret society, he experienced the influence of its liberal ideas. "He was indignant at serfdom and his only thought, his only desire was that the Russian people would be free." [2]

Glinka continued his musical studies. He took piano lessons from the famous Irish pianist-composer John Field. The lessons did not envisage anything beyond customary salon playing. Glinka became a regular visitor at aristocratic salons where music was a favorite pastime. He tried to compose and wrote variations on a popular theme from Joseph Weigl's opera *Der Schweitzerfamilie,* and variations for harp and piano on a theme by Mozart.

In 1822, Glinka graduated from the boarding school. After serving for a short time in a government position, he lived alternately in Petersburg and Novospasskoye. In Petersburg, Glinka played the piano in salons, accompanied singers, participated as a singer in private operatic productions, composed songs and variations on popular themes, and gained the reputation of a talented musical amateur.

During these years, however, music was more than salon entertainment for Glinka. In his childhood, he listened attentively to Russian folk songs sung by peasants or played by his uncle's orchestra. His interest did not diminish in later years. Glinka was always interested in the popular tunes and melodies he heard sung by a village coachman, at outdoor village celebrations and at gatherings of friends. He studied the compositions of Haydn, Mozart, Beethoven, Méhul, and Cherubini performed by his uncle's orchestra. He played them with friends in four-hand arrangements.

In Petersburg, Glinka became acquainted with the great literary personalities of his time. He met the poets Pushkin, Zhukovsky, and Delvig and the dramatist Griboyedov, who influenced Glinka's attitude toward art and the function of a creative artist in society.

Glinka's attempts at composition made him realize his deficiencies in musical theory. He took lessons in harmony, counterpoint, and musical analysis. He learned orchestration from personal experience with orchestral instruments. Glinka soon came to the conclusion that he had learned all he could from his teachers. He decided to continue his studies in Western Europe. In the spring of 1830, Glinka left for Italy.

There were several reasons Glinka went to Italy first. Among them were the Italian climate, the great traditions of Italian art and the Italian *bel canto*, then at the height of its development in the operas of Bellini and Donizetti, two composers Glinka met in Italy.

Although Glinka was charmed by Italian art, he reached the conclusion that southern *sentimento brilliante* (light-hearted melody) was not compatible with the strong and harsh feelings of northern Russians. During the three years Glinka lived in Italy, he composed a sextette for piano and strings in E flat major (1830), a "Trio Pathétique" in D Minor for piano, clarinet and bassoon (1833), and variations and divertimentos on themes from popular Italian operas. "The pieces which I composed to please the inhabitants of Milan," wrote Glinka, "convinced me that I was not following a path suitable for me, and that I could not sincerely be an Italian."

In 1832, Glinka began to plan a national patriotic opera. Two years later, in a letter to a friend, he confirmed his intention: "To give our theatre a composition of large dimensions . . . the most important thing is the subject. In any case, the subject will be completely national, and the music will also be national. I want that my dear compatriots should feel themselves at home . . . The problem we face is to develop our own style and to blaze new trails for Russian operatic music."

From Italy, Glinka went to Vienna where he became captivated by the dance music of Johann Strauss, the elder, and Joseph Lanner. From Vienna, Glinka went to Berlin to study theory with Siegfried Dehn. Dehn helped Glinka to systematize his theoretical knowledge and compositional technique.

In 1834, upon news of his father's death, Glinka hurried home. He returned after an absence of four years with an enriched musical background and important acquisitions in compositional technique. He was a mature composer who felt himself equipped to realize large and independent artistic problems.

Glinka's compositions of this period present a good idea of his creative individuality. He shared the middle class sentimentality of Russian cities. The favorite subjects of his songs are unrequited love, disappointed happiness, loneliness, cruel fate, precarious earthly happiness, hope for reconciliation in afterlife, and recollections of and regrets for the past. His smooth, flexible melodies show the influence of Italian cantilena. The piano accompaniments are colorful and descriptive.

Glinka's early instrumental compositions were written for the piano and harp, the two most popular instruments in Russian homes. The compositions are variations, dances, and melodic pieces in the style of John Field's nocturnes. Glinka also composed more serious works in classical design, including sonatas and chamber compositions.

Upon returning from his travels abroad, Glinka began to consider the composition of a national opera. The idea met with enthusiastic support among Glinka's literary friends.

The 1830's was the golden age of Russian literature. Pushkin, Lermontov, Zhukovsky, Delvig, Yazikov, Gogol, and other progressive writers recognized their cultural responsibilities to the Russian people. They realized that a national opera composed by an outstanding Russian composer would be an event of the greatest importance in Russian cultural life.

The subject of *Ivan Susanin* was recommended to Glinka by Zhukovsky. The story of Ivan Susanin, a peasant from the province of Kostroma, who gave his life to save his country from Polish invaders, was a suitable subject for a national opera. The epic image of Susanin received various interpretations in Russian literature. Official monarchist literature used the story to strengthen imperial autocracy. Progressive and freethinking Russian patriots regarded Susanin's heroic deed as an example of the idealism, dignity, and patriotism of the Russian people. Susanin's exploit was described in a ballad by the poet, Decembrist Rileyev (1825). In the ballad Susanin says to the Polish invaders:

> You thought you found a traitor in me.
> No Russian would betray his country.
> He loves his homeland,
> And he would never be disloyal.

Glinka became interested in the Susanin story and prepared the scenario of an opera. The libretto was written by Baron Rosen, a Russified German, whose literary style was an imitation of verbose eighteenth-century Russian poetry. Since Rosen was a staunch monarchist, he introduced ideas of loyalty to the throne into the libretto. Glinka's intention was to call the opera, *Ivan Susanin, a Patriotic*

Heroic-Tragic Opera. Under the pressure of Tsar Nicholas the First, however, who wanted the patriotic intention of the opera to be accepted as a glorification of tsarist autocracy, the opera was renamed *A Life for the Tsar.*

The story of the opera is based on an historical event which took place in the winter of 1612. Moscow was already liberated from the Polish invaders, but scattered detachments of Polish troops roamed the countryside. One of the detachments decided to capture Tsar Mikhail who lived in the vicinity of Domnino, a village in the province of Kostroma.

The operatic action takes place in the winter of 1612, during the final stage of the struggle to liberate Moscow and Russia from the Polish invaders. The first scene represents a street on Domnino, in which a gathering of the people's volunteer corps and villagers stand; among the villagers are Ivan Susanin and his daughter Antonida. Antonida hopes for the return of her fiancé Bogdan Sobinin as well as their forthcoming marriage.

A boat containing Sobinin and a group of soldiers sails up the river. Sobinin tells the villagers of the victories of his detachment and the success of the volunteer corps led by Minin and Pozharsky. He asks Susanin to let him marry Antonida. The villagers support Sobinin's plea. At first, Susanin decides to postpone the marriage because of Russia's sufferings from the invaders. But when Sobinin tells Susanin that the Poles in Moscow have been surrounded and that victory is imminent, Susanin consents to the wedding.

The next scene takes place in Poland. A ball is in progress at the castle of King Sigismund. The Poles are exulting in their power, boasting that they will conquer Russia and enrich themselves with plunder. Suddenly, a messenger arrives and informs the assembly that Minin's troops have defeated the Poles. The assembled guests decide to send a detachment of troops to capture Minin and occupy Moscow.

The scene shifts to Susanin's cottage. Preparations are made for Antonida's wedding. Peasants come to express good wishes and then leave to work in the forest.

A Polish detachment arrives and orders Susanin to guide them to Moscow. Susanin sends his adopted son Vanya to warn the Russian troops of the enemy. Susanin agrees to guide the Poles and leads them into an impenetrable forest.

Antonida's girl friends enter the cottage and find her in deep sorrow. Sobinin and the villagers also enter the cottage. When they learn that the Poles took Susanin with them, they decide to pursue the captors and rescue Susanin.

At night, Vanya arrives at a monastery settlement and awakens the Russian soldiers, who rush to pursue the enemy. Meanwhile, Susanin leads the Poles into frozen, snow-covered backwoods. The Poles decide to rest for the night. Susanin does not sleep. He knows that when the Poles discover his deceit they will murder him. He mentally takes leave of his family. In the cold winter morning, when the Poles realize they are lost in the forest and will perish, they murder Susanin.

The first presentation of *A Life for the Tsar* took place in Petersburg on December 9, 1836. This date is regarded as the birthday of the Russian national opera. In dramatic power, technical mastery and esthetic significance, Glinka's opera was superior to all previous Russian operas. *A Life for the Tsar* gave Glinka the reputation of an outstanding Russian composer.

In spite of the opera's approval by court circles, there were voices of disapproval. During the *première* of the opera, Glinka heard some members of the aristocracy express themselves in French, saying *"C'est la musique des cochers,"* meaning that the opera is coachmen's music. The court aristocracy was indifferent to Glinka's music and never recognized his musical abilities. His unsuccessful marriage and subsequent divorce caused him much humiliation. Failure to obtain moral support for his artistic endeavors brought on a feeling of frustration and disillusionment.

Glinka became friendly with the literary circle of the dramatist Kukolnik. There, he was met with respect and appreciation. The artistic level of Kukolnik's circle, however, was too circumscribed to understand the magnitude of Glinka's creative ideas. Glinka remained a lonely and frustrated person.

These were the conditions under which Glinka began to compose his second opera based on Pushkin's poem, *Ruslan and Ludmila*. He confided to Pushkin his intention to compose it and Pushkin agreed to provide the libretto with other collaborators. It took Glinka five years to write the opera.

In the opera, Svetozar, Prince of Kiev, is celebrating the marriage of his daughter, Ludmila, to Ruslan. Among the guests are two unsuccessful suitors, the young Khazar Khan Ratmir and the vainglorious

Farlaf. The singer, Bayan, predicts misfortune for Ruslan and Ludmila.

A crash of thunder followed by darkness interrupts the celebration. The guests are paralyzed with fear. When the darkness disappears, the guests find that Ludmila has been abducted by some evil power. Svetozar promises Ludmila's hand to anyone who will find her. Ruslan, Ratmir, and Farlaf depart in search of Ludmila.

Ruslan arrives at a cave inhabited by a kind magician, Finn, who informs Ruslan that Ludmila has been abducted by a terrible magician, the dwarf Chernomor. Finn foretells that Ruslan will eventually vanquish Chernomor. In a ballad, one of the most beautiful episodes in the opera, Finn tells Ruslan the story of his love for Naina, who turns out to be an evil sorceress.

Meanwhile, Farlaf scrambles out of a ditch, in which he has hidden, frightened by the dangers he encountered on the road. He regrets that he has undertaken the dangerous assignment. Suddenly Naina appears before Farlaf and promises to help him find Ludmila.

Ruslan continues the search. He arrives at a deserted battlefield and gives himself up to thoughts about the transitory quality of human life. He notices a large head and, after a brief struggle with it, takes possession of a magic sword concealed under the head.

The head is all that remains of Chernomor's brother, whom Chernomor treacherously destroyed. The head tells Ruslan that with the magic sword, he will defeat Chernomor, provided that Ruslan cut off Chernomor's long beard in which his magic power resides.

The next scene takes place in the magic castle of Naina. Naina's beautiful maidens entice tired travelers into the castle. Among them is Gorislava, who pines for Ratmir. Ratmir comes to the castle, but, as he is under Naina's spell, he fails to recognize Gorislava. Ruslan, enmeshed by Naina's charms, arrives at the castle. Suddenly Finn appears and saves the captives. The walls of the castle collapse. Ruslan resumes his search for Ludmila.

Ludmila is held captive in Chernomor's magic gardens. She does not enjoy the luxury of her surroundings. She longs for Kiev and a reunion with Ruslan. Ludmila is ready to die rather than submit herself to Chernomor.

A march, one of the most famous marches in Russian music, announces the arrival of Chernomor, surrounded by slaves and servants who dance for Ludmila's entertainment. At the height of the dances, a horn call is heard. It is Ruslan, who challenges Chernomor to combat. Chernomor plunges Ludmila into a deep sleep and rushes in to struggle with Ruslan. Ruslan cuts off Chernomor's beard with the magic sword and vanquishes the dwarf.

Ruslan finds Ludmila, but cannot awaken her from her sleep. Accompanied by Ratmir, Gorislava, and the freed slaves of Chernomor, Ruslan departs with the sleeping Ludmila for Kiev. While they camp for the night, Chernomor's slaves rush into Ruslan's tent to tell him that Ludmila has disappeared. Farlaf, helped by Naina, has abducted Ludmila and carried her off to Svetozar's palace in Kiev. Ruslan's friend, Finn, appears on the scene and gives Ruslan a magic ring which will awaken Ludmila.

Svetozar and the inhabitants of Kiev bewail the sleeping Ludmila, whom no one can awaken. Ruslan arrives and with a touch of the magic ring wakes Ludmila. The people of Kiev rejoice and glorify their country and their prince.

The first performance of *Ruslan* took place on December 9, 1842. The audience accepted the opera with indifference verging on general condemnation. Only a few music critics, who were close to Glinka, understood the significance of this operatic masterpiece.

The staging of the opera was surrounded by unpleasant experiences for Glinka. He had to agree to cuts and changes in the score. The singers were not adequately prepared and their inexperience in leading roles contributed to the failure of the *première*. The Tsar's family left the theater before the last act of the opera and the public accepted this action as an official disapproval of the opera. *Ruslan* was taken out of the repertoire. The opera was not performed again until after Glinka's death.

The failure of *Ruslan* was due to the originality of Glinka's musical style, to the preference of operatic audiences for Italian operas, and to the biased attitude of aristocratic circles toward Glinka. Even progressive literary and artistic circles were unsympathetic toward *Ruslan*. The cheerful and optimistic objectivity of the opera did not satisfy these artistic circles, interested in the baring of clashes and contradictions in Russian social reality. The controversy over *Ruslan* lasted for many years. The music critic Serov, who admired the music of *Ruslan*, doubted the opera's suitability for the stage. Serov's opinion was shared by Tchaikovsky. In a review "The Revival of *Ruslan and*

Ludmila," in *Russkiye Vedomosti* (1875), Tchaikovsky compared *A Life for the Tsar* and *Ruslan and Ludmilla*. He wrote that there was more musical material and of better quality in *Ruslan* than in *A Life for the Tsar*. Great works of art, however, are valued, not so much for the power of spontaneous creativity as for the perfection of form, the balancing of parts, and the successful blending of an idea with musical expression. Tchaikovsky concluded that *Ruslan* was not an operatic masterpiece. It was only a magic spectacle accompanied by excellent music, too difficult for execution. The opera violated the conditions for theatrical effectiveness and feasibility of vocal performance.

While working on *Ruslan,* Glinka created a series of compositions in various forms. In 1839, he composed "Valse Fantaisie," a composition which continued the symphonization of dance elements in *A Life for the Tsar*. The "Valse Fantaisie" influenced the development of waltz characteristics in Russian symphonic music.

In 1840, Glinka composed incidental music to Kukolnik's tragedy *Prince Kholmsky*. The music did not meet with public approval. Only after Glinka's death were the programmatic and dramatic elements of the music fully appreciated. The music to *Prince Kholmsky* was followed by a series of songs. Those songs composed to Pushkin's texts are masterpieces in Russian song literature.

During the summer of 1844, Glinka went abroad. His first stop was in Paris, where he lived till the spring of 1845. He met Berlioz who admired and respected Glinka's musical talent. Berlioz included selections from *A Life for the Tsar* and *Ruslan* in his concerts. Some time later, Glinka gave a concert of his compositions. In the *Journal de Débats* of April 16, 1845, Berlioz wrote that Glinka "has the right to occupy a place alongside the outstanding composers of his time." In a letter from Paris, Glinka wrote that he was the first Russian composer to acquaint the Parisian public with his name and with the compositions he composed in Russia for Russians.

While in Paris, Glinka decided to compose several orchestral compositions based on national dance and folk song materials. For this purpose, he went to Spain, whose national intonations and dance rhythms had always attracted him. During the two years Glinka spent in Spain, he studied Spanish folklore, attended national celebrations and festivals, became acquainted with performers of popular songs and dance music, and copied Spanish melodies characteristic of Spanish intonations. The result of these studies was the *Capriccio Brilliante sur la thème de la Jota Aragonesa*. Later, he used two *seguidillas*, which he heard sung by Spanish muleteers, for his *Souvenir d'une Nuit d'Été à Madrid*.

During the summer of 1847, Glinka returned to Russia. For a few months, he lived on his estate at Novospasskoye and then settled in Warsaw. Here he first sketched the *Souvenir d'une Nuit d'Été à Madrid* and then composed a fantasy on Russian wedding and dance songs, the *Kamarinskaya*. The *Kamarinskaya* is Glinka's artistic solution of the symphonization of Russian folk songs, an idea which always intrigued him.

During the winter of 1848, Glinka lived in Petersburg, but the hostility and intentional neglect he met with compelled him to leave there. A few years of wandering followed, during which Glinka composed songs and piano pieces. Around 1850, Glinka's admirers formed a circle to disseminate his musical ideas. Their efforts fell short of encouraging Glinka's sagging morale.

In 1852, Glinka left for Paris. He stopped over in Berlin and met Meyerbeer, at that time regarded as one of the greatest operatic composers. Glinka studied the music of eighteenth-century composers, especially the operas of Gluck. He composed parts of a programmatic symphony, *Taras Bulba*, based on Gogol's story of the same name. Dissatisfied with the score, Glinka destroyed it.

In 1854–1855, Glinka was back in Paris. He wrote his memoirs and made several orchestral arrangements, among them Weber's *Invitation to the Waltz*. In the spring of 1856, Glinka left for Berlin. His intention was to study medieval polyphony and to reform Russian church music. He died suddenly on February 15, 1857. His remains were brought to Petersburg and were interred in the Alexander Nevsky Monastery.

Glinka's most important compositions are the operas, *A Life for the Tsar* and *Ruslan and Ludmila*. *A Life for the Tsar* is a patriotic music drama based on historical facts. *Ruslan* is a musical fairy tale which combines fantasy with the imagery of the real world, the incredible and supernatural with the simple and commonplace and the mysterious and enigmatic with the natural joke and humor. Both operas are national in general conception, in stylistic components and in the method of musical-dramatic thinking.

In *A Life for the Tsar,* Glinka departed from customary operatic methods and traditions. Western European operas do not contain heroic plots similar to that of *A Life for the Tsar.* The idea of deliberate self-sacrifice in order to save someone else from impending danger occurred in French "rescue operas." However, heroic self-sacrifice in French rescue operas was usually based on motives of personality, love, attachment, or abstract justice. The happy ending in a rescue opera was usually based on melodramatic or sentimental reasons.

In Meyerbeer's "grand operas," the fate of heroic personages is intimately interwoven with fortuitous national or religious conflicts. Meyerbeer's heroes, engrossed in personal experiences, become victims of fateful circumstances.

Glinka's *A Life for the Tsar* has nothing to do with morality, virtue, and romantic heroism. The opera represents the people as the main force in historical events. The opening chorus indicates not only Susanin's character, but the triumph of a victorious people. Glinka shows the people as a great personality animated by a heroic and selfless love of the motherland. In this respect, Glinka followed in the footsteps of Pushkin who, in his drama *Boris Godunov,* reveals the fate of the people.

Stasov expressed the possibility that Pushkin's readings of *Boris Godunov* in Moscow and Petersburg were attended by Glinka, who might have been inspired by them to compose *A Life for the Tsar.* The historical periods of *Boris Godunov* and of *A Life for the Tsar* are closely related. The end of Boris' reign was followed by the reign of the first Romanov tsar. It is possible that Pushkin, who suggested the plots of *Dead Souls* and *The Government Inspector* to Gogol, inspired Glinka to compose *A Life for the Tsar.* Glinka's opinion of the spiritual greatness of the Russian common man echoed the idea, held by Pushkin's friends and the Decembrists, that the esthetics of Russian nationalism represented the richest source of national expression.

Susanin embodies the best qualities and aspirations of the common people. His drama is inseparable from the fate of the Russian people and the Russian state. His death represents the triumph of patriotism and love of one's country. His personal tragedy affects all people. In spite of Susanin's tragic fate, the opera's conception is optimistic. Susanin was a peasant man who lived and worked among the people and in a decisive moment, revealed the power and greatness of his character. In the words of Mussorgsky, Susanin is not a common muzhik;

"He is an idea, a legend, the powerful creation of necessity."

Susanin's relationship to the people is expressed in the opera's music. The part Susanin sings contains elements of authentic folk song intonations. The choruses contain musical quotations from popular peasant choruses. The opera contains two imposing choral scenes, one in the introduction and one in the finale. The method of framing a national epic opera with chorale scenes became traditional in Russian operatic art.

The concluding chorus in the finale, the *Slavsya* (Glory), is one of Glinka's greatest musical creations. It is probable that the strong marchlike rhythms of this chorus hark back to the 1812 marches, evoked by by the patriotic fervor of the war against the Napoleonic invasion. The musical and dramatic elements in *A Life for the Tsar* are clear and precise delineations of personality and situation, in independent musical presentations and episodes.

In creating musical themes which expressed Russian national musical imagery, Glinka employed generalized forms of songs which were derived from a study of the laws of national art. Glinka did not leave a written account of his studies of national popular songs. His music, however, reveals his tremendous knowledge and understanding of Russian folk songs.

Russian themes in *A Life for the Tsar* reflect musical peculiarities in national musical creativity. Glinka did not restrict himself to local musical elements. He did not favor any particular melodic pattern and used all national genres which would enhance the artistic conceptions of the opera.

Russian folk songs often reveal transformations of a particular tune or melodic fragment into various stylistic types. In Glinka's style, national tunes and melodic turns received new interpretations which he combined with other means of musical expression.

The classical perfection and simplicity of Glinka's music is sustained by the unfolding of the operatic plot. Dramatic situations are related symphonically by developments of significant themes and motives. The motive of the *Slavsya* chorus, in the epilogue, for example, first occurs in the introduction and then appears in climactic situations in the opera. The *Slavsya* chorus is, therefore, not merely a festive conclusion, but is also a logical climax of the musical and dramatic conceptions of the opera.

A Life for the Tsar represents a turning point in the development of

Russian operatic art. Glinka brought outstanding ideological content and popular national heroes into it. He was the first Russian composer to master large operatic forms and the prevailing expressive vocal and instrumental means. He was the first composer to create a national Russian opera notable for the unity of its style as well as for its musical and dramatic elements.

Ruslan and Ludmila carries on the traditions of the Russian epic fairy tale opera, with its elements of comic entertainment, which prevailed in the first years of the nineteenth century. The plot of *Ruslan* is characterized by a piling up of events and scenes, by a multiplicity of momentary imagery and by picturesque contrasts and enchanting sights. Glinka presents a succession of realistic imagery in a kaleidoscopic series of events. He contrasts lyric and comic elements and Russian and oriental elements. He depicts the mysterious, the fantastic and also the simple emotional experience.

Although the opera's personages act in imaginary and fantastic situations, they are characterized by vitality and truthfulness. Such are the noble Ruslan, the charming and graceful Ludmila, the affectionate Gorislava, the ardent Ratmir, the swashbuckling coward Farlaf, the introspective Finn, and the old Russian singer and gusli player, narrator of folk tales in Svetozar's palace, the wise Bayan. Svetozar is endowed with the attributes of the epic Prince Vladimir, "Bright Sun," of Kiev.

The fantasy of the plot is contrasted with the heroic imagery of Russian epic antiquity. As in *A Life for the Tsar,* every image or personality receives a distinct delineation in independent and complete musical representations and episodes.

In *Ruslan,* as well as the fairy tale operas of Rimsky-Korsakov, the development of national subjects from the Russian epos is invariably based on the principle of the inevitable triumph of justice over evil in the destruction of Chernomor, Kashchey, and Dodon. Faith in the victory of justice is supported by the manifestation of the generalized positive attributes of courage and fearlessness by Ruslan and Ivan Korolevich, by the keen-witted Sadko, and by the feminine charm of Ludmila, Tsarevna Nenaglyadnaya Krasa, and Lubava.

Pushkin raised the simple Russian folk tale, the *skazka,* to the level of great literature. In the poem *Ruslan and Ludmila,* which Pushkin wrote in his youth, he adopted a somewhat mischievous and witty attitude toward the heroes, endowing them with human weakness and frailty. Some years later, Pushkin contemplated rewriting the poem in a more serious vein. In this serious vein, Glinka reinterpreted the poem and described the actions and experiences of the heroes with affection, warmth and heartfelt excitement.

As a symphonic composer, Glinka first revealed his genius in the instrumental selections in his operas. Among them are the Polish dances in *A Life for the Tsar,* the oriental dances in *Ruslan,* Chernomor's march, and the overtures.

In 1834, Glinka planned a symphony based on Russian folk songs. He never completed the symphony, but composed the first movement which he called an *Overture Symphony.* The conception of the symphony anticipated, by fifteen years, the *Overture Fantasia Kamarinskaya* based on Russian folk songs.

The *Kamarinskaya* reflects elements of Russian national life and character. It is more than a vivid musical picture of life in a Russian village. It reveals the inexhaustible creative fantasy of the people and their national characteristics, including introspective mood, healthy revelry, and rich humor.

Glinka's method of symphonic development was new in Russian music. From a single melodic core, Glinka created a continuity of new intonational elements which led to new melodic formations. This creation was the result of Glinka's study of the peculiarities of Russian folk songs, in which the main tune is freely developed by members of the chorus.

The *Kamarinskaya* is a series of variations on two Russian folk songs, one a lyric, pensive wedding song, the other a lively dance song. Similar contrasts were found in compositions of Glinka's contemporaries. Glinka, however, noticed the common characteristics of the two songs including the descending scale movement within the interval of a fourth, often found in Russian folk songs. This enabled him to combine the tunes in the process of development.

Glinka embellished both tunes with supporting melodies in the manner of free improvisations practiced by peasant choruses. The transparent orchestration helps to reveal these improvisatory embellishments. The instruments are used in a manner which reminds the listener of national Russian instruments such as pipes, horns, and balalaikas. A humorous effect is achieved when the different tonalities, in which the dance tune appears, are accompanied by single tones sounded out of place by brass instruments.

The *Kamarinskaya* laid the foundation for Russian national symphonic music. This type of symphonic music was further developed by Dargomijsky, Balakirev, Mussorgsky, Rimsky-Korsakov, Borodin, Tchaikovsky, and Lyadov. Tchaikovsky summarized the idea in the following words: "There is a genuine Russian symphonic school. It is all in *Kamarinskaya,* just as an oak tree is in an acorn. For many years Russian composers will derive inspiration from this rich source."

The *Capriccio Brilliante sur la thème de la Jota Aragonesa* is a symphonic synthesis of various thematic elements in a complete, unified composition. Glinka based it on variations of a Spanish guitarist whom he had heard in Spain. Glinka preserved the peculiarities and sonorities of Spanish guitar music by means of a harp and pizzicato effects on string instruments.

The harmonic scheme of the accompaniment to the *Jota* is a succession of arpeggios of tonic and dominant chords. This is common in Spanish guitar music. Glinka combined these simple improvisational characteristics with the features of a sonata form development.

Souvenir d'une Nuit d'Été à Madrid is a colorful representation of contrasting musical episodes, based on four popular Spanish themes heard constantly in complete and independent thematic divisions. The ethereal orchestration of the introduction evokes the feeling of a sultry southern night. It forms a poetic and descriptive background for a series of vivid musical scenes from Spanish outdoor celebrations. Reviewing the composition Tchaikovsky wrote: "How much warm inspiration and luxurious poetic fantasy there is in this fascinating composition of our great artist! The extraordinarily original overture describing the transparent twilight of the approaching southern night; the passionately captivating sounds of the dance heard in the distance; the quickly changing episodes in the middle section in which is heard a mysterious prattle, a kiss, an embrace, and then, again, a calm under the cover of a fragrant, starry southern night."

In 1839, Glinka composed the "Valse Fantaisie" for piano. In 1845, he orchestrated it and in 1856, he completed a revised orchestration. The sincerity, smoothness, and lyricism of waltz music were appreciated in the Russia of Glinka's time. The main theme in the "Valse Fantaisie" is pensive and wistful. Instead of four measures in sentence structure, Glinka used three measures. This irregularity

evokes a feeling of restlessness and incompletion. The main theme is •
alternated with other tunes which evoke various psychological sensations, dramatically excited or charmingly refined and melancholy. As
a symphonic composition, the "Valse Fantaisie" laid the foundation
for the lyrical and psychological elements in Russian symphonic
music, expressing inner human experiences and emotions. Tchaikovsky's waltz music is a notable example.

In the incidental music to Kukolnik's drama, *Prince Kholmsky,*
Glinka anticipated the evolution of dramatic elements in nineteenth-
century Russian symphonic music. The drama is based on an historical event in Russian history in the fifteenth century. The main character in Glinka's music is the ambitious Prince Kholmsky. Livonian
(Baltic) knights use Kholmsky as a tool in their struggle with the
principality of Moscow. In order to persuade Kholmsky to declare
himself the independent ruler of the principalities of Novgorod and
Pskov, the knights use the beautiful and cunning baroness Adelgeide
who pretends she loves Kholmsky. The insincere love of Adelgeide is
contrasted with the devotion of the beautiful Jewess, Rachel, who sincerely loves Kholmsky.

The people of Novgorod and Pskov assemble in a *Veche,* a popular
assembly in ancient Russia, and repudiate Kholmsky's leadership.
Abandoned by Adelgeide, Kholmsky is disgraced.

A waltz-like, flexible theme describes Adelgeide and a powerful
theme characterizes Kholmsky. Glinka's somber and tragic music expresses the doom of Kholmsky and describes the psychological aspects
of the drama.

The War of 1812 awakened the hidden forces of the Russian people, later reflected in the poetry of Pushkin and the music of Glinka.
The bright and optimistic music of Glinka is spiritually related to
Pushkin's poetry and this music reflects the awakening consciousness
of the Russian people. Herein lies its spiritual wealth and content.
Glinka discovered, in the depths of Russian national life, the foundations of his music and imagery. Each of his images is, according to
Stasov, a complete picture, an incarnation of an epoch and of Russian
nationality. The effect of these images is a typical generalization, an
inalienable property of realistic art.

Glinka's music is an incarnation of Russian character and thinking.

Although the epic images of Susanin and Ruslan may seem, at times, different from Russian reality, they continue to live in Russian consciousness as examples of individuals who represent the best moral and ethical qualities of the Russian people.

Esthetics

The principles underlying Glinka's music are patriotism, democracy, and realism of artistic imagery. Although Glinka was acquainted with the Decembrists' leaders, he was not a political revolutionary. Wherever he lived, in the Russian village, in Italy or in Spain, he always regarded popular national sources as the true expressions of historical ideas of progress and development. The nationalism of his musical style is based on the unity of popular folk elements and national aspirations of the Russian intelligentsia.

Patriotism and love of country permeate Glinka's musical style. By drawing upon sources of Russian folklore, Glinka satisfied the cultural and artistic needs of his time. The main hero in *A Life for the Tsar* is a Russian peasant who personifies, as an historical force, the Russian people. The meaning of his opera is love of country and subordination of personal desires and passions to this ideal.

Glinka's main accomplishment is the creation of a Russian national musical school. He used Russian plots and he laid the foundations of Russian melody, harmony, polyphony, orchestration, musical form, and the art of musical performance. He fought the penetration of Italian and German influences into Russian music, but never failed to use the best that Western music had to offer.

Glinka's ideas and stylish traits transcended his era and were developed by later Russian composers: sincerity and lyricism by Tchaikovsky, patriotic imagery by Mussorgsky, majestic epos by Borodin, fantastic fairyland by Rimsky-Korsakov, variety of polyphonic devices by Taneyev and Glazunov, and refinement and elegance by Lyadov.

Glinka's aphorisms express his artistic views:

The people create music; we arrange it.
Coachmen are more practical than gentlemen.
One should compose in a manner comprehensible to experts and the ordinary public.
Feeling is inspiration from above. Form is beauty; it is the proportionality

of parts for the working out of the whole. Feeling creates the fundamental idea, but form clothes the idea with music. Feeling and form are the soul and body of music.
Sincere expression of feeling is the basis of artistic truth.

In his music, Glinka was faithful to his ideas. In *A Life for the Tsar* and *Ruslan and Ludmila,* in romances and in instrumental music, Glinka is a national composer. He raised Russian national music to the highest level of artistic expression. A *Life for the Tsar* anticipated the development of Beethovenian-Shakespearean dramatizations in Russian symphonic music. The climax of this trend was attained in Mussorgsky's music drama, *Boris Godunov,* which is a projection of vocal (speech) intonations combined with the Shakespearean method of social-psychological portraiture. *Ruslan and Ludmila* paved the way for Borodin's *Heroic Symphony* in B minor, the opera *Prince Igor,* and Rimsky-Korsakov's epic fairy tale music.

Glinka paid homage to musical romanticism. In his mature artistic period, he turned to realistic trends similar to Pushkin's in poetry and Gogol's in prose. In the typification of his operatic heroes, Glinka realistically represents characters from peasant life. Susanin is important; Atonida is graceful; Sobinin is bold and daring; Vanya is simple-hearted. Susanin's importance expresses stern heroism and patriotism. Sobinin's boldness is the courage of the Russian soldier. Antonida's grace is the incarnation of the idealism of the Russian woman.

The esthetic aspects in *Ruslan and Ludmila* represent the struggle of good and evil, of courage and cowardice, of honesty and perfidy, and the inevitable victory of justice. The heroes in the opera are carriers of truthful spiritual qualities.

In *Prince Kholmsky,* Glinka developed the drama of the struggle of patriotism with the charm of seduction. The idea resembles the plot of Gogol's novel, *Taras Bulba,* the drama of the conflict of social duty with personal predilections. Ensnared by the Polish noblewoman's beauty, Taras' son, Andrei, sacrifices his patriotism and duty to his country.[3]

As a musical painter of nature, Glinka is unique in Russian music. Musical descriptions of the wintry forest in *A Life for the Tsar* and of the wailing wind in the "head" and "Persian" scenes in *Ruslan and Ludmila,* are unexcelled in Russian music.

In the Spanish overtures, Glinka revealed himself a master of impressionistic effects. Alternating booming and soft echoes, decorative polyphonic designs and contrasting orchestral timbres, Glinka created the impression of a national Spanish holiday in the *Aragon Jota*. Approaching and receding tonal effects in *Recollections of a Night in Madrid* create the imagery of a night in which one hears the echoes of Spanish intonations.

Glinka is a superb master of musical intonations. Susanin's intonations express common sense, wisdom, and an inflexible will. Adelgeide's seductive melodies and the musical descriptions of Kholmsky's despair are intonational masterpieces. Farlaf's timidity and Ludmila's anger are intonationally realistic. Melody and timbre intonations, combined with rhythmic and harmonic effects, create a musical picture of the powerful, ridiculous, and the pitiful in Chernomor's march. Transformation of speech intonations into songlike manifestations and of realistic elements into artistic imagery, characterize Glinka's style.

Glinka was influenced by the esthetics of the "age of reason." His music is rationally constructed. Logic and balance of tonal elements are outstanding characteristics of his style. Emotional exhibitionism and improvisational coloring, affectation, exaggeration, pedantry, and shallow illustration are absent in his music. Everything is clear, reasoned out, and intelligible. Glinka emancipated expression of feeling in Russian music. Freedom of feeling and expression was a problem in Glinka's time. Glinka and Pushkin opposed the social hypocrisy and ostentatious official morality of the regime of Nicholas the First.

Glinka and His Contemporaries

The first place in Russian poetry belongs to Pushkin. Pushkin's contemporaries referred to him as "the sun of Russian poetry." The first place in Russian music belongs to Glinka. He is "the sun of Russian music."

Pushkin is the founder of Russian classic literature and Russian literary language. Glinka is the pioneer of Russian national classic music. His music is a perfect blend of ideological content and artistic value. Ethically and esthetically, the arts of Pushkin and Glinka are the best examples of Russian poetry and music.

Glinka's appreciation of national elements in music was influenced by nature, climate and life in the Russian village. His national esthetics was influenced by Pushkin. Like Pushkin, Glinka saw the common man as the only poetic personality in Russian history. When a group of aristocrats referred to *A Life for the Tsar* as "coachmen's music," Glinka answered: "This is good and even correct, since, in my opinion, coachmen are more capable than privileged people." Pushkin advised Glinka to learn the Russian language from Moscow women engaged in baking communion bread.

Like Pushkin in literature, Glinka became the guiding light for later Russian composers. Pushkin and Glinka have common characteristics: freedom of feeling and emotion, humanity and fraternity, appreciation of truth and beauty in human relationships, a sense of reality and deep awareness of national lyric and epic intonations.

The Decembrists appreciated Pushkin, but criticized him for lack of active rebellion against the Tsarist tyranny. The compromising attitude of Pushkin was later criticized by Chernishevsky, Dobrolyubov, and Pisarev (1850).

Pushkin was courageous and patriotic. He hailed freedom and condemned tyranny. In the message *To Chaadayev* Pushkin predicted the revolution:

> While fires of freedom within us burn,
> And hearts for honor beat,
> To our country let us give
> Fervent hopes of our spirit.
> Have faith, comrade,
> The star of happiness shall rise,
> Russia shall awaken from her sleep,
> And on the wreckage of autocracy
> Our names shall be inscribed.

In 1828, Pushkin answered his critics:

> No, I am not a flatterer
> When I praise the Tsar.
> I express my feelings freely,
> I speak the language of the heart.
>
> I am fond of him.
> He rules with courage,
> He revitalized Russia with
> War, hope, and work.

. . . . .

I lived in exile away from friends.
He stretched his regal hand,
And again I am with you.

He respects my inspiration,
He freed my thought.
Should not I in deep emotion
extol him?

Brother! I am not a flatterer.
A flatterer is sly.
He despises the people.

. . . . .

Woe to the country where
Slave and flatterer
Are near the throne.
And the poet, favored by heaven,
Stands silent with downcast eyes.

Pushkin's liberalism and revolutionary sympathies are revealed in the call for liberty in his poem "Freedom," in the human dream in "The Village," in his caustic epigrams against Russia's rulers and in his indictment of social conditions in the two novels, *Dubrovsky* and *The Captain's Daughter.*

Similar expressions of social protest are absent in Glinka's music. Although Glinka maintained ideals of national ethics and esthetics, he was not a revolutionary. Instead of exposing the social problems of Tsarist oppression, Glinka indulges dreams of idyllic patriarchal conditions. His music, despite its artistic greatness, ideologically lagged behind progressive Russian literature.

Gogol's comedy, *The Government Inspector,* with its sarcastic exposure of social and government corruption, appeared on the stage in 1836. This was the year in which Glinka composed *A Life for the Tsar,* a national patriotic opera which shunned revolutionary sentiments and presented the Tsar's relationship to the people in an idyllic light. This treatment gave Nicholas the First an opportunity to use the opera to enhance the idea of autocracy. Contemporary Soviet music criticism, despite the social neutrality of the opera, appreciates its musical and esthetic values.

In 1840, Lermontov's *A Hero of Our Life* and the poem, "Farewell,

Unwashed Russia, Country of Slaves, Country of Gentlemen," appeared. Simultaneously, Glinka, in the music to *Prince Kholmsky,* tried to create a heroic national social drama. The mediocrity of Kukolnik's plot prevented Glinka from attaining his objective. The composition is significant because it reveals Glinka's attempt to rise above the ideational possibilities of contemporary Russian music and create a national heroic style in music.

In 1842, Gogol published *The Greatcoat* and the first volume of his novel, *Dead Souls.* Here were two masterpieces of critical social realism. *The Greatcoat,* a protest against social inequality and injustice, was an indictment of the cruelty and bureaucratic petty tyranny of "important persons" and their indifference to the fate of humble and oppressed people in the lower strata of Russian society. The story marked the beginnings of the humanistic trend in Russian literature of the 1840's as expressed by Dostoyevsky's *Poor People* (1846). The theme was originally developed by Pushkin in the story *The Stationmaster,* in which a poor stationmaster of a provincial relay station drank himself to death vainly seeking the return of his beautiful daughter, Dunya, abducted by a wealthy Petersburg hussar, Minsky. *Dead Souls* unmasked serfdom and the bureaucratic regime of Nicholas the First. Herzen called *Dead Souls* "a bitter reproach and terrible confession of contemporary Russia. . . . Thanks to Gogol, we have seen at last the landed gentry leaving their palaces and country homes without masks and in their true colors, always intoxicated and gluttonous, undignified slaves of state authority, merciless tyrants of their serfs . . . sucking the blood of the people." [4]

In 1842, Glinka was completing the fairy tale opera, *Ruslan and Ludmila,* a treasury of national characteristics and realism, but alien to contemporary social problems in Russian reality. The year 1852 saw the appearance of Turgenev's *A Huntsman's Diary,* a realistic indictment of the evils of serfdom. In 1855, Chernishevsky wrote his dissertation, *Esthetic Relations of Art to Reality* in which he formulated principles of a revolutionary realistic Russian art truthfully interpreting life, passing judgment on reality, criticizing serfdom, and based on the idea that *the beautiful* is seen in life itself and in its development towards new and superior social forms. In 1857, the liberal, progressive ideas of Dobrolyubov's criticisms began to appear in the magazine, *Sovremmenik* (The Contemporary). The canvases of the painter Perov satirized Russian social and political realities. But Glinka's genius, despite the creative vigor, lost its purposefulness. The revolutionary tendencies of the Russian progressive intelligentsia baffled him. The progressive ideas of Pushkin, Gogol, Belinsky, Herzen, Chernishevsky, and Dobrolyubov left Glinka behind.

The esthetics of Russian painting and sculpture influenced Glinka's thinking. Two painters achieved distinction in Glinka's time: Brulov and Venezianov. The outstanding sculptors were Loganovsky and A. Ivanov. Ivanov's objectives were to oppose abstract academicism by depicting the imagery of Russian daily life. Brulov's famous painting is *The Last Day of Pompeii.* Like Glinka, Brulov was attracted to sunny Italy with its artistic traditions and emotions. The attraction of Glinka and Brulov to Italy was not motivated by a desire to imitate Italian art and music. They wanted to enrich Russian art and music with new methods and techniques. Glinka characterized this new Russian style as *sentimento brilliante,* the emancipation of Russian art from academic conditions.

In his *Neapolitan Paintings,* Sylvester Shchedrin acquainted Russian painters with Italian methods of special perspective. The poet Batyushkov enriched Russian speech with the plasticity of Italian melody, or, as Pushkin remarked, "with Italian sounds."

While Glinka realized his ideal of a Russian national music, Brulov, attempting to create a patriotic painting, *The Siege of Pskov by the Troops of King Stefan Batory,* failed to realize his conception. The brilliance and sophistication of Brulov's technique could not be reconciled with Russian national esthetics.

The heroes of Venezianov's paintings are esthetically related to Glinka's heroes in *A Life for the Tsar.* Unlike Glinka, Venezianov did not rise to heroic conceptions and remained within the boundaries of Russian daily existence and thinking.

The painter Alexander Ivanov (1806–1858) sought to escape from reality by utilizing religious ideas. His painting *Appearance of Christ Before the People* (1837–1857) is a protest against social oppression. Glinka's esthetics were alien to religious ideas in art.

The poetry of Pushkin, Zhukovsky, Batyushkov, and Baratinsky influenced Glinka. Glinka acknowledged his love for the sentimentality of Zhukovsky's poetry: "In evenings and during twilight I loved to dream at the piano; the sentimental poetry of Zhukovsky pleased me and moved me to tears. . . . I am indebted to Zhukovsky for many pleasant, poetic moments in my life."

Glinka was more sympathetic towards the monarchist loyalty of Zhukovsky than to Pushkin's revolutionary ideas. The national popular optimism of Glinka was alien to the Germanic romantic gloom and mysticism of Zhukovsky. Glinka was sympathetic with Zhukovsky's poems which are descriptive complaints about the transitory quality of happiness, fickle friendship, and unrequited love. Glinka set these poems to music.

The passionate emotions of sadness in Batyushkov's poems appealed to Glinka. The trio for piano, clarinet, and bassoon was inspired by Batyushkov's poetry, evidenced by Glinka's introductory words to the trio: *"Je n'ai connu l'amour que par les peines qu'il cause."*

Gogol's realism, relentlessly exposing the shady aspects of Russian life, was alien to Glinka's esthetics, but was later reincarnated by Mussorgsky, Rimsky-Korsakov, and Tchaikovsky. Gogol's Russian patriotism was related to Glinka's artistic ideals in *A Life for the Tsar.* Glinka tried to compose a programmatic symphony based on Gogol's novel *Taras Bulba.* The attempt failed because Glinka could not give up his idealism for Gogol's realism. Probably Glinka could not change his set traditions of musical creativity and become a pioneer of Russian musical realism. But the patriotic fervor of Gogol, expressed in the concluding sentences of *Dead Souls,* is musically incarnated in the concluding chorus, *Slavsya,* in *A Life for the Tsar:*

Russia, thou art like an animated troyka that will not be outstripped! The road underneath it moves like smoke, the bridges clang, and everything lags and is left behind.

CHAPTER 6

Dargomijsky

ALEXANDER DARGOMIJSKY carried on Glinka's principles of a national-realistic Russian opera and shared the growing interest of the Russian intelligentsia in social problems. His critical realism in Russian opera paralleled a similar trend in Russian literature and painting. The development of critical realism in opera compelled Dargomijsky to dispense with classical operatic devices and to use, instead, intonations of human speech, declamatory elements, folk songs, and city songs.

Dargomijsky was born on February 2, 1813, in the village of Dargomizh, his father's estate in the Province of Tula. His father, Sergei Dargomijsky, a man with a stern, skeptical disposition, was an illegitimate son of a Russian nobleman prominent during the reign of Catherine the Great. His mother, born Princess Kozlovskaya, was a cultured woman. She wrote poetry and cultivated in her son a love of French literature.

In 1817 the Dargomijskys settled in Petersburg where the future composer spent the rest of his life. Living in a large city and lacking contacts with the country influenced Dargomijsky's personality and musical creativity. Through the use of city songs, romances, and intonations of city speech, Dargomijsky developed an "urban" musical style, rather than an epic-heroic style like Glinka's.

As a child, Dargomijsky learned to play the piano and the violin. During the 1830's, Dargomijsky became known in Petersburg salons as a brilliant pianist and composer of romances and piano compositions, including mazurkas, waltzes, polkas, and variations on Russian songs.

In 1834 Dargomijsky met Glinka, who had returned from abroad and started to compose the opera *A Life for the Tsar*. Encouraged by

Glinka, Dargomijsky studied music theory and orchestration.

At that time, Dargomijsky did not sympathize with Glinka's ideas of a Russian national opera. He preferred the dramatic conflicts of French grand operas of Auber and Meyerbeer. Dargomijsky was interested in French romantic literature, especially the works of Victor Hugo. He decided to compose an opera, *Esmeralda,* based on Hugo's *Notre Dame de Paris.* Although he completed the opera in 1839, it was not until 1847 that it was first performed in Moscow's Bolshoi Theater.

During the winter of 1844–1845 Dargomijsky lived in Paris, and a study of French operatic genres changed his ideas about operas. He became convinced of the shallowness of French grand opera and at the same time realized the significance of Russian national art and culture. As a result, Dargomijsky formulated concepts of a democratic realism in music based on the principle that living reality is superior to artistic fancy and invention.

Dargomijsky first developed concepts of musical realism in a cycle of lyrical psychological songs which he composed in 1845–1850. The songs revealed the main characteristics of Dargomijsky's vocal style, truth and simplicity of musical expression through speech intonations and vocal declamations.

In 1855 Dargomijsky composed an opera, *Rusalka,* based on Pushkin's drama. The opera was the first significant Russian national opera after Glinka's *Ruslan and Ludmila.*

During the last years of his life, Dargomijsky composed a psychologically realistic music drama, *The Stone Guest,* based on Pushkin's drama.

Dargomijsky died in 1869. He was, in the words of Mussorgsky, "a great teacher of truth in music."

Dargomijsky aimed for realistic representations of human emotions and experiences. He did not regard an individual idealistically, as an embodiment of moral excellence, but as a personality revealing various traits and aspects in a social environment.

Musical representations of nature did not intrigue Dargomijsky. Such representations in music interested him only in connection with characterizations of moods, emotions, and situations, as, for example, in the music accompanying Laura's answer to Don Carlos in *The Stone Guest:*

Come, open the balcony.
How peaceful is the sky!
The warm air is still,
The scent of lemons and laurels fills the night,
The moon's lucent orb is in the dark-blue depths,
And watchmen's drawling calls shout: "clear."

The objectives of psychological realism compelled Dargomijsky to look for new means of musical expression. Although he composed vocal, chamber, and symphonic music, it was mainly in the opera that he tried to solve his musical and dramatic problems.

Dargomijsky's musical creativity in Russia coincided with Wagner's in Germany. In their musical objectives, they were opposed.

Wagner's art is a summary of economic, social, biological, national, and religious elements. *Tristan and Isolde* represents the triumph of instinct and the resulting annihilation of the individual. *The Ring of the Nibelungs* is a social and philosophical criticism of society. *Tannhäuser* and *Lohengrin* project the ideas of a pessimistic fate, and the eternal feminine ideal as the embodiment of salvation. *Parsifal* presents opposition between the sinful and virtuous.

These aspects are said to be revealed by Wagner's symphonization of the theater. As a musical dramatist, Wagner achieved the most in symphonic domains. The human voice in Wagner's dramas is subordinated to the orchestra, which is supposed to express the psychological basis of dramatic action.

Wagner expanded the function of the orchestra and his discoveries of the dramatic possibilities of instrumental timbres have influenced other operatic composers. Wagner underestimated his reform of the operatic orchestra. In his book, *Opera and Drama,* Wagner asserted that his orchestra took over the function of the chorus in Greek tragedy. In practice, the function of Wagner's orchestra is more important. The opinion of some Soviet music critics is that Wagner overestimated his reform of scenic dramaturgy.[1]

Dargomijsky's intonational realism destroyed the natural relationship among operatic genres and led to the "fetishization" of one genre at the expense of other genres. Tchaikovsky pointed this out in his newspaper articles and criticisms.[2]

Dargomijsky stressed the word as the carrier of meaning and poetic imagery. Word intonations express spiritual and emotional experiences. To Dargomijsky, human speech reflected feelings, emotions, and experiences. He tried to translate these speech intonations into the language of music. In a letter to a friend (1857), he wrote: "I wish the sound would express the word; I want the truth." Thus, while Wagner saw the means of musical expression in the orchestra, Dargomijsky found these means in the human voice, inseparable from the word.

Dargomijsky combined musical speech and melody in declamatory constructions. The melodic outlines of these constructions, rests, repetitions, and intervallic components emerge in the form of a melodious and expressive reading of the poetic text. The result is a melodic recitative, enriched with speech intonations. Dargomijsky stressed every intonational nuance and shade of expression and for each verbal phrase, he found a suitable musical thought.

Dargomijsky's melodic style does not resemble Wagner's continuous melody. The structural aspects of Dargomijsky's melodies are more complex than operatic arias and songs. His melodies are not successions of independent phrases or sections. They reveal an inner unity determined by the imaginative development of the text. Dargomijsky's melodies have a melodic symmetry, such as binary, ternary, or rondolike structures, rhyming with the verse constructions of the text.

Dargomijsky's intonational dictionary includes intonations which he heard in every phase of daily city life as well as in Russian music. He was familiar with song intonations which he heard in the city, such as adaptations of peasant songs and folk songs, indigenous city songs and tunes, and gypsy songs. These represent the reservoir of his intonational materials.

Dargomijsky's harmonic innovations were very important. Classical harmonic elements were already transformed in Glinka's music by augmented and diminished alterations of major and minor chords and intervals. This tonal thinking is characteristic of Dargomijsky's style. He uses unexpected harmonic progressions, combinations and modulations, often harsh and unpleasant. These tonal aspects weaken regular triad relationships. Instead, subdominant formations appear, harmonies which gravitate to the subdominant triad built on the fourth step of the scale. Dargomijsky also delays in the assertions of the tonic tone of the scale. In *The Stone Guest*, he anticipates vague impressionist effects.

Operas

Rusalka and *The Stone Guest* are Dargomijsky's outstanding operas. *Esmeralda* and the ballet, *The Triumph of Bacchus,* are of lesser significance.

Pushkin's *Rusalka* is a social, psychological drama of common people. Its aspects are significant in everyday life. It is a story of an unhappy, deceived girl. The national aspects of Pushkin's drama are represented by the characters and the popular turns of speech.

Dargomijsky increased the role of the people in the opera by introducing scenes from daily life absent in Pushkin's text. He expanded the peasant scene in the marriage celebration and added a new character, Olga, instead of Pushkin's nurse. Dargomijsky's music gives the opera a popular character, calling attention, in his words, to "dramatic elements." [3] One means of dramatizing the music is to make the singing resemble living human speech. In his review of *Rusalka,* Tchaikovsky wrote: "It is well known that Dargomijsky's power is in his remarkably realistic, and gracefully singing, recitative, which gives his opera the charm of inimitable originality." [4]

The drama centers on the miller, his daughter Natasha, and the prince. Natasha's tragedy is disclosed in the first act of the opera. The work opens with a vocal trio in which the miller, Natasha, and the prince express their feelings. The calculating miller, anticipating the unhappy end of Natasha's affair, thinks of the money the prince will give him. The prince is undecided about how to tell Natasha of the impending separation. In Pushkin's text, the prince is accused of willfully seducing the miller's daughter. In the opera, the prince is a suffering hero, a victim of circumstances more like a character in a French grand opera. Natasha is happy in her love for the prince, but a lurking suspicion makes her feel he no longer loves her. The three characters sing in melodious, declamatory recitatives characteristic of their personalities and emotions.

The opera's libretto avoids the coarse expressions which Pushkin deliberately used to enhance the drama's realism. The influence of French grand opera is evidenced in large choral and ensemble scenes, arias, ballet dancing, and in the charming mermaid scenes.

The miller is a peasant whose warnings to his daughter are

couched in a peasant singsong dialect. His peasant mentality is emphasized by music resembling peasant melodies: diatonic melodies and successions of short motives within the interval of a fourth. The absence of semitone progressions in his melodic recitative enhances the meaning of his exhortations. He is a coarse man, possessing a practical view of life. He is absorbed with thoughts of monetary gain. His attempts to teach rules of conduct to his daughter are humorous. These attempts are described by a dancelike refrain, with simple chordal accompaniment, which seems to bring out the miller's cunning.

The dramatic development begins with the prince's arrival. Natasha has a premonition of misfortune, but the prince's assurances dispel her grief. Popular intonations enhance the poignant imagery in Natasha's aria, "The Golden Time Has Passed."

Natasha is not yet aware of the prince's betrayal. A light polka-like melody expresses her happiness. A crowd of peasants appears on the scene. Three songs in folk song style are heard: a slow lyrical song, "Oh, Thou Heart," a round-dance (*khorovod*) song, "Braid, Oh Fence" and a dance song, "How We Brewed Beer on the Mountain."

The duet of Natasha and the prince is a masterpiece. Natasha's love and suffering are revealed by rhythmic pulses in the melody, modulations, changes of tempo, and orchestral effects. The prince, reproached by Natasha for his coldness, tells her he must leave her. The music conveys a feeling of misfortune. Natasha begins to understand the impending separation, but does not believe that anything can interfere with her love. She interrupts the prince with "No, no, no!"

A sudden modulation in the music indicates Natasha's realization of what is happening to her. The music suddenly stops, excepting a few orchestral chords. Timidly, Natasha asks the prince: "Are you getting married?" His evasiveness is represented in the music by altered, unstable harmonies. He answers ingratiatingly: "We princes are not free." The prince gives Natasha a pearl necklace and a bag of money and prepares to leave. Natasha's scream stops him: "I wanted to tell thee . . . I do not remember what." The melody breaks up into separate phrases, while the orchestra is silent. Natasha reveals: "I am going to be a mother." The prince consoles her and departs.

The miller soon arrives on the scene. He does not realize Natasha's emotional disturbance, her loneliness, and grief. He sees the presents and expresses his joy. A succession of short tunes describes the miller's thoughts of gain.

Natasha tells her father what has happened. He begins to understand everything. Natasha tells him: "You see, princes are not free to take wives according to their heart."

Natasha's love has turned into hate. She reproaches her father for encouraging her affair with the prince. She throws the presents into the miller's face, saying: "Here is the pay of the prince for the miller's kindness." She runs to the bank of the Dnieper and entreats the queen of the river. She then throws herself into the water.

In the second act, the curtain rises on the prince's marriage celebration. The bride and bridegroom are honored with traditional songs and toasts. The celebration is suddenly interrupted by the song of the drowned woman, heard behind the scenes. The guests have a premonition of trouble. The bride senses that the song augurs misfortune for her married life.

In the third act, the princess is pictured as an abandoned, suffering woman. Her fate seems to resemble Natasha's. Musically, the two women are described differently. Natasha's melodies convey will and power; the princess' melodies are lyrical and passive. Olga consoles the princess.

The prince meets the mad miller, who is now a man who has experienced misfortune. He is no longer comic and servile, but independent and proud, and he accuses the prince of murdering Natasha.

The weak, passive prince is now revealed as a sensitive dreamer indulging in recollections of a happy past and tormented by repentance. The music of the miller, although similar to his music in the first act, becomes wild and incoherent, reflecting his madness.

The miller imagines he has been changed into a crow and that he now has wings. A rising figuration, played by the violins, seems to represent the flight of a bird. The miller's wild joy is followed by a slow lyrical melody in which he pours out his grief. In his declamatory recitative, the miller stresses words which express the deep meaning of his misfortune: "Yes, *old* and playful I have become, it *feels well* to look after me . . . as a wild *beast* I wander alone . . ." The prince invites the miller to live in his palace. "No," answers the miller. "You will entice me and you will probably strangle me with a necklace."

In the fourth act, Natasha appears as a proud and revengeful mermaid, the mistress of fantastic surroundings in an underwater kingdom. Musical fantasy was not Dargomijsky's forte. The music of this scene lacks orchestral color and magic. The mermaid's aria reveals her hatred of the prince and her anticipation of revenge. The prince arrives on the scene. He hears an enticing call emerging from the river bottom. The melody, a lullaby, is a repetition of three sounds within an interval of a fourth. The prince is bewitched and perishes in the river.

In Pushkin's drama *The Stone Guest*, Dargomijsky found an ideal setting for a musical drama without traditional operatic effects. He saw in the play, not a tale of Don Juan's amorous adventures, but an emotional psychological drama involving Don Juan and Donna Anna. He decided to present their subtle emotional experiences, outbursts, and feelings in a psychologically realistic musical drama.

Dargomijsky was convinced of the scenic expressiveness of recitatives based on Pushkin's text and of the feasibility of merging verbal and musical texts, in which the music would follow the subtlest nuances and shades of verbal intonations.

Because of the plot's swift unfolding, accurate characterization of persons and the emotional power and intonational aspects of Pushkin's drama, Dargomijsky made very few changes in the text. *The Stone Guest* emerged as a new type of musical-dramatic composition: a chamber opera.

The opera does not contain traditional successions of operatic numbers. It is a continuous drama built exclusively on dialogues. The drama's vocal style is a declamatory musical recitative. Musical intonations describe nuances of the text. There are no arias and no significant melodic sections to distract the audience from the spontaneous development of the text. Every verbal phrase has a corresponding musical thought.

This does not mean that the composition is a monotonous recitative without melodious elements. The recitative in *The Stone Guest* possesses a rich melodic flexibility. Following Pushkin's dialogues, the vocal intonations and imagery reflect the emotional significance of speech. Dargomijsky uses an intonational structure based on intervals of diminished fifths, augmented fourths, and major and minor sevenths. These intervals seem to reflect the constantly changing character of speech. When the speech reflects romantic or lyrical aspects, the musical intonations assume various melodic configurations.

The orchestral accompaniment is subordinated to the psychological significance of the intonational musical texture. The accompaniment is mostly chordal. When important events are represented, for example, Don Juan recollecting his duel with the Commander, a trill in the bass represents the sword piercing the victim and a fragmented, chromatic scale represents the Commander's death.

The intonational flexibility of the musical drama is supported by a harmonic flexibility and a freedom of key relationships. Dargomijsky seems to improvise and wander through various tonalities. He tries to avoid complete cadences.

The composer gave individualized social characteristics to some persons in the drama. For example, he remarked in the score that Laura's second guest was "a narrow-minded aristocrat." Rimsky-Korsakov did not include this remark in the published edition of the score.

The musical characterizations are varied. Don Juan is an impulsive, capricious man susceptible to quick changes of mood. His intonations are changeable, impetuous, and explosive, especially in the scene with Donna Anna.

Leporello is coarse, querulous, sly, and mistrustful. He is characterized by common everyday conversational intonations. An example is the scene in which Leporello, afraid and with bated breath, delivers Don Juan's invitation to the statue.

The Commander is a symbol of moral values and retribution. He is portrayed by a flexible motive. Donna Anna is characterized by a smooth, somewhat choral theme, a musical image of a devout widow determined to renounce all earthly temptations. The arrival of the Commander and his knock on the door is represented by a whole-tone scale and an augmented triad.

The Stone Guest aroused differing reactions among Russian composers. Members of Balakirev's circle hailed the drama as the greatest accomplishment in musical-dramatic art. Tchaikovsky called it "the sorrow fruit of a dry, purely rational process of invention. . . . By sacrificing musical beauty for falsely understood conceptions of truthfulness in dramatic movement, Dargomijsky deprives a singer of all that is fascinating in singing, and himself of all abundant means of musical expression. . . . It is not necessary to search in art for a narrowly understood truth where a real apple tastes better than a painted one. It is better to search for that superior artistic truth which springs from the mysterious depths of man's creative powers, and finds expression in clear, intelligible, conventional forms. The pursuit of extreme naturalism in opera will eventually result in the complete negation of opera itself." [5]

By discarding traditional melodic forms, Dargomijsky impoverished the esthetic significance of the opera. At the same time, the opera gained in realism. It all depends on one's definition of artistic truth. Tchaikovsky's conceptions did not agree with Dargomijsky's. On the other hand it is interesting that, while composing *Falstaff*, Verdi kept the score of *The Stone Guest* as a handbook. [6]

Russian realistic opera did not follow the ideas of *The Stone Guest*. Dargomijsky's musical drama, however, remains a unique contribution to Russian musical literature. Its psychological realism, intonational discoveries, and daring harmonic means influenced many Russian composers. [7]

Rimsky-Korsakov's *Mozart and Salieri* (1897) is an experiment in the recitative-arioso style. The function of the orchestra in *Mozart and Salieri* is more important than in *The Stone Guest*. The vocal parts are more melodic. Rimsky-Korsakov was interested in the psychological drama of rivalry and envy and in the ethical principle of the artist's life, as expressed in Mozart's words: "Genius and villainy are incompatible." The plot of *Mozart and Salieri* interested Rimsky-Korsakov because of the problem of the interrelation of intuition and conscious mastery in musical creativity.

CHAPTER 7

Music Criticism: Odoyevsky, Verstovsky, Serov, Stasov, and Laroche

Odoyevsky

VLADIMIR ODOYEVSKY composed music and wrote articles on music education, Russian folk songs, and church music. In the 1830's he wrote two novels, *The Last Quartet of Beethoven* and *Sebastian Bach*. While enthusiastic about Russian national culture, he was influenced by German philosophy and romanticism. He hailed Glinka's *A Life for the Tsar* as the beginning of a new era in Russian music.

Verstovsky

Alexei Verstovsky, a composer of operas and a music critic, was best known for his opera *Ascold's Grave,* a story about Prince Svyatoslav and the pagan Northmen in pre-Christian tenth-century Kiev. As a composer Verstovsky was not as important as Glinka and Dargomijsky because his operas, with the exception of *Ascold's Grave,* were collections of songs, choruses, and dances popular in Russian vaudeville during the first half of the nineteenth century. In 1826 Verstovsky published an essay on Western European opera in which he revealed his sympathy for Italian opera and Gluck's operatic reforms.

Serov

Alexander Serov was a versatile musical personality in Russia in the second half of the nineteenth century. He was a talented operatic composer and a brilliant music critic. Serov's controversial style of music criticism, coupled with a sincerity and integrity of conviction, raised Russian musical criticism to a professional level comparable to Belinsky's style in literature.

Serov's operas link the operas of Glinka and Dargomijsky with the operas of Mussorgsky, Borodin, Rimsky-Korsakov, and Tchaikovsky. Serov's operas, although influenced by French grand opera, were important contributions to the development of Russian music in the nineteenth century.

Serov was born on January 11, 1820. His father was an important government official. Serov studied in a gymnasium and in 1835, he matriculated in the School of Jurisprudence. He learned to play the piano and the violon cello, and his appearances as soloist or ensemble player at concerts influenced his determination to choose music as a career.

Upon graduation in 1840, Serov accepted a position in the Department of Justice. In 1849, he resigned in order to devote himself entirely to music. This resignation resulted in a break with his father, who did not approve of his son's musical activities.

To earn a living, Serov wrote music criticisms and essays. He was an editor of a music magazine and a music lecturer in Petersburg University and the Imperial Musical Society in Moscow. Serov traveled in Europe, where he met Wagner. He returned to Russia, an enthusiastic supporter and propagandist of Wagnerian operatic reforms. His Wagnerian sympathies brought him into sharp conflict with Balakirev's circle and the music critic Stasov. In 1870, Serov went to Vienna as a representative of the Russian Musical Society to the celebration of the centenary of Beethoven's birth. Serov died on January 20, 1871, of a heart attack.

Serov was a self-taught composer. He composed three important operas: *Judith* (1863), based on the Biblical story of Judith and Holofernes, *Rogneda* (1865), based on a story of life in pagan Russia, and *The Power of Evil*, based on a drama by the Russian dramatist, Ostrovsky. The last opera was completed by the composer Nicholas Solovyov in 1871.

Although Serov's operas are heroic and effective, their characters lack individuality and psychological significance. In *Rogneda* and *The Power of Evil,* Serov developed national characteristics and intonations of city songs and romances. Serov's music, however, does not probe the significant aspects of Russian popular music and fails to disclose realistically Russian life and feelings. His music, a valuable contribution to Russian operatic art, was eclipsed by Glinka's *A Life for the Tsar* and *Ruslan and Ludmila.*

As a music critic, Serov possessed, in addition to musical experience, a background in literature, philosophy, and esthetics. He was the first Russian music critic to give music criticism a professional dignity, evidenced by his scientific analysis of artistic elements, and the sincerity and forthright quality of his opinions.

Serov's credo as a music critic was this: "Music is an art of expressiveness . . . the language of the soul, a reflection of man's psychological changes, and of inner spiritual and emotional life." "Real art is not concerned with outward effects; it tries to reflect man's world." "Beauty alone is not enough; beauty must be appropriate, and it must go hand in hand with truth. Without truth of expression music is only a rattle, more or less pleasant, but, at the same time, more or less empty." [1]

Serov's opinions reveal him to be a realist. He characterized Hanslick's contentions in *On the Beautiful in Music* as "sophisms and sly dialectics." Hanslick felt that the truthfulness of musical expression is nonexistent and that a musical idea has no meaning and, thus, requires only musical beauty.

Serov stressed the importance of the historical aspects of music criticism. "There never was a poet or an artist who was not influenced by prevailing ideas, tastes, and fashions, and who did not defer to them." [2] "An ideal work of an artist which has been created under the influence of prevailing ideas of a period, and which expresses a single phase or aspect of art, is not regarded by historical criticism as an everlasting law of beauty." [3] "The main objective of a music critic is to educate the musical taste of the public. The dissemination of musical knowledge among music listeners is the function of friends of art." [4]

Serov studied the symphonic music of Haydn, Mozart, Beethoven, Liszt, and Berlioz. He admired the music of Beethoven and wrote analyses of the Ninth Symphony and the *Leonora Overture*. In an opera, Serov demanded truth of expression and vitality of ideas. He was critical of Meyerbeer and Gounod, but admired Wagner in whose operas he saw the pinnacle of operatic development. "He who does not love *Tannhäuser* or *Lohengrin* does not love Gluck, Mozart, Spontini, Beethoven, and Weber. Wagner is an innovator and a reformer because no one before him has so clearly understood the unity of *poetry of the theater* and *poetry of music*. No one before Wagner has so successfully influenced music by drama, and drama by music." [5]

Serov failed to understand the importance of Glinka's music. He recognized Glinka's dramatic accomplishments in *A Life for the Tsar* and the epic, popular, and heroic aspects of the opera, but did not appreciate the significance of *Ruslan and Ludmila,* characterizing it as "a fancy dress concert of arias and romances."

Serov's musical tastes were classical. He preferred Gluck, Haydn, Mozart, and Beethoven. He cared less for Bach and Handel. Serov linked the music of Rossini, Weber, and Mendelssohn. He hardly cared for the music of Schubert, Chopin, and Schumann. He regarded Berlioz as an excellent orchestrator and Liszt as a brilliant arranger of piano transcriptions.

In 1856, Serov published an analysis of Dargomijsky's opera *Rusalka,* followed by a few articles on Glinka. After this, Serov's interest in Russian music became casual. Only in 1859, did he show more interest in Russian music. In his search for song materials for *The Power of Evil,* he studied Russian folk songs. In an article published in 1859, he wrote: "Who knows, perhaps in the Russian, in the depths of splendid Russian characters, rest artistic aspects which are destined to exceed those of the West, and which already shine in the brilliance of greatness and glory. Ivanov (a famous Russian painter whose masterpiece is the painting *Appearance of Christ Before the People*) and Glinka are excellent examples, the pledge of the magnificent future of Russian art." [6]

Stasov

The name of Vladimir Stasov is inseparable from Russian music during the second half of the nineteenth century. Stasov sympathized with the revolutionary-democratic ideas and cultural aspirations of the

Russian intelligentsia during the 1860's. A man with a tremendous musical, artistic, and esthetic background, Stasov shared the nationally popular ideas of Balakirev's circle and the Russian painters and sculptors of his time. He devoted his life and energies to fostering and propagandizing Russian national popular music.

Stasov was the son of a prominent Petersburg architect. He was educated in the School of Jurisprudence in Petersburg and studied piano with private teachers. Self-educated in the arts, he read books on art and art criticism, visited museums and art exhibitions in various European countries, and became a man with tremendous erudition and an encyclopaedic knowledge of literature and the arts. Stasov was influenced by the democratic philosophy and revolutionary ideas of Belinsky, Herzen, Dobrolyubov, and Chernishevsky. In the 1850's, Stasov became friends with Glinka and became an enthusiastic supporter of Glinka's music.

As a music critic, Stasov demanded from Russian artists and composers, truth of life, realism and originality. In *Twenty-five Years of Russian Art,* he condemned "pure" art and cosmopolitanism in art as inimical to Russian music as an expression of the life and spirit of the Russian people. "Art that does not issue from the roots of popular life, though it may not always be useless or insignificant, is, to say the least, certainly always powerless." In the article "Perov and Mussorgsky," Stasov praised the truthful representation of the life and feelings of the Russian people in Perov's paintings and in Mussorgsky's music.

In 1872, Stasov was appointed chief of the fine arts division in the Petersburg library. He published articles, reviews, and criticisms on current musical problems and compositions. He also published monographs on composers and artists. His work *Art of the Nineteenth Century* is a criticism of the arts from the point of view taken by realistic esthetics.

Stasov was the first biographer of Glinka. In a monograph published after Glinka's death in 1857, Stasov reviewed Glinka's music and analyzed its esthetic significance in the development of an independent Russian popular music.

Stasov was the first Russian critic to analyze the ideational significance of Mussorgsky's music. He suggested the plot of *Khovanshchina* to Mussorgsky for an opera and helped him write the libretto. Equally important are Stasov's articles on the compositions of Rimsky-Korsakov, Borodin, Dargomijsky, and the singer Chaliapin.

In the 1890's, Stasov defended the music of the younger Russian composers Glazunov, Lyadov, and Scriabin. The development of formalistic tendencies in Western music brought a series of critical articles by Stasov, "The Poor in Spirit" and "The Inn of Lepers," in which he condemned them. In an article, "An Answer to Two Statements About Music of the Future," Stasov ridiculed two assumptions, that which asserted "the criterion of a musical law is not in the ears of the consumer, but in the artistic thought of the producer" and "when theory does not agree with the practice of the world genius, it has no significance because art does not live in books but in the artistic work."

In his zeal for a Russian national popular music, Stasov underestimated the music of Tchaikovsky. Stasov failed to appreciate the dramatic and symphonic significance of Tchaikovsky's operas.[7] Stasov also underestimated some Western composers. He failed to understand the significance of Wagner's musical dramas in Western culture and the importance of Verdi's contributions to the opera.[8]

Laroche

Hermann Laroche was graduated from the Petersburg Conservatory in 1866. Among his teachers was Anton Rubinstein. From 1867 to 1870, Laroche taught at the Moscow Conservatory and from 1872 to 1879, at the Petersburg Conservatory. In 1868, he published a book, *Glinka and His Importance in the History of Music,* in which he analyzed Glinka's musical style and the national roots of his music. The book placed Laroche at the forefront of Russian music criticism.

In 1895, Laroche translated into Russian Hanslick's *Vom Musikalisch Schönen* (On the Beautiful in Music) and in the preface to the translation defended Hanslick's formalistic ideas.[9]

Laroche maintained that in order to achieve maturity and independence, Russian music should master the musical culture of past centuries and should repeat all stages of musical development which had taken place in Western Europe, beginning with the *a cappella* music of early polyphonic composers.

Laroche regarded the post-Beethovenian era in music as a period of musical decline. He considered musical design from 1600 to 1800 as a perfect example of musical form.

Laroche did not regard contemporary Russian composers very highly. The single exception was Tchaikovsky. Laroche's personal preconceived opinions, however, prevented him from fully appreciating the significance of Tchaikovsky's genius.

Laroche's criticisms lack consistency of view and opinion. He often wrote sympathetically about some aspects of Balakirev's circle, which, as a group, he hated. His constant vacillation between conservative academic tendencies and the accomplishments of Russian composers make his criticisms and essays contradictory and unreliable. However, in appreciating Glinka's traditions, Russian folk songs, and Tchaikovsky's music, Laroche disclosed his perspicacity as a music critic.

CHAPTER 8

Musical Trends

1860-1900

DURING THE 1860's, several well-defined musical trends emerged in Russia. The most important was represented by the New Russian Musical School, also known as "The Powerful *Kuchka*" (group). The leaders of the New School were Balakirev, Borodin, Cui, Mussorgsky, and Rimsky-Korsakov, often referred to as "The Five." Stasov, the music critic, was connected with the group. It was Stasov who first referred to the New School as "The Powerful Group." In a review of a symphony concert conducted by Balakirev in honor of Slavic delegations visiting Petersburg, Stasov wrote: "How much poetry, feeling, talent, and skill is in this small, but already powerful, '*kuchka*' of Russian musicians."

There were similar groups in literature and painting. The literary group included Chernishevsky, Dobrolyubov, and Nekrasov. These writers published the journal *Sovremennik* (*Contemporary*). The group of painters known as the *Khudozhestvenaya Artel,* or the *Peredvizhniki* included Kramskoy, Perov, Yaroshenko, and Repin. These painters were democratic realists who painted realistic scenes in Russian life and exhibited their paintings in mobile (*peredvizhniye*) art galleries.

In the absence of a well-developed social life or freedom of professional organization in Russia, circles or groups of artists provided the only means for the effective collection of the experiences of artists.

The *kuchka* regarded itself as heir to the musical heritage of Glinka and Dargomijsky. Their principles and ideas were set forth in articles and musical reviews written by Stasov and Cui.

According to Stasov, a characteristic feature of the New School was "the absence of prejudice and of blind faith." "Beginning with Glinka," wrote Stasov, "the Russian musical school is distinguished by an independence of thought and view on what has been heretofore created in music." This independence of thought and a critical attitude towards authoritative opinion was characteristic of the foremost Russian cultural trends of this period.

Russian democratic ideology of the 1860's, as set forth in the writings of Belinsky, Chernishevsky, and Dobrolyubov, demanded a common-sense attitude toward facts and ideas, a verification by reason, and the development of a world outlook on national bases.

The members of the "Balakirev Circle" applied these principles to music. They were innovators who analyzed classical principles in music, transforming them in the light of contemporary Russian conditions. In their attempts to reform the musical language, "The Five" were sympathetic to the most radical musical romantics, including Schumann, Berlioz, and Liszt.

Stasov felt that one of the main aspects of the freedom and independence of thought characterizing the outstanding Russian composers was "their desire for truth and sincerity of experience" and their opposition to the false and artificial in music. Stasov's words underline the realistic tendency of the New School. Stasov connected this tendency with Dargomijsky's principle that in vocal music, "the sound should directly express the word"; a melodic conversion of natural speech intonations should be aimed for. According to Stasov, "Dargomijsky was the founder of realism in Russian music."

The practical musical activities of the circle were more comprehensive than the musical theories of its members. While the members of the circle accepted Dargomijsky's rational and analytical approach to reality, they also adopted the bases of Glinka's all-embracing realism.

Another feature of the New School was its nationalism. In their compositions, "The Five" developed themes from Russian history, folk tales, and legends, heroic *bylinas,* and contemporary peasant genres. They favored features of Russian national music and discovered in folk songs a source for the creation of new and original expressive means and devices. Members of the circle transcribed and studied Russian folk melodies. The problem confronting them was the method of arranging folk songs. They tried to extract the principles of harmonization from the character of the melodies. Balakirev and

Rimsky-Korsakov did much work arranging folk songs and both published valuable collections of them.

The circle's interest was not solely limited to Russian folklore. It studied and used Spanish, Serbian, Jewish, Ukrainian, Tatar, Armenian, Georgian, Persian, and Arabian national subjects and melodies. "In connection with the national Russian element," wrote Stasov, "there is another element that is a characteristic of the New Russian Musical School. This is the oriental element. Nowhere in Europe does it assume such an important role as it does among our musicians. This is not surprising when one considers the totality of oriental influences and characteristic colorings in manifestations of Russian life."

Another feature of the New School was its bent toward programmatic music. The circle's members were influenced by nineteenth-century Russian literature, characterized by a concreteness of imagery and an objectivity of content. "The Five" rejected separation of the arts. They maintained that both music and painting were equal to literature in the embodiment and expression of the varied manifestations of reality. The views of "The Five" were similar to tendencies in Western romantic music. According to Stasov, the main contribution of Berlioz and Liszt was the fine literary articulation and concreteness of their instrumental music.

The innovations and nationalism of the *kuchka* were opposed by the Russian Musical Society and its conservatories in Petersburg and Moscow. The main representative of this trend was Anton Rubinstein, who stressed the importance of the great traditions of the past and of classical music for the development of Russian music. Rubinstein accepted the romantic music of the first half of the nineteenth century, represented by Schubert, Mendelssohn, Schumann, and Chopin, but he rejected contemporary musical innovations.

This veneration of the past by Rubinstein and his supporters gave their views an academic coloring. Rubinstein's ideas often reflected the views of the "Leipzig School" founded by Mendelssohn. Rubinstein's position, however, had positive value because it stood as a counterpoise to the one-sided views of "The Five" who often underestimated the musical heritage of the past. "The Five" declared the principles of classical esthetics old and scholastic, even dead, and the compositions of Bach, Haydn, and Mozart childish, naive, dry, and soulless.

The objective of the Russian Musical Society was to develop a mastery and appreciation of the music of the past as a basis for normal musical growth. The members of the *kuchka* favored freedom of creativity and rejection of traditions. They denied the usefulness and necessity of conservatories. They were hostile to the Petersburg Conservatory and regarded it as a brake on musical progress.

The main point of disagreement between the two trends was the question of how to develop a Russian musical art. Rubinstein believed that a mastery of Western European musical classicism was of paramount importance. He often ignored the specific conditions which influenced the development of Russian music as well as the relationship of these conditions to national life and music. He failed to take existing national traditions in Russian musical culture into account.

Rubinstein's failure to establish roots in Russian national musical traditions was the reason his own music exerted a limited influence on Russian composers. His struggle for classical traditions and principles helped establish the foundations of a musical professionalism in Russia.

Tchaikovsky, a graduate of the Petersburg Conservatory, absorbed the best features of Rubinstein's musical curriculum, but without its academic limitations. Tchaikovsky received, in the conservatory, a thorough musical training, a command of musical forms, and an excellent understanding of the musical experiences of the masters. In his compositions, Tchaikovsky interpreted these features and principles on the bases of Russian national traditions.

Tchaikovsky was a national composer and, like the members of Balakirev's circle, was influenced by Glinka's musical traditions. The content of Tchaikovsky's music, its imagery, themes, and subjects, are taken from Russian reality. He was sensitively attuned to Russian social ideas and Russian literature. The influence of Russian folk songs is significant in his music. He was aware of modern trends in Western music and his attitude toward them was restrained and objective.

Disagreement between Tchaikovsky and "The Five" was not produced by differences concerning a Russian national musical art, but by the conflict waged over the principles of musical composition. Tchaikovsky did not approve of the radical innovations of "The Five." His musical principles were restrained and classical. In programmatic music, Tchaikovsky preferred general emotional outpourings to concrete emotional descriptions of reality. Subjective lyrical expressions in Tchaikovsky's music did not appeal to "The Five."

However, in the historical development of Russian music, the trends represented by Tchaikovsky and "The Five" converged.[1] As years went by, the members of Balakirev's circle gained in public recognition. They soon gave up the exclusive and exaggerated ideas and views they held during the 1860's. On the other hand, the Russian Musical Society also changed. A new generation of conservatory graduates brought up on classical traditions was attracted to Russian national ideas and inspirations.

In 1867, Balakirev was invited to conduct the orchestra of the Russian Musical Society. The concert repertoire included the names of Glinka, Dargomijsky, and Rimsky-Korsakov. Balakirev lasted only two years as conductor of the orchestra. His removal temporarily returned the conservative group of the Russian Musical Society to power. In 1871, Azanchevsky, a Russian musician, became director of the Petersburg Conservatory. He offered a professorship in composition and theory to Rimsky-Korsakov.

As a teacher at the conservatory, Rimsky-Korsakov combined his solid academic training with the advanced traditions of the New Russian School. Rimsky-Korsakov's contribution is the synthesis of these two trends. This synthesis finally set the educational policy of the conservatory for the last quarter of the nineteenth century.

The teaching of composition in the Moscow Conservatory was at first influenced by Tchaikovsky and Taneyev. In the 1880's, Arensky and Ippolitov-Ivanov, two pupils of Rimsky-Korsakov, joined the teaching staff of the conservatory and introduced Rimsky-Korsakov's ideas and methods into the musical curriculum.

While different trends in Russian music gradually merged during the last quarter of the nineteenth century, the powerful *kuchka* began to disintegrate. It soon ceased to represent a group of composers bound by unique aims and ideas. The circle's disintegration was hastened by Balakirev's retirement due to an emotional disturbance. There also were disagreements about methods of composition among members of the circle.

The decrease of differences, resulting from the merger of various musical trends, was unacceptable to Mussorgsky. Mussorgsky's ideas of a democratic musical realism represented a radical position within Balakirev's circle. He opposed any compromise which would jeopardize the original ideas of the *kuchka*. He regarded the softening of the circle's original stand as a betrayal. Mussorgsky never fully appreciated the importance of classical traditions and Western romantic forms for the development of a Russian musical art.

The majority of the *kuchka* thought Mussorgsky's musical methods were inartistic. Rimsky-Korsakov and Cui thought that the unusual characteristics of Mussorgsky's musical style were due to his ignorance of music theory and a coarse naturalism. Mussorgsky was left alone to advocate a realistic Russian national musical art of and for the people.

As the end of the nineteenth century approached, important changes were taking place in Russian political, social, and artistic conditions. The revolutionary organization, "People's Freedom," was losing its influence and significance. Russia was beginning to feel the effects of industrialization. New revolutionary leaders, Plekhanov and Lenin, educated in Marxist social philosophy, emerged. In 1883, the first Marxist group, calling itself "Emancipation of Labor," was organized in Petersburg. In 1887, Lenin was expelled from Kazan University and went into exile.

Literature describing Russian life and social conditions began to appear. In 1880, Dostoyevsky completed *The Brothers Karamazov*. The first stories of Chekhov were published in 1884. Nadson's poem, "Life," describing the contradictions of existence, was published in 1886:

> Life is sorrow and temptation,
> It is bright and lustrous,
> It is darkness and shame.
> Life is a seraph and a drunken reveler,
> Life is an ocean and a crowded prison.

Tolstoy's novels and dramas exposed and condemned social conditions: *The Death of Ivan Ilyich* in 1884, *The Power of Darkness* in 1886, and *The Fruits of Enlightenment* in 1887.

The paintings of Repin, Surikov, Shishkin, Levitan, and Serov were realistic representations of Russian nature, life, and history. The music of Mussorgsky, Borodin, Rimsky-Korsakov, and Tchaikovsky was established as an art of world significance.

CHAPTER 9

Balakirev

LIKE ANTON RUBINSTEIN, Mily Balakirev was a composer, piano virtuoso, conductor, teacher, and organizer of musical activities. He was born on December 21, 1836, in Nizhni-Novgorod. His father was a middle-class civil servant. Balakirev's musical gifts revealed themselves at an early age and his mother taught him to play the piano. At the age of ten, he studied piano with Dubuque, a pupil of John Field.

An important influence on Balakirev's musical development was his acquaintance with a Nizhni-Novgorod landowner, Oulibishev. Oulibishev was a musical enthusiast who published significant biographies of Mozart and Beethoven. Balakirev participated in musicals held in Oulibishev's home where works by Glinka and Western composers were performed. In Oulibishev's music library, Balakirev studied the scores of Western composers.

After graduation from the Noblemen's Institute in Nizhni-Novgorod, Balakirev matriculated in the mathematics faculty of Kazan University. He became known in Kazan as a brilliant pianist, and he earned a modest living giving piano lessons. At this time, Balakirev had already composed romances and piano compositions, among them, a fantasy for piano and orchestra based on Russian folk songs and a piano fantasy based on themes from Glinka's *A Life for the Tsar*.

In 1855, Balakirev left Kazan University and went to Petersburg. Through Oulibishev, he became acquainted with Glinka who not only hailed Balakirev, but even called him his successor.

In 1856, Balakirev gave a series of concerts. At one concert, he played his Allegro in F Sharp Minor for piano. At the same time, he read and studied to improve his literary and critical background. He became friendly with the eminent Russian critic and biographer Vladimir Stasov. Together with Stasov, he read the works of Belinsky, Dobrolyubov, and Herzen. Stasov introduced Balakirev to the music of Schumann and encouraged him to study the music of Glinka.

Thoughts of a national art related to and expressing Russian reality and national aspirations were rampant among Russian intelligentsia during the 1860's. Such ideas stimulated young progressive groups in various artistic fields. During the 1850's, Balakirev became friends with Cui and Mussorgsky. A few years later, they were joined by Rimsky-Korsakov and Borodin. In the beginning of the 1860's, the "Balakirev Circle" was formed.

In 1857, Balakirev composed an overture, based on a Spanish march theme given to him by Glinka. This was followed in 1858 by an overture on three Russian themes. The two overtures disclose Balakirev's preference for Glinka's musical traditions. The first overture reveals the influence of Glinka's *Spanish Overture* and the second, of Glinka's *Kamarinskaya*.

In 1858, Balakirev began composing music for Shakespeare's *King Lear*, a composition which occupied him three years. The dramatic, romantic excitement of the music as well as its descriptive aspects reveal the influence of Berlioz, a composer who at that time exercised a tremendous influence in the circle.

In 1862, Balakirev composed the *1000 Years* overture commemorating the founding of the Russian state in 862. In 1877, Balakirev renamed the overture *Symphonic Picture,* more in accordance with the music's dramatic nature. In a later revised edition, he called the overture *Rus,* a national epic poem describing the grandeur of Russia and the then popular call of Herzen upon Russian intelligentsia to go to the people.

During the summer of 1860, Balakirev traveled on the Volga River and transcribed folk songs. The result was a collection of forty published in 1866. He was also attracted by oriental folklore. In 1862, he visited the Caucasus and wrote a series of compositions embodying the characteristic dynamics and rhythms of Caucasian melodies. Among these, the most famous is the piano fantasy, *Islamey,* completed in 1869 and the symphonic poem, *Tamara,* completed in 1882.

In 1862, under Balakirev's leadership, the Free Music School was founded as a center to propagandize national Russian music. His musical activities in the school were primarily devoted to conducting.

In 1867, on the anniversary of Glinka's death, he conducted *Ruslan and Ludmila* and *A Life for the Tsar* in Prague. As a result of this journey, he composed a symphonic poem, *In Chehia*.

When Anton Rubinstein left the Russian Musical Society, Balakirev was invited to conduct the society's concerts during the two seasons 1867 to 1869. However, without any explanation, he was dropped by the society. This, coupled with lack of financial support for the Free School, compelled him to give up musical activities and take employment with the Warsaw railroad.

Balakirev was deeply affected by this experience. Originally a sociable, energetic person and a good mixer, he now began to avoid people. He lost interest in surrounding reality. This psychic change was not unexpected. Accompanying Balakirev's dynamic will power it would often reveal his emotional instability and fluctuation of mood. Periods of activity were sometimes followed by periods of depression. It is probable that the constant struggle for existence and the implementation of his artistic ambitions brought on the crisis. He began to exhibit disappointment, skepticism of his own abilities, and thoughts of death.

A transformation also took place in Balakirev's social ideas and views. His enthusiasm of the 1860's for social reform met with reactionary suppression. The disappointment and defeat experienced in his struggle for artistic ideals, brought about his withdrawal from liberal-democratic positions. He became a monarchist and a mystic. His religious inclinations verged on bigotry and sanctimony.

In 1874, Balakirev gave up his activities in the Free School, and Rimsky-Korsakov took his place. Balakirev became aloof from his former friends, who, in turn, became suspicious of him. Only at the close of the 1870's, did Balakirev begin to emerge from this torpidity. Together with Rimsky-Korsakov and Lyadov, he prepared new editions of *A Life for the Tsar* and *Ruslan and Ludmila* for publication. In 1882, he resumed leadership of the Free School.

However, this "revival" was temporary. In 1883, Balakirev was appointed conductor of the Court Chapel. During this period (1883–1893) his composing was insignificant. A creative upsurge took place around 1895. Between 1895 and 1900, Balakirev composed two symphonies (C major and D minor), a number of romances, a sonata in B minor, and a Spanish serenade.

In 1897, Balakirev headed a special commission which prepared a group of Russian folk songs, collected by expeditions of the Russian Geographic Society, for publication. He also prepared a collection of *Thirty Songs of the Russian People* and worked on a piano concerto, originally sketched in 1861. Balakirev died on May 16, 1910, and the concerto was completed by Lyapunov, a gifted composer-pianist and friend.

As a piano composer, Balakirev was superior to the other members of the circle. However, of all his piano compositions, only two became popular: the rhapsody-fantasy, *Islamey* (the name of a Kabardine dance in the Caucasus) and the transcription of Glinka's song "The Lark." This general lack of popularity surrounding Balakirev's piano compositions is due to the character of his music.

A remarkably gifted musician, a leader, and an inspirer of Russian composers, Balakirev was eventually eclipsed by his collaborators. This happened for two important reasons: the narrowness of Balakirev's life experiences and his inability to extend his interests out of the field of music into general social experience and daily contact, indispensable conditions for a composer aspiring to express life and reality in music. As a composer, Balakirev expressed a purely musical impression, not an experience of life and reality. This narrowed his imaginative creativity and for his last years, a wall was formed between himself and Russian realities.

Although sympathetic, kind, and always willing to extend a helping hand to anyone, Balakirev was oversensitive, susceptible to illusions, skepticism, and disappointment. Quick to take offense, he often exaggerated the shortcomings of people, became intolerant, irritable, and embittered.

His emotional inadequacies and lack of spontaneity were compensated for by his enormous will power. Balakirev knew he could never fully project emotional or spiritual impulses and develop his creative insight. This realization often made him doubt his ability as a composer and reproach himself and his friends. He was keenly affected by disagreements and quarrels with friends and he took refuge behind a cover of arrogance verging on despotism. He tried to find comfort in religion and failed. Musical creativity became, for Balakirev, a self-sufficing pursuit with which he proudly and defiantly opposed the world.

In his music, Balakirev succumbed to depersonalization and intellectualization of feelings. His music often expresses a philosophical attitude toward life rather than a personal outpouring of feeling. It seldom expresses the passion of love or despair. At most, it is sentimental or an art of abstract individualism.

Balakirev could not fill large musical forms with significant emotional content. His prolix and repetitive musical forms are a compromise between symphonic and chamber characteristics.

Balakirev's inability to create significant emotional imagery led him to devise musical themes which he combined with genuinely inspired melodies. This method diminishes the artistic quality of the music and dampens the listener's attention. Balakirev's brief emotional outbursts were not suited for large musical forms which depend on continuous and uniform musical inspirations. When the emotional outbursts became exhausted, Balakirev resorted to intellectual compositional techniques which could never replace genuine feeling.

Balakirev's intellectual compositional pursuits are exemplified by impulsive dynamic aspects, tone color, and contrived modulational elements, as, for example, in *Islamey*.

In short musical forms, Balakirev often embodies imitations of emotional states. These imitations express sympathy with an emotion but not the genuine feeling. The brevity of emotional outburst affected Balakirev's thematic developments, which do not possess culminating emotional points followed by periods of rest and contemplation. His uniform thematic developments are successions of short musical conceptions within the confines of large musical forms.

Gifted with a phenomenal musical memory, Balakirev often resorted to stylistic imitation. This was an inadequate compensation for the lack of emotional inspiration which often plagued him. Nevertheless, Balakirev's piano music rose to the level of a great art. Interpreting and transforming the influences of Weber, Field, Schumann, and Chopin, Balakirev created his own distinct piano style which, despite the diversity of musical influences, possesses unique aspects.

The most outstanding feature in Balakirev's style is the preservation of Glinka's esthetic traditions, exemplified by the clarity and suppleness of Balakirev's tonal flow. Another feature is the decorative tracery of the musical texture which requires a strong finger technique from a pianist. Balakirev was sparing in the use of the piano pedal because he preferred clear harmonic outlines and disliked excessive sentimentality.

His piano compositions often embody polyphonic intonations of folk song elements, such as turbulent runs in oriental music and charming supporting tunes and musical tracery often found in Russian folk songs. Balakirev developed a Russian national piano style based on his studies of Russian folk songs which he treated programmatically. His synthesis of folk songs with their harmonic and tonal bases is his most important contribution to the development of Russian classical music.

Pictorial elements make Balakirev's piano music unique in Russian art. Compared to Balakirev's piano style, the styles of Glazunov and Lyadov lack dynamic significance. Scriabin's music is often effeminate. Rachmaninov's style is harmonically and polyphonically complex. Metner's style is encyclopaedic in its harmonic logic and polyphonic interweaves, in its lyrical concentration and emotional constraint. Balakirev's music is seldom emotionally original. It is predominantly intellectual music in which emotional aspects and feelings are rarefied. One cannot help admiring the clarity of his musical conceptions, his musical mastery and the exacting standards of a great musical master.

Among Balakirev's programmatic orchestral compositions, the symphonic poem *Tamara* (1867–1882) is outstanding. It is based on a poem by Lermontov.

In the deep Daryal gorge, where the Terek burrows in darkness, there stands a tower on a high black rock. In this tower there once lived queen Tamara. She was beautiful as an angel, but treacherous and malicious as a demon.

Through the midnight fog there glowed a golden light in the tower inviting a traveler to rest through the night.

And Tamara's voice was heard. It was full of longing and passion. It had a powerful charm, a strange power.

The voice attracted the soldier, the merchant, and the shepherd. The door would open for him, and he was met by a gloomy eunuch.

On a soft feather bed, bedecked with brocade and pearls, Tamara waited for the guest. Two cups of wine fizzed before her.

The ardent hands entwined; mouth clung to mouth; and strange, wild sounds were heard there through the night, as if a hundred passionate youths and women gathered there for a night wedding feast, or for a great funeral feast.

But as soon as the rising sun scattered its rays on the mountains, gloom and silence reigned there again.

Only the thundering Terek in the gorge of Daryal broke the silence. Wave dashed against wave; wave hurried wave.

And with a cry they hurried to carry the voiceless body. Something white glimmered in the window, and "forgive" was heard from there. And the parting was so tender, the voice sounded so sweet, as if it promised the delights of a meeting and the caresses of love.

In *Tamara*, Balakirev combined the effects of Liszt's orchestral and harmonic style with the colorful and exciting development of oriental musical elements. The thematic materials of the symphonic poem are saturated with ingredients of Caucasian musical folklore which retain their original flavor. The poem is colorful and rhapsodic. It consists of three parts: an introductory andante maestoso representing the gloomy Daryal gorge with the swirling Terek, an allegro moderato representing the night orgy in the castle, and a concluding andante in which the rising morning and the silence of nature, disturbed by the roaring Terek, are pictured.

In *King Lear* (1858–1861), Balakirev evokes, through symphonic means, the dramatic conceptions of Shakespeare's drama. The characters of the tragedy are musically described by a system of leading motives. Situations, such as the storm and battle, are descriptive musical episodes. The treatment of the drama is a romantic representation of a restless grieving hero who will find peace and reconciliation only in death. Every section of the score is an independent musical picture representing a phase in the play's dramatic development.

As the leader of a New Russian Musical School, Balakirev incorporated the fundamental elements of the school's style into his music. In accordance with Glinka's national traditions, Balakirev used national musical elements: Russian folk songs and oriental folklore. At the same time, he adopted the contemporary Western musical devices developed by Berlioz, Liszt, Chopin, and Schumann. Perhaps his most notable orchestral contribution was the adaptation of Russian musical elements to the dramatic and tone-color devices of Liszt and Berlioz.

Although other members of the circle surpassed and eclipsed Balakirev in musical creativity, many of Balakirev's compositions remain outstanding examples in the heritage of Russian classical music.

CHAPTER 10

Borodin

ALEXANDER BORODIN belonged to Balakirev's circle whose members wrote music characterized by the daring innovation and interpretation of Russian and oriental folklores. The courageous and optimistic character of Borodin's music reflects the heroic aspects of Russian history and epic poetry. His style is distinguished by clear musical textures and a wealth of tone color.

Borodin was influenced by the nationalism of Glinka's music. In the opera *Prince Igor,* in symphonies, and in chamber music, Borodin carried on the national traditions of Glinka's *Ruslan and Ludmila.* The epic narrative episodes and the tranquil developments of musical imagery in Glinka's music are also characteristic of Borodin's style in which these elements receive an original interpretation.

Borodin was born in Petersburg on October 31, 1833. He was the illegitimate son of an Imertine prince, Luka Semyonovich Gedeonov, and a *petit-bourgeois* woman, Avdotya Konstantinovna Antonova. As was customary with illegitimate offspring of Russian aristocrats, the child was registered as the son of Gedeonov's serf, Porfiry Borodin, and thereby received his surname.

The boy was brought up in the home of his mother. He learned to play the piano, flute, and violoncello. His musical development was stimulated by attending symphony concerts at the university, by participating in chamber music ensembles and by two-piano playing with friends. Thus, Borodin acquired an acquaintance with classical and early romantic literature, mainly by means of the music of Haydn, Beethoven, and Mendelssohn.

In 1850, Borodin enrolled in the medical-surgical academy. His interests were centered in chemistry. In spite of scientific pursuits, Borodin continued to study music. During his student years, he composed songs and instrumental pieces. In order to master the technique of composition, he studied counterpoint and composed fugues.

In 1854, Borodin was graduated from the medical academy and two years later, he interned in a medical hospital. During this time, he enlarged his circle of musical acquaintances. He met Mussorgsky, at that time a young man without definite musical views and ideas, and the music critic Stasov, who advised Borodin to study the music of Glinka.

In 1859, Borodin was sent abroad for three years to do postgraduate work in chemistry. The sojourn in Germany had a tremendous influence on Borodin's musical growth. New musical impressions changed his views and sympathies. In 1859, despite his enthusiasm for Glinka, he regarded Mendelssohn as the greatest musical authority. Mendelssohn was soon supplanted by Schumann to whose music Borodin was introduced by Catherine Protopopova, a talented pianist whom Borodin later married.

Borodin became acquainted with the operas of Weber and Wagner. He was dazzled by the brilliance and magnificence of Wagner's orchestral technique. Originally a follower of the moderate Mendelssohnian tradition, Borodin soon became an enthusiastic follower of the advanced musical romanticism of Schumann, Berlioz, and Liszt.

While abroad, Borodin composed several compositions. Among them was a Quintet for Piano and Strings in C Minor in which Borodin revealed the epic narrative qualities of his later musical style.

In November, 1862, Borodin returned to Russia and was appointed adjunct professor of chemistry in the medical-surgical academy. At this time, he became friendly with Balakirev's circle which was very active in musical events. Borodin's ties with the circle were not fortuitous. His world outlook, musical views and ideas, appreciation of Glinka's nationalism, and preference for the romanticism of Schumann, Berlioz, and Liszt made a *rapprochement* inevitable with the progressive trends of Russian music represented by the *kuchka*. Eighteen hundred and sixty-two signaled the beginning of Borodin's mature period in musical composition, which lasted twenty-five years.

In his scientific and teaching career, Borodin remained in the academy until his death in 1887. He educated a generation of scientists, practical workers, and teachers. His reputation in the academic world was that of an outstanding scholar, scientist, and fascinating lecturer.

He was active in public affairs and always remained a magnanimous friend and patron of young people.

An ardent advocate of higher education for women, Borodin was one of the founders of a medical school for women (1872). He lectured there on chemistry for the next fifteen years. Borodin's activities testify to his progressive ideas. During the 1860's, he was active in the Russian liberal, sociocultural movement.

When Borodin joined the Balakirev circle, he was already a thoroughly educated musician. His friendship with Balakirev helped Borodin realize his own creative abilities in music. The result was his First Symphony in E Flat Major, composed in 1867. In this symphony, Borodin successfully integrated Western romantic trends with Russian nationalism, imagery, and musical intonations. The music of the symphony is a confident, optimistic expression of a feeling of power and grandeur. On January 4, 1869, the symphony had its *première* at a concert of the Russian Musical Society under Balakirev's direction. This was Borodin's first public appearance as a musician. The success of the symphony determined Borodin's future career as a composer.

In the years 1865 to 1870, Borodin and the members of the Balakirev circle made great progress in composition. During this period, Borodin wrote some of his best compositions.

During 1868 and 1869, Borodin substituted for César Cui in the capacity of a music critic for the *Petersburg Gazette*. He wrote several reviews in which he set forth the aims and ideas of the Balakirev circle.

After the First Symphony, Borodin composed a series of songs (1867–1870). Some of the texts were written by Borodin himself: "The Song of the Dark Forest," "The Sleeping Princess," and "The Sea Princess." The songs are interesting because of their imagery, freedom of harmonic devices, and ingenuity of tonal textures. They anticipate the imagery, devices, and forms which Borodin later developed in *Prince Igor*.

In 1869, Borodin busied himself with his two greatest compositions: the Second Symphony and the opera *Prince Igor*. The story of Prince Igor was called to Borodin's attention by Stasov who wrote the general plan of the libretto with additions from ancient chronicles found in the Ipatiev Monastery. Borodin's aim in the opera was a truthful representation of historical events and persons. In order to obtain ideas and information about the times and events narrated in

The Lay of Prince Igor, Borodin studied Russian literature, history, and folklore. He wanted to compose an epic Russian opera in the style of Glinka's *Ruslan.* In historical realism and dramatic description of events, *Prince Igor* is on common ground with Mussorgsky's *Boris Godunov* and Rimsky-Korsakov's *Pskovityanka,* two operas which carried on the traditions of Glinka's *A Life for the Tsar.*

Borodin worked intermittently on *Prince Igor.* In 1870, he interrupted work on the opera because his attention was absorbed by the Second Symphony, completed in 1876. The symphony is Borodin's greatest achievement in instrumental music. The quiet grandeur of Russian national epos is incarnated in the vivid, pictorial, and monumental musical style of Borodin.

Borodin's First Symphony echoes classical traditions and Schumann's romanticism. In the Second Symphony, Borodin found his personal musical language, free from Western influences. According to Stasov, Borodin had a program for the Second Symphony. Basing his opinion on Borodin's remarks, Stasov called the symphony "heroic," a title it has retained. Mussorgsky compared the Second Symphony to Beethoven's *Eroica.* The comparison does not refer to resemblance of musical aspects in Borodin's and Beethoven's symphonies, but to their common heroic idea.

In 1872, Borodin collaborated with Mussorgsky and Rimsky-Korsakov in composing an opera-ballet, *Mlada,* commissioned by Gedeonov, the director of Imperial Theaters. The opera's plot, based on Slavic mythology, appealed to the epic heroic character of Borodin's genius. *Mlada* was never performed and Borodin later incorporated his musical contribution into *Prince Igor.*

Around 1880, Borodin's musical activities began to lag. In letters to friends, he complained of fatigue and the pressure of manifold duties. Borodin's mental depression was the result of a heart condition and disillusionment with social conditions brought on by political reaction following the liberal reforms in 1861. In the academic field, Borodin clashed with government bureaucracy. The Balakirev circle was disintegrating because of differences of opinions among its members. These events deeply affected Borodin. He became aloof and introspective. He turned his attention to chamber music compositions, best suited to express intimate lyrical moods.

In 1885, Borodin composed his Second Quartet in D Major. A clear and perfect musical construction, an effortless and spontaneous melodic flow, and a smooth harmonic texture make the quartet one of the best-known compositions in chamber music literature.

During these years, Borodin composed several songs, one of which is the well-known *Arab Melody* based on his own text. He also composed an andante for a string quartet on the theme B-La-F (1886), the name of the music publisher Belayev. This work was done in collaboration with Rimsky-Korsakov and Glazunov. A Little Suite of seven piano pieces composed in collaboration with Rimsky-Korsakov, Cui, and Lyadov is another example of Borodin's musical works around 1885.

In 1877, Borodin visited Liszt in Weimar. On May 20, 1880, with Liszt's encouragement, Borodin's Symphony in E Flat Major was performed in Baden-Baden. In 1885, his compositions were performed at a concert of Russian music in Belgium.

On February 15, 1887, Borodin died of a heart attack.

Although Borodin's musical output was not large, all his compositions have a distinct stamp of originality. In the words of Stasov: "Borodin's talent, which is equally great in symphony, opera, and song, is characterized by power, impetuosity, passion, tenderness, and beauty."

Borodin's style has an optimistic outlook, a grandeur of dimensions, and a wealth and variety of musical invention. The harmonic texture of his music is always clear. The unity of dramatic expression and tonal imagery is similar to the unity of these elements in Glinka's music.

In 1875, Borodin wrote: "Many people feel sorry that Rimsky-Korsakov turned back and plunged into a study of musical antiquities. This is understandable. Rimsky-Korsakov developed differently from me. He began with Glinka, Liszt, and Berlioz, became satiated with their music, and turned to regions that retain an interest of novelty. I began with the old people, and, in the end, came over to the young generation."

Borodin always thought in terms of large musical dimensions and generalized forms. In his instrumental compositions, large and small, one feels his orderly grasp of the entire composition. He called himself a symphonic composer and described himself as follows: "By nature I am a lyricist and a symphonist, and symphonic forms attract me." Almost all of Borodin's instrumental compositions bear a vivid picturesque quality making it easy to discover their programmatic meanings, which are generalized, not particularized. For this reason, Borodin preferred classical construction schemes to the episodic and fragmentary nature of Liszt's and Berlioz's musical forms. Free romantic forms, advocated by some members of Balakirev's circle, did not appeal to Borodin. In his symphonies and quartets, Borodin retained the classical four-movement scheme. The only difference was that he used a scherzo for the second movement. This, however, was not Borodin's innovation, because Beethoven used a scherzo for the second movement of the Ninth Symphony.

Mussorgsky's objective was to attain a spontaneous realization of a "living person in living music," a representation of a human individual as such, with all his characteristics and manifestations. Borodin's characters are generally collective types whose individual qualities are of secondary importance.

This characteristic resulted in a difference of musical-expressive means, as employed by Mussorgsky, Dargomijsky, and Borodin. Dargomijsky and Mussorgsky resorted to changeable intonations of human speech, not easily susceptible to accurate fixation. Borodin, on the other hand, preferred stable, expressive, and complete melodic forms. These aspects of Borodin's creative genius evoke a national character in his music. The mighty heroic images of Russian national folklore, full of healthy vitality and wholesome emotions, appealed to Borodin. He often romanticized these images. Popular epic themes predominate in *Prince Igor* as well as in Borodin's symphonic and vocal compositions. These epic themes are vividly and truthfully integrated into Borodin's musical genres. In spite of the impression of orchestral color and harmonic aspects, the basic expressive method of *Prince Igor* is a spontaneous, naturally flowing melody.

Borodin's music abounds with the rhythmic, melodic, and harmonic patterns of Russian tunes. There are no literal quotations of folk songs in Borodin's music because he preferred to generalize representations and forms of musical expression rather than reproduce the typical or significant meanings of Russian national music.

Borodin was interested in the cultures of oriental peoples with whom Russia had historical ties and he studied their poetry and music. Oriental elements received varied expression in Borodin's music. Oriental folklore is reflected in the Polovetsian Dances in *Prince Igor* and in the orchestral poem, *In Central Asia*. Borodin's use of oriental musical effects was not limited to special occasions determined by scenic and programmatic considerations. Elements of oriental musical cultures became a part of his musical style, endowing it with a distinct originality.

Prince Igor

As an epic heroic opera, *Prince Igor* is similar to Glinka's *Ruslan and Ludmila.* Despite the difference in plots, *Ruslan,* a fantastic fairy tale, and *Prince Igor,* a realistic historical event, the musical and dramatic conceptions of the two operas are similar. The basic principle in both *Prince Igor* and *Ruslan* is a succession of separate, complete musical pictures, which determines the character of musical forms.

The plot of *Prince Igor* is taken from an epic work of ancient Russian literature, *The Lay of Igor's Host,* a work which called for unity among the Russian people in defense of their country. The story tells of the battle between Igor's host and the steppe nomads, the Polovtsy, and describes Igor's patriotic exploit.

Prince Igor is a national opera. Its meaning is disclosed by Igor's aria while in captivity and by the arias of his wife, Yaroslavna, waiting and hoping for her husband's safe return.

The story is a defense, written against the nomads of the Russian steppes as well as against feudal and princely divisions and jealousies. The opera stresses the idea of a strong state as the foundation of national unity and vitality, and negates the idea that the "Russian people" is a primeval force which cannot be controlled and unified.

Borodin compared two worlds in the opera: the enslaved, nomadic world of the Polovtsy and the world of the working Russian peasants and soldiers led by a Russian prince who, as a leader, embodies the qualities of a national hero. Igor's image is that of a prince-soldier described in the old Russian chronicles. He is a warrior leader, bearer of the idea of Russian statehood, and defender of the homeland. Yaroslavna is the image of those Russian women who fought against Tatar invaders at the side of their husbands on the ramparts of Russian cities. Yaroslavna's "Lament" in the opera is a restrained epic expression of sorrow, a lament narrated in old Russian chronicles.

Borodin did not create a musical image of the Polovtsy which would brand them as miserable, decrepit enemies. On the contrary, they are shown to be a strong and courageous people who belong to a different sociohistoric formation. Khan Konchak and his wife, Konchakovna, are passionate, brave, and sincere.

Borodin romanticized and even ennobled the image of Khan Konchak. He created a nostalgic picture of nomadic life in the steppe. When Igor escapes from Konchak's camp, he is motivated not by torture, fear of death, or imprisonment. Igor's escape is motivated by a sense of duty to his people and country. This conception was not an easy one for Borodin to fulfill. He had to avoid creating a feeling of hate for the invaders in the audience. The spectator, although charmed by the primeval bravery of the Polovtsy, their life, dances, and the beauty of their southern nature, still prefers the ethical motives of Igor, his sense of duty and moral obligation.

In the last scene, in which Borodin depicts the destruction of Igor's city, Putivl, when Yaroslavna sings her "Lament" and the peasants pray for the return of their Prince, the feelings of the audience turn away from the nostalgic pleasures of life in the nomadic camp. The sympathies turn to thoughts of one's country, to Yaroslavna's reunion with Igor, and the glorification of the national state in the final chorus.

There is also another facet to Borodin's conception of the opera. He does not portray Russian nationalism as a conquering, subduing force. He reveals, through music, that the East, as a cultured entity, is entitled to its own development and recognition and that through art, various cultures can achieve understanding, equality, and solidarity.

Busy with his duties as a professor of chemistry, Borodin composed sporadically. He jotted down musical sketches and fragments, which are often confusing and difficult to decipher. After his death, his friends, trying to reconstruct his musical ideas, often missed the special characteristics that were typically Borodin's. *Prince Igor* was completed by Rimsky-Korsakov and Glazunov after Borodin's death.

Borodin expressed in 1876 these ideas about operatic composition: "In my views on operatic art I always differed from some of my colleagues. I love singing and cantilena, not recitative. I love complete, rounded, broad musical forms. In my opinion, small forms and meticulous details have no place in an opera and its decorations. Everything must be written with broad strokes, with clarity and vividness, for practical singing and for orchestral performance. Voices are more important than orchestral playing. I cannot judge if I shall be able to fulfill my aspirations, but in its direction my opera will be nearer to

Ruslan than to Dargomijsky's *Stone Guest*. For this I can vouch."[1]

Borodin rejected an operatic art based on declamatory principles. He adhered to Glinka's views of an opera with completely separate numbers and a predominance of cantilena over recitative.

The chorus is an important element in *Prince Igor*. The abundance of choral scenes impelled Stasov to call *Prince Igor* a "national music drama similar to Mussorgsky's *Boris Godunov* and *Khovanshchina*." Borodin's treatment of choruses is different from Mussorgsky's. Mussorgsky dramatically delineates excited crowds of people by singling out separate choral groups and clashing one against the other and by introducing solo parts into choral groups. Borodin treats the chorus as an indivisible group. The musical texture is mainly chordal-harmonic. Wherever Borodin resorts to polyphonic devices, he employs imitations of phrases by different voices, a method preferred by Glinka in operatic ensembles.

Borodin's choruses evoke an atmosphere of Slavic antiquity. Severe and resolute tone progressions based on the pentatonic scale endow the choruses with power and grandeur. Such are the choruses, "Glory to the Red Sun" in the prologue and "For Us, Princess, It Is Not the First Time" in Yaroslavna's chamber (in the second picture of the first act). In the chorus of the boyars, "Be Courageous, Princess, We Do Not Bring Good News," Borodin employs the Phrygian mode (an ascending scale of an octave: *e, f, g, a, b, c, d, e*), which gives the music an epic severity reminiscent of ancient Slavic melodies.

There are other choruses in which Borodin describes the plight of peasants suffering oppression and calamities. For example, the chorus of girls in the first act ask the reckless debauchee, Prince Vladimir Galitzky, to release their girl friend. Gliding chromaticisms express intonations of lamentation.

Another peasant chorus describes the sorrows brought on by the bloody raids of the Polovtsy. This chorus, a series of slow, drawn-out melodies, written in the natural minor scale with supporting free polyphonic interweaves and variations, characteristic of Russian folk songs, expresses boundless grief.

For the music of the Polovetsian scenes, Borodin composed melodies with folk song characteristics. He studied tunes heard and written down by the Hungarian traveler Gunfalvi among the Polovtsy, who settled in Hungary after leaving the steppes between the rivers Don and Dnieper in Southern Russia. Borodin did not utilize the tunes literally, but used them as examples for his own melodies.

The music in the oriental episodes in *Prince Igor* is of three different types. The first type contains chromatic elements, lavish melodic ornamentations, intervals of augmented seconds, and complex harmonies which evoke a feeling of passion and languor. This type of music is related to Arabian-Iranian musical cultures. Examples are the chorus of the Polovetsian girls and the cavatina of Konchakovna.

The second type is characterized by an acerbity of harmonic progressions, sharp rhythmic accentuations, and vivid melodic intonations. To this type belong the dance of the boys and the chorus, stressing angular melodic outlines and empty harmonies, sung by the Polovetsian patrol.

The third type is the music describing the Polovetsian camp. It is characterized by a peaceful, smoothly flowing diatonic melody reminiscent of Russian folk songs. An example of this music is the dance and chorus of the girls in the finale of the second act.

The delineation of personalities in *Prince Igor* corresponds to the epic pictorial type of the opera. Borodin reveals characters of persons not through action, struggle, and conflict, but in a detached portrait-like manner. Hence the predominance of monologues, reflective soliloquies and confessions, all in the form of arias. Beginning with Glinka, reflective monologues have been popular in Russian operas. Examples include the arias of Susanin, Ruslan, and Boris Godunov.

Igor's aria, "Neither Sleep Nor Rest," sung in the second act, reveals his character. The thematic material of the aria is associated with Igor's role and thereby becomes something like a leading motive.

Yaroslavna's "Lament" in the last act is a succession of stanzas with variational elements. The lament creates a lyrical, charming and, at the same time, majestic image of Yaroslavna.

Symphonic elements in the opera are represented by the Polovetsian dances and orchestral parts. The form of the overture is similar to the overture in Glinka's *A Life for the Tsar*. It is of the sonata-allegro design, featuring a succession of musical-thematic images of the operatic personalities presented, not dramatically, but as different pictorial representations.

The Polovetsian dances are in the form of a suite. They are projected on a grander scale than the oriental dances in Glinka's *Ruslan*. Borodin's dances represent an independent symphonic composition as effective as Rimsky-Korsakov's *Scheherazade*. Borodin re-creates varieties of melodic turns of oriental tunes, emphasizing their capricious patterns and rhythms, in colorful romantic harmonies and orchestration.

In the dances, Borodin exhibits remarkable variational and contrapuntal mastery by combining simultaneously different melodies. The dances are designed as successions of contrasting melodic episodes which enabled Borodin to achieve a thrilling dynamic climax.

Symphonic Compositions

Borodin's Symphonies in E Flat Major and B Minor are linked to the same heroic imagery of national Russian folklore reflected in *Prince Igor*. This content determines the aspects of Borodin's symphonic compositions: breadth of musical conceptions and unity of construction combined with vivid musical imagery and pictorial qualities. Like all other members of the Balakirev circle, Borodin wanted to saturate instrumental music with colorful pictorial elements characteristic of the decorative sparkle and glitter of the harmonic and orchestral colors in Liszt's music.

A resemblance of Borodin's juxtaposition of independent musical images to Liszt's methods of composition is corroborated by Stasov's quotation of the program of the B Minor Symphony as related to him by Borodin. "Borodin used to tell me that the first movement represents a gathering of *bogatyrs*, Russian epic heroes; the andante describes Bayan, an ancient Slavic bard; and the finale is a feast of *bogatyrs* accompanied by the sound of a *gusli*, an ancient Russian psaltery, and the rejoicing of large Russian crowds."

The B Minor Symphony is a series of independent musical pictures, united by an artistic idea and an inner relationship of content. The plot of the symphony is not a complete literary dramatic story with consecutive developments similar to those in Berlioz's programmatic symphonies.

Alternation of separate pictures, without strict subordination to a single, consecutively developed story, is the basis of the style of Rimsky-Korsakov's *Scheherazade, Spanish Caprice,* and *Easter Overture.* It is characteristic of Liszt's symphonic style and also of Glinka's *Ruslan,* used as a model by Borodin and Rimsky-Korsakov.

Alternation of epic pictorial episodes assumed different guises in the styles of Borodin and Rimsky-Korsakov. Rimsky-Korsakov was interested in the contrasts of the outward features of pictorial representations, brought about by rhythmic and harmonic devices, orchestral timbres, and structural techniques. A symphonic suite, consisting of free and complete episodes or movements, offered the best means to attain such contrasts.

Borodin proceeded from a single, unique symphonic conception or idea. The alternating musical images and episodes in his symphonies constitute a continuous development of this idea by different musical incarnations and versions. The symphonic forms of the sonata style offered the best means to unfold Borodin's conceptions.

In his First Symphony, Borodin was influenced by the music of Beethoven and Schumann. The scherzo of the symphony, with its pulsating rhythm and sharp accents, is reminiscent of the scherzo in Beethoven's *Eroica*. The ponderous and powerful syncopations in the development and coda of the finale are similar to syncopations in Beethoven's Fourth Symphony.

Beethoven's influence was not limited to external resemblances. Borodin adopted some of Beethoven's symphonic devices, such as mounting dynamic preparations which precede main points in the musical form and organ points on the dominant tone that give a strong dynamic quality to the musical texture.

The influence of Schumann in Borodin's First Symphony is noticeable in the short, rhythmic aspects of Borodin's themes. The theme of the symphony's last movement is reminiscent of the main theme in the finale of Schumann's D Minor Symphony. The development of the first allegro in Borodin's symphony is based on repetition of a concise and resilient rhythmic figure. This device was employed by Schumann in the first movement of his Symphony in E Flat. The difference between Borodin's and Schumann's themes is Borodin's use of a rhythmic figure based on an interval of a fourth. This interval relates Borodin's theme to a similar rhythmic formula in Glinka's overture to *Ruslan*. The interval of a fourth is generally characteristic of Russian folk songs. A "swinging" fourth in Russian music is often a musical means of reproducing the sounding of church bells.

The use of this rhythmic figure by Borodin is in consonance with the national heroic conception of his music. A swinging fourth in the opening theme of the finale in Rachmaninov's Third Piano Concerto represents the "church bells" effect that sometimes occurs in Rachmaninov's music.

The Trinity, by Andrei Rublev (about 1420), reveals the Byzantine influences which prevailed in Russian religious paintings and church music.

LEFT: Alexander Alabiev (1787–1851), composer of romances and music for the theater and vaudeville. BELOW LEFT: Alexander Varlamov (1801–1848), singer and composer of romances reflecting the experiences of ordinary people. BELOW RIGHT: Alexander Gurilev (1802–1856), outstanding composer of popular Russian romances.

Mikhail Glinka (1804–1857), founder of the Russian national musical school. His operas *A Life for the Tsar* and *Rusland and Ludmila* reflects many facets of Russian life.

Alexander Dargomijsky (1813–1869), whose critical realism in his operas *Rusalka* and *The Stone Guest* paralleled the critical realism in Russian literature and painting

Mily Balakirev (1836–1910), composer, piano virtuoso teacher, and organizer of musical activities, whose *Balakirev Circle* fostered Russian music based on national ideas and traditions

Alexander Borodin (1833–1887), composer of symphonies, romances, chamber music, and the opera *Prince Igor*

ABOVE: Alexander Pushkin (1799–1837), the great Russian poet whose drama *Boris Godunov* was set to music by Mussorgsky. LEFT: Mikhail Lermontov (1814–1841), an outstanding Russian poet and novelist of the early nineteenth century whose lyrics were set to music by many Russian composers.

Modest Mussorgsky (1839–1881), the founder of democratic realism in Russian music

Nicholas Rimsky-Korsakov (1844–1908), composer of operas and symphonic compositions

Peter Tchaikovsky (1840–1893), one of the greatest Russian composers of symphonies, operas, and ballets

Alexander Glazunov (1865–1936), a leading Russian composer of symphonies and ballets

Sergei Rachmaninov (1873–1943), whose music reflects Russian life and culture in the end of the nineteenth and beginning of the twentieth centuries

Alexander Scriabin (1871–1915), whose early music resurrected romantic elements of the music of Chopin and Schumann

ABOVE: Sergei Prokofiev (1891–1953), composer of operas, symphonies, ballets, and piano music. RIGHT: Dmitri Shostakovich (1906–), an exponent of critical realism in Soviet music.

Dmitri Kabalevsky (1904–), who attempts in music to represent the patriotism and moral integrity of Soviet people

Aram Khachaturyan (1903–), who reflects the phase of Soviet music which seeks to develop cultural and spiritual aspirations of Soviet nationalities

The Bolshoi Theater in Moscow, rebuilt in 1856, three years after the first building was destroyed by fire

Moscow State Conservatory, founded in 1866 by the Russian Musical Society. The Conservatory honors Tchaikovsky by bearing his name.

Appearance of Christ Before the People by Alexander Ivanov (1806–1858), is a protest against social oppression, later reflected in the music of Mussorgsky, Tchaikovsky, and Rachmaninov.

The Last Day of Pompeii by Karl Brulov (1799–1852), who, like Glinka, was attracted to sunny Italy with its artistic traditions and emotions

In the Field by Alexei Venezianov (1780–1847), whose subjects, Russian peasants, are esthetically related to the characters in Glinka's *A Life for the Tsar*

The Execution of the Streltsy by Vasili Surikov (1848–1916), represents the Red Square in Moscow in 1698. Tsar Peter, mounted on a horse, watches the execution of the Streltsy who revolted against his reforms, the subject of Mussorgsky's opera *Khovanshchina*.

Refreshment at Mitishchi by Vasili Perov (1833–1882), reflects the realistic art trends favored by Russian intellectuals and members of *Balakirev's Circle,* especially Mussorgsky.

Ivan Grozny and His Son, Ivan by Ilya Repin (1844–1930), represents the drama of Tsar Ivan the Terrible, a subject that also intrigued Mussorgsky.

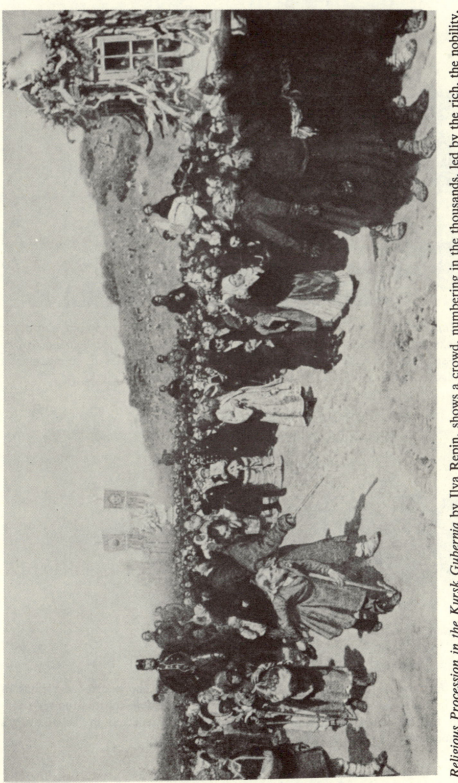

Religious Procession in the Kursk Gubernia by Ilya Repin, shows a crowd, numbering in the thousands, led by the rich, the nobility, and the police. The esthetic meaning of the painting is "the truth" as Mussorgsky envisaged it.

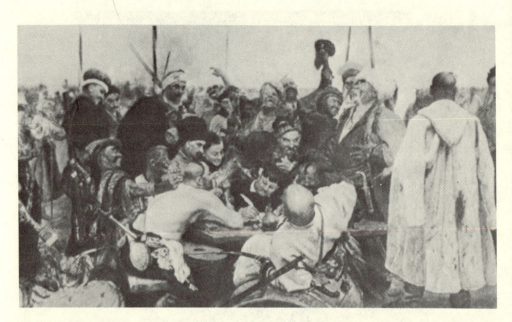

The Zaporozhtzy Write a Letter to the Sultan of Turkey by Ilya Repin, shows the Cossacks laughing over their daring reply to the Sultan, who had demanded their submission. In the center of the painting is the Ataman, Ivan Serko, an incarnation of Golgol's Taras Bulba and of the heroic types in Borodin's music.

Barge Haulers on the Volga by Ilya Repin represents the people as victims of social injustice, echoing Borodin's belief in the inexhaustible spiritual power residing in the Russian people, and the human anguish reflected in Tchaikovsky's symphonies.

The harmonic texture of Borodin's First Symphony was influenced by the daring modulations and chromatic alternations in Western romantic music. In addition, the symphony contains harmonic patterns of Russian national music: chords built on fourths and polyharmonic formations. These polyharmonic formations are produced by a simultaneous sounding of dominant-subdominant and tonic-dominant triads. However, such harmonic stratifications interfere with the dynamic flow of Borodin's music.

In his thematic developments, Borodin preferred rhythmic metamorphoses of themes and doubling of metrical patterns with slower tempos. The slowing up of tempo enhances the epic narrative features of the music.

Borodin's Second Symphony in B Minor surpasses the First Symphony in stylistic unity and importance of thematic materials. The conception of the symphony possesses greater consistency and originality. It evokes a feeling of courage, power, and determination. Borodin's characteristic musical imagery and peculiarities of musical thought receive mature and vivid incarnations in the Second Symphony, which is a remarkable example of an epic heroic composition in nineteenth century Russian music. Its themes possess a distinctive originality. Their tonal aspects, though characteristically national and folklike, are Borodin's original tunes. The themes in the andante are smooth, fluent, and wavelike. The main theme in the scherzo is short, tense, and dynamic. The main theme in the finale is steplike, energetic, and pentatonic. The secondary themes in the symphony are short and pentatonic. The second theme in the main allegro movement combines some of the characteristics discussed. There is a theme with oriental elements in the trio of the scherzo.

Color effects of romantic harmony and other harmonic aspects of Russian folk songs, occurring in the First Symphony, are used extensively in the Second Symphony. The harmonic patterns of Russian folk songs used in the Second Symphony are triadic progressions of II, III, and minor IV, of V and III, or III and I. All these progressions are in root positions. These harmonic patterns evoke a feeling of archaic severity and grandeur.

An interesting feature of the Second Symphony is Borodin's preference for major scales with alterations of the sixth and seventh steps. By these means, members of the Balakirev circle created oriental effects. Borodin used such alterations in the trio of the scherzo and the concluding section of the finale.

The tonal aspects of the Second Symphony are colorful. Borodin grouped tonalities whose tonics are separated by intervals of seconds and thirds. The changes are sometimes sudden, that is, without modulational bridges. There is, for example, the "opposition" of B major and D flat major tonalities in the transition to the second theme in the exposition of the last movement. The statement of the second theme in the last movement is first in A major, then in C sharp major, and finally in the basic tonality of D major.

Borodin preferred the tonalities of B minor and D flat major. The development section of the first movement, the trio of the scherzo, and the last movement are in the tonality of D flat major. The D flat major triad, its enharmonic equivalent, the C sharp major triad, and the B minor triad form the Phrygian cadence widely used by Russian composers beginning with Glinka. This cadence is often a harmonic feature in Russian folk songs.

Thematic developments in the Second Symphony are rhythmic and variational transformations combined with changes of tempo, tonalities, and orchestral effects. The music is endowed with power, dynamic contrast, and sweeping drives commensurate with the heroic conception of the symphony.

By simultaneously using all orchestral choirs in unisonal passages, Borodin creates majestic effects. In the andante, the harp imitates the *gusli,* an instrument associated with the epic image of the bard, Bayan.

Borodin prefers to use an orchestral choir as a group. He rarely uses individual instruments in solo capacities. The exception is the woodwind choir whose instruments Borodin uses individually for folk song and epic effects.

The symphonic picture, *In Central Asia,* is a short composition characterized by a sparsity and simplicity of musical materials. The orchestration, deliberately sustained in monotonous colors, is light and transparent. The tonal and harmonic aspects of the composition are simple.

There are two themes in the symphonic picture, one Russian, the other oriental. Neither is developed or transformed but are presented consecutively and then repeated with contrapuntal additions.

The design of the composition is determined by the program. In the monotonous sandy desert of Central Asia, a Russian tune is heard for the first time. The clatter of horses and the measured footfall of camels are heard accompanied by an oriental song.

The vast desert is crossed by a native caravan guarded by Russian soldiers. The caravan, in perfect security, makes its long journey and slowly disappears behind the horizon. The peaceful melodies of Russians and natives merge into a single tune and, echoed by the desert, die away in the distance.

A sustained E tone creates an image of a boundless desert. A regularly swinging figure played by plucked strings describes the slow and heavy tread of horses and camels. The music expresses a mood evoked by the contemplation of a mournful and monotonous desert landscape. In this symphonic picture, Borodin expresses elementary aspects of musical impressionism.

Borodin's two string quartets in A and D major are lyrical outpourings of peaceful and contemplative music within traditional classical designs. It is possible that, as a scientist, Borodin felt himself at his best in a type of music requiring intellectual mastery of musical form and technique of composition. In the A Major Quartet, Borodin is interested in principles of classical construction of musical thought. The main motive is a thematic passage taken from Beethoven's string quartet, opus 130, which is expanded by Borodin. The first movement is a perfectly balanced sonata form in which Borodin introduces polyphonic passages. By means of an extensive fugato, a typically Beethovenian device, the movement achieves a tense and dramatic culmination. Another fugato appears in the andante con moto. Double counterpoint is extensively used in the finale. Despite Beethovenian influences, the thematic materials of the quarter reveal Russian national influences.

The second quartet is famous for its melodic qualities. The popularity of the quartet is due to the second movement, the "Nocturne," one of Borodin's best inspirations. The "Nocturne" sounds like a peaceful and drawn-out Russian song. Thematic developments in the D Major Quartet are simple. This simplicity, however, is compensated for through the use of colorful harmonies and extensive modulations.

Borodin portrays the Russian people as the fairy tale epic hero, the *bogatyr* who represents spiritual and physical power, a symbol of a glorious past and of a great future. Thereby Borodin paid tribute to the idea prevalent during the 1860's among Russian peasant dem crats that the Russian people are "a great personality animated by a single idea" of the inexhaustible spiritual power dormant in the common people. Lyrical imageries in *Prince Igor* and in the Second Symphony reflect feelings of masses of people and of epic heroes.

Unlike Beethoven's thematic developments, Borodin's developments are not projections of struggles, conflicts, and antagonisms of thematic aspects, but syntheses of contrasting themes achieving unified musical conceptions. Borodin was less interested in the dramatic possibilities of the sonata form and more in its logical affinity to the epic and narrative qualities of his music. Beethoven's lyricism is often heroic in the sense that it reflects heroic emotions. Borodin's smoothly flowing lyrical themes are characterized by expressive aspects peculiar in his epic themes. However, some of Borodin's lyric themes in the string quartets and in *Prince Igor* express intimate, personal aspects. Here Borodin's lyricism is a gentle, caressing narrative or a languorous contemplation different from the passionate, impetuous lyricism of Tchaikovsky and Rachmaninov. Borodin's whole-hearted and sensitive hero rising above the turmoil of passions differs from the anguished Raskolnikov in Dostoyevsky's *Crime and Punishment*.

Borodin's epic hero is powerful because he is inseparable from the Russian soil, the boundless Russian steppe, reflecting Gogol's words in *Dead Souls:* "Should not a *bogatyr* be here, where there is room for him to turn around and walk along?" A similar thought is found in Nekrasov's *Who Lives Well in Russia?:* "You think, Matryonushka, a muzhik is not a *bogatyr?*" In his story "The Steppe," Chekhov describes a road as "something unusually wide, sprawling like a *bogatyr*," which seems appropriate for Russian epic heroes. In this sense, Borodin's *Prince Igor* and the Second Symphony are generalizations of the historical destinies of the Russian people.

National characteristics in Borodin's music are enhanced by intonations and rhythms found in Russian narrative speech, tales, and ceremonial rites; by melodic turns of fourths, fifths, sixths, and octaves expressing power and boldness; and by a static "trampling" of the unisonal main theme in the Second Symphony which seems to convey an idea of a persistent war-cry, a declaration to the crowd. Such themes were not original with Borodin: unisonal declarations open Beethoven's Fifth Symphony. Schumann's First Symphony, Liszt's First Piano Concerto, and Tchaikovsky's Fourth Symphony. However, in Borodin's symphony, the "trampling" theme with its swinging emphasis on the tonic tone is a reminder of a powerful, stern Russian antiquity and of ancient *bylina* tunes. The C natural followed by the D sharp (the enharmonic equivalent of E flat) recalls distant tonal deviations in Russian peasant songs and the Phrygian tetrachord with a lowered fourth found in oriental music.

Borodin substituted the epic Russian *bogatyr* for Beethoven's revolutionary hero. Instead of Beethoven's passionate ideological quests, Borodin expressed Russian national consciousness, nature, and ancient mode of life. Borodin's epos differs from Wagner's and Bruckner's. Wagner's *Ring of the Nibelungs* projects socioeconomic conceptions; *Tristan and Isolde* unfolds the metaphysics of love. Bruckner's pantheism is hardly heroic and does not reflect social questions of his time.

Borodin is one of the greatest representatives of Russian music in the nineteenth century and his music exercised a strong influence on its future development. He carried on the traditions of Glinka and, at the same time, enriched Russian music with an original style. His style evolved from the integration of Western classic-romantic traditions with features of Russian folk songs and oriental folklore.

Borodin and Tchaikovsky were the founders of the Russian symphony. The epic grandeur and pictoriality of Borodin's symphonic style received further development in the music of Soviet composers such as Myaskovsky, Shaporin, Khachaturyan, and in the music of various nationalities within the Soviet Union.

CHAPTER 11

Mussorgsky

MODEST MUSSORGSKY was the champion of democratic realism in Russian music. His music, based on realistic concepts, represents and expresses the sufferings, hopes, and joys of the common people, the spiritual and psychological aspects of their daily existence and the disasters and calamities which overwhelm them.

Mussorgsky conceived realism to be a truthful reflection of life in artistic imagination and representation. "Life wherever it is; truth no matter how unpleasant it is; and sincere, courageous conversation with people—this is my objective." He believed that art should be educational in its purpose and functional in society. "Art as a means of conversation with people, not as an aim in itself."

Mussorgsky's views were influenced by the intellectual, social and philosophical milieu of the 1860's in Russia. His artistic objectives reflected the materialistic art philosophy of Chernishevsky who, in his essay, "Esthetic Relations of Art to Reality" (1853–1855), advocated art as a representation of people, actions, and feelings as they were in real life.

Mussorgsky was born on March 1, 1839, in the village of Karev in Pskov province. His father was a prosperous landowner who, in later years, met with financial reverses. His mother, who loved music and occasionally wrote poetry, was her son's first piano teacher.

As a child, Mussorgsky loved to sit at the piano and improvise music for the fairy tales his nurse told him. Daily contacts with peasants, their customs, songs, and dances, made an indelible impression on the boy.

At the age of ten, Mussorgsky entered a military school in Petersburg and upon graduation in 1856 became an officer in the Preobrazhensky regiment. Mussorgsky became acquainted with Dargomijsky and Balakirev. His friendship with Balakirev was a decisive influence in Mussorgsky's musical career. Under Balakirev's guidance, Mussorgsky studied the music of Russian and Western composers and tried to compose in various genres.

Realizing that his future was in music, Mussorgsky resigned from the army. To support himself, he became a clerk in various government offices, an occupation he followed during his short life.

Mussorgsky's first serious compositions were songs which he called "compositions from Russian national life—musical pictures of national individuality in songs." "Sirotka" (The Orphan), "Svetik Savishna" (Darling Savishna), a song about the love of a *yurodivy* (a queer man) for a girl named Savishna, "A Lullaby for Yeremushka," and "Kalistrat." He also composed satirical songs: "The Flea" (words by Goethe), "The Billy Goat" and "Seminarist" (a seminary student sings in a church melody about a girl he has met).

Mussorgsky's genius as a reformer of the music drama was first revealed in *Boris Godunov*. This opera was preceded by three unfinished operas: *Oedipus*, based on a play by Sophocles, *Salambo*, based on a novel by Flaubert, and *The Marriage*, based on a play by Gogol.

Mussorgsky completed *Boris Godunov* in 1869 and submitted the score to the management of the imperial theaters. The management found the music's progressive national ideas unacceptable and rejected the opera in 1871. Mussorgsky made alterations in the opera, but did not change its ideas of freedom and of the people as a powerful force in Russian history. The management again rejected the opera.

Excerpts from the score were often performed at musicals in private homes at which singers from the Mariinsky Theater attended. One of the singers, Platonova, informed the management of the Imperial Theaters that if the opera were not approved by the management, she would leave the Mariinsky. Gedeonov, the director of the theater, thereupon ordered the staging of *Boris Godunov* on January 24, 1874.

Attacks on Mussorgsky's national realistic style, difficulties of self-support, and the political reaction which suppressed the liberal democratic movement all undermined his health. Nevertheless, he did not relinquish the efforts directed toward attaining Russian realistic art. In 1872, he began the opera *Khovanshchina*, based on events occurring during the revolt of the Streltsy in the seventeenth century. In the plot of *Khovanshchina,* Mussorgsky found similarities between Russian past and present. The main idea in the opera is that political reforms are fruitless unless accomplished with the participation of the people. "Man is a social animal and cannot be anything else. In masses of people, as in an individual person, one can find traits which seem to elude us. To observe and to study these traits, to bring them out, this is the problem. I shall try it in *Khovanshchina.*"

Simultaneously with *Khovanshchina,* Mussorgsky worked on the opera *Fair of Sorochinsk* (1874), based on Gogol's story. For a realistic representation of peasant life in southern Russia, Mussorgsky studied Ukrainian tunes and melodies.

Besides opera, Mussorgsky composed a piano suite, "Pictures at an Exhibition" (1874), choral works, an orchestral fantasia, "Night on Bald Mountain" (1867), and several song cycles: "The Nursery" (1868–1870), a cycle of seven pictures of child life; "The Dance of Death" (1875–1877), a cycle of four songs; and "No Sunlight" (1874–1875), a cycle of six songs.

Mussorgsky died on March 16, 1881, after a month of lingering illness. He was a lonely victim of poverty and physical sufferings.

As a representation of Russian social and political realities in music, Mussorgsky's style depends on the exact meaning of words and on intonation, in short, on the psychological aspects of a literary text. As a critical realist, Mussorgsky is related to Dargomijsky.[1] Like Dargomijsky, Mussorgsky was interested in the experience of daily life. The plots of Mussorgsky's vocal compositions reflect the life of common people.[2] Here Mussorgsky followed the democratic ideas prevalent in Russian literature during the 1860's. However, unlike Russian writers and painters, Mussorgsky did not simply portray the life, morals, and manners of common people. He created generalized images of masses of the people representing a powerful force in Russian life. Mussorgsky sought the key to the emergence of these forces in the momentous occurrences of Russian history.

Mussorgsky was the first Russian composer to whom a mass of people was *a personality,* endowed with thoughts, feelings, and a will. Thus, Mussorgsky was able to regard past and present events in Russian life and history as expressions of meaningful and logical processes involving masses of people.

Mussorgsky studied the psychological and emotional experiences of a human personality. "A living man and a living music," was Mussorgsky's explanation of his artistic principles. The representation or description of psychological imagery in Mussorgsky's music depends mainly on the expressive qualities of a human voice, on sound as an expression of a word. To accomplish this end, Mussorgsky usually employed melodic recitatives based on natural speech intonations. His recitatives reflect psychologically accurate meanings of the speech of characters in his musical conceptions. He often reproduces speech intonations by melodic-declamatory means.

In 1876, in a letter to the music critic Stasov, Mussorgsky wrote: "A study of human speech led me to melody created by speech, that is an incarnation of recitative in melody. I should like to call it a sensible, justified melody."

Although Russian folk songs influenced Mussorgsky's style, he was mainly interested in their psychological and intellectual meanings, which reflected the life of common people. To Mussorgsky, national rhythmic, melodic, and harmonic features of folk songs were aspects of expressive peasant speech, which he developed by musical means. Hence, the originality of Mussorgsky's musical style distinguishes him from other nineteenth-century Russian composers.

Mussorgsky's style was also influenced by the styles of Berlioz, Liszt, and Schumann: Berlioz's programmatic articulation and orchestral tone color, Liszt's philosophical thought and romantic harmony, including alterations and distant modulations, and Schumann's rhythmic contrasts. The harmonic language of Mussorgsky anticipates Western impressionism.

Mussorgsky rejected schematic outlines and designs in music. He saw no point of reconciliation between standard musical designs, like the logical and rational schemes of the sonata style, and the representation of life in all its manifestations. "Where there are people, there is life, and there is no place for preconceived paragraphs and articles."

Esthetic values had relative value for Mussorgsky because he believed they were as inconstant as were the spiritual-emotional elements in the life of people. He rejected the idea that there were immutable laws in art. To Mussorgsky, art was inconstant because it had to conform to the spiritual and emotional experiences of man. Mussorgsky looked for musical forms suitable to embody his musical conceptions.

In songs, Mussorgsky used simple ternary or variational designs. In his operas and in the symphonic picture, *Night on Bald Mountain,* Mussorgsky used variational principles. Complex musical structures in his operas resulted from psychological and dramatic situations unified with verbal and visual components.

The synthesis of Mussorgsky's musical style is found in *Boris Godunov.* It is a realistic music drama in which music is subordinated to expression of psychological-emotional experiences and dramatic action. Here, Mussorgsky successfully created a feeling of vitality and sincerity in the characters he represented.

Boris Godunov

The development of Mussorgsky's national music-drama, *Boris Godunov,* is based on the intrigues of *boyars,* rebellious actions of the people, and the personality of Tsar Boris. The drama of Boris himself occupies the greater part of Mussorgsky's attention. Boris' serious thoughts in the arioso, "My Soul Sorrows," in the coronation scene, are expressed in music which conveys the feelings of an unusual person. In the chamber scene of the second act, Boris is disclosed as a loving father, and while discussing the geographic map of Russia with his son, he is also revealed as a wise ruler. The musical intonations stressing sounds which represent thoughts create the impression that Boris is an exceptional, humane, and sincere person.

In the monologue, "I Have Attained to Highest Power," Boris reveals his strong character. But in the following scene, in which Shuysky appears, Mussorgsky's objective becomes clearer. Here the composer is concerned with the ethical problem of Boris' personality. Boris' humanity is tainted by the compunctions of conscience. Mussorgsky is concerned with the problem of Dmitri's murder: was it premeditated or was it an unpremeditated mistake which stains Boris' humanity?

As a composer, Mussorgsky distinguished between a musical art created by rules, laws, and regulations and one based on ethical foundations. The latter instance would include the notion of truth about "man," for example. Therefore, *Boris Godunov* was not an ordinary opera but the expression of a composer, personally responsible for his musical creativity. This, to Mussorgsky, was the over-all objective of a Russian artist. Thus, in *Boris Godunov,* while following Pushkin's drama, Mussorgsky discloses his own reflections on human truth against the background of historic events.

Boris' image, whether innocent or criminal, is always the truthful revelation of a human personality. This is especially true in Boris' confession scenes, "Farewell" and "Death," where the spectator actually sympathizes with him.

Although Mussorgsky, like Pushkin, accepted the version contending that Boris engineered Dmitri's murder, the composer truthfully reconstructs the contradictions existing between Boris and surrounding reality as well as the emerging repentance in Boris' inherent humanity. It is difficult to avoid feeling compassion for Boris. Mussorgsky's music is not artificial or contrived. It comes from the heart of a composer, dictated by an emotional penetration into the life and thoughts of Boris and an understanding of his personality.

Mussorgsky demanded truth, realism, and vocalization based on the musical laws of human speech. The truth of scenic representation, as a reflection of reality, logically fulfills Mussorgsky's demands. For Mussorgsky, the musical theater can only be based on truthful human intonations, sounds representing thoughts.

The human voice and its intonations determined the emotional style and meaning of speech and melody for Mussorgsky. The origins of Mussorgsky's harmonic style are human intonations, presented as sounds reflecting spiritual and emotional processes. Mussorgsky sought to discover a Russian melodic foundation for Russian opera in the musical laws of Russian language and speech, in the intonations of Russian men and women. This meant melodies created by the sounds of talking. It could best be described by the statement: speech sings, singing speaks.

Mussorgsky's writing for voices, with its pauses and rhythmic divisions, grew from emotional necessities, not scholastic considerations. For this reason, his musical textures sound natural, delightful, new, and typically Russian.

There is no sentimentality in the music of *Godunov*, no deliberate originality, and no pursuit of tonal effects. What one experiences in this national music-drama is a series of images and representations strongly evoked by the music. There is no landscape painting in the music-drama, yet the feeling of Russian soil and nature is always present. There is no abstract thinking in this music, or what in symphonic compositions would be called thematic development. There is simply a convincing stream of thoughts revealed in musical images. Mussorg-sky called this truth in music, truth in art.

Glinka, founder of the Russian national opera, realized that the language of the common people, despite the differences of various dialects, always retained a singing, intonational quality. Russian versification is rooted in the imagery and picturesque quality of popular verse. In popular verse, the metric foot, the word, and the image are inseparably linked, from a melodic point of view. A Russian verse may be syllabic or tonic, but this is only part of the problem. The versifications of many old Russian folk songs are fundamentally semantic and based on the quantity of images and significant expressions in the verse. Each expression can be regarded as a metrical unit having a principal accent preceded and followed by an indefinite number of unaccented syllables.

Glinka was the creator of the Russian "musical-poetic" intoned verse and language. He felt the above factors and, though he avoided the baring of metrical schemes, he introduced melodic designs into the rhythmic, intoned meaning, thus enveloping the verse with a melodic chiaroscuro. He singled out, or shaded, word-links and watched the intonation of Russian vowels. This is the basis of the rhythmic beauty in Glinka's melodies. Similar qualities characterize the verses of Pushkin, for whom the mere sounding of a word reflected intonational meaning.[3]

The creative principles of Dargomijsky were based on the singing quality of Russian words. The Russian dramatic theater, during the nineteenth century, was inexorably moving towards the representation of truth in Russian reality by means of the intonations of words. Russian opera, therefore, could not imitate Western operatic forms. The musical forms of arias, ensembles and recitatives in the Russian musical theater had to be developed on the basis of qualities of Russian speech intonations.

Mussorgsky's achievement is the mastery and development of the wealth of intonations in Russian speech as a source of meaningful inflections in intercourse among people by means of sounds. This, to Mussorgsky, was the truth of pronounced melody. For the music of *Boris Godunov* Mussorgsky sought voice intonations of operatic characters in the imagery and verses in Pushkin's drama. At no time did Mussorgsky attempt to paraphrase Pushkin's verses into a melodic structure.

There are similarities between the artistic styles of Pushkin and Mussorgsky. The syntax of Pushkin's poetry gradually assimilated the forms and idioms of speech of the common people. The literary school of the Russian poet-historian Karamzin condemned the mixing of abstract literary syntax with forms and idioms of common speech. The poet Zhukovsky did not approve of Pushkin's merging literary styles with the spoken Russian language. But it is this simple, natural syntax of ordinary Russian speech which gives Pushkin's poetry its expressiveness, simplicity, and national characteristics. The short sentences and phrases within Pushkin's style are dynamic and expressively diversified. They contain the intoned and rhythmic varieties of popular speech.

Similar qualities characterize melodic elements in Mussorgsky's music. Mussorgsky "heard" intonations of common speech in Pushkin's drama. He integrated these intonations into accepted norms of musical construction, thereby transmitting Pushkin's spirit and culture to the Russian musical stage. Varlaam's speech discloses his ingenuity, innate humor, and cunning. He seems to enjoy his facetious remarks and the manner in which he delivers them. In *Boris Godunov*, Varlaam's floral recitatives, whimsical and sinuous, are accompanied by chromatic harmonies which accentuate the above characteristics. Tsar Boris' melodies are sometimes characterized by leaps and acerbic dissonantal sonorities in the orchestral accompaniment which seem to reflect the dreadful imagery of Boris' soliloquies and utterances. When Rimsky-Korsakov edited *Boris Godunov*, he only repeated what Zhukovsky did to some of Pushkin's verses. As a sensitive musical stylist, Rimsky-Korsakov did not understand the unrestrained musical talent of Mussorgsky.

Mussorgsky's orchestration of *Boris Godunov* has a meaning consonant with the plot and development of the music-drama. The genre scenes are artistic embodiments of objective reality as Mussorgsky saw and heard it. Having a clear perception of the psychological development of the characters in *Boris Godunov*, the characteristic traits of their behavior, and their outward appearance, Mussorgsky carefully described the poses, gestures, and movements of persons on the stage. He did not envisage various scenes pictorially, but as living theatrical presentations and pantomimes. Conceptions of stage actions not only influenced the formation of musical structures in the drama, but the orchestration of the music as well. The orchestration acquired the expressiveness of a gesture and the feeling of stage movements, as envisaged by Mussorgsky.

Mussorgsky employed orchestral sonorities to reflect the dynamics of emotional realism in dramatic situations. For this purpose, he preferred a flexible orchestral palette with frequent changes in light and shade and in timbre, avoiding orchestral splendor and decorative effects.

Mussorgsky conceived the Coronation Scene, not as a magnificent grand opera presentation, but as a passing phase in the evolution of the plot. The Coronation Scene follows the mutterings of the crowd that "We are ordered to howl, we shall howl in the Kremlin." Rimsky-Korsakov, misunderstanding Mussorgsky's conceptions, changed the Coronation Scene into a magnificent operatic spectacle in the tradition of nineteenth century grand opera.

Mussorgsky's meager instrumentation for the Coronation Scene suggests that he did not want to portray a happy and popular event, but a forced celebration, a compulsory coronation. The people glorified the new Tsar unwillingly. Such a conception justifies the dramatic meaning of the ensuing monologue of Boris: "My Soul Sorrows." To show the uncertainty and doubts of the people, the *boyars,* and the Tsar, Mussorgsky ended the Coronation Scene on a C major chord with the fifth of the chord, G, in the melody. This produces a feeling of incompleteness. Rimsky-Korsakov changed the ending by placing the root of the chord, C, in the melody, thereby giving the music a positive, determined feeling. Many other changes introduced by Rimsky-Korsakov nullified the esthetic conceptions of Mussorgsky.

Besides Rimsky-Korsakov's orchestration of *Boris Godunov* there is also an orchestration of the opera by Shostakovich. It is interesting to compare the three versions.

Mussorgsky's orchestration is characterized by a discontinuity of orchestral timbre. This method reflects the improvisational character of Mussorgsky's music. Different musical variants in the score of *Boris Godunov* are not fortuitous occurrences, but reflections of similar variants prevailing in Russian folk songs, in which each new variant represents a new penetration of the emotional expressiveness of the music. Improvisational features are fundamental qualities in Mussorgsky's musical style.

Improvisation, as a principle of construction in musical form, demands the coexistence of the effects of surprise and maximum inner conformity to these effects in the tonal texture. This is the principle in commedia dell'arte, in the style of Domenico Scarlatti, and in the last piano sonatas of Beethoven. It is the fundamental principle of construction of free musical forms.

Shostakovich, with his feeling for musical continuity, is not reconciled to the improvisational discontinuity of timbre in Mussorgsky's orchestral episodes. While preserving Mussorgsky's attention to the expressiveness of different orchestral voices, Shostakovich unified these voices through common relationships of orchestral group timbres so that the entrance of every voice timbre has its own particular significance. Shostakovich changed the movement of orchestral voices in Mussorgsky's score and, at the same time, preserved the spirit and meaning of Mussorgsky's musical and dramatic intentions. He achieved the accentuation of different orchestral expressive elements which Mussorgsky had in mind, but by different means.

Rimsky-Korsakov, on the other hand, smoothed out the sharp, rugged outlines in Mussorgsky's score with an unruffled movement of harmonic elements and orchestral timbres. Rimsky-Korsakov's academic ideas, however, diminished the sharpness of emotional and dramatic experiences embodied in Mussorgsky's intonations, which were expressions of ideas and thoughts in music.

Esthetics

Mussorgsky advocated a popular musical art which would express the life and experiences of common people. His artistic creativity is based on the function of intonations which, as musicalized thoughts, emerge from sounds amidst the realities of existence. Mussorgsky demonstrated that a true musical intonation is always a "living" intonation of the emotional and spiritual experiences of people.

Mussorgsky studied speech intonations because he was interested in the environmental, social, and psychological aspects of human relations. Whenever he tried to represent, in music, the intonations of general programmatic qualities, his methods and schemes became traditional. He made important contributions to the study of national intonations, intonational features of social groups, of characters, and of spiritual and emotional states.

Mussorgsky successfully demonstrated that musical intonations took precedence over musical forms. He showed that intonations created form, but form never created intonations. However, in his efforts to prove the superiority of intonations, Mussorgsky underestimated the importance of musical form.

Mussorgsky believed in the superiority of content over form and technical refinements. A composition without intelligible content was, to him, music without ideas and significant imagery. Such music was an example of routine methods and traditions for which he had no use.

As an example of significant art, Mussorgsky mentioned the sculptures of Antokolsky and the paintings of Repin and Perov: [4]

People seem to be so alive that the spectator is eager to become acquainted with them. Compared to this art, contemporary music lacks vitality and meaning.[5]

Mussorgsky believed that the backwardness of contemporary music was due to adherence to traditions which formed boundaries, which kept music in a state of stagnation. He did not equate music with sculpture or painting. He acknowledged that music had its limitations of expression, because sounds were not artistically equal to the brush or the chisel.

The music envisaged by Mussorgsky was an art of profound psychology, not of sensuous tonal textures. He condemned representation of physical beauty in painting and sculpture, because he believed that an artist's mission was to probe the subtlest aspects of human nature and of the masses of humanity:

Man is a social animal and cannot be anything else. In masses of humanity there always exist traits which no one has yet discovered. The function of art is to find and study these traits.[6]

Mussorgsky defended intonational and structural innovations in his operas and program music:

The form and character of *Night on Bald Mountain* are Russian and original. . . . I am interested in a re-creation of popular fantasy, free from German profundity and academic routine, and nurtured by Russian bread.[7]

The first scene in my opera *The Marriage* should serve as an experience in a dialogue opera. . . . I tried to delineate intonational changes which appear in the dialogues of acting persons.[8]

Art will find tremendous opportunities in Russian nature. I have crossed the Rubicon in *The Marriage*. I should like acting persons on the stage to speak as persons in real life so that the character and effect of their intonations, supported by the orchestra, would artistically reproduce nuances of speech. The sounds of human speech, as true revelations of thought and feeling, should become true artistic music. This is my ideal. It represents living prose in music through the re-creation of simple human speech.[9]

If one should break away from operatic traditions and represent, instead, musical conversation on the stage, then *The Marriage* is an opera. If my music truthfully re-creates human thoughts by sounds, and feelings by simple speech, then my composition is musically artistic.[10]

When Mussorgsky met Tchaikovsky, he characterized him as "the worshipper of absolute beauty." The two composers could not agree on the function and meaning of music.[11] At this period, however (1872), Tchaikovsky's music was favorably regarded by Balakirev's circle, of which Mussorgsky was a member.

Tchaikovsky described his attitude toward Mussorgsky in a letter to Madame von Meck (January 5, 1878):

Mussorgsky is more talented than the other members of the circle. He is a man of narrow views. He believes blindly in his genius and in the preposterous theories of the circle. His character is somewhat base. He enjoys coarseness, roughness, and uncouthness. His outbursts of talent are not without originality.

In Soviet esthetics, Mussorgsky is regarded as a materialist who rejected idealistic esthetics which favored the romantic appreciation of music as an art of moods and abstract mystical reveries. Mussorgsky is regarded as a composer who created a musical art which served and expressed the interests of society.

Mussorgsky's realism is not the scientific realism of Communist philosophy and esthetics. His realism developed the realism of progressive romanticism initiated by Pushkin, Gogol, and Lermontov. They regarded romanticism as an expression of protest, struggle, and emotion, and not merely a manifestation of moods and mystical reveries. The realism of these writers was not a substitute for romanticism, but a subordination of the romantic world of dreams to the world of reality.

Mussorgsky's esthetics continued the objective perception of the world in Russian art and literature. The visionary, futile, and abstract aspects of romanticism were discarded. The features of romanticism which embodied perceptions of realities in life were retained in a new realistic art. These features of romanticism were pointed out by Belinsky in 1843:

The sources of romanticism are in life. Where there is life, there is man; and where there is man, there is romanticism. In its essential meaning, romanticism is the inner spiritual world of man, the innermost life of his heart. The secret source of romanticism is in the breast and heart of man. Feeling and love are manifestations, or actions, of romanticism. Therefore, every man is a romantic.[12]

Mussorgsky believed in the common people. He advocated musical art as an expression of Russian national culture. He had vague ideas of peculiarities in the development of Russian history and of connections of the past to the present. However, he demanded that historical operas should recognize and reveal the influence of past events upon contemporary Russian social and political conditions. During the 1860's, the struggle between the Tsar and the *boyars* was a historical account without any significance in contemporary Russian social and political conditions. However, the rebellious discontent in the Time of Troubles (1598–1613) had a concrete sympathy in the 1860's. This discontent Mussorgsky projected in *Boris Godunov:* the powerful rebellious spirit of the common people in the Kroman Scene which concludes the music drama was the first musical incarnation of a popular uprising in the Russian opera and it was especially meaningful against the background of unfolding Russian social and political realities.

CHAPTER 12

Rimsky-Korsakov

NICHOLAS RIMSKY-KORSAKOV was influenced by the nationalism of Glinka's music. His creative work was based on Russian national art in which he found representations congenial to his optimistic outlook. The sources of Russian folklore, especially the folk song, intelligible to diverse masses of listeners, helped Korsakov form his musical style.

Korsakov is one of the greatest Russian operatic composers. While continuing the musical traditions of Glinka, he created new operatic forms linked to the artistic imagery and stylistic aspects of Russian national art, its poetry and folk song. He is regarded as an outstanding composer of programmatic symphonic music, in which he created consummate pictures of nature, and of Russian life and customs.

In addition to his activities as a composer, Korsakov taught composition and orchestration in the Petersburg conservatory. For several decades, he surrounded himself with the most gifted musical talents in Russia.

In the world of music and music education, Korsakov enjoyed immense prestige, both as an authority and a composer. His personal and artistic qualities courageously and unselfishly devoted to principles and ideals, earned him the respect and loyalty of friends, colleagues, and students.

Korsakov was born on March 6, 1844, in Tikhvin, a town in the province of Novgorod. He was the son of a retired governor, Andrei Petrovich Rimsky-Korsakov. The musical talent of the future composer revealed itself at an early age. At the age of six, the boy took piano lessons with a local teacher. At the age of eleven, he made his first attempts at composition.

In 1856, Korsakov enrolled in the Naval School in Petersburg, a private institution for officer training. He continued his music studies by taking piano lessons every Sunday with a Mr. Ulich. In 1859, Korsakov began taking lessons with a well-trained and cultured teacher, Mr. Kamille, who encouraged his pupil's interest in composition. Under Kamille's direction, Korsakov composed a sonata-allegro movement, variations and sketches for the first movement of a symphony.

Kamille introduced Korsakov to Balakirev and the original members of the circle—Cui, Mussorgsky, and Stasov. Balakirev advised Korsakov to compose a symphony based on his previous sketches. Balakirev's guidance was the first school of composition for Korsakov, but the lessons were more in the nature of consultations than studies of theory and analysis. Balakirev helped Korsakov make up deficiencies in musical education.

While in naval school, Korsakov read and studied Russian literature. In his *Chronicles,* he writes with enthusiasm of Belinsky and Dobrolyubov, the most progressive writers of the period. He became acquainted with the writings of Chernishevsky, one of the greatest Russian estheticians, and with the *Kolokol* (The Bell), a revolutionary newspaper published by Herzen in London.

From 1863 to 1864, the students of the naval school went on a sea voyage around the world. In the spring of 1865, the clipper *Almaz* (Diamond), on which Korsakov was an officer, returned to Petersburg. Memories of the sea and of foreign countries left an indelible impression on him. In his *Chronicles* he wrote enthusiastically of his travels in poetically inspired descriptions.

Upon his return, Korsakov resumed his friendship with Balakirev who insisted that Korsakov complete the symphony on which he was working for several years. In December of 1865, the symphony was performed by an orchestra conducted by Balakirev, and this event determined Korsakov's musical career. A few more years remained before resignation from the navy enabled Korsakov to devote his career to composition.

In 1866 and 1867, Korsakov composed two overtures, one on three Russian themes, the other on Serbian themes. During the summer of 1867, he composed a symphonic poem, *Sadko,* which contained the main features of his symphonic style: a national, popular plot based on the *bylina* (a Russian epic story); themes based on Russian folk songs and dances; tone painting of sea pictures and fantasy of fairyland representations. Thirty years later, Korsakov utilized the thematic materials of this symphonic poem in his opera *Sadko*.

In 1868, Korsakov completed his second symphony, a symphonic suite entitled *Antar*. Like *Sadko, Antar* is characterized by programmatic aspects, fairyland subjects, and tone painting. It contains oriental features enhanced by authentic oriental melodies. The romantic aspects of *Antar* include its colorful harmonies, its representations of Antar who forsakes human society for a hermit's life in the desert, and its suitelike compositional construction based on several leading motives heard consecutively throughout the work.

After composing *Antar*, Korsakov turned his attention to operatic forms. His first opera, *Pskovityanka* (The Woman from Pskov), completed in 1871, was based on a plot suggested by Balakirev and Mussorgsky. The libretto was criticized by the government censor who told Rimsky-Korsakov to eliminate references to republican ideas. A greater obstacle was presented by the censor's request to omit the depiction on stage of members of the Tsar's family, in this case, Ivan the Terrible. Eventually, this request was canceled. In the choice of an historical subject for the libretto, the importance of giving parts to masses of people and the predominance of recitative aspects in the opera, Rimsky-Korsakov was influenced by Mussorgsky's *Boris Godunov*. *Pskovityanka* disclosed Korsakov's bent for the fabulous as well as for tone painting in operatic forms.

Azansky, director of the Petersburg conservatory, offered Korsakov a professorship to teach orchestration and composition. Korsakov hesitated, feeling inadequately prepared to teach music. In his *Chronicles,* he wrote: "I, the author of *Sadko, Antar,* and *Pskovityanka,* compositions that were well written, did not sound badly, and were approved by the public, was an amateur musician who knew nothing. . . . The insistence of friends, coupled with my own delusion, triumphed. I was young and confident. My confidence was encouraged and I accepted the offer."

Teaching made Korsakov realize his technical shortcomings and he began to study music theory. Stimulus was provided not only by pedagogical activities, but also by personal factors. After completing *Pskovityanka*, Korsakov found himself in a state of creative stagnation and crisis. The reason was his unpreparedness in music theory. He wrote in his *Chronicles:* "The absence of harmonic and contrapuntal training which I realized after composing *Pskovityanka* put an end to my compositional fantasy."

The encouragement and advice of Tchaikovsky helped Rimsky-Korsakov organize his studies to which he applied himself with his usual perseverance. During one summer, he composed dozens of fugues. He studied the works of old contrapuntal masters, especially of J. S. Bach whose importance was deprecated by the Balakirev circle. At the request of Glinka's sister, L. E. Shestakova, Korsakov, together with Balakirev and Lyadov, prepared revised editions of *Ruslan and Ludmila* and *A Life for the Tsar* for publication. The study of these operatic scores had, in the words of Korsakov, "a wholesome influence which led me, after contrapuntal complexities and the strict style, to the path of contemporary music."

Of singular importance in the development of Korsakov's creative talent was a study of Russian folk songs which he made at the behest of an amateur collector of songs, T. E. Filipov. The result was a book of "Forty Folk Songs Collected by T. E. Filipov and Harmonized by N. A. Rimsky-Korsakov."

Simultaneously Korsakov worked on his own collection of "One Hundred Russian Folk Songs." The book contained songs taken from old collections by Prach and Stakhowich, but with new harmonizations by Korsakov. The book also included songs which Korsakov heard as a child in Tikhvin and songs written down by him and other musicians.

At this time, Korsakov began to display his love for ceremonial and play songs which attracted him "as the oldest musical examples reaching into ancient pagan times and presenting their essential aspects."

The five years following the completion of *Pskovityanka* were for Korsakov years of study, of self-improvement, and intellectual growth. The compositional efforts of these years are not significant. Neither the Third Symphony nor the chamber works composed during this period represent important musical contributions.

In 1872, Korsakov married Nadezhda Purgold, a very gifted pianist. In 1873, he accepted an offer to supervise brass bands in the Navy Department, a position which improved his financial situation.

In 1874, Korsakov assumed leadership of the Free Music School established by the Balakirev circle. He took charge of the chorus and orchestra, and thereby gained experience as a conductor. In 1881, when Balakirev assumed direction of the school, Korsakov left. In 1884, he resigned as music supervisor in the Navy Department.

In 1878, Korsakov composed *A Night in May,* an opera of great artistic power, based on Gogol's story of the same name. The story, with its colorful scenes of Ukrainian peasant lore, inspired Korsakov to compose an opera dealing with life and customs in a Ukrainian village. In this opera, he created superb lyrical characters (Ganna and her lover Levko) as well as comical ones (the tipsy Kalenik and the pompous village chief, Golova). At the same time, the opera extensively develops the fairyland elements in Gogol's story, the Rusalki (the mermaids) scenes, for example. As in *Pskovityanka,* national aspects of music are sustained throughout the opera and various episodes are built on authentic Ukrainian tunes.

A Night in May signified a turning point in Korsakov's style. He turned away from historical subjects toward national fairyland fantasy and ceremonial and playful episodes, clothed in gentle musical lyricism. This new style is best exemplified in the opera *The Snow Maiden* (Snegurochka), composed in 1880 and 1881 and based on a dramatic fairy tale by the Russian dramatist, Ostrovsky. Korsakov called *The Snow Maiden* his Ninth Symphony. It represents a consistent development of his artistic principles. The plot of the opera is national and linked to Russian folklore, as are the images of Snegurochka, Lel, Kupava, and Berendey.

The opera reveals Korsakov's bent for Russian pagan antiquity and old rites and ceremonies. His love of nature is expressed in pantheistic glorifications of the powers of nature, personified by fairy tale characters. His harmonious, bright, and optimistic world outlook is expressed in the music's lucidity and in the opera's moral conception, demonstrating the victory, in nature, of good forces over evil. The music is so interwoven with national folk songs that it is often difficult to draw dividing lines between authentic folk melodies and the composer's original themes. *The Snow Maiden* completed the first stage of Rimsky-Korsakov's operatic style.

For the next ten years, Korsakov concentrated on symphonic music: a *Skazka* (a tale) based on the prologue to Pushkin's *Ruslan and Ludmila;* a piano concerto on a Russian theme (1883); a fantasy on Russian themes for violin and orchestra (1886–1887); *An Easter Overture* (1888), and his best symphonic compositions, *A Spanish Caprice* (1887) and *Scheherazade* (1888). During these years he also edited the works of Mussorgsky and Borodin.

Skazka and *Scheherazade* are programmatic compositions. In

Skazka, Korsakov turned to Russian folklore. The epigraph to *Skazka* is the opening stanza from Pushkin's *Ruslan and Ludmila:*

At the curving seashore stands a green oak.

The charming and gentle music of *Skazka,* representing a bewitched forest, mermaids, Baba Yaga (a witch in Russian folklore) and her hut mounted on chicken legs, resembles the music of *The Snow Maiden.*

The music of *Scheherazade* is characterized by a decorative splendor befitting the fantastic wonders in the Arabian tales. Oriental colors and picturesque qualities are more consistently sustained in *Scheherazade* than in *Antar.*

The *Easter Overture,* based on themes from Russian orthodox liturgy, is not entirely imbued with religious sentiments. According to Korsakov, his aim was to describe the "legendary and pagan aspects" of the season. The dance-like music in the concluding section describes "unrestrained joy" characteristic of Korsakov's interest in ancient Slavic pagan ceremonies.

The *Spanish Caprice* is based on several authentic Spanish dance tunes. In Korsakov's words: "The opinion of critics and the public that the *Caprice* is an excellently orchestrated piece is incorrect. The *Caprice* is a splendid composition for orchestra. Change of timbre, successful selection of melodic patterns and figured designs appropriate for every instrumental family, masterly cadenzas for solo instruments, rhythm of percussion instruments, etc.—represent the essence of this composition, not its musical finery." [1]

The *Spanish Caprice* is a uniquely effective study for orchestra. It represents Korsakov's utmost achievement in colorful and masterful orchestration. With the exception of a small composition, the *Dubinushka* (The Cudgel), the *Spanish Caprice* and *Scheherazade* complete Rimsky-Korsakov's work in the orchestral-symphonic field.

In 1883, Balakirev, conductor of the Court Chapel Chorus, invited Korsakov to assist him, and he held the position until 1894.

Around 1885, Korsakov developed a friendship with a wealthy timber merchant, Belayev. Belayev's Petersburg home became a regular meeting place of musicians, including many of Korsakov's pupils. Korsakov was considered to be head of the *Belayev Circle.* He participated in the work of the music publishing house established by Belayev to publish works of Russian composers. In 1886, when Belayev organized the Russian Symphonic Concerts to popularize Russian music, Rimsky-Korsakov became the official conductor.

In 1889, Korsakov resumed his interest in operatic composition by composing *Mlada* on the subject of an unfinished opera he wrote in 1872. *Mlada* was written with Cui, Borodin, and Mussorgsky. The libretto, based on legends of Baltic Slavs, was prepared by the director of Imperial Theaters, Gedeonov, and by the dramatist Krylov. The objective was not an opera imbued with national elements, but a brilliant and fantastic spectacle in the tradition of grand opera. The plot includes a mysterious murder, Mlada's apparition, ghosts, the struggle of good and evil spirits, the appearance of Cleopatra, a mysterious night scene in Triglava (three-headed) mountain, the destruction of a temple, and a flood.

Korsakov was deeply interested in pagan antiquity, sorcery, and the ceremonial aspects of the plot, which, however, did not present opportunities for the realistic delineation of acting persons. Although not one person in *Mlada* received characterizations similar to those in *The Snow Maiden* and *Night in May,* Korsakov's genius was superbly revealed in the descriptive features of the music. For the first time, Wagner's influence was noticeable in Rimsky-Korsakov's style as it was in his later operas.

The composition of *Mlada* was followed by a crisis. In his letters to friends, Korsakov complained of a decline in his creative work and he expressed doubts about his future activities as a composer. These reflections were enhanced by his disappointment in the composers of Balakirev's circle, whose compositions he characterized as cold and sterile.

With doubt and pessimism besetting him, Korsakov decided to summarize, in book form, the development of Russian music, including his own compositions as well as those of Borodin and Mussorgsky. His idea was to introduce the book with a discussion of esthetic problems. With this in mind, Korsakov decided to study philosophy and esthetics. These studies, however, did not produce practical results. After the death of his two children, the composer became more dispirited and discouraged. This mental crisis lasted until 1894.

In 1894, Korsakov resumed work on a new opera, *The Night Before Christmas,* based on Gogol's story. The plot renewed his interest in national folklore. In this opera, completed in 1895, Korsakov remained true to his favorite subject—pagan antiquity and ancient

Slavic deities. Kolyada and Ovsenya, mentioned in Russian and Ukrainian ceremonial songs, are the deities. In Gogol's story, Kolyada and Ovsenya personify the good forces of nature. They are opposed by the evil forces of nature, including witches (Solokha), devils, and sorcerers (Patzyk).

Esthetically, *The Night Before Christmas* is related to *The Snow Maiden,* in which the thought of struggle between good and evil forces and the victory of the former over the latter is naturally blended with the subject of the opera. In *The Night Before Christmas,* the same thought is skillfully projected into Gogol's story.

Ceremonial and fantasy scenes gave Korsakov what he called an opportunity "to write a lot of interesting music," including the flight of Vakula mounted on the devil's shoulders, the dance of the stars, and other fantastic episodes. The picturesque national Ukrainian color is sustained throughout the opera.

Korsakov's artistic power was fully revealed during the years following the completion of this opera. Several operas followed, one after another, each a masterpiece of Russian operatic art.

In 1895 and 1896, Korsakov composed an opera on the subject of the *bylina* about Sadko. Stasov participated in the elaboration of the opera's plan. *Sadko* is an opera-*bylina*. Korsakov's operas are known for the leisurely development of their plots and each scene has its individual characteristics. These features are even more prominent in *Sadko.* The epic narrative aspects of the opera are enhanced by declamatory recitatives.

The vivid fairy tale colors and masterful tonal representations in *Sadko* surpass anything that Korsakov had previously composed in the operatic field. The fantasy of *Sadko* is blended with the plot and the imagery of Russian national epic poetry. In the originality of its style and the maturity of its consummate craftsmanship, *Sadko* is the equal of *The Snow Maiden. Sadko* concluded Rimsky-Korsakov's middle period of composition.

After *Sadko,* Korsakov turned his attention to vocal composition. In 1897, he composed forty songs, several choruses, and vocal ensembles. These songs are lyrical, serene, and restrained. The piano accompaniments are descriptive and, together with the melody, are closely knit with the meaning of the words.

In the same year, Korsakov composed music to Pushkin's drama, *Mozart and Salieri,* in which Korsakov adopted Dargomijsky's technique in *The Stone Guest*. The opera is written in an arioso-recitative style with arioso elements predominating.

In 1898, Korsakov composed a one-act opera, *Boyarina Vera Sheloga,* an account of Vera Sheloga's meeting with Ivan the Terrible. Korsakov took the story from a second (unpublished) edition of *Pskovityanka* (1870). He regarded the composition as an independent opera and as a prologue to *Pskovityanka.*

Vera Sheloga was followed by *The Tsar's Bride,* a dramatic and dynamic composition. In this opera features absent in Korsakov's previous operas are revealed: flexibility of recitative, melodic sweep of cantilena, greater attention to the human voice, and the expressive possibilities and greater importance of vocal ensembles.

The opera, *The Tale of Tsar Saltan,* composed in 1899, is based on Pushkin's tale. The popular character of Pushkin's *skazka* is wittily and skillfully projected in the opera. The scenes of fantasy in *Tsar Saltan,* whose descriptive music resembles similar episodes in *Sadko,* are very important. Among them are the scene of Tsarina Lebed (Swan) and the introductions to the four acts of the opera. These introductions are extensive symphonic pictures.

The next opera, *Servilia* (1900–1901), is based on a drama by the Russian writer Mey. It describes the clashes of the first Christians with pagan Rome. The music is not related to national Russian music but reveals Italian and French operatic influences. Several episodes are written in Greek modes. Although the opera is skillfully composed, it is not an inspired work.

From 1901 to 1903, Korsakov composed *Pan Voyevoda* (Sir Governor). This opera, one of Korsakov's few melodramatic compositions, lacks outstanding scenic representations. The composer's objective, to write an opera with a national Polish atmosphere, lacks inner conviction. The Polish effect is sustained by external features: the mazurka and polonaise.

Simultaneously with *Pan Voyevoda,* Korsakov worked on Kashchey Besmertny (Kashchey the Immortal). Kashchev is the evil and bloodthirsty Tsar in Russian folklore, whose realm is at the other end of the world. Coming on the eve of the 1905 revolution, the opera assumed political significance. Kashchey's realm and prisoners symbolized Tsarist autocracy. *Burya Bogatyr* (Storm the Hero), who threw off Kashchey's oppression, symbolized the force which would overwhelm Russian autocracy. The concluding words of the opera,

"Storm opened the gates for you," seemed to anticipate the revolution. The opera's style reflects a treasure of musical effects which characterize Korsakov's fairy tale operas.

During 1903 and 1904, Korsakov composed an opera-legend, *The Legend About the Unseen City Kitezh and the Maid Fevronia*. The plot, adapted from Russian legends, is a web of semihistorical and fairy tale features. The fairy tale aspects sometimes assume a mystical meaning.

Korsakov responded sympathetically to the 1905 revolution. Together with other musicians, he signed an open letter, published in the *Russian Musical Newspaper,* requesting certain political freedoms. He sympathized with student demonstrations in the Petersburg conservatory and opposed the attempt of its Director, Bernhard, to suppress student activities. The Board of Directors of the Russian Musical Society, which supervised the conservatory, dismissed Korsakov. As a protest, Glazunov, Lyadov, and other professors resigned from the conservatory.

In the fall of 1905, conservatories were granted a measure of autonomy. Glazunov, a pupil and friend of Korsakov, was elected director, and, at his invitation, Korsakov rejoined the conservatory.

The revolution was reflected in Korsakov's last opera, *Zolotoy Petushok* (The Golden Cockerel), composed in 1907. The story of the opera is provided by a fairy tale by Pushkin which Korsakov used to express deeper symbolisms.

Zolotoy Petushok is a satirical opera. Dodon is a stupid and bestial Tsar. His sons are imbeciles and his *boyars* are slow-witted advisers. All of them symbolize Tsarist autocracy, destined to perish. "I hope to bring shame on Dodon," wrote Korsakov. The plot of Pushkin's tale is very compact. There is no traditional hero in the story and there are no miraculous transformations. Everything in the tale is determined by a definite conception. Separate motivations in the plot's development assume the characteristics of daily reality. Pushkin proposed to speak ironically of the Tsar by creating a sharply delineated grotesquerie concealing a bitter satire. Dodon "rules the state lying on his side with arms folded." An example of Korsakov's satire is revealed in the "Lullaby" which Amelfa, Dodon's housekeeper, sings as she puts the Tsar to sleep. The "Lullaby" is Schubert's famous "Military March" adumbrated with Russian intonations. The words which Amelfa sings are:

> A daily nap is good for the health,
> Lie down, I shall chase away
> The bothersome flies
> From the face of the Tsar.

What Pushkin only hints at, Korsakov gives a musical representation in the opera. The image of the Shemahanskaya Tsarina gave Korsakov an opportunity to sum up oriental influences in Russian classical music. Korsakov's music changes the impression of fantastic imagery to a feeling of sinister reality, almost palpably visual. The spectator is left in doubt whether the Tsarina was conspiring with the astrologer. The Tsarina's image is that of a cruel and commanding woman who uses her beauty to bewitch the senile Dodon. The astrologer represents either a fantastic being using his magic power for personal aggrandizement or a force condemning the corrupt social conditions in Dodon's realm.

The Tsarist censor understood the opera's satirical meaning. In 1909, after many difficulties and textual changes, *Zolotoy Petushok* was finally allowed to be presented, but Korsakov did not live to see the performance. He died of a heart attack on June 7, 1908.

Korsakov taught approximately two hundred students. Among them were Glazunov, Lyadov, Stravinsky, Spendyarov, Gnessin, Steinberg, Prokofiev, and Myaskovsky. Korsakov's teaching reflected his personality. He cultivated a love for a wholesome and truthful art, stating that "the most fantastic imagery in art is successful only when its roots are normal, earthly sensations." Korsakov expected integrity and definite objectives from students. He respected the creative individuality of a student. His own individuality never weighed on students and he encouraged independence of creative aims. His books, *Foundations of Orchestration* (edited and published after his death by Steinberg), and the *Textbook of Harmony,* have been used as texts for many decades.

Carrying on Glinka's traditions, Korsakov formed his personal musical style. His optimistic outlook on the world found familiar imagery and representations in Russian national art, in epic poetry, in pantheistic pagan mythology, in ancient Slavic worship of the sun, and in ceremonial plays and songs associated with the cult of the Sun. Love, spiritualization, and incarnation of nature in Korsakov's compositions are the results of his interest in pantheistic mythology.

The predominance of operatic forms in Korsakov's music is due to his love of Russian national art. Neither the symphony nor chamber music offers as much scope and freedom for the realization of elements of Russian folkore, fantasy, and national genre scenes as the opera. These elements are inseparably interwoven in Korsakov's operas, whose fantasy grows out of realistic foundations and is rooted in earthly sensations as it is in Russian epic poetry.

Russian epic poetry is the source of dramatic elements in Korsakov's operas. The leisurely, independent, narrative developments in Korsakov's operatic plots are due to the influence of epic sources in Russian folklore and to Glinka's example in *Ruslan and Ludmila*. Developing the *Ruslan* tradition further, Korsakov created varieties of operatic genres: historical, fairy tale, *bylina,* and legendary operas. In *Kashchey* and *The Golden Cockerel,* Korsakov imbued the fairy tale opera with political allegory.

The lyrical tendencies in Korsakov's style grew out of genre elements in national poetry. Hence his preference for gentle feminine representations. Female characters in Korsakov's operas are attractive because of their purity, gentleness, kindness, and emotional stability. Snegurochka, Marfa, Fevronya, Militrisa, Tsarevna Nenaglyadnaya Krasa (Darling Beauty), Tsarevna Lebed (Swan), Volkhova, and Pannochka: all these female characters are incarnations of the gentle and kind woman of Korsakov's imagination. Even Kashcheyevna, wife of the cruel Kashchey, sheds tears of tender emotion. Servilia, who is not a Russian woman, is nevertheless representative of Korsakov's vision of an ideal woman.

The epic narrative character of Korsakov's artistry determined his preference for programmatic representations in symphonic and operatic compositions. Influenced by Russian mythological poetry and its animistic qualities, Korsakov connected nature pictures with supernatural beings personifying, in popular belief, good and evil forces in nature. In his first original composition, the musical picture, *Sadko,* there is already a blending of popular fairy tale fantasy with Korsakov's favorite subject—lakes, rivers, and sea.

The images of the Tsar of the Sea and of Volkhova in *Sadko* and of Storm the Hero in *Kashchey* personify phenomena in nature. The operatic subject in *The Snow Maiden* is an allegorical representation of the destructive and beneficent forces of nature. Many episodes in Korsakov's compositions are simultaneously pictures of fantasy and representations of nature, the representations of the water elements in *Sadko,* for example. The snow storm in *Kashchey* and the sea in *Scheherazade* also illustrate this dualism. In these scenes, there is no separation between the fantastic and pictorial qualities.

His delineations of nature reveal the even-tempered artistic personality of Korsakov. His compositions include representations of manifold aspects of nature, including representations of angry elements. The shipwreck scene in *Scheherazade* is an example. Korsakov, however, prefers nature in its quiet and peaceful aspects. Even in his songs, lyrical imagery blends with serene contemplations of a peaceful nature.

National Russian art decisively influenced Korsakov's artistic trends and the essential features of his musical language, closely related to Russian folk songs. Many folk songs, authentic or altered, appear in his compositions, especially in the operas. Imbued with the spirit of Russian folk songs, Korsakov created in his operas original melodies which cannot be distinguished from authentic folk songs.

Structural elements of national Russian melodies, pentatonic turns and intonations of fourths, fifths, and seconds, for example, are also characteristic of Korsakov's original melodies.

Oriental music is an important feature in Korsakov's operatic and symphonic compositions. In *Antar* and *Mlada,* he introduced authentic oriental tunes. Through studies of the music of Eastern countries, Korsakov was able to create generalized musical representations of the East in arabesque, chromatic, and complex melodic patterns. An excellent example is "The Song of India" in *Sadko.*

A preference for programmatic imagery determined the fundamental aspects of Korsakov's harmonic and modulational patterns. In his love for harmonic colors, he was a follower of Glinka and Western romantics, especially Liszt. He also employed patterns of classical tonic-subdominant-tonic functions (I-IV-V-I), combining them with independent groups of subordinate harmonies. In his modulations, Korsakov preferred tonalities separated by diminished, minor and major third intervals.

Korsakov often preferred subdominant patterns. This could be explained by the generous color possibilities of subdominant (plagal) harmonies and their relatively static character which seemed to agree with Korsakov's serene and contemplative moods. Plagality and prominence of subordinate harmonies are also characteristic of many Russian folk songs.

Korsakov's music derives a distinctive quality from augmented and diminished scale patterns which do not fit into minor and major scales. Similar patterns are found in Chopin's mazurkas, in Liszt's rhapsodies, and in scenes of fantasy in Glinka's *Ruslan*. Secondary dominants are prominent in Korsakov's compositions. Beginning with the symphonic picture *Sadko* and the *Antar Suite,* chromatic elements become important in Korsakov's music. In his later compositions, Korsakov integrated different scale patterns.

In Korsakov's style, set means of musical expression, often of deliberate contrast, correspond to the worlds of fantasy and earthly life. Attempts to depict the extraordinary in music compelled Korsakov to look for unusual expressive means. These he found in harmonic patterns which did not, as a rule, fit into the diatonic scale system. In representations of earthly scenes and expressions of human emotions, Korsakov preferred diatonic and modal means.

The gloomy realm of Kashchey is described by somber chromaticisms and a chain of major thirds which forms a whole-tone scale. A sustained diminished fifth in the basses adds to the feeling of hopeless despair. Tsarina Nenagladnaya Krasa, held in captivity by Kashchey, is described by a sad theme in a minor key.

There are differences between delineations of the earthly world and the world of fantasy. Fantastic beings are often represented by melodies of an instrumental character, containing unusual intervallic skips and leaps devoid of the intonational components of the human voice. These melodies are suitable for an instrument rather than the human voice. Some scenes of fantasy, the wonders in *Tsar Saltan,* for example, are described by music which Korsakov usually reserves for earthly scenes.

Being a rational thinker, Korsakov insisted on logic, cohesion, and order in musical forms. He recoiled from romantic freedoms in music. His musical forms are esthetic in the sense that they reveal perfect unity of expression, purpose and tonal means.

In his operas, Korsakov favored either uninterrupted development of action, as in *The Golden Cockerel,* or division of the opera into complete episodes, as in *The Tsar's Bride, The Snow Maiden,* and *Sadko.* In either case, Korsakov aimed at unity and logical completeness of sections.

Independent symphonic pictures in the operas contribute to their leisurely narrative and epic character, the orchestral interludes in *Tsar Saltan,* the battle of Kerzhenetz in *Kitezh,* and the dream of Dodon and the procession in *The Golden Cockerel,* for example.

Korsakov's symphonic compositions are embodied in clear and logical forms. Absolute music was not Korsakov's domain because it did not offer sufficient scope for the unfolding of his programmatic musical imagery. Striving for perfection, Korsakov often used the sonata form without classical restrictions of design. In his thematic developments, Korsakov leaned towards repetition, variation, and sequential devices. Thematic recurrences are numerous in his style. His music is usually emotionally subdued, often contemplative, unexcited, and colorful. He illustrates different aspects of a musical thought and leans towards the epic traditions in Glinka's music.

Korsakov is one of the greatest masters and poets of the orchestra. The orchestra is interwoven with the pictorial and colorful character of his music. The impression of color and brilliance which Korsakov's music leaves with audiences is the result of the fundamental qualities of his orchestral writing: wealth and variety of timbres, clarity and simplicity of orchestral thought, and economy of orchestral means. The sources of Korsakov's orchestral technique were Glinka, Liszt, Berlioz, and Wagner.

Leading motives were employed by Korsakov in operas and in programmatic symphonic music. His system of leading motives differs from Wagner's. Korsakov's leading motives are not symbols, as Wagner's are, but musical characterizations of phenomena and persons. His leading motives are melodies, chords, or instrumental timbres. The *Leshy* (woodgoblin) in *The Snow Maiden* is announced by the simultaneous sounding of two augmented triads by muted French horns.

By changing leading motives in accordance with scenic requirements in opera or in accordance with programmatic intention in symphonic compositions, Korsakov obtained powerful and flexible means of artistic expression. His preference for program music, for refinement and variety of harmonic color, and for orchestral tone painting, relates him to Western musical romanticism. At the same time, his music is interwoven with Russian folklore and the traditions of Glinka. Korsakov's musical achievement was the integration of elements of Western romanticism with national Russian music.

Sadko

Sadko is an opera-*bylina*. *Bylinas* and fairy tales are different genres of Russian folklore. Fantasy dominates a *skazka;* in a *bylina,* fantasy is often combined with events which took place in a particular historical era.

The story of *Sadko* takes place in the ancient City of Novgorod, with its rich merchants, noisy crowds, wandering blind singers, mountebanks, and visiting foreigners. The hero of the story is a young *gusli* player and singer, Sadko. At a banquet, Sadko reproaches the guests for being sluggish and not leaving Novgorod to travel in faraway countries. Angered by Sadko's words, the merchants reply:

> How dare he teach and reproach us?
> How dare he aspire to be our equal?

The arrogant merchants do not wish to follow Sadko's advice. Sadko continues:

> Novgorod lives in time-honored customs;
> Live according to the olden times.

A poor *gusli* player will not change the customs of grandfather's days. Sadko will never again sing at banquets in Novgorod.

The next scene takes place on the lonely shore of Lake Ilmen. Sadko bewails his fate:

> Hear me, unstable wave!
> Hear me, thou wide expanse!
> Listen to my bitter lot,
> Listen to my cherished wish.

It seems that Lake Ilmen has heard Sadko. The reeds become noisy and lake waters become rough. Sadko beholds a flock of white swans and gray ducks swimming on the lake. Before his amazed eyes, they change into lovely maidens and step ashore. It is Volkhova, the daughter of the Tsar of the Sea, with her sisters and girl friends. For a long time, Volkhova has heard Sadko's songs from the depths of the lake. The girls disperse in the forest. Sadko remains with Volkhova, fascinated by her beauty.

After declaring their mutual love, Sadko and Volkhova part. Volkhova gives Sadko a magic present: when he casts the net into

Lake Ilmen, he will catch three golden fish.

Sadko returns home in a thoughtful mood. His wife, Lubava Busla-yevna, joyfully greets him. But Sadko, full of recollections of his meeting with Volkhova, pushes his wife away.

The next scene takes place near the landing place on Lake Ilmen. A crowd of people fill the square near the pier. The inhabitants of Novgorod surround foreign visitors and examine their beautiful merchandise. There are blind singers, buffoons, and soothsayers. Prominent citizens of Novgorod, leaders of the city government, and rich merchants arrive on the scene. The merchants and the "fathers of the city" are concerned about how they will pacify Sadko and the crowd of urban poor which is ready to follow him.

Sadko enters the square and is greeted with laughter. He is not embarrassed by the greeting. He tells the merchants and "fathers of the city": "I know a miracle of miracles which is in Lake Ilmen; it is the golden fish in the lake." Sadko offers a wager to the merchants and the "fathers of the city": Should his net catch the golden fish, the Novgorod stores, with their rich wares, shall belong to Sadko; should he not catch the golden fish, the merchants shall have his head. His challenge is accepted. No one ever saw golden fish in Lake Ilmen and the merchants are certain that Sadko shall have lost his head. The net is cast, and, to the consternation of the merchants, it brings up three golden fish. Sadko has won the wager and has become owner of the merchants' treasures in Novgorod.

Sadko is magnanimous. He returns the stores with their wares to the merchants. He is very rich because the catch brought up by the net has turned into gold in the presence of the crowd on the shore.

Sadko gathers a group of friends, loads several ships with merchandise, and departs to trade in foreign countries. Before departure, Sadko asks the Varangian, Indian, and Venetian guests to tell him about their countries. Nezhata, a young *gusli* player from Kiev, makes up and sings a *bylina* about Sadko's deeds and the miracle on Lake Ilmen.

The next scene represents the broad expanse of the sea at sunset. Sadko's ships appear, sailing under full sail, and they disappear in the distance. Only one ship, "The Falcon," with Sadko on board, stands still with lowered sails. Sadko and his friends understand that the Tsar of the Sea requires tribute. They throw barrels with silver, gold, and pearls into the sea; but the ship does not move. It seems that the ruler of the sea wants another kind of tribute: one of the passengers will have to go into the depths of the sea. They prepare to cast lots. Sadko's lot is the lightest of all, a feather made of hops. The lots are cast into the sea and the sailors are amazed when they see that all lots float on the surface of the sea while Sadko's feather has sunk as a stone. This means that the Tsar of the Sea wants Sadko. Sadko takes leave of his friends and is lowered into the sea on an oaken board. Immediately the sails of the ship rise into the wind and the ship begins to move.

Sadko descends to the bottom of the sea and is greeted by the Tsar of the Sea. For twelve years, Sadko has sailed the seas and never paid tribute to the Tsar. Volkhova intercedes for Sadko. The Tsar asks Sadko to sing and play the *gusli*. He likes it so much that he decides to give his daughter, Volkhova, in marriage to Sadko.

Sadko sings an honor song for the Tsar and Tsarina. The Tsar asks Sadko to play a dance song. The wild dance stirs the sea and ships perish in the turbulent waves. At the height of the wild dance, the Old Mighty Bogatyr appears, knocks the *gusli* out of Sadko's hands, and the sea quiets down. The Old Mighty deprives the Tsar of the Sea of power over water domains. Sadko and Volkhova are ordered to rise to the surface of the sea. Volkhova takes leave of her parents.

The concluding scene takes place on the shore of Lake Ilmen. Volkhova, bending over the sleeping Sadko, sings a lullaby. Upon the order of the Old Mighty, Volkhova sacrifices herself for the happiness of Sadko and the City of Novgorod. The morning fog changes Volkhova into a river.

Sadko awakens and hears the voice of Lubava. The spell of the underwater kingdom is broken. Sadko greets his wife. His ships are sailing on the Volkhova river. The amazed inhabitants of Novgorod greet Sadko and his friends.

The Snow Maiden

The story takes place in the enchanted kingdom of the Berendeys. The peaceful existence of the Berendeys is disturbed by Snegurochka, the daughter of Father Frost and Beautiful Spring. For fifteen years, Father Frost has concealed Snegurochka in inaccessible dark forests, guarding her from his enemy and rival, Yarilo the Sun. This angers

Yarilo the Sun and he vents his displeasure on the Berendeys by depriving them of his beneficent rays. The summers are shorter and colder and the earth has lost its fertility.

Living in the dark forest, Snegurochka sometimes hears the song of the shepherd Lel and is intrigued by the human world. With the consent of Father Frost and Beautiful Spring, Snegurochka visits a Berendey settlement where she meets Mizgir. Mizgir falls in love with Snegurochka. Snegurochka cannot reciprocate Mizgir's love because Father Frost did not give her "warmth of heart." She runs away from Mizgir. Mizgir follows her into the forest; but Leshy, a friend of Father Frost, distracts Mizgir's attention and Snegurochka escapes.

Snegurochka understands that she lacks feelings experienced by human beings. She asks her mother, Beautiful Spring, to help her. Beautiful Spring gives Snegurochka a magic garland which will help her experience the feeling of love. On the first day of summer, at dawn, Tsar Berendey greets young couples who wish to get married. Among the couples, Berendey recognizes Snegurochka and Mizgir. Snegurochka's happiness, however, is shortlived. Having learned the "fire of love," she is helpless against the revenge of Yarilo the Sun. While the people enjoy the warm rays of the morning sun, Snegurochka melts and disappears. Mizgir, in despair, throws himself into the lake and drowns. The wise Tsar Berendey understands that the destruction of Snegurochka has turned away the anger of Yarilo the Sun, who revenged himself on his enemy and rival, Father Frost. The country of the Berendeys will again enjoy happiness and prosperity. Berendey, Lel, and the people sing a hymn of praise to Yarilo the Sun.

Two worlds are contrasted in the opera: the world of fantasy represented by Father Frost, Leshy, and Beautiful Spring and the real, "earthly" world represented by Mizgir, Kupava, Bobyl-Bakula and Bobylikha, who befriend Snegurochka and the people of Berendey's realm. Snegurochka, Lel, and Tsar Berendey are semimythical, semireal persons. The world of fantasy represents the incarnation of the forces of nature. Old Tsar Berendey represents popular wisdom; Lel, the art of music; and Yarilo the Sun, the creative principle in nature. The meaning of the fairy tale lies in the struggle between the hostile and beneficial forces of nature and their effect on human beings. This idea is common in Russian folklore.

Symphonic Style

Korsakov's symphonic style embodies fairy tale fantasy, representations of nature, and imagery of Russian and Eastern folklore. Pictorial and colorful aspects, prominent in Korsakov's operas, are even more prominent in his symphonic compositions.

The musical sources of Korsakov's symphonic style are Western musical romanticism and Glinka's *Ruslan* and his symphonic compositions. Korsakov's best symphonic compositions are *Scheherazade, Antar, Sadko, Skazka,* and the *Spanish Caprice*. The *Spanish Caprice* is a national symphonic composition based on authentic Spanish themes and tunes. It is reminiscent of Glinka's *Spanish Overtures*.

Korsakov was not successful in all music. His symphonies and piano concerto do not disclose great originality and artistic power.

The significant features of Korsakov's symphonic style were first revealed in the musical picture, *Sadko,* and further developed in Korsakov's adaptations of aspects of Western musical romanticism to Russian folklore. Tone painting in *Sadko* is as highly developed as it is in Korsakov's mature symphonic style. It is not fortuitous that thirty years later, Korsakov included the music in the opera, *Sadko*. In his *Chronicles,* Korsakov writes that in *Sadko,* he was influenced by Liszt's harmonic style, modulations of tonalities separated by diminished thirds, for example, (D flat major to B major in the introduction). A scale of tone-semitone progressions represents Sadko's rapid descent into the sea. Korsakov points out that the laconic quality of the music in *Sadko* is its main shortcoming and attributes it to "lack of technical experience."

Antar is a more romantic composition than *Sadko*. The image of Antar, disillusioned in life and dissatisfied with everything, is reminiscent of romantic literary imagery in Berlioz's *Fantastic Symphony* and *Harold in Italy*. Antar is a prototype of a frustrated and disillusioned young man in early nineteenth century literature. Berlioz's influence is evident in the colorful aspects of the *Antar Suite* and in the unification of the movements by musical themes representing Antar and Hule Nazar. The *Antar Suite* does not contain sad moods and pessimistic reflections on the fate of a hero. The idea of a strong personality seeking solitude was not Korsakov's intention. Psychological interpretation of the hero, his thoughts, and feelings recedes into the background and gives way to colorful musical episodes. According to Korsakov, the music of the *Antar Suite* expresses the sense of power and the sweetness of revenge. "I understood that by means of external representations I could successfully express sweetness of revenge and sense of power, the first as a picture of a bloody battle, the second as a picture of magnificent surroundings of an oriental sovereign."

The plot of *Antar* gave Korsakov an opportunity to compose a series of colorful, descriptive episodes. Of the four movements, the fourth which describes the delights of love, is considered the best.

The principle of Korsakov's program technique in *Antar* and *Sadko* is based on the development of a plot in contrasting musical pictures or episodes. He used this principle in his later compositions. *Skazka* is a series of musical episodes based on Russian folklore, including characters such as Baba Yaga, mermaids, witches, and Leshy.

Scheherazade is a series of musical episodes based on the Arabian tales "1001 Nights." In his *Chronicles,* Korsakov points out that the program in *Scheherazade* consists of separate, unconnected episodes and pictures scattered among the four parts of the suite. He mentions only five main episodes or parts in the first edition of *Scheherazade:* The Sea and Sinbad's Ship, The Tale of Prince Kalender, The Prince and the Princess, The Festival at Bagdad, and the Shipwreck. Because of the small number of musical themes in *Antar* and *Scheherazade* and the epic narrative character of the programs, the musical forms of the two compositions are cyclical designs, closer to the suite than the symphony. Originally called a symphony, *Antar* is often referred to as a suite.

Neither *Antar* nor *Scheherazade* is an arbitrary connection of different parts. The general programmatic conception and the common rhythmical aspects of thematic materials unify the compositions, which could be called symphonic poems or program symphonies with the elements of a suite.

The unifying element in *Scheherazade* is a musical refrain occurring in Scheherazade's theme. This refrain underlies the epic narrative character of the suite and the fact that it is Scheherazade herself who narrates the story. The occurrence of this refrain throughout the composition gives it a well-conceived unity.

In *Scheherazade,* Korsakov made extensive use of the elements of sonata style designs. The first movement is a free sonata form. The absence of a development section is compensated through the use of dynamic developments in the exposition and opening of the recapitulation. In the recapitulation, the theme of the sea, an altered version of the theme of Sultan Shakhriar, is interwoven with the rhythmic figure of a triplet, belonging in the subordinate theme. This triplet supposedly represents sea whitecaps.

The second movement is a complex three-part form (ABA) with the middle section, B, in a free sonata form. The fourth movement is in rondo-sonata form design in which the coda repeats the introduction and sea episode in the first movement.

Korsakov employed leading motives in his symphonic compositions. There are only two motives in *Antar* and they always retain their meaning and association with the representations of the heroes—Antar and Hule Nazar. There are several leading motives in *Scheherazade*. Since the program of the suite does not represent a unified plot, it would appear that Korsakov was not too concerned with the significance of meaning of leading motives. The motives in *Scheherazade* are not always identified with the same imagery. Korsakov explained it as follows: "It is useless to look in my suite for leading motives closely identified with the same poetic ideas and representations. On the contrary, in the majority of cases what appear to be leading motives are only musical materials and motives for symphonic development. These alternating and interweaving motives are scattered in the suite movements. Emerging in a new light, describing each time new aspects, and expressing different moods, the same motives and themes are suitable for different images, actions, and pictures."

Korsakov's statement indicates that artistic potentialities inherent in a musical thought were more important to him than its connection with a definite poetic image. The powerful introductory motive describing the stern appearance of Sultan Shakhriar is, after a few measures, heard in the sea episode. The subordinate theme in the movement is an altered version of Scheherazade's theme.

In some large-scale compositions of Beethoven, Brahms, and Tchaikovsky, a germ of the main theme appears in the introduction to or beginning of the first movement. This is true in Beethoven's *Pathétique* and *Les Adieux Sonatas* and the Fifth Symphony, in Brahms' First and Second Symphonies and in Tchaikovsky's Sixth Symphony.

The appearance of a motivic or rhythmic figure from the main theme facilitates perception of thematic development or transformation. Korsakov used this principle in *Scheherazade,* sacrificing the programmatic significance of themes for the sake of symphonic unity based on thematic transformation. It is possible that Chopin's Ballades, symphonic canvases for the piano developed by thematic transformations and variations, influenced Korsakov.

Shakhriar's theme undergoes several transformations. It first appears as a powerful, stern theme in the introduction. In the following episode, its meter changes from 6/4 to 2/2 pulsations. The swinging, wavelike accompaniment gives it a gentle and peaceful character.

In the middle section of the second movement, Shakhriar's theme assumes a warlike character. In the epilogue of the fourth movement, the theme is set forth as it is in the introduction, but it does not sound as stern. It is a quiet, peaceful theme, heard against a pianissimo accompaniment of double basses and violoncellos, suggesting, according to Korsakov, a change in Shakhriar, who no longer threatens Scheherazade with death.

Although Korsakov's interest was in musical unity rather than the meaning of leading motives, thematic likeness sometimes indicates affinity of musical themes. Kalender's theme in the second movement does not resemble Scheherazade's theme. Nevertheless, a cadenzalike figure, growing out of Kalender's theme, is reminiscent of Scheherazade's theme. The closeness of the two themes is enhanced by the refrain representing Scheherazade as the narrator throughout the suite and Kalender as the narrator in the second movement.

Since the subjects of Antar and Scheherazade are based on Eastern tales, the musical themes of these compositions are oriental in character. There are three genuine Arabian tunes in *Antar* but the leading motive of Hule Nazar is Korsakov's. Although there are no genuine oriental tunes in Scheherazade, a few melodies sound oriental and are characterized by ornamentations used in Eastern music, such as the interval of an augmented second in the Prince's theme in the third movement. The theme of the Princess in the third movement brings to mind a languid oriental dance. The main theme in *The Bagdad Festival* sounds like a swift, impetuous oriental dance.

The oriental atmosphere in *Scheherazade* is enhanced by harmonic and orchestral means. The sustained intervals of a fifth imitate the sound of oriental instruments. The second theme in the third movement is rhythmically accentuated by a tambourine, flute, plucked strings, triangle, snare drum, cymbals, and a kettledrum.

Korsakov often associated tonalities with colors. In the choice of tonalities for *Scheherazade,* Korsakov was guided by notions of tonalities which, in his imagination, were associated with the colors of the sea and the sky: E major for light blue, B major for dark blue, E flat major for dark–gray blue, F major for green, and A major for rose.

Musical contrasts in *Scheherazade* are achieved not by dynamic surges, anticipations, cumulations, and consummations as in Beethoven's symphonic style, but by thematic and orchestral contrasts. The stern motive of Sultan Shakhriar is contrasted with the tender melody of Scheherazade. Epic narrative episodes alternate with pictorial episodes. A violin solo is contrasted with orchestral sonorities. Orchestral tutti are contrasted with limpid woodwinds, sustained by a background of double basses and pizzicato on violoncellos and violas. The picture of a stormy sea is contrasted with the representation of a ship sailing a calm sea.

These contrasts in *Scheherazade* achieve an artistic unity which compensates for the absence of dynamic elements similar to the cumulative dynamics which Beethoven brings to a climax in the final movement of a symphony.

Korsakov's orchestral writing is the outstanding feature of his symphonic style. In the introduction to his textbook on orchestration, Korsakov wrote: "How wrong are those who say that this or that composer orchestrates a composition perfectly; or that a composition is excellently orchestrated. Orchestration is the soul of a composition. The composition itself is orchestrally conceived, and in its early stages it already promises well-known orchestral colors characteristic only of its creator." This statement is more applicable to Korsakov than any other Russian composer. Korsakov's symphonic imagery is often inseparable from its orchestral realization.[2]

Korsakov's symphonic compositions are orchestrated simply, clearly and with a wealth and variety of color and timbre effects. Korsakov individualizes instruments, singly or in groups, especially the woodwinds, and thereby achieves light and transparent sonorities. He loves to use solo instruments accompanied by small instrumental groups which often attain independent significance. An important feature in Korsakov's orchestrations is the rhythmic and colorful character of percussion instruments, especially in oriental episodes. Contrasts of the entire orchestra with groups of instruments or with solo instruments enrich the sonorities of Korsakov's symphonic compositions.

Korsakov was one of the outstanding Russian composers of the second half of the nineteenth century. His creative work, nurtured by the traditions of Russian musical classicism and principles of Western romanticism, is an artistic contribution of world-wide importance. Korsakov is a musical portrayer of Russian national manners and morals, storyteller, historian, and musical landscape painter. His original and optimistic symphonic style combines expressive and representative elements. His orchestra often conjures up imaginative representations of what one "hears" and "sees" in sound imageries evoked by his musical-historical landscape paintings.

Korsakov's symphonic style is original and optimistic. The subjectivism of Western romanticism was alien to his personality. The pictorial episodes in Berlioz's *Fantastic Symphony* and *Harold in Italy* emphasize the loneliness of the hero. Pictorial episodes in Korsakov's symphonic compositions are independent musical representations. His aim was not to represent the hero against the background of nature, but to represent nature itself, as in the episode of Sindbad's ship in *Scheherazade*. Disclaiming interest in the hero and his fate, Korsakov preferred descriptive and colorful musical episodes, based on fairy tale subjects. An atmosphere of holiday splendor and rejoicing envelops *Scheherazade* and the *Spanish Caprice*.

Korsakov's music influenced the early period of Stravinsky. It influenced Lyadov, Glazunov, and many other Russian composers. It also influenced the development of French and Italian impressionism. The colorful programmatic resourcefulness of Debussy, Ravel, and Respighi is, without doubt, indebted to Korsakov.

CHAPTER 13

Cui

CÉSAR CUI shared the principles and objectives of Balakirev's circle, but was not deeply attached to Glinka's national traditions. As a composer, Cui was mainly influenced by Western romanticism. Not having an outstanding musical individuality, Cui did not re-create Western influences. His music is often a rehash of Chopinesque and Schumanesque stylistic intonations.

Cui's musical imagery is far removed from the national representations of the circle. His musical style seldom reveals Russian folk song elements which characterize the music of his friends in the circle.

During the 1860's, Cui became the spokesman for the circle and propagandized its national principles. His role in the practical development of its musical conceptions was of no particular significance.

Cui was born in Vilno on January 6, 1835. His father, a French officer in the Napoleonic invasion of 1812, settled in Russia after the war. His mother was Lithuanian. Cui began to study music at the age of ten. His favorite composer was Chopin, and under that influence he composed a Mazurka in G Minor. He studied harmony and counterpoint with the Polish operatic composer, Stanislav Moniuszko. The studies were interrupted by the departure of Cui's family to Petersburg.

Cui matriculated in the Military Engineering Academy. He graduated in 1857 and received an instructorship in the academy. In 1878, he was appointed professor of fortifications.

Cui's musical pursuits were purely amateurish. His interests in music were awakened by Balakirev whom he met in 1856. Balakirev introduced Cui to Glinka's music and guided him in the study of scores of Western composers.

In 1857, Cui met Dargomijsky. At musicales in Dargomijsky's home, Cui was introduced to the realistically expressive vocal style of his host's music. Dargomijsky's style of translating words into tonal expression was different from Italian *bel canto,* in which beauty and quality of tone were more important than dramatic and declamatory components.

In 1857, Cui composed a scherzo for two pianos on the theme BABEG and CC, the letters of his bride's surname, Bamberg, and the Latin initials of his name. The variations show the influence of Schumann's "Abegg Variations" and the "Carnaval."

The scherzo was followed by the opera *The Captive in the Caucasus,* based on Pushkin's poem of the same name. The lyrical, salon-like aspects of the music appeared in Cui's later operas. *The Mandarin's Son,* a one-act comic opera in the French style of Daniel Auber's light operas, was composed in 1859.

Cui's most important composition is the opera *William Radcliffe* (1861–1868), based on a drama by Heine. Its romantic plot was recommended to Cui by Balakirev.

Cui worked on *William Radcliffe* at a time when the operatic principles of Balakirev's circle were not sufficiently crystallized. The opera aims at continuous development of plot and music. Cui used melodic recitatives and nuances of verbal intonations, devices which he probably learned from Dargomijsky's opera *The Stone Guest.*

William Radcliffe was presented in the Mariinsky Theater in Petersburg on February 14, 1869. In spite of the absurdities of its romantic plot, the opera was hailed by Cui's friends in the circle as an example of musical and dramatic truth.

The plot of the opera is an excellent example of German romantic literature in the beginning of the nineteenth century. It is full of fatalism, doom, horrors, mysterious interference of supernatural powers, nightmares, and murders.

The action takes place in MacGregor's ancestral castle in Scotland. Many years ago beautiful Betsy loved Edward Radcliffe, who returned her affection. One day, as a joke, Edward frightened Betsy. When she sang to him, "Why Is Thy Sword Bloody, Edward?" Edward suddenly appeared at her window and sang in reply, "I Have Murdered My Beloved."

Betsy rejected Edward and married MacGregor. Edward married another girl. However, Betsy and Edward continued to meet secretly.

When MacGregor learned of these meetings, he ordered that Edward be killed. Only an old servant, Margaret, saw Edward's corpse. Betsy died soon after.

Betsy's daughter, Mary, was brought up by Margaret who often sang to the child the sinister song, "Why Is Thy Sword Bloody, Edward?"

Edward's son, William, visits MacGregor's castle. He meets Mary and falls in love with her. When he tries to confess his love to Mary, she turns away from him with revulsion. At this moment, William suddenly recalls the mysterious vision which had been confronting him since childhood: vague figures of a man and a woman extending their hands to one another with entreaty and suffering. In the features of Mary, William recognizes the apparition of the woman.

William swears that Mary will belong only to him. He murders two of Mary's bridegrooms and both times he appears at Mary's window with the bridegroom's ring.

MacGregor offers Mary's hand in marriage to Lord Douglas. During the marriage celebration, William's messenger brings Douglas a challenge to fight a duel near The Black Stone, the spot where William murdered the two bridegrooms.

However, fate is no longer propitious for William. The spirits of the murdered bridegrooms interfere and William's sword is deflected. He falls down, pierced with Douglas's sword, but is still alive. He is carried into MacGregor's castle.

In the meantime, Margaret reveals to Mary that MacGregor had murdered Edward. Margaret is horror-stricken by William's resemblance to Edward. Mary throws herself into the embrace of the wounded William. When Mary utters the name of Douglas, William, in a fit of anger, plunges his knife into her and kills her. The noise attracts MacGregor who is also killed by William. Then William plunges the knife into himself and he falls dead. Douglas and the guests find three corpses.

Cui used leading motives in the opera. There are motives of William, apparitions, and of doom. It is not a system of motives in the Wagnerian sense. To reveal dramatic situations, Cui resorted to thematic transformations, a device successfully used by Berlioz and Liszt. Modulations and orchestral effects enhance dramatic moments in the opera. All these devices and effects were means which the New

Russian School regarded as indispensable in the evolution and revival of operatic forms.

In his musical style, Cui is a romantic miniaturist. He expressed himself best in short lyrical miniatures and this aspect of his talent prevented him from attaining great symphonic developments. His operas consist of successions of small musical forms, or frescoes, which detract from the general musical impressions of his work. The tremendous philosophical conceptions of Berlioz and Liszt were alien to Cui's talent. Whatever orchestral arrangements he achieved in the grand romantic style, bear an outward resemblance to Liszt's and Berlioz's musical canvases. His style is elegant, refined, sentimental, and restrained.

His songs and piano compositions are Schumannesque or Chopinesque. They are suitable for salon or domestic consumption, but not for the concert stage. They possess neither the dramatic and rhythmic impetuosity of Schumann nor the lyrical expressiveness of Chopin.

Cui's fame rests mainly on his critical writings. As a music critic, Cui expressed the views and ideas of the national school of music. His reviews and criticisms revealed the national, patriotic sentiments of Balakirev's circle and its evaluation of Western musical culture. The range of Cui's criticisms included baroque, classical, romantic, and Russian composers.

Cui's writings refute the opinion that the circle held unqualified admiration for the music of Berlioz, Liszt, and Schumann. The circle rejected Wagner's ideas as being of no consequence to Russian music.[1] They were critical of Liszt, Berlioz,[2] and Schumann and found some aspects of Beethoven's music [3] unacceptable. The circle even criticized the music of Glinka and Dargomijsky. The New Russian School did not blindly accept musical authority. It subordinated musical creativity to the urgent ideological and artistic problems of Russian reality.

Although Cui generally expressed various opinions which agreed with those of the circle, he was, in his own right, a critic and thinker with a creative individuality. In newspapers, Cui always defended the interests of the New Russian School. He was not always objective in his judgments. His personal tastes and sympathies often colored his criticisms and reviews. He regarded pre-Beethovenian music as an old-fashioned art alien to contemporary perception.

Cui was not a profound musician-philosopher. Therefore he was not able to grasp and analyze a subject in the totality of its aspects. As a music critic, he was often superficial and one-sided, praising or censuring a composition, but missing its inner meaning and significance.

His criticisms were keen and pointed. His musical evaluations became more accurate, the more they reflected the collective opinions of the circle. In retrospect, Cui often was the scapegoat of the circle. The thoughts and ideas of Balakirev, Mussorgsky, Borodin, and Rimsky-Korsakov were published by Cui and ascribed to him.

Cui possessed a detached, cold, and calculating mind. His devastating remarks reveal a firm, unswerving person, but, at the same time, a man of somewhat narrow-minded convictions and principles. He often succumbed to the temptation to enrage an adversary rather than present the pros and cons of a composition.[4] His peremptory remarks often roused indignation, but managed to convert people to the ideas of the New Russian School.

The topics covered by Cui's criticisms included problems of musical esthetics, theory, history of music, and musical content. He also analyzed the function of words in musical imagery and the problem of opera and music drama. His stylistic approach toward these topics was polemical, not analytical.

Cui's views and ideas changed somewhat during the 1870's. During the 1860's, he was the spokesman for the circle. During the 1870's the circle disintegrated because of the irreconcilable views of its individual members. Although "The Five" did not give up their main idea of an independent Russian musical culture, personal attitudes and tendencies made a collective expression of opinion impossible. This situation affected Cui. Although he shared the aspirations of the circle, his writings during the 1870's assumed a more personal expression and he was no longer too embarrassed to oppose his former colleagues.

Cui's attitude toward Glinka and Dargomjjsky never wavered. He regarded them with veneration as the founders of Russian national music. He criticized Balakirev for the faults and weaknesses in his musical forms. He criticized Rimsky-Korsakov for the weaknesses of emotional structure, schematic features in small and large musical forms, and lack of melodic originality in his music. Rimsky-Korsakov's work in the Petersburg Conservatory, however, evoked Cui's sympathetic response.

Cui was enthusiastic over the originality of Borodin's talent, but he condemned the ruggedness of his style, his harmonic and orchestral combinations, and capricious rhythms. Cui admired Mussorgsky's talent, but deprecated his realism and some features in his music such as absence of symphonic form, excessive freedom of modulations, and irregularity of harmonic progressions which produced harsh tonal combinations.

Cui praised Tchaikovsky's chamber and piano music, but not his symphonic and operatic forms. It would be incorrect to presume that "The Five" did not understand Tchaikovsky's music. They appreciated his musical gifts, but did not approve of some ideological tendencies in his music. Cui pointed out that Tchaikovsky's symphonic music contained a wealth of themes, developments, harmony, and instrumentation. His criticism asserted that Tchaikovsky was not selective in his choice of thematic materials which often included quite ordinary themes.[5]

As for Anton Rubinstein, Cui characterized him as a "German" composer, a successor of Mendelssohn, who absorbed two aspects of Russian national music: melancholy and the lively dance characteristics of the *trepak*.

Cui's criticisms of Western composers were varied. He admired Chopin, but never changed his critical attitude toward Mendelssohn,[6] Wagner, Liszt, Brahms,[7] and Verdi.[8] He praised the music of Saint-Saëns,[9] and here Cui expressed himself as a Russian of French descent.

Cui died in 1918. The last member of "The Five," he witnessed the rise of Stravinsky, Scriabin, and Rachmaninov. But Cui already belonged to the past. His esthetics, a combination of the beautiful with the truthful, emotional, restrained, and refined, was the result of his personal creative limitations. He preferred music that was graceful rather than powerful, harmonically and melodically simple and structurally logical. His democratic nationalism did not include strong critical condemnations of Russian social and political realities. He sometimes expressed unfavorable opinions of contemporary social conditions. Unlike Rimsky-Korsakov, who openly sympathized with the revolution in 1905, Cui was a reserved and cautious man, favoring objective contemplation rather than active participation in revolutionary events.

CHAPTER 14

Anton Rubinstein

ANTON RUBINSTEIN was a great pianist, an outstanding composer and conductor, and an organizer of music education in Russia. His activities laid the foundation for musical development in Russia during the second half of the nineteenth century.

Rubinstein was born on November 16, 1829, in the village of Vikhvatinets in the Podol province of southern Russia. His father, Grigori Romanovich, was an educated person who spoke several European languages. His mother, Kaleria Christoforovna Levenstein, was born in Prussian Silesia where, according to Rubinstein, she received a good education, mainly in music. In 1830, when Tsar Nicholas issued a ukase against the Jews, Rubinstein's grandfather, Roman Rubinstein, baptized the entire family. Soon after, they moved to Moscow.

When Rubinstein was six years old, his mother gave him his first piano lesson. According to Rubinstein, the piano repertoire consisted of compositions by Hummel, Hertz, Mosheles, Kalkbrenner, Czerny, Diabelli, and Clementi. When Rubinstein was eight years old, his musical education passed into the hands of Alexander Ivanovich Villoing, one of the best piano teachers in Moscow. "He was my only teacher in music," Rubinstein recalled. "After him I did not have other music teachers, except in music theory."

Rubinstein's first public appearance as a pianist took place on July 11, 1839. He played the "Allegro" from Hummel's A Minor Concerto, the fantasy "Moses" by Thalberg and Liszt's "Chromatic Gallop." The Moscow journal *Galathea* noted the remarkable technical maturity of Rubinstein and his ability to disclose the composer's idea. In the winter of 1840, Rubinstein was taken to Paris, ostensibly to study in the conservatory. He was not accepted there, however, because of his youth and his advanced musical training.

Rubinstein gave several concerts in Paris, where his piano playing met with the approval of Chopin and Liszt. These concerts were followed by an extensive tour which took him to Holland, England, Germany, and the Scandinavian countries. His playing was imitative of Liszt's virtuoso style. "There was at that time a manner of virtuosity," wrote Rubinstein. "Liszt headed this movement. In my playing I imitated Liszt. I adopted his mannerisms, his movements of the body and hands, the throwing back of his hair, and, in general, all the fantastic devices which accompanied his playing."

In 1843, Rubinstein returned to Russia to continue his triumphs. The Tsar invited him to play at the Winter Palace and he then played a series of concerts in Petersburg and Moscow. However, Rubinstein's mother decided to continue the musical education of Anton and his brother, Nicholas, in Berlin. There Rubinstein studied counterpoint with Siegfried Dehn, who ten years earlier taught Glinka. During the year and a half Rubinstein lived in Berlin, he mastered the technique of composition and became firmly attached to the classical musical traditions which characterized Mendelssohn's school. Rubinstein's first composition, a piano étude, "Undine," published in 1843, was favorably reviewed by Schumann.

In 1846, Rubinstein went to Vienna. "I gave piano lessons there, mostly for pennies. I lived on the top story of a big house. It often happened that for two or three days I did not have money to pay for dinner. There were hardly any furnishings in the apartment, but every corner and the floor were littered with my compositions. I composed everything: oratorios, symphonies, operas, and songs. I also wrote literary, critical, and even philosophical papers. In my garret I even wrote something like a newspaper for a single reader, myself."

Rubinstein's friendship with Liszt began in Vienna. Liszt visited Rubinstein in his garret. The Russian reported, "He treated me in a friendly manner, and he invited me the same day to dinner, which was very apropos."

In 1848, Rubinstein was again in Berlin. Because of revolutionary events, however, he left and returned to Russia, where he lived from 1849 till 1854. He gave piano lessons and concerts and he also composed. He acquired the repertoire and authority of a professional musician. Grand Duchess Helena Pavlovna introduced Rubinstein in court circles and he became the "court pianist." He composed several operas: *Dmitry Donskoy, Hadji Abrek* (to a poem by Lermontov), *Siberian Hunters,* and *Fomka the Fool. Dmitry Donskoy* was presented in Petersburg in the spring of 1852, but was discontinued after four performances. The opera, with the exception of the overture, is lost but it aroused a lively discussion in newspapers about Russian national music. The critic Stasov condemned the comparison of *Dmitry Donskoy* with Glinka's operas. This was the beginning of the antagonism between Rubinstein and the New Russian School of Music.

In 1854, Rubinstein went to Germany. He took his compositions with him, including two symphonies (one of them entitled the *Ocean Symphony*), three piano concertos, several string quartets, and piano compositions. He met with a friendly reception from Liszt, who helped him produce *Siberian Hunters* in Weimar. The friendship with Liszt lasted till Liszt's death in 1886. The two musicians were diametrically opposed in their views and tastes. Liszt opposed Rubinstein's traditionalism; Rubinstein opposed the "new music" of the Weimar school and Wagner's art. Rubinstein's refusal to participate in one of the annual Weimar music festivals led to a break with Liszt which lasted several years.

Rubinstein's European concert tour was a triumphal success. In a review of his performance in Paris, Saint-Saëns wrote: "It seemed as if the race of 'piano gods' has disappeared, when one beautiful day there appeared posters with the name of Anton Rubinstein. He made his debut with his concerto in G major. The next day he was a celebrity, and at the second concert the hall was crowded to suffocation. I was present at the concert, and I harnessed myself into the chariot of the conqueror."

In 1855, Rubinstein published an article on Russian music in the Vienna magazine *Blätter für Musik, Theater, und Kunst* in which he minimized the significance of developments in Russian national music and asserted that Glinka failed to create a Russian national opera. "Russian folk songs," wrote Rubinstein, "are exclusively melancholy and monotonous. This monotony has been the stumbling block for composers." The failure of *A Life for the Tsar* and of *Ruslan and Ludmila* was due, according to Rubinstein, to Glinka's attempt to relate his music to Russian songs. Rubinstein regarded Dargomijsky, who had already composed the opera *Rusalka,* as one of the weakest

Russian composers of the first half of the nineteenth century.

The article plagued Rubinstein for many years. In the 1880's, Rubinstein declared: "I always admired Glinka, and I always placed him on a level with Beethoven. Nevertheless, I am accused that I criticized Glinka. . . . Should something like this be ascribed to me, I have said it thirty-five years ago, and during this time I changed my opinion."

Six years later, Rubinstein published an article on Russian music in the Petersburg magazine *Vek* (Century). He condemned the amateurish character of Russian musical life and its dependence on foreign musicians. Rubinstein saw a solution of the problem in the establishment of a conservatory for the dissemination of a musical culture based on Western traditions.

In later years, Rubinstein's views on Russian music changed. In his book, *Music and Its Representatives,* he gave a glowing appraisal of Glinka's art. As a conductor, Rubinstein included in his programs the compositions of Russian composers based on Russian themes.

Rubinstein's home in Petersburg became the center of weekly concerts at which Rubinstein, professional musicians, and amateurs played for guests and friends. Eventually these people formed, in 1859, the nucleus of The Russian Musical Society. The first directorate of the society consisted of five members: Vyelgorsky, Rubinstein, Kashkin, Kologrivov, and D. Stasov. Rubinstein was the only professional musician in the directorate and he assumed the management of the society.

The first concert season of the society opened in 1859. Rubinstein was the conductor, choirmaster, and soloist. He continued these activities till 1868.

The Petersburg Conservatory was officially opened on September 8, 1862, with Rubinstein as director. The cherished wish of every piano student in the conservatory was to become a member of Rubinstein's piano class. His directorship lasted five years, until 1867 when he submitted his resignation. There were two groups in the conservatory. One group of professors, led by Rubinstein, believed that the function of the conservatory should be the education of outstanding artists. Another group, led by Davidov, believed that the conservatory should concentrate on the education of average, well-trained musicians who would disseminate musical culture throughout Russia.

Davidov's view was more progressive than Rubinstein's. It is also possible that Rubinstein resigned because the directorship interfered with his activities as pianist and composer.

From 1870 till 1880, Rubinstein made several concert tours in Europe and America. His fame as a pianist equal in ability to Liszt was firmly established. Rubinstein was a romantic pianist with an amazing gift of interpretation and with a superlative technique.

"He overpowered with Michelangelian pertinacity and with a leonine grasp. . . . He overcame the mechanical aspects of the keyboard, and he could evoke from it a musical imagery . . . sounding like voices of poetry, intonations of anger, and ecstasy of an enraptured soul of a prophet. . . . His leonine hands ordered the keyboard to deliver his passionate, temperamental thought, the life of the artist. . . . People thrilled at the indescribable excitement of the music during Rubinstein's musical revelations. . . . What was this quality? What distinguished Rubinstein's playing? Every pianist generally plays himself, but in Rubinstein's case this "I" embraced the whole world of music, as if the music became the lyrical creation of a single poet, of a sincere soul, retaining the peculiarities of the music of Chopin, Schumann, and of other great composers. . . . The singing quality of his playing and the transformation of the piano into a human organ of speech, into a voice-like melody which penetrated everything, was the source of a feeling of warmth, power, caress, grandeur, and of romantic sensation in Rubinstein's playing. One accepted his playing as a great art of an instrumental *bel canto* . . . when intonations evoked by his hands attained the heights of poetic imagery. . . . The wind quietly, but unrestrainedly, flew over the solitary grave of the obscure man who was just buried (the funeral march and finale of Chopin's sonata). Lovers' meetings, crowds of masqued people eager to live, youths enjoying themselves (Schumann's "Carnaval"). Torrents of violent power rushing down from a gigantic rock (Chopin's Étude in A Minor). In Rubinstein's fingers Bach's fugues sounded like timeless music beyond centuries, thought after thought, constancy of human broodings. . . .[1]

Rubinstein was one of the most prolific Russian composers. The complete list of his works contains about two hundred compositions, not including arrangements and transcriptions. More than half of his compositions are operas, symphonies, concertos, sonatas, and songs.

As a composer, Rubinstein was not sufficiently critical of himself. He did not possess the critical instinct in the choice of musical materials. Many of his compositions abound in remarkable musical thoughts interspersed with superficial musical materials. Another shortcoming is the monotony of Rubinstein's methods of musical exposition and the poverty of his harmonic and polyphonic thinking.

In a letter to Rubinstein, Liszt reproached him for being a composer of quantity and careless in his creativity: "I respect your compositions and I find much to praise in them . . . with a few critical observations. Your excessive productivity did not afford you spare time to disclose more individuality in your compositions and *complete* them. It has been justly said that it is not sufficient *to make* a composition; one should *complete* it."

In his *Basket of Thoughts,* Rubinstein vindicated his position. "There are artists who devote a lifetime to one composition in order to make it perfect. There are others who throughout their lives create innumerable compositions which are, however, far from being perfect. These last seem to me more logical. There cannot be absolute perfection in a man's composition. However, in imperfect compositions one could find enough beauty worthy of appraisal. There is something sympathetic in the fertility of creativity because it is naïve. At the same time, the faith that one could create something perfect carries in it the seal of conceit."

A few of Rubinstein's compositions have survived. They are the "Persian Songs," the operas *The Demon* and *Feramors,* and some piano compositions, such as "Melody in F" and the romance, "Evening in Petersburg." In his tendency to complete a composition, Rubinstein often left the intonational substance of a lyrical moment unfinished. This weakness is found in his small and large musical forms. He "draws" melodic outlines and hurriedly fills in the schemes with music. Occasionally, a brilliant musical thought will flash, only to be followed by successions of improvisational components which bring the composition to an end.

The reason his opera *The Demon* survives is its inclusion of successful musical ideas. The spaces between these ideas are shorter than in many other compositions. The key to Rubinstein's music resides in the "singing" qualities of his melodies, experienced as pronunciations of an image-bearing speech. This is how Rubinstein played the piano, and this is how he wrote his music. If one penetrates the meaning of Rubinstein's melodic imagery, his music will reveal him as a great master.

Through Rubinstein, Russian music was introduced to the stylistic aspects of Western composers. He had perfect mastery of the classical traditions of composition. His style was influenced primarily by the styles of Schumann and Mendelssohn and partly by the styles of Chopin and Liszt. His musical creativity was important in the assimilation of Western romantic influences by Russian music in the middle of the nineteenth century.

Around 1850, Rubinstein had already composed two symphonies, the symphonic poem *Faust,* and the "Persian Songs." The songs anticipated the song styles of Borodin, Cui, and Tchaikovsky. The opera *The Demon,* completed in 1871, is similar in many respects to the operatic style of Tchaikovsky.

The professional approach to musical composition established by Rubinstein in the Petersburg Conservatory was of tremendous importance to Russian composers. This is evident in the styles of Rimsky-Korsakov, Tchaikovsky, Glazunov, and Taneyev.

It would be wrong to assume that the sources of Rubinstein's music were rooted only in Western romanticism. Rubinstein was interested in the intonational manifestations of Russian everyday musical life, such as songs and instrumental "music-making." Many of his songs are reminiscent of the styles of early Russian song composers, Alabiev, Gurilev, and Dargomijsky. The song genres of these composers were enriched in Rubinstein's melodic style by Western romantic influences, especially the influence of Schumann. Rubinstein's songs originated melodic elements which were later developed into an original Russian style in the music of Tchaikovsky.

Rubinstein's contributions to Russian music were outstanding. He was, however, gradually eclipsed by Tchaikovsky, Borodin, Mussorgsky, and Rimsky-Korsakov, whose ideas and concepts were more vital in originality and inspiration to a musical art expressing Russian life and culture.

Operas

The lyrical style of Rubinstein's operas, *Feramore* (1863) and *The Demon* (1871) was influenced by Western operatic traditions. *Nero* (1877) and *The Maccabees* (1875) are heroic romantic operas. *The Merchant Kalashnikov* (1879) and *Dmitry Donskoy* (1852) are Russian historical operas.

Rubinstein composed many operas on characteristic national plots:

Fomka the Fool, Hadji-Abrek, and *Siberian Hunters* (1853); *Revenge* and a gypsy opera, *The Children of the Steppe* (1865); *The Parrot* (1884), a comic opera based on an Eastern fairy tale and *Goryusha* (1889), based on a plot from Russian life in the seventeenth century; spiritual operas: *The Lost Paradise* (1850), *Babel* (1869), *Sulamith* (1883), *Moses* (1887), and *Christ* (1893).

During the second half of the nineteenth century, the operatic field was dominated by Wagner's music dramas and the French lyrical operas of Gounod, Thomas, David, Bizet, Delibes, Saint-Saëns, and Massenet. Rubenstein was influenced by the French lyrical romantic style. His spiritual operas never became popular because the spiritual opera did not attract public attention. Only *Feramors* and *The Demon* have retained their popularity.

The plot of *Feramors* is an Eastern love intrigue which takes place in Bokhara. The Indian princess, Lalla Rukh, has arrived in Bokhara where she is supposed to marry the king. She falls in love with the singer Feramors. The grand Vizier, Faladin, discovers Feramors near the tent of the princess, arrests him, and sentences him to death.

Lalla Rukh, who has not met her bridegroom, hopes to ask him to save the life of Feramors. The marriage procession and the appearance of the king bring about a happy solution of the intrigue. The king is the singer Feramors.

The hero of Lermontov's poem, "The Demon," is a fallen angel, a romantic representation of a titan fighting God, harboring a hatred toward heaven. The Demon is an image of complex feelings and ideas, skepticism and social injustice. The poem, an exposure of defects in human society, and the struggle of calculating egoism with romantic idealism, is a representation of the Byronesque character of the early nineteenth century.

Rubinstein's Demon, a majestic, stern image tortured by loneliness, craves for love and happiness when he sees Tamara:

> And again he understood the sacredness
> Of love, goodness, and beauty.

After a short symphonic introduction, the curtain rises and the stage reveals a rugged mountain range. Voices of spirits in hell call upon the Demon. They are followed by voices in heaven glorifying the beauty of the world. The Demon appears on the top of a rock and delivers a monologue full of tragic disappointment, bitterness and despair:

> Cursed world! Contemptible world!
> Unhappy, detestable world which I hate!

An angel appears and tries to reconcile the Demon with heaven. The Demon, incapable of humility and forgiveness, answers the angel:

> I want freedom and passion.

The second scene takes place near the castle of Prince Gudal on the bank of the river Aragva. Girls with pitchers leave the castle and sing:

> Every evening we go to fetch water in Aragva.

The girls are joined by Gudal's daughter, Tamara. The Demon's figure appears on the rock. He sees Tamara for the first time and her image awakens in him long-forgotten dreams. No one sees the Demon, but Tamara experiences a strange alarm. She stops to listen to a mysterious voice singing:

> I, the free son of heaven,
> Shall take you into the world above,
> And thou shalt be the queen of the universe,
> The eternal friend of mine.

Tamara sees the Demon, but he suddenly disappears. Frightened, Tamara calls the girls. They did not hear the singing. Tamara, in a deep reverie, returns to the castle repeating the Demon's words.

The third scene is a gloomy ravine in the mountains. The caravan of Synodal, Tamara's bridegroom, appears. Synodal is hurrying to the marriage ceremony in Gudal's castle. A mountain landslide has detained him. Synodal sends a messenger to inform Gudal that he will arrive in the castle tomorrow afternoon.

But Synodal will never see his bride. When he and his followers fall asleep, the Demon foretells Synodal that he will perish at the hands of his enemies. Indeed, the enemy is near. Robbers, guided by the evil power of the Demon, fall upon the travelers, and Synodal is mortally wounded. Before he dies, he sees the majestic figure of the Demon.

The fourth scene takes place in Gudal's castle. Everyone is excited because a messenger has just announced that Synodal will arrive the same day. Tamara is pensive. All night long she heard a mysterious voice and she thought she saw the Demon.

The celebration is suddenly interrupted by a wailing sound and the lifeless body of Synodal is carried into the room. Tamara cries over the dead body of her beloved. While a chorus prays for the soul of Synodal, Tamara hears a mysterious voice which tenderly and affectionately sings:

> Do not cry, my child,
> Do not cry in vain!

Gudal orders the removal of Synodal's body. Exhausted, Tamara falls asleep. The Demon appears at the head of the bed, and in her sleep Tamara hears his voice:

> In the aerial ocean,
> Without rudder, without sail,
> Choruses of heavenly bodies
> Quietly float in the fog.

Tamara awakens. She is terribly confused. She does not want to yield to the mysterious power of supernatural charms which try to subdue her. She begs her father to let her go to a convent and find spiritual peace. Gudal accedes to her demand.

The fifth scene takes place near the wall of the convent. The Demon, ready for love, with his soul open to accept goodness, thinks the new life he has hoped for has arrived at last. His old adversary, the angel, blocks the Demon's way. The angel fails to deter the Demon. With the words

> I here possess and love

the Demon enters the convent.

The sixth scene takes place in Tamara's cell. It is night. The walls of the cloister did not give peace to Tamara. The mysterious, fascinating and frightening image is in her thoughts. "Who is he?" asks Tamara. When the Demon appears, Tamara, frightened, turns to him with the same question: "Who art thou?" The Demon answers:

> I am he to whom thou has listened
> In the quiet midnight,
> I am the king of knowledge and freedom,
> I am the enemy of heaven,
> I am the evil of nature, and now, look,

> I am at your feet!
> With tender emotion, I brought thee
> A pure prayer of love,
> My first earthly martyrdom,
> My first tears!

Tamara listens with a growing sympathy. "Oh! If thou would only understand my grief and my sufferings," continues the Demon. Tamara does not conceal her pity: "Sufferer, I am compelled to listen to thee with a secret joy." She wants to believe that the road to goodness is open to the Demon. She requests him to renounce evil forever. The Demon solemnly swears:

> I swear by the first day of creation,
> I swear by its last day.

Tamara still tries to resist the Demon, but she cannot. "I am in thy hands," she tells him. The Demon kisses Tamara. A chorus of angels is heard calling Tamara. She falls dead. The death of Tamara has deprived the Demon of power over her soul, and has ruined his dreams. He is not destined to find happiness and to start a new life:

> And again he remained arrogant,
> Alone, as before, in the universe,
> Without hope, without love!

The seventh picture is the apotheosis. Angels carry Tamara's soul to heaven:

> With a terrible price
> She atoned for doubts.
> She suffered, she loved—
> And paradise was open for her love!

Rubinstein's Demon is a tragic, and, at the same time, lyrical image. The Demon's emotion, love, and suffering are unfolded in the music and apprehended by listeners as strong, sincere human feelings. Rubinstein's Demon is not a standard lyrical hero. He is the strong, courageous Demon of Lermontov's imagination.

Rubinstein knew and understood oriental music. Oriental intonations are heard in Synodal's scene and in the dances in Gudal's castle. *The Demon* contains many beautiful melodies, dynamic effects, dramatic situations, and contrasts, all of which ensured the survival of the opera.

Symphonic Compositions

Rubinstein's symphonic compositions, like his operas, contain a variety of musical values. He preferred large symphonic forms, but did not possess a marked capacity for thematic development. The possibilities of his thematic conceptions do not correspond to the scope of his symphonic forms. His sonata style lacks resiliency, concreteness, and dynamic momentum in the Beethovenian sense.

The looseness of Rubinstein's sonata-allegro forms is increased by a lack of polyphonic methods, by repetitions of structural aspects, and by monotony of instrumentation. In his symphonic tastes, Rubinstein adhered to the classical-Mendelssohnian traditions of the Leipzig school.

Rubinstein's best symphony, the *Ocean Symphony,* is a cycle of seven movements representing contrasting lyrical and descriptive episodes. Despite its name, the symphony does not have a definite literary program. It is nearer to Mendelssohn's concert overtures and the *Italian* and *Scotch Symphonies.*

Color and mood predominate in Rubinstein's symphonic music. Image-bearing musical expressions, as in Beethoven's *Coriolan, Egmont,* and *Leonora Overtures,* are absent. Rubinstein's symphonies aroused interest, but not enthusiasm, in Balakirev's circle. Mussorgsky referred to the *Ocean Symphony* as "Ocean! Oh Puddle!" In 1861, the critic Stasov, with the *Ocean Symphony* in mind, suggested to Balakirev a Russian water-mythology based on the story of a Novgorod merchant Sadko as a plot for a composition. The plot was later used by Rimsky-Korsakov.

Songs and Piano Compositions

Rubinstein's songs are composed to texts by Russian and German authors. In his songs, Rubinstein adhered to the song traditions of Schubert, Schumann, and Mendelssohn. Russian lyrical intonations did not lend themselves to Rubinstein's sensibility. He was more successful with lyrics by Heine, Goethe, and others.

Rubinstein's piano compositions consist of romances, scherzi, nocturnes, serenades, barcarolles, and cycles of characteristic landscape elements, the "Kameny Ostrov," for example.

In large piano forms, Rubinstein composed four sonatas, five concertos, and a concert piece for piano and orchestra. The most famous concerto is in D minor.

Rubinstein's piano style was not very original. Influences of Mendelssohn and Schumann predominate. Sometimes Lisztian and Chopinesque devices appear.

Rubinstein's piano style, however, has exercised a tremendous influence on the evolution of Russian piano music from household music-making towards mastery of European pianism. The piano styles of Balakirev, Tchaikovsky, and Rachmaninov are indebted to Rubinstein's pianism.

Rubinstein initiated professional musical education in Russia. At the same time, he built the foundation for musical mass education. In retrospect, the disagreements and antagonisms between Rubinstein and Balakirev's circle are not important. Rubinstein and they had one purpose in mind: the development of an independent Russian musical culture.

The aloofness of the Petersburg Conservatory from national musical aspirations was gradually overcome. Rubinstein was probably the only Russian musician who could have accomplished the historical mission he set for himself. In addition, he was a superb organizer and administrator, qualities which helped him develop Russian musical culture to unprecedented heights.

CHAPTER 15

Tchaikovsky

DURING THE second half of the nineteenth century, the nationalism of Balakirev's circle was represented by "The Five": Balakirev, Cui, Borodin, Mussorgsky, and Rimsky-Korsakov. Peter Ilyich Tchaikovsky did not belong to the circle. He did not approve of the militant nationalism of "The Five." Tchaikovsky was a nationalist, but his musical principles were restrained and classical. He did not conceal his admiration of Western musical achievements, and, as a graduate of the Petersburg conservatory, he believed in a thorough training in musical theory and composition.

Tchaikovsky did not propagandize his principles and did not attempt to enlist sympathizers for his ideas. Nevertheless, he created a school of composition, which, like Balakirev's circle, influenced Russian music and its future development.

During Tchaikovsky's life, his Western sympathies were thought to be opposed to the ideas of "The Five." In retrospect, the differences between Tchaikovsky and "The Five" are of no significance. Tchaikovsky and "The Five" represented various aspects of Russian nationalism, and all these men absorbed, in their own way, Western musical influences. The common features in the styles of these composers are preference for subjects from Russian life and for a musical realism.

The sympathies of Balakirev's circle were with Berlioz's and Liszt's "music of the future." The musical forms, technical aspects, and orchestral techniques of Berlioz and Liszt were regarded by the circle as proof that German classical academicism and musical intellectualism were no longer significant. The circle believed that the free programmatic styles of Liszt and Berlioz formed a basis for the development of Russian national music. The circle did not realize that the cultural and spiritual background of Western musical romanticism was inimical to Russian realities. It failed to understand that the symphonic poem of Liszt and the dramatic symphony of Berlioz were esthetically opposed to Russian musical nationalism with its glorification of peasantry and folklore. Eventually "The Five" succeeded in substituting national realism for Liszt's and Berlioz's romantic exaltation.

"The Five" preferred national Russian customs, epos, and fantasy. Their artistic ideas were similar to the ideas of the *peredvizhniky*—the painters Kramskoy, Perov, Yaroshenko, Surikov, and Repin whose paintings represented Russian history, reality, and the life of common people.

Tchaikovsky was drawn towards the Russian intelligentsia, but not the revolutionary group. He was attracted by the literary group whose chief representatives were Tolstoy, Dostoyevsky, and Chekhov. Like these writers, Tchaikovsky was interested in the spiritual and emotional aspects of a human personality. Among "The Five" only Mussorgsky, like Perov among the *peredvizhniky,* was interested in the social and individual aspects of personality.

Tolstoy analyzed the psychic processes of passions and emotions, their forms and their laws. Tchaikovsky and Tolstoy possessed the genius to disclose the dialectics of the soul, the origin and development of feelings and psychological states.

Instead of analyzing social and political problems involving the peasantry and ruling powers, Tolstoy and Dostoyevsky were interested in man's relationship to society and the world. Man and his inner, psychological self-analysis and self-criticism became the subject of their writings. The conclusions and solutions reached by Tolstoy and Dostoyevsky revealed the differences between Western and Russian sociocultural realities.

Tchaikovsky's Sixth Symphony reflects Russian sociocultural realities at the end of the nineteenth century. The symphony does not express pessimism, resignation, and despair. The content of its dramatic imagery is an assertion of the power of life over death.

Dostoyevsky, in *Crime and Punishment,* emphasized the folly and futility of a revolt by a freedom-loving personality by contrasting defiance with submission and servile obedience. Tolstoy preached nonresistance toward evil, not hopeless pessimism. Tchaikovsky did not accept either Dostoyevsky's submissiveness or Tolstoy's conciliatory moral, philosophical, and religious formulas, especially his moral preaching. Tchaikovsky turned nonresistance and fatalistic resignation into a protest against reality.

Tolstoy and Dostoyevsky sought to merge their personalities with the common people. Raskolnikov, in *Crime and Punishment,* and Bezukhov, in *War and Peace,* do not think, in personal terms, of the "I," but in terms of the collective "We," the people. This was, to Tchaikovsky, Tolstoy, and Dostoyevsky, the key to understanding the meaning and purpose of life.

Tchaikovsky sought a new reality among peasants. One feels the strength of the peasantry and the village in the abandon of the scherzo in the Sixth Symphony. The answer, truth as an expression of the collective "We," Tchaikovsky found among the people. This is his nationalism in which he is spiritually related to Levin in *Anna Karenina* and Bezukhov in *War and Peace,* neither of whom finds the answers to moral questions in society or philosophy. Both characters realized that a Russian peasant had a better insight into the meaning of life than an educated intellectual in Moscow or Petersburg or a Western personality steeped in abstruse philosophy.

In 1872, Tchaikovsky wrote:

Everyone knows that quite often a clumsy peasant has a more sympathetic perception and knows how to behave himself better than an elegant nobleman dressed in a swallow-tailed coat.[1]

For the main theme in the finale of his Second Symphony, Tchaikovsky used the Ukrainian folk song, "Zhuravel." For the main theme in the finale of the Fourth Symphony, he used the folk song, "In the Field Stood a Birch Tree" and contrasted it with the theme of fate in the symphony. Thus, Tchaikovsky indicated that unity with the people was the source of man's inexhaustible strength. Tchaikovsky felt his loneliness and found happiness in submerging his personality in the collective "We" of the Russian people.

The Russian peasant often thinks in collective terms. Loneliness is not a Russian characteristic, but rather a Western European attitude. Goethe's Faust and Nietzsche's Superman are lonely individuals. Tchaikovsky's feeling of loneliness was the result of of the depressing Russian realities of his time and it became the link between his musical style and the West. In expression of the bitterness and poignancy of contemporary reality, he was on common ground, not with extreme Russian musical nationalists, but with Western romantics. This is the reason his music remains popular in the Western world.

For Dostoyevsky, the humble folk, the common run of people, are the impoverished and the victims of adverse fate. The tragedy of the common man is the lack of protection of his rights. It is the tragedy of martyrdom, not of struggle and heroism. Unlike Tolstoy, Dostoyevsky did not trust life, and he sympathized with the humble man. He saw the tragic contradictions and circumstances besetting him, and found no way out of the dilemma. The sun will never rise. One must withdraw oneself and submit.

For Dostoyevsky, the common man is weak, passive, and an object of compassion, which cannot help him. The contradictions are insoluble. The common man's attempts to become a free personality are not only doomed to failure, but are actually a crime because the road to freedom is through violence, and violence is always a crime. Crime is followed by punishment. At first it is a guilty conscience; then the established order punishes the violator.

Tolstoy does not succumb to hopeless pessimism. In Platon Karatayev, the modest peasant in *War and Peace*, Tolstoy reveals heroic aspects concealed in the inner character of man. These aspects are neither garish nor striking. However, in this modesty is a concealed power. In historical perspective, it is a pledge of escape, a means for common men to become great men, creators of a new life and masters of their destiny.

Although the quality of feelings and thoughts in Dostoyevsky and Tolstoy differs from the psychic world of Tchaikovsky, the three masters are artistically related by their ability to transmit prolonged psychological processes expressing various states and characteristics of emotional life and reality.

The main theme in Tchaikovsky's music is man's struggle for happiness, love, and enjoyment of life against the fatal predestination which confronts him. This theme is expressed in the first movement of the Fourth Symphony. Life is a continuous alternation of gloomy reality and transient dreams and visions of happiness. The festive finales in the Fourth and Fifth Symphonies do not represent a positive solution of the problem. They represent a temporary removal of the problem through the enjoyment of happiness among the people.

In Tchaikovsky's music, victory is always on the side of a formidable and impersonal power which fatally entails struggle and death. This philosophy of Tchaikovsky's music is consistently developed in his large compositions, especially the Sixth Symphony and in the opera *Queen of Spades*.

Maxim Gorky's words, "active pessimism," describing a pessimism which protests violence and evil, can be applied to Tchaikovsky's music. The dreams of Chekhov's heroes about a better and happier life have become, in Tchaikovsky's music, a struggle between a passion for life and a depressing fate.

The violence with which Tchaikovsky revolts against death is a measure of his love of life. The most pessimistic pages in his music do not plunge the listener into despair and disappointment with life and men. The variety, power, and straightforward quality of Tchaikovsky's feelings, his tense and spontaneous outbursts in defense of life's rights, and the urge to resist all that hinders life are the distinguishing qualities of his music.

Tchaikovsky was a musical realist, not a musical naturalist. He did not believe that artistic truth was identical with the truth of life. He maintained that instead of copying reality, art should truthfully reflect life situations and human characters in specific forms and representations.

Tchaikovsky rejected Hanslick's formalistic esthetics which reduced music to sounding forms without specific content and ideas.[2] He championed ideological content in music. In the relationship between content and form, Tchaikovsky stressed the importance of content in determining the musical form. Because of the importance of content, he maintained that all music was subjectively or objectively programmatic. He believed that his main function as a composer was to achieve a truthful representation of emotional experiences. "It seems to me that I have the gift to express sincerely and truthfully in music feelings, moods, and representations evoked by a text. In this sense I am a realist and a native Russian man."[3]

Tchaikovsky did not reject traditional musical forms and did not create new musical forms. His innovations and experiments with traditional forms were generated by the content of the composition. He championed national traditions in Russian music. He fought and criticized the dominance of Italian opera in Russia as well as slavish adherence to Western operatic influences. His realism reflected his creative principles. In symphonies and operas, Tchaikovsky revealed, in dramatic developments, the inner world and the spiritual life of man.

The symphony gave Tchaikovsky an opportunity to disclose his creative imagination and fantasy. Although the scenic conditions in an opera circumscribed Tchaikovsky's inspiration, the opera attracted him by its possibilities to direct communication with masses of people.[4] In the symphony and the opera, Tchaikovsky created generalized artistic representations with individual characteristics. He dramatized the symphony and individualized its musical imagery. He generalized operatic concepts and achieved the symphonization of the opera, the unity of musical development in the entire opera and in individual scenes.

It is not surprising that Tchaikovsky called the symphony "a musical confession of a soul." In his last three symphonies, Tchaikovsky disclosed every conceivable mood, emotional state, thought, and feeling. The content of the last three symphonies is the emotional drama of man: man's attempt to attain happiness, his clash with reality and fate, and his struggle with hostile social conditions. Tchaikovsky symphonically disclosed the unsolvable contradictions existing between a personality and an unfavorable social environment.

Tchaikovsky's heroes were ordinary people whom he understood and with whom he sympathized. He disclosed the personality and the individual emotional world of Onegin, Lensky, and Tatyana in *Eugene Onegin* and of Herman, Liza, and the Countess in *Queen of Spades*.

Tchaikovsky's music is interwoven with Russian national culture. His melodic style had been influenced by Russian folklore. In his Second Symphony, First String Quartet, finale of the Fourth Symphony, First Piano Concerto and *The Snow Maiden*, Tchaikovsky used authentic folk melodies. Although authentic folk melodies were not used in the Fifth and Sixth Symphonies, the connection with Russian national sources assumes intonational characteristics. Tchaikovsky's melodies often reflect the influence of musical culture and customs in Russian cities.

Tchaikovsky's melodies and themes are very individual and bear the imprint of his personality. They are expressive and reproduce and transmit moods, thoughts, psychological states, dramatic elements, developments of the heroes' feelings as well as those of Tchaikovsky himself. The melodies are seldom regular musical periods or sentences. They are usually constructed of small links, motives, or fragments which Tchaikovsky builds into an overflow of feeling by means of sequences, intonational changes, chromatic additions, suspensions, simultaneous contrasting movement of upper and lower voices and resolution of the tension by dividing the melodic structure into individual links, motives, and figures.

Tchaikovsky considered himself a musical lyricist. He saw the virtue of artistic works in their spontaneity and their freedom of emotional expression. He recognized the importance of self-criticism and outside criticism only when a composition had survived a period of time. He believed that a composer could objectively judge his music only when a sufficient period of time had elapsed during which spiritual and emotional travails connected with the composition had been forgotten. "Critics will never succeed in making a man do, even in a lifetime, that which he will never regret."

When Taneyev criticized the Fourth Symphony for its "ballet and dance aspects," Tchaikovsky wrote to him: "I positively do not understand why the expression *ballet music* could contain something reprehensible. I cannot see why a symphony should not include episodically a dance melody even with an intentional nuance of coarse comism." The idea of lyrical programmaticism, as the base of his symphonic artistry, was formulated by Tchaikovsky in a letter to Madame von Meck (March 1, 1878) in which he discussed the Fourth Symphony: "How can I describe the indefinable sensations which one experiences while composing an instrumental work without a definite subject? It is a purely lyrical process. It is a musical confession of a tormented soul that unburdens itself in sounds as a lyric poet expresses himself in verses."

Tchaikovsky expressed his idea of program music in another letter to Madame von Meck (December 5, 1878). "What is program music? Inasmuch as you and I do not acknowledge music which is an aimless game with sounds, from our viewpoint all music is programmatic. In a narrow sense this means symphonic or instrumental music which illustrates to the public a subject in a program and bears the name of the subject. . . . I find that the inspiration of a symphonic composer is either subjective or objective. In the first case a composer expresses in music sensations of joy and suffering just as a lyric poet pours out, so to speak, his own soul. In this case a program is not only superfluous, but it is not even possible. It is a different case when a musician reads a poetic work, or is affected by a picture of nature, and wishes to express in a musical form the subject that inspired him. Here a program is necessary. . . . Anyway, from my viewpoint both types of music have the same reason for existence, and I do not understand people who recognize exclusively one of the two kinds."

Tchaikovsky further expanded his idea of a realistic, understandable musical lyricism in another letter to Madame von Meck (August 18, 1880). "I would like with all the power of my soul that my music spread, and the number of people who loved it and who found in it consolation and support, grew."

Tchaikovsky's musical esthetics was conservative. He sought to preserve the bases of classical music. His admiration for Mozart is well known. At the same time, he criticized blind adherence to traditions in neoclassicism and, in a friendly remark, he referred to his pupil Taneyev as "Bach from the neighborhood of the fire station." Taneyev's residence in Moscow was not far from a fire station.

Tchaikovsky did not subscribe to the objective realistic programmaticism of "The Five." He did not approve of Laroche's rejection of programmaticism altogether because Laroche's views were similar to Hanslick's. Tchaikovsky evolved his personal lyrical programmaticism, subjective in form and realistic in content.

Unlike "The Five," Tchaikovsky regarded Russian folk songs as raw musical material suitable for musical development. He did not agree with the attitude prevalent in Balakirev's circle that Russian music was superior to Western music; and, at times, he pointed out the backwardness of Russian music. At the same time, he belittled the significance of Wagner and Brahms because he did not approve of the pathos of the first or the rational methods of the latter, two traits which Tchaikovsky thought could lead to decadence in Western music.

The vitality and survival of Tchaikovsky's music are due to its human appeal. The attraction and influence of his music are equally manifested in his operas, ballets, symphonies, symphonic overtures, songs, chamber compositions, and small piano miniatures.

Tchaikovsky's melodies possess an emotional persuasion independent of the size and form of the composition. At the same time every composition invariably reveals the intellectual and esthetic constancy or Tchaikovsky.

The greatness of Tchaikovsky's music is recognized all over the world. The development of traditions in interpreting his music is proof that every generation, while changing its interpretive attitudes, feels new qualities in his music consonant with spiritual and emotional aspirations of the times.

Tchaikovsky's music is Slavic in its expressive qualities and classic in its organization and form. His imaginative thinking in music is one of the richest sources of subtle emotional nuance and experience. It is the best evidence of the freshness, vitality, and conviction of his music.

Tchaikovsky is a musical orator who influences audiences, not by pathos and rhetoric, but by emotional suggestions concentrated in the particular turns and lilts of his melodies, that is, in his musical intonations. The significance of these intonations transcends national boundaries and becomes universal. In the words of the Soviet critic Asafiev, "The appeal of Tchaikovsky's intonations is different from those of Schubert, Beethoven, Chopin, Schumann, and Brahms. It echoes voices of people one loves, of friends, of a mother, a father, whose kindness and endearments mean so much to everyone." [5]

Tchaikovsky's lyricism contains emotional characteristics which, in the relationships among people, represent a distinctive dictionary of the intonations of sympathy, interest, compassion, romance, and friendliness. Tchaikovsky is a sensitive psychologist, equal to the greatest Russian writers and poets including Tolstoy, Dostoyevsky, Chekhov, and Pushkin. This is remarkably revealed in Tatyana's letter scene in *Eugene Onegin,* in which Tchaikovsky sympathetically and caressingly discloses emotional conflicts and experiences. These qualities are present in the Sixth Symphony, in the *Romeo and Juliet Overture* and in *Francesca da Rimini.* Impetuous melodic flashes are followed by lyrical themes full of heartfelt sympathy, love, and humanity. These qualities relate Tchaikovsky to Dante and Shakespeare.

As an operatic composer, Tchaikovsky is unique in Russian music. In *Eugene Onegin,* in *Queen of Spades,* and in his ballets, Tchaikovsky is a master of dramatic collisions growing out of psychological situations. In this sense, Tchaikovsky's operas are related to the plays of Chekhov and the psychorealistic productions of Stanislavsky in the

Moscow Art Theater.

Tchaikovsky's musical psychorealism can be traced to Robert Schumann, whose music exerted a profound influence on nineteenth-century Russian composers. Schumann's emotional impressions of reality and introspections are musically expressed in nervous, improvisational imagery calling forth the listener's participation in the emotional experience.

Tchaikovsky's place in Russian music is that of a musical stage producer of human emotions. He is a symphonic dramatist who raised melody to the status of thought in dramatic forms.

Peter Tchaikovsky was born on the 20th of April, 1840. His father, a graduate of the Military College of Mines, managed the Kamsko-Votkinsk Works. Tchaikovsky spent his childhood in Votkinsk, at present a town in the Udmurt Soviet Socialist Republic. His musical education began at an early age. He was receptive to music, intelligent, but did not reveal exceptional musical gifts. In 1850, his mother took him to Petersburg and registered him in the preparatory class of the School of Jurisprudence. A sensitive child, Tchaikovsky missed his family and the domestic environment. He developed a bent for reminiscences that persisted for the rest of his life. The letters of the ten-year-old boy reveal many psychological traits of the future composer.

In 1859, Tchaikovsky graduated from the School of Jurisprudence and accepted a position in the Ministry of Justice. During these years, his musical abilities became more pronounced. He participated in the school chorus directed by Lomakin who, together with Balakirev, organized the Free Music School.

Tchaikovsky took piano lessons and became a proficient pianist. He composed a sentimental song, "My Genius, My Angel, My Friend." His musical activities were of an amateurish, salonlike character.

The nineteen-year-old Tchaikovsky was interested in Italian operas, ballets, dancing parties, and strolls in Summer Garden and Nevski Prospect, the main thoroughfare in Petersburg, during the "fashionable" hours of the day. "It makes me laugh," he wrote many years later, "how I suffered that I could not quite become a man of fashion."

The year 1861 found Tchaikovsky undecided about his future. His career in the Ministry of Justice was not successful. He failed to get a promotion and was worried about the future and his financial security. "How shall I finish," he wrote to his sister, "what does the future

hold for me? It is terrible to think about it. I know that sooner or later
I shall smash myself to smithereens. Meanwhile I enjoy life as well as I
can. During this fortnight I have unpleasantness from all directions,
my work is bad, and my money is spent." Then he added a significant
postscript: "I began to study thorough bass and my work is progress-
ing successfully. Who knows, perhaps within three years you will hear
my operas and sing my arias."

Tchaikovsky seriously turned his attention to music and, in the fall
of 1861, began to attend the newly established music classes of Anton
Rubinstein. While studying music, he continued working in the Ministry of Justice. During the summer of 1862, he hoped to get a promotion, but was unsuccessful. He registered in the conservatory and in
the beginning of 1863, quit his job in the Ministry of Justice.

Tchaikovsky changed his mode of life. He was no longer a man of
fashion but a serious student who discovered himself and was determined to devote his life to music. His teachers in the conservatory
were Zaremba in harmony and counterpoint and Rubinstein in instrumentation. According to Laroche's recollections, Tchaikovsky was
somewhat opposed to his teachers because of their musical conserva-
tism. Zaremba, a pupil of the German theoretician Adolf Marx, was
influenced by Mendelssohnian traditions. The advanced ideas of
nineteenth century romantic music were hardly known to Zaremba.
Rubinstein adhered to classical traditions and did not permit his students to study orchestrations of romantic composers. Nevertheless, the
influence of Rubinstein's personality on Tchaikovsky was fruitful.
Tchaikovsky learned his compositional technique and professional
discipline from Rubinstein.

During his years at the conservatory, Tchaikovsky enlarged his
acquaintance with musical literature. Among Western composers, he
preferred Schumann. Among Russian composers, he admired Glinka.

While a student at the conservatory, Tchaikovsky composed an
overture to Ostrovsky's drama, *The Storm*. This composition revealed
dramatic and national aspects which became characteristic of Tchaikovsky's musical style. He also composed two overtures, one in F
major, the other in C minor, "Characteristic Dances" for orchestra, an
allegro for a string quartet, a sonata and variations for piano and his
graduating composition, a cantata on Schiller's *Ode to Joy*, suggested
to Tchaikovsky by Rubinstein.

The opinion of music critics of the cantata was unfavorable. The only dissenter was Laroche who wrote to Tchaikovsky: "All that you have accomplished I regard as a preparatory and experimental work of a schoolboy. Your creative works will probably begin within five years, and your mature classical compositions will surpass all that we have since Glinka."

Tchaikovsky graduated from the conservatory in 1865. In 1866, Tchaikovsky moved to Moscow and accepted a professorship in the Moscow conservatory, of which Nicholas Rubinstein was the director. Laroche, who had also moved to Moscow, became a friend of Tchaikovsky and a staunch advocate of his music.

Tchaikovsky's first important composition in Moscow was the symphony, *Winter Dreams* (1866). He worked hard on the symphony and made many alterations in the score to please his former teachers, Zaremba and Rubinstein, with whom he consulted while composing it. Eventually, Rubinstein rejected the symphony, declaring it unworthy to be performed in its entirety. This caused Tchaikovsky to adopt a skeptical attitude toward Petersburg composers and musicians. At the same time, Moscow audiences hailed Tchaikovsky warmly. The *première* of *Winter Dreams* in Moscow in 1868 under the direction of Nicholas Rubinstein was very successful.

An artistic circle in Moscow organized by Nicholas Rubinstein and Ostrovsky included many prominent musicians, poets, and writers. They held frequent meetings at which new literary works by Ostrovsky, Pisemsky, Pleshcheyev, and Sologub were read. Meetings were also devoted to performances of quartets, trios, and solo compositions. Tchaikovsky often attended these gatherings and became friendly with Ostrovsky who, besides being a dramatist, was keenly interested in Russian music, especially in old peasant songs.

The friendship with Ostrovsky was important to Tchaikovsky in another sense. Ostrovsky's love of folk songs was motivated by his interest in dramatic portrayals of Russian life, customs, and morals. Ostrovsky studied folk songs and contemporary music in Russian cities, as well as romances and arrangements of folk songs. This "everyday music" Ostrovsky heard in Russian cities was incorporated into some of his dramas.

Tchaikovsky's tastes for national song materials were influenced by the preferences of the artistic circle. The result of his friendship with Ostrovsky was the opera *Voyevoda* (the governor of a province in ancient Russia). The *première* of the opera took place in Moscow in

1869. The presentation was unsuccessful because of inadequate preparation. After five performances, the opera was taken off the repertoire. Eventually Tchaikovsky destroyed the score.

In 1868, Tchaikovsky became friendly with Balakirev's circle. The reason for the *rapprochement* was Tchaikovsky's defense of Rimsky-Korsakov's *Serbian Fantasy,* which was severely criticized in the Moscow Journal *Antract* (Interlude). This was Tchaikovsky's debut as a music critic. From 1872 to 1876, he wrote reviews and criticisms for the Moscow newspaper *Russkiye Vedomosti* (Russian Records).

Tchaikovsky's friendship with the circle was strengthened by common interest in Russian music and the latest achievements of Western composers. His compositions were discussed by the circle. The Second Symphony, with its variations on the Ukrainian folk song, "Zhuravel" (The Crane), and the *Romeo and Juliet Overture,* met with enthusiastic approval in the circle.

Tchaikovsky was critical of the musical ideas of "The Five." He approved some of Balakirev's and Rimsky-Korsakov's compositions. Balakirev's advice and criticism of Tchaikovsky's compositions undoubtedly influenced Tchaikovsky.

In 1868, Tchaikovsky composed a symphonic poem *Fatum* (Fate), which he dedicated to Balakirev. The *Romeo and Juliet Overture* was suggested to Tchaikovsky by Balakirev. In a letter to Tchaikovsky (October 4, 1869), Balakirev described the programmatic conception and plan of the overture and the character of its themes. Indicating the psychological basis of symphonic program music, Balakirev analyzed the creative process from the *idea* to the *music* as a deliberate intonational incarnation of programmatic content.

Tchaikovsky refused to show the overture to Balakirev until it was completed. Tchaikovsky disapproved "collective creativity" and criticism of a work in the process of composition as practiced by members of the circle.

The overture was Tchaikovsky's first great symphonic composition. Its musical ideas and the dramatic intensity of their development anticipated the psychologism of realistic lyricism in Tchaikovsky's mature symphonic style which emerged in the years 1875 to 1880.

In 1869, Tchaikovsky composed a lyric romantic opera, *Undine,* on a text by the poet Zhukovsky. The opera was rejected by the Mariinsky Theater in Petersburg and Tchaikovsky destroyed the score.

During 1870 to 1876, Tchaikovsky composed three string quartets, the opera *Oprichnik* (a guardsman in the reign of Ivan the Terrible), incidental music to Ostrovsky's fairy tale *Snegurochka* (The Snow Maiden), in which Tchaikovsky used authentic Russian songs, the *Swan-Lake Ballet,* the symphonic poem *The Tempest,* the piano concerto in B flat minor and the opera *Vakula the Smith,* based on Gogol's story, in which Tchaikovsky used authentic Ukrainian songs. In 1887, Tchaikovsky rewrote *Vakula the Smith* and renamed it *The Little Slipper or Oxana's Caprice.* In 1876, he composed *Francesca da Rimini* on Dante's text. In *Francesca,* Tchaikovsky revealed his mastery of Liszt's symphonic method of composition.

These compositions of Tchaikovsky's first period reveal a variety of thematic features, genres, and stylistic derivatives. Subjects from Russian life and history in *Voyevoda* and *Oprichnik,* Russian lyricism and fantasy in symphonies, quartets, *Vakula the Smith* and *The Snow Maiden* and romantic subjects in *Romeo and Juliet* and *Francesca da Rimini.* Stylistically, Tchaikovsky's music of this period reflects the influence of Beethoven, Glinka, Dargomijsky, Gounod, Meyerbeer, Schumann, and Liszt.

Comments by members of Balakirev's circle pointed out Tchaikovsky's eclecticism. Stasov regarded Tchaikovsky's creative versatility as a regrettable result of Rubinstein's method of music education which supposedly trained students in mediocre principles of composition.

Tchaikovsky was not an eclectic. He was able to assimilate and reinterpret creatively all that was vital and important in the music of his time. The criteria by which Tchaikovsky evaluated musical styles were based on the vitality of an artistic trend. He vigorously opposed music in which he felt a predominance of rationality over inspiration. He opposed the music of Wagner who "forgot that truth of life and artistic truth are two completely different truths." He criticized Dargomijsky's music drama, *The Stone Guest,* as an example of a recitative opera without music. He did not approve some of the aims of "The Five." However, he rejected some of the aims of Taneyev and Laroche, who were anti-Wagnerian and anti-Balakirevian. Tchaikovsky preferred contemporary musical trends and did not share Taneyev's and Laroche's love of medieval music. His compositions were created on a basis of individual interpretation of theme, subject, and style. Although Tchaikovsky's creative individuality does not sufficiently assert its independence in his first compositions, his bent for psychological content and artistic means suitable for this content is clearly evident.

Characteristic of Tchaikovsky's nature was a revolt against reality, a defiance that would not endure self-deception and compromise. In a letter to the music publisher Jurgenson in 1877, Tchaikovsky wrote: "I am a man who passionately loves life and just as passionately hates death. I cannot live without working, but as soon as I complete a composition and I am ready to relax, instead of rest I feel anguish and morbidness. I think about the vanity of life. I fear the future and I regret the irrevocable past. I try to understand the meaning of existence. . . . I am destined to have doubts all my life and to look for a way out of contradictions. . . . You can see that I am full of contradictions and, having arrived at a mature age, I have arrived at nothing. I did not rest my turbulent spirit in religion or philosophy. Indeed, had it not been for music, I would have lost my mind."

Tchaikovsky's letters between 1870 and 1880 reveal how irrepressible the intensification of his emotional crisis was. Even passing spells of melancholy gradually grew into a tragic, persistently haunting feeling of doom. In 1877, at the height of his musical creativity, Tchaikovsky wrote: "My only joy is to plunge into the past. . . . I have grown old. . . . I have lived my life."

These moods reflect the conditions of Tchaikovsky's life. Although in Moscow he was surrounded by friends who admired and appreciated his music, he could not escape the feeling of intellectual dullness and humdrum existence. In a letter to a friend, Klimenko (1872), Tchaikovsky wrote: "Now we go to the conservatory, now we meet sometimes and jointly give toasts, and, practically speaking, we are in the blues, as we were last year. As a matter of fact, the blues make life a burden to us." Tchaikovsky often complained that he had no one with whom to share his burden.

The event which staggered Tchaikovsky and brought him unbearable mental tortures and to the brink of suicide was his marriage in 1877. In the fall of 1877, Tchaikovsky was in a state of mental collapse. He left for Petersburg and from there, friends took him abroad. That year was a turning point, during which his individuality as a composer matured and his ideas and creative principles were clearly defined. A feeling of doom, a violent protest against fate, a hopeless yearning, a romantic dream of life, love and nature, boundless elation and exaltation tempered with a quiet melancholy became characteristic of Tchaikovsky's imagery as revealed in the Fourth Symphony and

Eugene Onegin. Identical imagery, but to a lesser extent, is found in Tchaikovsky's compositions of the previous decade: in the highly dramatic *Francesca da Rimini,* in *Romeo and Juliet,* and in *The Tempest,* with their contemplative lyricism and passionate qualities of musical theme.

The intensification of Tchaikovsky's tragedy was paralleled by his preference for large-scale generalized philosophic conceptions in symphonic compositions. The esthetic conceptions of the Fourth Symphony and *Eugene Onegin* are similar: antagonism of life and death; of happiness and destructive fate. In *Eugene Onegin,* these qualities are represented by the youth, love, and hopes of Tatyana and Lensky; the death of Lensky, and the final meeting of Tatyana and Onegin.

Tchaikovsky settled in Clarens, on Lake Geneva, in Switzerland. "I do not care to see anyone," he wrote, "I am afraid of everyone, and I can hardly work." Realizing that he could not resume teaching at the Moscow conservatory, he resigned his professorship. During the next eight years, from 1877 to 1885, Tchaikovsky spent the winters abroad and the summers on the estate of his sister in Kamenka, near Kiev.

Tchaikovsky's complete devotion to composition was made possible by the yearly allowance of 6000 rubles given him by Nadezhda von Meck, the widow of a wealthy railway engineer. This friendship lasted thirteen years. Tchaikovsky never met Madame Von Meck, but he corresponded with her.

During the early 1880's, Tchaikovsky was satisfied with his freedom, with his work as a composer, and with the growing recognition of his compositions. He became interested in Shakespeare's *Romeo and Juliet* as a subject for an opera. "This is the most suitable subject for my musical character," he wrote to his brother. "There are no Tsars, no marches, there is nothing that constitutes the routine of an opera. There is only love, love, and love." In 1879, however, he became interested in the subject of Joan of Arc. He returned to Clarens where he composed the opera *The Maid of Orléans.* His next operas were *Mazeppa* (1883), based on Pushkin's poem *Poltava,* and *The Enchantress* (1887), based on a play by Shapjinsky.

Tchaikovsky's name became known throughout Russia. In 1884, *Eugene Onegin* was successfully presented in Petersburg under the direction of Napravnik. The Fourth Symphony, *Francesa da Rimini,* the Third Suite, and his concerto for violin and orchestra were performed in many European cities.

Tchaikovsky's character underwent a marked change. He became sociable and more active in artistic pursuits, appearing as conductor of his own compositions. In 1887 and 1888, he made a triumphant tour of Germany, France, England, and Bohemia. He was enthusiastically received in Prague, where he was greeted with a serenade and a torch parade in front of the balcony of the house at which he stayed. In 1892, he was elected a corresponding member of the French Academy. Cambridge University conferred the honorary degree of Doctor of Music upon him.

In 1885, Tchaikovsky settled in the region of the town of Klin near Moscow. At first he lived in the villages of Frolovskoye and Maidanovo and then at Klin where his home is at present a national museum.

Tchaikovsky's last years were characterized by agonizing emotional torments. However, these emotional torments were no longer due to the external aspects of Tchaikovsky's life. They appeared unaccountably and often assumed the character of abstract moral and philosophical reflections. "I stay at home," he wrote in his diary, "and I am remorseful of something. The meaning of this remorse is that life passes and approaches its end, and I have not hit an idea. I even try to banish the fateful question, do I live and act justly?"

He was deeply moved by Tolstoy's *Confession* and *The Death of Ivan Ilyich*. About the *Confession* Tchaikovsky wrote: "I was impressed that the torments of doubt and of tragic perplexity which beset Tolstoy and which he so marvellously described in his *Confession* were well-known to me." Tchaikovsky called *The Death of Ivan Ilyich* "a work of genius, but extremely agonizing." Almost every entry in the diary during the last years of Tchaikovsky's life contain references to anguish, sadness, and despair. As early as the 1870's, his mental depression became more aggravated. "It is amazing," Tchaikovsky wrote to his brother, "that I have not lost my mind from the murderous, phenomenal, appalling depression."

The *Manfred Symphony* (1885) was the first of Tchaikovsky's last tragic compositions. The Fifth Symphony (1888) continued the program and design of the Fourth Symphony. This final period came to an end with the opera *Queen of Spades* and the Sixth Symphony. The fate of Herman, the hero in *Queen of Spades,* is a representation of the main idea in Tchaikovsky's music, the clash of forces of life with invincible death. The progress from the elegiac grief and duel in *Eu-*

gene Onegin to the tragedy in the fourth scene of *Queen of Spades* represents the evolution of Tchaikovsky's ideas during the last thirteen years of his life. *Queen of Spades* reflected the personal world of Tchaikovsky's moods. While composing the last scene, he actually cried over Herman's fate.

In 1891, Tchaikovsky composed the one-act opera *Iolanthe* and in 1892, the *Nutcracker Ballet*. The first sketches of the Sixth Symphony were composed in the same year, but he became dissatisfied with the music and destroyed the score. In the beginning of 1893, he wrote to his nephew Davidov: "You know that last fall I destroyed a symphony which I partly composed and orchestrated. I did a good thing because there was not enough good music in it. It was an empty succession of sounds without any inspiration. During my travels it occurred to me to write a symphony with a program which will remain an enigma for everyone. This program is very subjective. During my wanderings I mentally composed it and cried over it."

The Sixth Symphony was completed in August, 1893. Its content did not remain a riddle. Its subject is similar to that of the Fourth and Fifth Symphonies and the *Queen of Spades*. The Sixth Symphony is more tragic. Tchaikovsky compared the finale of the symphony to a requiem. Because of its tragic poignancy, the Sixth Symphony surpassed, in emotional contrasts and culminations and in variety of imagery, everything Tchaikovsky had previously composed.

On October 7, 1893, Tchaikovsky left Klin for Petersburg to conduct the new symphony. The concert was not successful. Five days later he became ill. In the evening, doctors diagnosed cholera. During the night of October 24, Tchaikovsky died.

Esthetics

Uncompromising struggles between good and evil, darkness and light, and love and death are reflected in Tchaikovsky's music. Love and kindness triumph in *Swan Lake* and *Sleeping Beauty*. Loyalty and faith conquer the king of mice and his fantastic hosts in *Nutcracker*. Love of life and happiness restore the vision of the blind princess, Iolanthe. Although Liza and Herman perish, the idea of eternal human love underlies *Queen of Spades*.

The programmatic basis of Tchaikovsky's last three symphonies is the conflict between the hope and aspiration of man and the obstacles he encounters in life. The program of the Fourth Symphony is man's struggle against fate in order to attain happiness. In this symphony, Tchaikovsky advises man to lean upon the common people among whom he will find simple and strong joys. This was Tchaikovsky's interpretation of the finale of the symphony in a letter to Madame von Meck: the solution is man's submergence of his personality in the mass of people.

The word "fate," used by Tchaikovsky, does not mean that he believed in the existence of a fatal or mystical power which prevented the attainment of happiness. The concept of "fate" in Tchaikovsky's thinking was a complex of objective factors or causes which prevented a free individuality from attaining happiness.

The Fifth Symphony, composed ten years later, represents the solution of the problem of life as the triumph of "the will" over suffering, doubts, and anxieties. In the finale of the symphony Tchaikovsky attempted to give a symphonic conclusion in a Beethovenian manner. However, the result achieved by Tchaikovsky is ambiguous: it could represent the triumphant victory of the will over fate, or the victorious procession of a triumphant fate. It is possible that this ambiguity was felt by Tchaikovsky who liked this symphony less than his other symphonies. The seemingly controversial solution of the finale testifies to the uncertainties in ethical and esthetical questions in Russian reality which Tchaikovsky experienced but found unsolvable.

After five years, Tchaikovsky composed the Sixth Symphony, which represents a tragic solution of the same problems. In this symphony, Tchaikovsky expressed the feelings of Russian men and women who experienced the oppression of Russian social and political realities. The symphony is a fervent call for a free development of human personality. With overwhelming realism and truth, Tchaikovsky expressed feelings and thoughts common to men and women: a search for happiness and creative activity, dreams, struggles, recollections, and finally, death.

The Sixth Symphony is not a pessimistic composition. It is "tragic" in Beethoven's musical use of the word. The symphony represents a positive assertion of life and active struggle. The thought of death in the finale of the symphony is not a negation of life. The imagery associated with suffering and despair evokes an understanding response from the listener. It is a protest against the futile, destructive forces in the world. It is a fervent desire to live and enjoy life. Death is inevitable. But stronger than death is the eternal creative and constructive action that leads mankind from darkness into light.

An interesting interpretation of the last three symphonies was given by Asafiev who characterized them as three stages of a declining lyrical emotional force. A dull, immovable, and threatening power intrudes into man's unfolding spiritual life in the Fourth Symphony, which is the first stage. The cold, paralyzing breath of this power, growing and developing alongside man's aspirations and meditations, is felt in the Fifth Symphony, which is the second stage. The final stage is represented by the Sixth Symphony. The unknown dark power, which cannot be separated from the suffering personality, drags that personality to death and to disappearance in a creative enthusiasm and passion.

In a letter to Taneyev (March 27, 1878), Tchaikovsky wrote: "I agree with you that my Fourth Symphony is programmatic, but I do not see why you regard this as a defect. I fear the opposite, that is, I would not like that my symphonic compositions were empty musical games with sounds, rhythms, and modulations. My symphony is programmatic, but it would be impossible to describe it in words. To attempt to describe it would appear comic and ridiculous. Should not a symphony be the most lyrical of all musical forms? Should it not express that which escapes from the soul and begs to be expressed, but for which words are superfluous? My thought in the symphony could be understood even without a program. . . . Essentially, my symphony imitates Beethoven's Fifth Symphony. However, I did not imitate Beethoven's musical thoughts, but only his basic idea. . . . There is not a single line in my symphony which I did not feel keenly, and which does not echo the deepest stirrings in my soul."

These words represent the esthetic qualities of Tchaikovsky's symphonic music. He regarded a symphony as a musical form which could best express the gamut of human feelings. The bases of his symphonies are lyrical, philosophical, and psychological conceptions.[6]

Tchaikovsky was a master of all symphonic resources. *Romeo and Juliet, Francesca da Rimini, Manfred* and the ballets are colorful and descriptive musical canvases. He did not care for a detailed symphonic program. While composing *Manfred*, he wrote to Taneyev (June 13, 1885): "I do not know the outcome of *Manfred*. I am dissatisfied with myself. It is a thousand times more pleasant to compose without a program. When I compose a program symphony, it seems to me that I am deceiving the public."

Passive contemplation was alien to Tchaikovsky's personality. His emotions were spontaneous and explosive. In his music, he favored tense dramatic conceptions in purposeful dynamic developments. The bases of his symphonic compositions are lyric and philosophic ideas. He avoided abstract imagery and arbitrary play of the imagination. His symphonic ideas are unfolded in expressive images, which can be understood by many people.

The concreteness of Tchaikovsky's musical imagery is enhanced by his use of genres popular in Russian everyday music. His lyricism is often expressed in genres of the dance and song. The main theme in the first movement in the Fourth Symphony is in movimento di valse.

Glinka was the first Russian composer to develop popular genres used in Russian everyday music. The *Kamarinskaya* was as important to Tchaikovsky as it was to "The Five" and the *Valse Fantaisie* anticipated waltz characteristics in Tchaikovsky's music. Glinka's music influenced the development of Tchaikovsky as a national composer and as a symphonic lyricist. Tchaikovsky summarized Glinka's influence in the following words: "There is a genuine Russian symphonic school. It is all in *Kamarinskaya,* just as an oak tree is in an acorn." [7]

The programmatic principles of Berlioz, based on the representation of all the details in a plot or subject, did not appeal to Tchaikovsky. Tchaikovsky was closer to the traditions of general philosophic conception in Beethoven's music (*Egmont, Coriolanus, Leonara,* the Fifth and Ninth Symphonies) and in Liszt's symphonic poems (*Les Préludes, Two Episodes from Lenau's Faust,* and *Faust Symphonie*). He did not care for decorative effects in music. To Tchaikovsky, a literary program was valuable only if it contained lyrical and psychological qualities which appealed to him (*Romeo and Juliet*). Such programs enabled him to concentrate on representations of emotional structures through expressive means, rather than through tone color and design.

In *Romeo and Juliet,* Tchaikovsky revealed the content of the drama by concentrating on important components of imagery and the main features of action. In the overture, despite the tragic denouement, love and passion triumph over evil and death. The result is a perfect synthesis of music and poetry.

The first part of the *Manfred Symphony* represents Manfred's wanderings and his search for some positive foothold in reality. He is attempting to find a way out of the uncertainty of existence. The escape is far away, the road is uncertain and perilous, and the view is obscured. Manfred is caught in the riddle of existence, the insignificance of all that man hopes and strives for in life. In the end he is faced with cruel death. In Tchaikovsky's music, Manfred's passions and emotions seem to exhaust themselves in the hopeless, almost painful, sighs of the first theme.

This subjective development represents Tchaikovsky's lyrical perception of the world, emphasizing an expression of emotional and spiritual excitement. The second and third parts of *Manfred* are objective in their representations and in tone painting, and therefore inferior to the first part.

In *Francesca da Rimini* the passion of love is conquered by cruel punishment. Nevertheless life is beautiful and wonderful in the recollections of happy moments of love and passion.

The romantic symphony, after Beethoven, lost the social and ideological significance of Beethoven's heroic conceptions. Post-Beethovenian passive romanticism stressed the struggles and contrasts of psychological sensations and sentiments or the descriptive genres in Mendelssohn's *Italian* and *Scotch Symphonies*. Brahms was interested in containing romantic esthetic forms within classical designs. Romantic symphonic music was often characterized by the predominance of color effects at the expense of content, as in the symphonies of Berlioz, the symphonic poems of Liszt, and the tone poems of Richard Strauss.

After Beethoven, Tchaikovsky was the first composer whose music exercised a tremendous social influence, although the heroic ideology of Beethoven's music was alien to Tchaikovsky. Tchaikovsky's interest was concentrated on eternal human problems, such as man and fate, struggle for happiness, and life and death. His musical representations are simple and truthful answers to the emotional and spiritual aspirations of mankind. His music sounds like human speech.

Symphonies

Tchaikovsky's first three symphonies are not distinguished by philosophical thoughts. The symphonic cycle does not reveal unity and purposefulness of thematic development. The symphonies are successions of narrative episodes whose emotional qualities are characterized by elegiac moods, a radiant lyricism, and a festive holiday spirit.

The romanticism of these three symphonies is reminiscent of descriptive pictorial genres in Mendelssohn's symphonies and passive contemplations in Schumann's symphonies. Although Tchaikovsky's symphonies follow the traditional designs of classical symphonies, their contents are lyric descriptions of subjects taken from Russian nature. They are based on intonational materials connected with Russian everyday life and music. The symphonies reveal Tchaikovsky's bent for symphonic developments based on the dynamic growth of a musical idea. These elements eventually compelled Tchaikovsky to break away from schematic musical constructions.

The First Symphony, *Winter Dreams* (1866), is a series of symphonic impressions of Russian northern landscapes. It is a lyric cycle of mood pictures, which develops a favorite subject in Russian poetry, namely, the impressions of traveling on a Russian road in winter, a coachman's song, a monotonous tinkling of a bell, and a heartfelt longing. Tchaikovsky's music reveals a poetic feeling for nature and a fidelity of representation.

The first movement, "Dreams on a Winter Road," is a succession of reveries and charming flashes of imagery. The music creates the feeling of constant movement on a road, not a headlong run, but a leisurely ride on a boundless Russian steppe.

The second movement, "The Gloomy Land, the Foggy Land," is a musical elegy which might have been inspired by Pushkin's traveling verse:

> The moon picks its way
> Through rolling mists,
> Pouring a wistful light
> On melancholy glades.

Elegiac moods often occur in the compositions of Tchaikovsky, Borodin, Mussorgsky, Rimsky-Korsakov, and Rachmaninov. They are reflections of life with its joys and sorrows. Had this music been a reflection of subjective fantasies, it would have been forgotten long ago. The music lives because it reflects Russian history, feelings, thinking, and aspirations in musical intonations which represent emotional truth to Russians in every walk in life. For the same reasons, the music of these composers appeals to people all over the world.

The third movement is an impetuous and mysterious scherzo which might have been inspired by Pushkin's verse:

> The sky is dark, the night is dull,
> Clouds whirl and curl,
> The moon becomes invisible,
> Illuminating the swirling snow.

The scherzo is a musical impression of silence in a wintry forest and of the stillness of night broken by falling snow. The middle section of the scherzo is a waltz, the first symphonic waltz composed by Tchaikovsky.

A festive finale based on two Russian songs concludes the symphony. One of the songs is an authentic folk song, "The Flowers Bloomed." The movement is one of the first examples of Russian festive symphonic finales developed on the basis of Glinka's symphonic music, namely, the overture to *Ruslan and Ludmila* and the *Kamarinskaya*. All of Tchaikovsky's symphonies, with the exception of the Sixth, are concluded with festive finales.

The Second and Third Symphonies (1872 and 1875) represent a further evolution in Tchaikovsky's style away from schematic classical designs and toward esthetic symphonic forms suitable for his musical lyricism. The two symphonies are suitelike in construction. The movements include a variety of genre characteristics based on authentic Russian songs and Tchaikovsky's original melodies in folk song style.

One of the themes in the first movement of the Second Symphony is a Ukrainian variant of the famous song, "Down the River Mother-Volga." The second movement is based on a folk song "Spinner, Spin." The finale is a sonata form combined with colorful variations on a popular Ukrainian folk song, "Zhuravel." When the symphony was edited in 1879 and 1880, Tchaikovsky rewrote the first movement in a tense, dramatic Beethovenian manner.

The Third Symphony consists of five movements. The opening allegro is a festive, dancelike movement with dramatic episodes. The second movement is a waltz. The third movement is an elegy. The fourth movement is a romantic scherzo. The finale is a polonaise.

The underlying ideas of the last three symphonies are man's struggle against fate, suffering, and despair, and the desire to live and enjoy life. These thoughts are best developed in the first movements by musical themes which denote the opposition of tragic reality to dreams of happiness as well as man's attempt to reconcile dream and reality. To Tchaikovsky, the contrast between tragedy and happiness was not an abstract concept, but the reality of life which he wanted to express in his music.

The Fourth Symphony (1877) is a Russian symphony and a European composition of Russian symphonic culture. Its style breaks with classical principles of the development of cadential, metrical, and motivic elements. Instead, thematic developments become successions of moods and imaginative representations in a unity of feelings and tonal medium. The symphony is a continuity of emotional drives and musical lyricism climaxed by the festive abandon of the finale.

The Fifth Symphony (1888) is a chronicle of the emotional strains and experiences of life, a work in which Tchaikovsky discloses his mastery of the language of musical timbres and intonations. Its melodies, as carriers of representations of mental life, reveal the characteristics of narrative and speech intonations, especially in the emotional excitement of the andante movement.

The finale of the symphony is a musical representation of social significance. It is a series of scenes of multitudes of people, of man immersed in the impersonal experiences of a mass of people, of man driven by the compelling action of a crowd.

The Sixth Symphony (1893) is Tchaikovsky's greatest achievement. In both its form and the intensity of emotional and dramatic developments, the symphony is unique in musical literature. As an instrumental drama, it does not represent clashes of characters and events. It is an account of conflicts and clashes of feelings, of the experiences of a personality amidst the struggles and contradictions of existence.

Tchaikovsky's sincere and emotional creativity never substituted dreams and fantasies for realistic personal experiences. The symphony is Tchaikovsky's confession, not an attempt to create a visionary, utopian reality. It is a statement of the tragedy and contradictions besetting Tchaikovsky who was suffocating in the social atmosphere of Russian reality.

The overpowering emotional effect of the symphony is due to the sincerity and expressiveness of the music in general as well as its melodies which evoke the emotional response of the listener. There is a spiritual relationship between the music and the harrowing loneliness described in some of Chekhov's stories and in Tolstoy's *The Death of Ivan Ilyich,* the latter of which affected Tchaikovsky very much.

Symphonic Themes

Tchaikovsky's symphonic themes are usually based on tones of major and minor scales. Chromatic tones, that is, additional sharps and flats, occur in developments and in culminating cadential passages, both of which are the extended harmonic points of rest. The themes are contrasted by various tempos and scales. The main theme in the Sixth Symphony is marked allegro and the subordinate is marked andante. As a rule, Tchaikovsky preferred traditional scale relationships. The Sixth Symphony is predominantly in the B minor tonality and the related D major tonality. The main theme in the Fourth Symphony, however, is in A flat major and the subordinate is in B major.

The main themes in the first movements of the last three symphonies are structurally and esthetically similar. In the Fourth and Sixth Symphonies, the main themes are tense, unstable, and impulsive, creating a feeling of aspiration mixed with fatalistic hopelessness. The main theme in the Fourth Symphony (Moderato con anima, in movimento di valse) exemplifies some of Tchaikovsky's favorite intonations: motivic fragments based on intervals of seconds representing an imagery of sadness and sorrow, enhanced by sequential contrasts of elation and depression. Although the motives are selective for thematic developments, this is inapplicable to this theme since emotionally and esthetically it is unified and indivisible. The main theme in the Fifth Symphony (Allegro con anima), derived from the introductory fate theme, is a quiet narrative theme played by a doleful clarinet and bassoon against a background of abrupt harmonies played by strings.

The main theme in the Sixth Symphony consists of two parts, the first an abrupt thrust of short motives, the second a descending melody which contrasts with the active upward motion of the first part. Like Beethoven, Tchaikovsky used an imbalance of tonic and dominant elements to create a feeling of indecision.

A descending melody along the steps of a minor scale was a favorite pattern of Tchaikovsky's, designed to express sorrow and frustration. The intensity of emotional effects is increased when the melody descends from an unstable tone, such as the dominant, or is embellished with ties and chromatic passing tones.

In the Sixth Symphony, when the main theme is repeated in the exposition, the first part is transformed into an ascending scalelike pattern which comes to rest on F sharp, the dominant tone of B minor, the basic tonality of the symphony. This produces a tense and restless emotional effect.

Main themes are contrasted by smoothly flowing subordinate themes of two types. The first type is a romantic melody, usually a theme of love, peaceful contemplation, or exaltation. Such is the subordinate theme in the first movement of the Sixth Symphony, which recalls romantic love themes of Liszt, Schumann, and Wagner.

The second type, represented by waltz patterns, occurs in the Fourth and Fifth Symphonies. A smoothly flowing, soaring waltz movement was one of Tchaikovsky's favorite stylistic devices. Through waltzes, Tchaikovsky created images of the ideal, the feminine, and the beautiful. In the Fifth Symphony, the waltzlike movement is intensified by ties and passing tones in a gradually ascending melody.

Main and subordinate themes in the expositions of first movements are presented in independent contrasting sections which are often in three-part forms with short developments in the middle part. Such are the main themes in the Fourth and Fifth Symphonies and the subordinate theme in the Sixth Symphony.

The contrast between main and subordinate themes is enhanced by linking episodes. Bridges in Beethoven's symphonies fulfill a dual function: they elaborate the main theme and lead to the subordinate theme. In Tchaikovsky's symphonies, the episode which follows the main theme is not the bridge leading to the subordinate theme. The actual transition to the subordinate theme is accomplished by a short passage which represses the excitement of the main theme and introduces the peaceful subordinate theme. Similar short passages occur in Schubert's *Unfinished Symphony*, in which they link various romantic episodes. Such short musical links bear out Tchaikovsky's comment on the Fourth Symphony: "Is it not better to turn aside from reality and sink into a dream?"

Fate Themes

A "theme of fate" was a third theme which Tchaikovsky added in his last symphonies. The introductions to the Fourth and Fifth Symphonies are constructed from fate themes, which have a symbolic significance. The gloomy fanfare in the introduction to the Fourth Symphony is probably a representation of a stern impersonal force or a trumpet call on the Day of Judgment. A similar fanfare introduces the fate theme in the Fifth Symphony. The funereal harmonization of the theme arouses associations of death and funeral services. A similar funereal fate theme is introduced in the development section in the first movement of the Sixth Symphony. In his comments on the Fourth Symphony, Tchaikovsky wrote:

The introduction is the thematic core of the symphony and, undoubtedly, its main thought—fate. It is the fatal power that prevents the attainment of happiness and jealously watches that well-being and peace would never be complete and without clouds. It is like the sword of Damocles which hangs over the head and poisons the soul. It is invincible, and no one can ever subdue it. One must submit and grieve in vain.[8]

The fate theme in the introduction to the Fourth Symphony is built on tones of the tonic chord. The same tonic tones are pivotal in the main theme of the first movement. The rhythmic pattern of the fate theme anticipates the rhythmic aspects of the main theme and its motives. The fate theme in the Fifth Symphony is a series of doleful intonations of intervals of seconds, thirds, a fifth and sixth descending step by step, evoking a feeling of sadness and sorrow. Somber timbres and harmonies in low registers intensify the melancholy intonational effect.

In the development section of the first movement of the Fourth Symphony, the peaceful subordinate theme and the stern fate theme are contrapuntally combined, as if Tchaikovsky's intention was to represent emotional confusion. The fate theme appears in the finale of the symphony.

In the Fifth Symphony, the fate theme appears in all movements. Whenever the optimistic tenor of the music reaches a culmination, the fate theme intrudes, thus destroying the dream and asserting a feeling of tragic reality. Examples of this effect occur at the beginning of the development in the first movement of the Fourth Symphony and in the recapitulation in the andante movement of the Fifth Symphony. The fate theme is not only used as a tragic contrast, but as a transformed theme which enhances the festive imagery. The fate theme in the Fifth Symphony changes from a minor to major tonality in the third movement and into a festive march in the finale.

The Sixth Symphony does not contain a unifying symbolic fate theme. Instead, Tchaikovsky used the Beethovenian cyclic method. The theme in the middle section of the allegro con grazia is related to the theme of the finale. Both themes are related to the descending melodic pattern in the main theme of the first movement. The three thematic variants are in the B minor tonality.

Thematic Development

Tchaikovsky is the successor to Beethoven's symphonic traditions. His preference for philosophic conceptions expressed in dynamic developments is similar in nature to Beethoven's esthetics. If Tchaikovsky had not continued Beethoven's symphonic traditions, his symphonies would have become lifeless symphonic schemes.

There are similarities in Tchaikovsky's and Beethoven's thematic developments. Both preferred dynamic treatment of symphonic forms, especially of the sonata form, development of expressive elements in a theme and dynamic intensification preceding cadential climaxes.

Emotional unity characterizes the themes in Tchaikovsky's last three symphonies. Although the themes are lyrical, they are, nevertheless, divisible into phrases and motives. The emotional unity of a long lyrical theme cannot be subjected to contrasting analyses and syntheses of classical developments. While a phrase or a motive can be subjected to logical developmental processes, the emotional unity of a lyrical theme is not divisible into emotional parts or fragments. Therefore, Tchaikovsky's symphonic developments chiefly represent the contrasts and comparisons of cumulative emotional states rather than the manipulation of thematic motives.

Beethoven's thematic developments are logical "dialectic" analyses and syntheses of thematic elements in classically constructed themes. Beethoven's themes possess a variety of emotional facets imbued with an imaginative musical conception, rather than a single emotional unity. His thematic developments become struggles and contrasts of emotional qualities, culminating in the victory of a definite emotional position.

In Tchaikovsky's symphonies, contrasts of extensive and unified emotional states dominate the tonal flow. The effect of such emotional states is intensified or weakened by means of dynamics, harmonic elements, and orchestral timbres (strings for lyricism, woodwinds for contemplation, and brass for power). Tchaikovsky's symphonic forms represent successions and contrasts of emotional cycles. The appearance of such emotionally unified themes and their inability to fit logical thematic developments characterizes the first movement of Schubert's *Unfinished Symphony*.

Beginning with the Fourth Symphony, Tchaikovsky's thematic developments disclose realistic intonational elements in which thoughts and imagery become sounds which displace the schematic features of classical developments. His developments are often intensifications of the intonations of main themes, rendered in accumulations of rising dynamic tonal waves. The climactic wave is reached before the return to the recapitulation. The final coda, as a second development, is the culminating point of the movement. Individual thematic groups sometimes become complete and independent constructions in three-part song forms or in dance forms.

Tchaikovsky unified movements in a symphony and episodes in a symphonic poem by the use of leading motives. Examples are the Fourth and Fifth Symphonies and the *Manfred Symphony* and *Francesca da Rimini*. The symphonic poem appealed to Tchaikovsky because, through the use of leading motives, it became an ideal medium for a musical synthesis in symphonic form.

Tchaikovsky preferred continuity of musical development. He favored complete musical-philosophical conceptions. Combinations of philosophical generalizations with concrete musical imagery relate his style to the romanticism of Liszt and Wagner.

While intensifying the excitement of thematic intonations, Tchaikovsky often contracts the theme by gradually narrowing its tonal range until the emotional possibilities of the theme seem to be exhausted. This is found in the first movement of the Fourth Symphony in which the theme is enriched by chromatic elements and is gradually contracted. The contractions eventually reduce the theme to repetitions of two thematic tones.

In the first movements of the Fourth and Sixth Symphonies, the development and recapitulation merge in the main theme. Only when the peaceful and songlike subordinate theme is heard is the listener aware of the entry of the recapitulation.

The development in the first movement of the Sixth Symphony is one of Tchaikovsky's greatest inspirations. Powerful orchestral fanfares destroy the tranquility of the preceding adagio movement and are followed by the first tonal wave. The opening motive of the main theme is developed in fugato style. Accumulations of dynamics lead to the first culminating point and are answered by a descending scale-like melody played by the brasses. These descending melodies are derived from the second part of the main theme.

A short chorale episode is followed by a new tonal wave whose rhythmically intensified rising sequences modulate through a series of tonalities. The chorale, played by three trombones and a trumpet against a repeated triplet figure on string basses, seems to remind the listener of inevitable death.

The gloomy timbres of brasses marking the coming of death have been used by Tchaikovsky in other compositions. Three trombones, a tremolo of strings, and a sustained tone on a bassoon represent the coming of death in *Francesca da Rimini*. Lensky's death in *Eugene Onegin* is announced by three trombones and a sustained tone on a bassoon. A chord played by French horns, trombones, and tuba against a background of pulsating double basses marks the death of the Countess in *Queen of Spades*.

The climax of the tonal wave following the chorale episode is met by a descending syncopated melody played by strings. A third wave merges with the recapitulation and leads to a new and more intense culminating point. A whirlwind of sequences, enhanced by a temporary disappearance of tonal focus, evokes associations of emotional confusion and a symbolic submission to elemental forces.

The culmination of the third wave is a sustained F sharp, the dominant tone of the B minor tonality. The tragic meaning of the passage is enhanced by exclamations of trombones answering strings and woodwinds. The questions and supplications in the development are answered by the tragic music of this section.

Middle Movements

Middle movements in the last three symphonies are esthetically similar to subordinate themes in the first movements. They evoke images of love, remembrance, and contemplation of nature. The forms of these movements are usually genres of songs and dances, especially of the waltz.

The andantino of the Fourth Symphony is a song in the form of a series of variations, and it is esthetically similar to the adagio of the First Symphony. The scherzo of the Fourth Symphony, enlivened by pizzicato of strings, is a lively sketch of Russian village life, a song, and a march of merry peasants.

The andante of the Fifth Symphony is one of Tchaikovsky's most beautiful compositions. The melody with its contrapuntal accompaniment is a song of love. Tchaikovsky used similar polyphonic accompaniments in the waltz of the Fifth Symphony.

The allegro con grazia of the Sixth Symphony is waltzlike in character. Its quintuple metrical pattern resembles similar patterns in Russian folk songs. The even and uneven measures enhance the smoothness and fluency of the waltzlike motion. The middle section of the movement is an expression of deep sadness characterized by sighs and complaints. Dynamic accentuations and unstable harmonies enhance the feeling of grief. Gradually, the graceful waltz theme slips into mournful meditations and the dancing images again absorb the listener's attention. Recollections of the middle section conclude the movement.

Finales

An outstanding feature in Tchaikovsky's first three symphonies is the contrast between the first and last movements. Esthetically, this contrast represents the submersion of the personal emotional state in the revelry and abandon of the finale. Whether this contrast is a typically Russian psychological characteristic is debatable.

The finales of the Fourth and Fifth Symphonies are festive musical canvases of popular celebrations, which contrast strongly with the subjectivity and introspection of preceding movements. Their thematic components are popular genres of Russian songs and dances.

There is, however, a difference in the treatment of the finales.

In the First and Third Symphonies, the finale is the last movement in the symphonic cycle. In the Fourth Symphony, the finale summarizes and dramatizes the emotional experiences delineated in the preceding movements. The variations in the finale of the Second Symphony are colorful transformations of the theme. The variations on the folk song, "In the Field Stood a Birch Tree," in the finale of the Fourth Symphony, change the lyrical intonations of the song from a rejoicing to a sorrowful mood. This type of alteration is found in many of Tchaikovsky's themes. The folk song helps bring out the subjective psychological ideas of the symphony.

The finale of the Fifth Symphony departs from the subjective lyricism in the preceding movements. The introduction of a transformed fate theme enhances the meaning of the finale as a representation of the emotional experience of a multitude of people. The fate theme unifies the finale with the esthetic content of the symphony, namely, the baring of the emotional strains and experiences of life.

The realization of the tragic idea in the Sixth Symphony and the desire to subordinate it to expressive musical elements led Tchaikovsky to substitute a mournful adagio for a festive finale, thus illustrating concentration of psychological motives.

The finale is a summary of images, representations, and lyrical intonations which have appeared in Tchaikovsky's symphonic and operatic compositions. The first theme is a succession of sighs, supplications, expressive melodic turns accompanied by unstable seventh chords and accumulations of poignant sequences.

The second theme consists of intonations of sighs and supplications accompanied by a pulsating figure played by French horns which suggest heart palpitations.

The recapitulation of the first theme enhances the intonations of sighs and supplications. Chromatic runs enhance the intonations. A short chorale section played by trombones and tuba, ending in pianissimo, seems to suggest a prayer. The gamut of human passions, emotions, hopes, desires, and aspirations have come to rest.

The tragedy of the finale is increased by the festive march in the preceding scherzo. The splendor of the march and the funereal weeping in the finale draw the curtain on the drama. The Sixth Symphony demonstrates the perfect unity of concept and its realization.

Operas

In his operas, Tchaikovsky did not follow commonly accepted operatic devices and formulas. He adapted the operatic experiences of Western composers to his musical needs and evolved an individual operatic style. Tchaikovsky created representations of people whose spiritual and emotional reactions were familiar to Russian audiences.

In an operatic libretto, he always demanded a dramatic situation found in everyday life and spiritual and emotional experiences of ordinary people. The plots of his operas generally present dramas and emotional conflicts from everyday life. Operatic scenes with psychological elements always engaged Tchaikovsky's attention. Examples are Tatyana's letter scene in *Eugene Onegin,* the duet of Mazeppa and Maria in *Mazeppa,* the meeting of Nastya and the Prince in *The Sorceress,* the love scene in *The Queen of Spades,* and the duet of Iolanthe and Voldemon in *Iolanthe.*

Tchaikovsky's operas are related to Western lyrical operatic genres. He loved the operas of Gounod and Massenet. He admired the realism of Bizet's *Carmen,* the simplicity of its plot, the concentration of action on a single dramatic element, the clarity of its melodic style, and the emotionalism of its music. Similar qualities characterize Tchaikovsky's operas.

There are no spectacular effects in Tchaikovsky's operas. Their plots concentrate on several culminating scenes with monologues and duets of a lyrical or psychological content. Like Gounod and Bizet, Tchaikovsky employed the forms of arias, popular songs, and dances.

The musical constructions of Tchaikovsky's operas often resemble the forms of his large symphonic compositions. They reveal a continuity and purposefulness of dynamic developments and a concreteness of imagery in scenes and episodes.

The orchestra in Tchaikovsky's operas is the vehicle for thematic development. Sometimes the orchestra carries out independent musical functions in addition to supporting the lyrical demands of vocal parts, such as Tatyana's letter scene. Although Tchaikovsky was influenced by Wagner's orchestral methods, he did not aim at overwhelming symphonic effects.[9] He created full, dynamic sonorities with limited orchestral means and preserved balanced relationships between vocal and orchestral parts.

The melodic elements in Tchaikovsky's operas have been influenced by the lyrical styles of Glinka and Dargomijsky. The realism and psychology of scenes and episodes in Tchaikovsky operas resemble similar occurrences in Dargomijsky's opera, *Rusalka*. Tchaikovsky further developed the traditions of the music drama, which Dargomijsky created in *Rusalka*.

Tchaikovsky created an individual type of Russian realistic opera, with tense dramatic situations and emotional experiences and with distinctly Russian musical idioms and intonations.

Eugene Onegin

The best features of Tchaikovsky's operatic style are found in *Eugene Onegin,* composed in 1877 and 1878. It was his first opera in which lyrical and psychological elements formed the basis of the plot. Tatyana is the prototype of all female characters in Tchaikovsky's operas. *Eugene Onegin* contains typical components of his operatic forms, melodies, and orchestral techniques.

Pushkin's novel in verse is a difficult subject for an operatic libretto because it does not contain elements of scenic action. Tchaikovsky realized the difficulties and referred to *Onegin* as a series of lyrical scenes.

The novel attracted Tchaikovsky because he wanted to concentrate on an intimate, but powerful drama. The mood and genre of Pushkin's novel agreed with Tchaikovsky's emotional life, hence the emotional spontaneity of the music. *Onegin* is not an opera of situations, but of moods which reveal the emotional life of the heroes. The lyrical scenes do not require large operatic ensembles. *Onegin* is dominated by intimate forms of the romance, aria, and duets which reveal introspections and reflections of the heroes.

The absence of forceful situations in the operatic plot is compensated by a variety of musical and scenic images. The libretto and music concentrate on the love of Tatyana, Onegin, and Lensky.

During Pushkin's life, many of his poems, stories, and verses appeared on stage in the form of ballet, melodrama, and vaudeville. Undoubtedly Pushkin saw some of these presentations, but his attitude toward the theatrical settings in not known. He probably did not object because he never voiced objections.

Pushkin gave his permission for the staging of *Tsygane* (Gypsies).

The composers Verstovsky and Vyelgorsky wrote the music for the song of Zemphira, the gypsy girl. Court circles in Petersburg did not approve the setting of *Tsygane* because of its suggestion of the ideas of freedom. The presentation was therefore discontinued.

The first theatrical presentation of *Eugene Onegin,* which took place in the late 1840's, was a makeshift affair. According to Tchaikovsky's own words, he was deeply moved from early years by the poetic image of Tatyana. In 1877, after completing the opera, Tchaikovsky declared that "Onegin would not be interesting in the theater." His skepticism was due to the difficulties of adapting accepted operatic forms to Pushkin's text.

Tchaikovsky defended his choice of *Onegin* for an opera by stressing the poetic characterizations in the novel, the spontaneity of the emotional experiences of the heroes, the drama of Lensky's death, and the romantic fate of Tatyana. He created an appealing image of Tatyana because he sympathized with her feelings. The intense sincerity of Tatyana's feelings vindicated the symphonic dimensions of the musical setting of her letter scene. After completing the letter scene, Tchaikovsky decided to compose the opera. The music was composed in a single outburst of inspiration because Tchaikovsky felt that Pushkin's realism agreed with his own experience and idealism.

Eugene Onegin, a Petersburg dandy and a habitué of society drawing rooms, inherits the estate of his uncle. He arrives at the village and establishes himself in the spacious home, formerly occupied by his uncle.

He meets Lensky, the landowner of a neighboring village. Lensky, a romantic poet educated in Germany and an ardent admirer of Kant, Schiller, and Goethe, is in love with Olga. Olga, a flighty girl whose portrait, in the words of Pushkin, can be found in any novel, is a daughter of the Larins, a neighboring family. Olga's sister Tatyana is a quiet and dreamy girl who prefers solitude, reveries, and contemplations of nature. Lensky invites Onegin to visit the Larins.

Tatyana falls in love with Onegin and writes a letter to him in which ·she confesses her love. Onegin receives the letter and meets Tatyana. He tells her that he appreciates her sincerity, but he does not care for married life; should he even fall in love with her, his affection will be temporary and life with him will only bring her unhappiness.

Some time later, Lensky and Onegin visit the Larins again to attend the celebration of Tatyana's birthday. At the dinner table, Onegin sits opposite Tatyana. He is annoyed by her confusion and anxiety. He decides to revenge himself on Lensky. After dinner, Onegin dances and flirts with Olga. When Lensky asks Olga for the next dance, she answers that she had already promised it to Onegin. Lensky is hurt and leaves the house to challenge Onegin to a duel with pistols. They fight the duel and Lensky is mortally wounded.

A few years have passed. Onegin has left his village to travel abroad. Olga has married a dashing uhlan. Tatyana and her mother are visiting relatives in Moscow who hope to arrange a suitable marriage for her. Tatyana meets a wealthy general (in the opera he is Prince Gremin) and marries him. They settle in Petersburg where the general's wealth allows them to entertain lavishly Petersburg society.

Meanwhile Onegin has returned from abroad and lives in Petersburg. He receives an invitation to a reception at the palace of the general, who happens to be a friend of his. Onegin sees a beautiful woman in the reception room and asks the general who she is. The general tells Onegin that she is his wife, the former Tatyana Larina, and introduces him to her.

Onegin is stunned by Tatyana's beauty, dignity, and bearing. Tatyana is cool, polite, and collected. She acknowledges that she knew Onegin many years ago.

Onegin realizes that he is hopelessly in love with Tatyana. Tatyana treats him with respect and aloofness. Onegin writes her a letter confessing his love, regrets for his past mistake when he did not realize he actually loved her, and asks Tatyana to grant him an interview.

They finally meet. Onegin sees Tatyana in the room crying. He falls on his knees and kisses her hands. Tatyana listens to his confession of love. She reminds him of the past and tells him he acted nobly in rejecting her love many years ago. Tatyana admits that she would have preferred life in the village to the pomp and glitter of Petersburg drawing rooms. She concludes with the words: "I love you (why deny it), but I belong to another, and I shall be forever faithful to him." Tatyana leaves the room. The sound of the general's spurs is heard in the distance. Onegin is stunned as if struck by thunder.

The main character in the opera is Tatyana. A short orchestral prelude introduces the audience to Tatyana's emotional world, a world of anxiety and languor. The meandering introductory melody with chromatic changes and unstable triplets is a musical representation of Tatyana's maiden dreams. This theme appears as a leading motive in the culminating episodes of the opera. It appears in the first scene in which Tatyana remarks, "How I love to be carried away somewhere to the accompaniment of these sounds," and also in the second scene before the appearance of Onegin.

The development of Tatyana's character reaches a climax in the letter scene. The dreamy and caressing music, at times excited and passionate, reveals the spiritual image of Tatyana.

The waltz in the sixth scene portrays Tatyana as a woman of the world whom Onegin sees at the reception at Gremin's palace. The seventh scene reveals the intimate spiritual world of Tatyana as Gremin's wife. Her remarks and the arioso "Onegin, at that time I was younger," do not possess the ardor of the music in the letter scene. Tatyana sings: "Happiness was so possible" in a sorrowful, descending melody typical of Tchaikovsky's tragic themes, against a sustained B flat tone in the orchestra which stresses the futility of the situation. Onegin's replies become passionate. His excitement affects Tatyana and her music reveals the struggle between proud restraint and suppressed love.

As in Pushkin's novel, the opera does not present Lensky as a versatile personality. The fifth scene, devoted to Lensky, is full of sorrow and its main feature is Lensky's aria:

> Where, o where are you the golden days of my spring?
> What will the coming day bring to me?

The elegiac character of the music reveals Lensky's romantic nature.

Unlike Pushkin, Tchaikovsky did not sympathize with Onegin's personality. In the first two scenes, the music stresses Onegin's studied restraint and politeness. His aria in the third scene, in which he asks Tatyana "You wrote to me?" is cold and calculated, compared with the emotional admission of Tatyana. Only in the last scenes does Onegin's part become emotional and only then is his melodic line impetuous, passionate, and reminiscent of the music in Tatyana's letter scene. In the finale, Onegin's music is excited and abrupt and it concludes with his despairing outburst, "Shame, anguish. . . ."

The background of the opera is a series of Pushkin's idyllic pictures of nineteenth century Russian life in provinces far removed from the glitter of society life in Petersburg and in Moscow.

Idyllic pictures of Russian life form the background of the romantic experiences of the heroes. Examples are the song of peasants in the first scene, the girls' chorus in the third scene, and the shepherd's music at the end of the second scene.

The second scene consists of Tatyana's long monologue, framed at the beginning and the end by dialogues with her nurse Fillipovna. The scene, a revelation of Tatyana's psychology and personality, was unprecedented in nineteenth century Russian opera. One could question whether Pushkin's heroine, living in a village mansion in a remote Russian province, could experience life as deeply as Tchaikovsky's Tatyana. There is no doubt, however, that the essence of Tatyana's character is perfectly revealed by Tchaikovsky's music in the letter scene.

Tatyana is disturbed and cannot fall asleep. She asks Fillipovna to describe her life as a serf girl. Fillipovna's story, a recitative in restrained narrative tones, is a realistic representation of the peasant psychology of Russian serfs. Fillipovna's recitative is followed by the excited musical theme of Tatyana's languor:

> Oh! nannie, nannie, I suffer, I languish,
> My dear one, I cry, I am ready to sob!

The melody, with its frequent modulations and sequence of motives, resembles Tatyana's theme in the opera's introduction. Tatyana confesses to Fillipovna:

> I am not sick, nannie . . . I am in love. . . .
> Leave me . . . leave me . . . I am in love.

The background of this dialogue is sustained by the musical motives of Tatyana and the nurse. An episode follows in D flat major. The ascending melody, characterized by restless rhythms, chromatic changes, unprepared retardations representing sighs, and a gradually accelerated tempo ends on A flat as a tonic tone accompanied by the rustle of syncopations on string instruments.

The letter scene is a succession of several musical episodes. The tonic cadence ending each episode is, at the same time, the beginning of a new episode in a new tonality. In the D flat major episode, Tatyana sings as she writes the letter:

> Imagine, I am here alone and no one understands me,
> My reason is strained and I think I shall die.

The sincerity of the melody discloses Tatyana's intimate thoughts. Her love is the result of a strong urge for a better life in which she would reveal her rich emotional qualities. The D flat episode ends on an enharmonic C sharp minor tonic, the beginning of a new episode which, in turn, modulates to a D minor episode.

The D minor episode, moderato assai quasi andante, accompanies most of the letter writing. The quiet melody consists of two parts: an ascending melody and a melody which descends by intervals of fourths and fifths. The music creates a mood of sadness.

When Tatyana comes to the word "another," the melody modulates into a colorful C major episode. The possibility of another man outrages Tatyana:

No, I would not give my heart to anyone else in the world.

The scene ends with a musical representation of dawn. An intense tremolo of string instruments on an ascending melody ends on a powerful C major chord. The early morning sun fills the room. At the same time, the C major chord, as an affirmative background to Tatyana's passion, represents the triumph of love.

Representations of daily life in various scenes are interwoven with emotional characterizations of persons and situations. The duet of Olga and Tatyana, "Did you hear?" is composed in the style of a Russian sentimental romance, popular at the beginning of the nineteenth century. The melody is interwoven with Tatyana's theme in the introduction of the opera, a representation of Tatyana's emotional world with its maiden reveries. The excited but melancholy mazurka in the scene of the ball at the Larins' mansion is the emotional background for the quarrel between Lensky and Onegin.

Tchaikovsky introduces realistic touches into the dance music at the Larins' ball. The provincial gentry is characterized by a simple waltz with a choral accompaniment. Some episodes in the waltz have descriptive touches. The G major episode both imitates a hunter's horn and represents replies of elderly landowners. The melodious B minor episode is a representation of the mothers and the playful episode in G major describes the young girls. For the verses of Monsieur Triquet, Tchaikovsky used the music of a song written by the French composer Beauplan; the song was popular in Russia at the beginning of the nineteenth century. To describe the ball at Gremin's palace, Tchaikovsky used a polonaise and an écossaise.

The forms of the lyrical scenes are free musical constructions which blend with dramatic situations and actions. Most of the scenes are complete musical constructions of the arioso-romance type. When Tchaikovsky uses recitatives, he joins statements, questions, and replies into melodic groups, unified by orchestral accompaniment. The dialogue between Lensky and Olga, for example, is heard against the background of the melody of Lensky's arioso; the quarrel between Lensky and Onegin takes place against the background of a mazurka.

The melodies in the various scenes are unified by a single thematic mood and without traditional schematic elements. The music in Tatyana's letter scene is an example. This principle of musical construction enabled Tchaikovsky to achieve a unity of dramatic and musical elements.

Eugene Onegin is a revelation, by symphonic means, of emotional tonal elements which characterize the heroes in Pushkin's novel. The lyrical scenes are constructed of musical links of psychologically interwoven monologues, dialogues, and ensembles, which make usual operatic procedures and recitatives superfluous. In all of Tchaikovsky's operas, arias, ariosos, duets, and ensembles emerge, not from external dramatic motivations, but from the uninterrupted dramatic flow of a psychological drama. This is especially characteristic of *Eugene Onegin*.

In its musical realism, *Eugene Onegin* equals the best accomplishments of Russian realistic literature in the nineteenth century. As a representation of psychological realism in the Russian musical theater, *Eugene Onegin* is equal in importance to similar achievements by the dramas of Ostrovsky and Chekhov, and by the dramatic presentations in Stanislavsky's Moscow Art Theater.

The Queen of Spades

Pushkin's story "The Queen of Spades" is a psychological study. The hero of the story is Herman, an army engineer of German descent.

During a card game at the home of Naroumov, an officer of the Horseguards, Herman hears Tomsky tell an anecdote about his eighty-year-old grandmother, Countess Anna Fedotovna. Some sixty years earlier, while living in Paris, the Countess lost a fortune playing cards with the Duke of Orléans. Her husband refused to honor the debt. The Countess asked the Count of Saint Germaine to loan her money to cover the loss. Instead, the Count of Saint Germaine told her a secret of three cards which, when played one at a time on three successive days, would win back her card losses. The Countess played the three cards and won.

Tomsky told his friends that his grandmother never divulged the three lucky cards to her sons, one of whom was Tomsky's father.

Herman watched the card game. He did not play because he could not afford to lose. He was impressed by Tomsky's tale and decided to ask the Countess to name the three cards. He began courting Liza, a poor companion of the Countess, and received an invitation to visit her one evening at around midnight.

Herman went to the Countess' house, but did not keep his appointment with Liza. Instead, he found the entrance to the bedroom of the Countess. He saw the Countess sitting in a chair. He left his hiding place, introduced himself to the Countess, and pleaded with her to help him by naming the three cards. The Countess, paralyzed with fear, did not answer him. Herman pointed a pistol at her and threatened to kill her unless she revealed the three cards. The Countess slumped forward dead.

A few days after the funeral, Herman awoke during the night. He heard someone open the door. He saw a woman, dressed in white, enter his room. The apparition approached his bed. It was the Countess. She named the three cards: a three, a seven, and an ace. She told Herman to play only one card on each successive day and then never play again. She forgave him for causing her death and asked him to marry Liza.

Herman went to a card game at the home of Chaplinsky. He placed forty-seven thousand rubles on a closed card at his side. The card was a three. Chaplinsky began to deal and turned over a three. Herman turned over his card and won. The next evening, he came to the game and placed ninety-four thousand rubles on a closed card at his side. The card was a seven. Chaplinsky began to deal and turned over a seven. Herman won. On the third evening, Herman came to the game and placed all his winnings on a card at his side. Chaplinsky began to deal and turned over an ace. "My ace wins," said Herman and turned over his card. "Your queen lost," said Chaplinsky. Herman looked at the card which was at his side: it was the queen of spades. He had made a mistake. He looked at the card and thought the queen winked and laughed at him. "Witch," screamed Herman. He lost his mind and was placed in an insane asylum.

It is probable that Pushkin was inspired to write the story by the prevailing fad for card playing in Russian social circles. Pushkin knew renowned gamblers who won and lost fortunes and who became victims of their fatal passion for cards. In those times, card playing often resulted in tragedy. A daring gambler, willing to risk a fortune on the turn of a card, was regarded as a hero and surrounded by an aura of glory.

Herman, a man with a Napoleonic visage and a consuming passion to get rich, was an unusual character in the Russian literature of Pushkin's time. Pushkin describes Herman's character and pesonality, but deliberately omits his work and family life.

Herman is a renegade, a mediocre person without moral values, a man totally consumed by a passion for financial gain. He is ruthless and is ready to commit a crime in order to achieve his purpose. Only once, when he saw the girl he deceived, "something like remorse echoed in his heart and became silent again." His action is calculated and he creates the impression of a scoundrel, but not of a lunatic. Only when he lost on the third card did Herman reveal his insanity.

With all his repelling characteristics, Herman wins the reader's sympathy. He deserves pity because he is doomed from the very beginning. He wants to gamble and be certain of winning. The more deliberate his calculation, the more he gives himself away to his criminal plans. Herman pretends to be in love with Liza, the oppressed ward of the Countess, and, if necessary, would be ready to become the lover of the loathsome Countess.

Tchaikovsky decided to compose an opera based on Pushkin's story when he realized the psychological and musical significance of the scene in the bedroom of the old Countess. This scene, representing the struggle of man and his fate, determines the subject of the opera. In the person of Herman, Tchaikovsky saw a lonely individual who struggled to conquer fate and to achieve financial independence. In the personality of Liza, Tchaikovsky did not see a woman of the world but a sincere and sensitive girl, an image he could easily portray in music.

In the epigraph to the story, Pushkin wrote: "A Queen of Spades denotes secret hostility." The meaning of this epigraph coincides with the themes of the Fourth, Fifth, and Sixth Symphonies, of *Romeo and Juliet,* and of *Manfred.* Tchaikovsky could not fail to see the significance of the thought and he used it to express his ideas of life and death in operatic form. Hence the contrasting images of Herman and the Countess. The struggle for the fullness of life, however, is incomplete without a pure and ideal love. Thus, the image of Liza emerges. She is motivated by strong impulses and knows only two solutions— love or death.

Tchaikovsky's libretto stresses the tragic tensions of Pushkin's personages. In the music drama, these tensions are increased to a degree at which they almost become palpable and real. The libretto made changes in Pushkin's story. The action takes place not during the reign of Alexander the First, but during the last years of Catherine the Second. In Pushkin's story, Herman uses Liza as a means of gaining access to the Countess; in the first half of the opera, Herman is madly in love with Liza; instead of being a poor companion of the Countess, Liza is her granddaughter. The opera reveals Herman as a man for whom gambling is a means of acquiring money which will enable him to secure the social standing to which he aspires.

In spite of these differences, Pushkin's Herman and Tchaikovsky's Herman represent the same personality. This is evident in the second half of the opera, especially in the fourth and fifth scenes. Herman's conversation with the Countess is practically a repetition of Pushkin's text. The card game in Chaplinsky's house follows Pushkin's description.

In the second half of the opera, the love element is not important. Herman no longer loves Liza. Since in Pushkin's story, Herman was never in love with Liza, the opera does not contradict the story. Only in the final scene of the opera, when Herman stabs himself after losing his bet on the third card, does he re-express his love for Liza and the love motive is heard in the orchestra. The apotheosis of love, the transfiguration of the dying hero in a moment of lucidity, was Tchaikovsky's concession to operatic tradition.

As a development of feelings and passions, the music drama overshadows the duality of impressions. The staging, costumes, and decorations represent the period of Catherine the Second; the thinking of the personages and the characteristics of the acting belong to a later historical period.

The action of the drama centers around Herman. All other persons, including Liza, are subordinated to Herman and enhance his characteristics.

The central point in the opera is the fourth scene. Based entirely on

Pushkin's text, it reveals the ruthlessness of Herman's fatal passion.

The curtain rises on the dimly lighted bedroom of the Countess. Against an intermittent pizzicato in the double basses, muted violins play a repeated triplet motive on C sharp. The absence of tonic cadences and the constant repetition of the triplet evoke a foreboding of danger. The fateful and ominous impression created by the continuous repetition of the motive is interrupted by a melodious phrase, the motive of Herman's suffering and anguish, played by woodwinds and, at times, by strings.

Herman enters the bedroom through a secret door. His recitative phrases, uttered against the sustained triplet motive, enhances the excitement and anticipation of danger:

Everything is as she (Liza) told me. . . . What now? Am I afraid? No. It is decided. . . . I will worm out the secret from the old woman! . . . And if there is no secret? Perhaps it is the raving of my sick soul?

Herman sees a portrait of the Countess on the wall:

Here she is, the Moscow Venus! Some secret power joins me to her. I feel that one of us will die. . . . I look at you and I hate you, but I cannot turn away my gaze. . . . I would like to run away, but I have not got the strength. . . . The searching look cannot tear itself away from the terrible, but wonderful, face! No . . . we cannot part without a fateful meeting.

The tempo of the music increases.

> Steps . . . someone is coming. . . . The die is cast. . . .

Herman conceals himself behind the curtain of the boudoir. The Countess and her chambermaids enter the room to the accompaniment of a scherzolike episode. The music enhances the sinister atmosphere. The girls sing a folklike melody to the following words:

> Our benefactress, did she go for a walk?
> Our dear one wants to go to sleep!
> She is tired. Was there someone else better?
> Perhaps someone younger, but not as beautiful as she.

Tchaikovsky is not as realistic as Pushkin, who makes Herman witness the "disgusting mysteries" of the Countess' toilet for the night. In the opera, the Countess enters the room wearing her nightgown and cap.

Liza enters the bedroom on her way to her room where she expects to meet Herman. The love motive, played by the orchestra, signifies that Liza still loves Herman, while he no longer loves her.

The grumblings of the Countess are successfully revealed by the music. To the accompaniment of a minuetlike rhythm, the Countess recalls her visit to Versailles where she danced with members of the French aristocracy. The monotonous rhythm of the music suggests the ghastliness of the past. For the old woman, the suggestion of gallantry in the music is a stimulus for recalling the past when she sang, danced, had lovers, and enjoyed life. Now she is tired of the world and only faint echoes and memories of the past are left. When the Countess mentions the name of the King, a short rustling pianissimo passage, like a gentle breeze, is heard in the orchestra.

Then a musical anachronism appears. The Countess sings an aria from Grétry's opera, *Richard the Lionhearted,* composed in 1784. Tchaikovsky changed the tonality of the aria from F minor to B minor, deleted the middle major episode, slowed the tempo, and re-wrote the accompaniment in order to evoke a subdued impression in consonance with the spirit of the scene.

In 1784, the Countess must have been seventy years old. It is doubtful that the King would have been interested in the singing of a seventy-year-old woman. Artistically, however, the melody is very appropriate in the bedroom scene. The charm of the melody is too emotional for an old woman who is marking her days. The scene reveals the spiritual bankruptcy of all who oppose Herman: the dead grapple with the living.

Herman's monologue discloses his spiritual world. He calls his soul "sick" and mentions the fatal power that binds him to the Countess. In Herman's request to name the three cards is the essence of his corrupted personality. He does not want to face life with its successes and failures. He does not want to struggle to make a living. He wants the power to control reality, but is afraid of the vicissitudes of life.

Herman and the Countess are hostile to each other, but are mutually attracted. Even in the first scene of the opera, when the Countess sees Herman for the first time, she asks: "What a terrible man! Where does he come from?" In the bedroom scene, Herman looks at the picture of the Countess and answers her: "I look at you and I hate you, but I cannot turn away my gaze. . . . We cannot part without a fateful meeting."

Herman's monologue is actually a dialogue in which the Countess' answers are given by the orchestra. In the scene, she does not say a word, although in Pushkin's story, in answer to Herman's importunities, she answers him: "It was a joke."

The expressive orchestral figures answer in the name of the Countess. The themes have a physiological aspect when they represent the heartbeats of the Countess and her deathly fear.

Herman prays, implores, and finally threatens the Countess. The music is a revelation of the power of relentless fate. The answer of the Countess is a firm refusal, played by the orchestra. Herman whips out a revolver: "Old witch," he says, "I shall compel you to answer me." The Countess' heartbeats are heard in the orchestra. Chords played pianissimo by trombones and trumpets represent the last gasp of the dying woman.

Herman does not notice her death. "Stop being foolish, do you want to name the three cards? Yes or no?" The French horn and the woodwinds become softer. There is a sudden orchestral exclamation by double basses and violoncellos, an E sharp in a low register, Herman suddenly realizes that the Countess is dead. "She is dead . . . and I did not discover the secret!"

The coda of the music (moderato assai) recalls the funereal coda in the first movement of Beethoven's Ninth Symphony. Liza enters the room. The character of the music changes, but the rhythm is the same. She realizes what had taken place. "Monster, murderer," she exclaims to Herman. This is her answer to Herman's passionate confession in the second scene of the opera when Herman addresses her with the words, "Beauty, Goddess, Angel . . ."

The bedroom scene contains the essence of the drama. The orchestra expresses the thoughts and feelings, the mournful fate of a perishing man and of his wretched victim.

Ballets

The nineteenth century ballet comprised two dance forms: a "classical" dance without outstanding expressive aspects and a characteristic dance with pictorial or representational features.

The main types of dances were lyrical adagios and rhythmical allegros. There were solo dances, called "variations," dance ensembles, called "Pas de deux," "Pas de trois" as well as other names and a "corps de ballet" danced by all participants. Individual dances representing various moods and characterizations were grouped in cycles. A cycle was concluded with a lively dance.

There were pantomimes with musical accompaniment. Musical episodes accompanied scenic actions, pictorial representations, mute monologues, or dialogues and gestures.

Of great importance was the dance-action, "Pas d'action." It was an eighteenth century genre with dance and pantomime. There also were "ballet variations," small solo dances without variations or modifications of previous dance forms. Ballet variations had nothing in common with musical variations. There were "adagio" and "allegro" dances. In classical ballets, the terms adagio and allegro indicated slow and fast dances, not musical conceptions of tempo. There were various speed indications in ballet adagios and allegros: andante, moderato, lento, vivo, presto.

Tchaikovsky introduced reforms into the classical ballet. For example, his ballet variations are sometimes accompanied by musical variations. He retained classical genres and forms, however, because they represented vital aspects of classical choreography. Tchaikovsky respected tradition in art and was critical of forced or artificial reforms, especially those of Wagner. Tchaikovsky respected artistic factors acceptable to the public, which have become meaningful and significant to masses of people. In his ballets, Tchaikovsky preserved all that was vital and capable of artistic and musical development.

The development of traditional forms of ballet music is conspicuous in Tchaikovsky's waltzes. Waltzes, waltzlike movements, and adagios are the main forms in his ballets. The stirring, exciting rhythm of his ballet waltzes evokes a soaring romantic feeling. Such are the two waltzes in Swan Lake, the A major in the first act and the A flat major in the third act. Such is the B minor waltz in the first act of Sleeping Beauty and the "Waltz of the Flowers" in Nutcracker. Waltzlike rhythms characterize various episodes in Tchaikovsky's ballets, for example, the "Pas de deux" of Aurora and Désiré in the finale of Sleeping Beauty and the dance of Aurora with a spindle in the same ballet.

Tchaikovsky's waltzes are charming, melodically captivating, and dramatically suggestive. Thematic divisions of the waltzes are lyrical expressions. Each section of the waltz movement enhances perception of melodic repetitions by new tonal means, orchestration, and development of thematic materials. These symphonic characteristics can be found in many of his waltzes. The "Waltz of the Flowers" is characterized by an increasing melodic expression of themes. The climax is reached in a B minor theme played by violoncellos in the middle section. Digression from original musical representations makes the return of original themes in the recapitulation very effective. New symphonic development and transformation of themes enhance the emotional content of the coda. In waltzes, Tchaikovsky invariably attains a continuity and effortlessness of melodic flow which, when combined with emotional tension, makes the waltz a miniature symphonic poem.

Tchaikovsky's "adagios" represent moments of lyrical concentration. In their expressive emotional content, the adagios resemble lyrical moments in his symphonies. Tchaikovsky's adagios reveal his marvelous melodic gift and ability to make his music meaningful. The adagio of the four princes in the first act of *Sleeping Beauty* consists of three statements of the main theme. Each repetition is a new and more intense expression of love for the Princess. Intermediate episodes enhance the anticipation of the return of the main theme.

In the adagio of Odette in the second act of *Swan Lake,* the recapitulated main theme, played by a violoncello, is accompanied by a new theme played by a violin. This enhances the lyrical expression of the music by transforming the melody into a duet of two instrumental timbres.

Another factor which distinguishes Tchaikovsky's ballets from traditional classical ballets is that the musical form of movements in classical ballets stresses structural aspects rather than dramatic factors. Unity of design and content in Tchaikovsky's ballets unfolds feelings which heighten the attention and response of an audience to developments on the stage.

In orchestrations of his ballets, Tchaikovsky used instrumental timbres so that the effect of an instrument would best reveal the dramatic or emotional significance of a situation or representation. In lyrical episodes, Tchaikovsky used violins, violoncellos, and oboes. In culminating points following lyrical episodes, Tchaikovsky used a heavier instrumental palette.

Dance characteristics in classical ballets were often of an impersonal nature, that is, without significant relationship to content. Tchaikovsky's music inspires choreographic interpretations of his ballets. His dances afford opportunities for representation of characters and acting persons. He evokes characteristics of an era and an environment, the old dances, (minuet, saraband, gavotte, and farandole), for example, in *Sleeping Beauty*. He creates a world of fantasy in the dancing of fairy Karobos' retinue and in the dancing of mechanical dolls in *Nutcracker*. Tchaikovsky brought concreteness, refinement, and accuracy of representations to the ballet, unknown in classical ballets. National dances, the trepak, for example, in *Nutcracker* are not stereotyped representations, but the incarnation of realistic elements. The cat, the kitten, and the finale of *Sleeping Beauty* are original representations in music. The variations of the fairies in Aurora's christening scene in *Sleeping Beauty,* the "Waltz of the Snowflakes" in *Nutcracker* are felt as realistic representations in music.

Pantomimes in Tchaikovsky's ballets are lyrical episodes which afford a multiplicity of interpretations. One can almost "feel" the "growing" Christmas Tree in Clara's vision in *Nutcracker*.

Tchaikovsky solved the problem of dance as action, "Pas d'Action." A creative choreographer finds in the music an inexhaustible source of dance interpretations and constructions.

Tchaikovsky's ballet reforms were made possible by the emotional and dynamic aspects of his music, by his ability to integrate musical lyricism with realistic elements, and by his understanding of the way to create scenic situations that will capture the attention of a theatrical audience.

Tchaikovsky's music is neither heroic nor epic. It is humane music which expresses love, compassion, truth, and justice. Hence the wholesome effect of his music and its growing popularity among listeners all over the world. It is an art which speaks of the beautiful and the good in life.

The appeal of Tchaikovsky's music to all people is a result of his ability, as a composer, to raise the commonplace and the ordinary in life to the level of dignity and self-respect.

Tchaikovsky speaks of the emotions of ordinary people, the joys, sorrows, tribulations, and struggles one encounters in daily existence. The road to happiness is not strewn with roses. Thus, Tchaikovsky's music speaks from heart to heart. It is a call to something better, more beautiful in life.

These elements were not new in Tchaikovsky's music. Tchaikovsky, through his art, was able to find simple, convincing musical means and intonations which have the articulation of speech. The hero in Tchaikovsky's music is the common man. Tchaikovsky was not a disciple of Schopenhauer's philosophy. He expressed the eternal problem in his music: the clash between dream and reality, the transitory quality of human experience, and the vanity of existence.

Tchaikovsky is a Russian national composer. The Russian character of Tchaikovsky's music is not something which can be described in words; it can only be heard and felt. Even his Romeo and Juliet, his Manfred, and Francesca are Russian in their emotional experiences. There is a great deal of Onegin in Romeo and a great deal of Tatyana in Juliet.

If Beethoven is the greatest dramatic symphonist, Tchaikovsky should be called the greatest lyrical symphonist. The lyricism of nineteenth century romanticism in music found its greatest exponent in Tchaikovsky, the symphonist.[10]

Tchaikovsky is a realist as well as a lyricist. One cannot listen to his music without experiencing an imaginative transformation. The imagery in his music becomes real and personal. One seems to recall something forgotten or slumbering in the subconscious. The recollection has become real, almost palpable to the imagination. The result is that a listener thinks: I have also experienced it; it is true.

Tchaikovsky's lyricism attains the quality of speech in the clarity of its imagery and representations. The most important factor in his style is the emotional unity of his symphonic conceptions which become enhanced by the concrete quality of intonational components and orchestral timbres.

A contemporary of Tolstoy, Dostoyevsky, and Chekhov, Tchaikovsky expressed the psychological insights of Tolstoy and Dostoyevsky and the humanity of Chekhov in his music. He also reflected the esthetic ideals of the great Russian realist painters Levitan, Repin, and Kramskoy.

"There is a deep connection between a concentration of creative powers in an individual with an aptitude for symphonic creativity, and the potentialities of a prevailing culture, or the explosive energy of a culture. The explosive situation in the Rhineland toward a seething France played a tremendous role during Beethoven's childhood and youth. The psychology of popular indignation and of passionate, emotional resistance of sensitive, receptive people to oppression and brute force influenced the accumulation of the tragic principle in Tchaikovsky's symphonic creativity. This did not result in revolutionary activity. Identical pressures and resistances could in one case bring forth Repin's painting *Barge Haulers on the Volga,* and in another case the burning anguish of Tchaikovsky's symphonies." [11]

CHAPTER 16

〜

Lyadov

ANATOLY LYADOV was devoted to the development of Russian realistic music. He carried on the traditions of Glinka and of the "powerful *kuchka*" and based his musical creativity on Russian life and folklore. A pupil and friend of Rimsky-Korsakov, Lyadov was friendly with Balakirev, Borodin, and Stasov. When Balakirev's circle was dissolved, Lyadov joined the "Belayev Circle."

Mitrofan Belayev, a wealthy timber merchant and a music lover,[1] became interested in Russian musical activities after a performance of Glazunov's First Symphony in 1882. He became acquainted with Rimsky-Korsakov at whose house often assembled composers of the older generation, including Borodin, and the younger generation of composers who were pupils of Rimsky-Korsakov. Balakirev and Cui rarely attended.

After the dissolution of Balakirev's circle, weekly Friday meetings, held at Rimsky-Korsakov's house, became a tradition of the musical life of Petersburg. Belayev often came to these meetings. In March, 1884, he organized a concert featuring Glazunov's compositions and founded the Russian Symphonic Concerts. In the same year, Belayev established the "Glinka Prize," a yearly financial award for a composition by a Russian composer. In 1885, he established a music publishing house to publish Russian music.

Rimsky-Korsakov, Glazunov, and Lyadov formed the music committee of the "Belayev Circle." The function of this committee was to select a Russian composition for publication and performance at the Russian Symphonic Concerts. Lyadov's activities as a musical editor made him an important member of the committee, especially after the death of Rimsky-Korsakov.

233

Lyadov loved and arranged Russian folk songs. He often used national melodies and intonations in his compositions. As a composer, Lyadov set for himself exacting esthetic standards. His music is without emotional outbursts and it combines sincere feeling with beauty and refinement of form. His esthetic principles were related to those of his favorite writers, Pushkin and Turgenev, and composers, Glinka and Tchaikovsky.

Lyadov's sensitive nature was hurt by the political reaction and suppression which characterized the reign of Tsar Alexander the Third. However, like many members of the intelligentsia, Lyadov realized the hopelessness of opposing Tsarist oppression.

In the 1880's, after reading Tolstoy's *Anna Karenina,* Lyadov accepted some of Tolstoy's teachings. During the summer, when he lived in the country, he would dress like a muzhik and join the peasants working in the fields.

Lyadov preferred solitude and avoided publicity. Like many of Chekhov's characters, he felt the monotony and drabness of his contemporary life. "The prose of life preys upon me slowly, but surely. It is my worst enemy." [2] Lyadov's aloofness from social life made him secretive and fearful of emotional manifestations. His reluctance to express opinions and pass judgments on Russian social and political realities was responsible for his inimical attitude toward the music of Mussorgsky, the poetry of Nekrasov, and the paintings of the *peredvizhniki.* Lyadov found inspiration and spiritual consolation in the fantasy of Russian folklore and in nature. He is one of the greatest masters of pictorial representations in Russian music.

Lyadov's symphonic fairy tale miniatures and orchestral arrangements of folk songs are among his best compositions. *Baba Yaga, Kikimora, Enchanted Lake* and *Eight Russian Folk Songs* are musical settings of Russian folklore.

Russian *skazkas* (fairy tales) and popular superstitions form the bases of the symphonic pictures, *Baba Yaga* and *Kikimora.* Baba Yaga is the old witch in Russian folklore. She lives in the forest, in a cottage standing on a chicken leg. She rides in a mortar driven by a pestle, and with a broom she covers up the traces. Kikimora is a supernatural creature, a *domovoy* (a creature living in every house) endowed with the shape of a woman.

Lyadov loved Russian fairy tales. "Give me a *skazka,* a dragon, a *leshy* (a supernatural being having a man's shape and living in a forest) and I shall be happy," wrote Lyadov in one of his letters (1907).

Russian poets, writers, artists, and musicians loved *skazkas*. Maxim Gorky wrote that *skazkas* gave him hope of a new and better life ruled by a free and fearless power. "As I grew older I understood the distinction between the *skazka* and the boring life of greedy, grasping, envious people." [3]

Russian fairy tales usually reveal a striving for goodness and victory over evil forces. *Skazkas* and *bylinas* (Russian epic songs about heroes) are national realistic reflections on the truth of life. This is how Lyadov understood Russian fairy tale imagery.

Lyadov's *Baba Yaga* and *Kikimora* are programmatic, with short quotations explaining the plot of the composition. *The Enchanted Lake* has no programmatic notes; it is a musical representation of a Russian landscape full of magic sound effects and emotional exhilarations. The symphonic miniatures, "Eight Russian Folk Songs," are superb orchestral arrangements of Russian songs.

Lyadov was a composer of small miniatures, realizations of a poetic image. In his recollections of Lyadov, Asafiev states that Lyadov did not believe he had an inner justification of the music of a long, extended composition. To his friends Lyadov observed: "After listening to a small composition you will leave without blaming the author and you will experience a desire to come to the next concert." [4]

Lyadov's programmatic works are free improvisatory compositions, avoiding standard classical designs. Instead of long, emotional, dramatic symphonic developments, these works follow Lyadov's imaginative impulse which never fails to arouse interest and tension.

Lyadov carried on the tradition of Balakirev's circle. As a musical landscape painting, *The Enchanted Lake* perpetuates similar traditions in the operatic and symphonic music of Glinka and Rimsky-Korsakov. Prototypes of *Baba Yaga* and *Kikimora* are in Glinka's musical description of the realms of Chernomor and Naina in *Ruslan and Ludmila*, in Rimsky-Korsakov's *Sadko*, *The Tale of Tsar Saltan*, and *Skazka*, in Mussorgsky's *Night on Bald Mountain* and *The Cottage on Chicken Legs* and in Dargomijsky's *Baba Yaga*.

Among the many fairytales about Baba Yaga, Lyadov chose the story of Vasilisa the Beautiful. A merchant had a beautiful daughter, Vasilisa, whose mother had died when Vasilisa was a child. As the mother was dying, she blessed Vasilisa and gave her a magic doll which would advise the child in time of need or misfortune. Soon after, Vasilisa's father married a widow who had two daughters. The evil stepmother hated Vasilisa and decided to exhaust Vasilisa with backbreaking work. However, the doll helped Vasilisa.

One dreary day in the fall, the candle went out in the house. The stepmother sent Vasilisa to Baba Yaga to get a fire to light the candle. Baba Yaga detained Vasilisa, and every day the old witch gave Vasilisa more work. When Baba Yaga realized that Vasilisa was a blessed daughter, she let her return home, giving her a skull with luminous eyes. Vasilisa returned home and the same night, the luminous eyes in the skull burned the stepmother and her two daughters. Vasilisa went to live with her grandmother and helped her weave linen cloth and sew shirts. Vasilisa's handwork was so beautifully done that the grandmother presented it to the Tsar. The Tsar desired to see Vasilisa. He was enraptured with her beauty and married her.

For his symphonic miniature, Lyadov took the part where Vasilisa went to see Baba Yaga. Baba Yaga's cottage was surrounded with a fence of human bones. On the fence were stuck human skulls with luminous eye sockets. The doors of the gate were human legs. Instead of a bolt, there were human hands. Instead of a lock, there was a mouth with sharp teeth.

At daybreak, Baba Yaga looked through the window. The sun rose and the luminous eye sockets were dimmed. Baba Yaga left the cottage and whistled. Suddenly a mortar, a pestle, and a broom appeared. Baba Yaga sat in the mortar and flew away driven by the pestle, covering up her traces with the broom.

For the program of the composition, Lyadov took Baba Yaga's swift flight in the dense, dark forest, accompanied by the sound of splitting trees, mysterious noises and rustlings, and crackling of dry leaves.

The composition opens with a shrill whistling sound of piccolos, flutes, oboes, and clarinets, followed by three whole-tone scale fragments with an ascending chromatic series of augmented triads. Baba Yaga's gloomy and mysterious realm has awakened.

Baba Yaga is represented by a diatonic melody played by a bassoon, accompanied by the rustling rumble of kettledrums and sustained by a French horn pedal tone and low strings.

Lyadov uses chromatic elements to represent the world of fantasy and diatonic components to express the real world. Chromatic threads permeate the harmonic and intonational design of the tonal texture within the complete symphonic picture. Chromaticisms represent the initial swayings of Baba Yaga's mortar, the flight, the driving pestle, and the sweeping broom.

The middle of the composition is a representation of Baba Yaga's swift flight in the forest. Rustling sounds in the music represent the crackling of dry leaves; harsh sounds represent the splitting trees. The final coda, played by the entire orchestra, gradually dissolves in diminishing dynamics. The end is a shrill, whistling sound of woodwinds. Baba Yaga has flown over the forest like a storm and has disappeared.

Kikimora

The plot of *Kikimora* is based on superstitions in Russian mythology. Every month in the calendar has some wonders connected with it. When the rooks arrive in March, Kikimoras (house spirits) become docile and incantations will drive them out of the house. In Russian mythology, Kikimoras are evil gods of the underworld. They create trouble, destruction, and evil. As a child, a Kikimora is carried away by devils to the other side of the world where it lives in the abode of a magician in the Stone Mountains. The magician feeds Kikimora with dew. He washes Kikimora in a steam bath with a silken besom. Kikimora is lulled to sleep by a cat which tells stories about the human race. From evening till midnight, the magician arranges games at which Kikimora is entertained, such as blind billy-goat and blind man's buff. From midnight till daybreak, Kikimora is rocked to sleep in a crystal cradle.

After seven years, Kikimora has grown up. It is thin and black and has a thin voice. Its body, which cannot be distinguished from a straw, will not age for a hundred years. During summer and winter, it walks around without clothes.

Kikimora knows all cities, suburbs, and villages. It knows everything about humans and their sins. It is friendly with witches and magicians and it plots evil for the human race. Unseen, Kikimora enters a peasant's cottage and takes up its abode behind the stove. It clanks and clatters from morning till night and whistles and hisses from evening till midnight. It weaves hemp and twists silk from midnight till dawn. It torments the peasant and every other human being.

For the plot of the composition, Lyadov chose the part of the story describing Kikimora's life with the magician in the Stone Mountains and the crystal cradle. Unlike *Baba Yaga, Kikimora* contains several themes corresponding to the different representations in the story. Lyadov achieved a remarkable articulate quality in the musical representation of fairy tale heroes and their actions. It is therefore appropriate that Lyadov called *Baba Yaga* and *Kikimora* "symphonic pictures."

The music of *Kikimora* opens with a slow introduction followed by a fast scherzo. The tense, mysterious introduction transports the listener's imagination into the magic realm of the magician in the Stone Mountains. A lullaby melody played by an English horn accompanied by strings is a musical representation of the cat rocking Kikimora's cradle. The introduction ends with the theme of the crystal cradle played by the ringing, bell-like tones of a celesta. The world of fantasy is represented by chromatic elements: the magician by augmented triads, and Kikimora by a diminished triad, a tritone, whose weird sound represents evil spirits. The lullaby is a diatonic melody.

The second part of the symphonic picture is a fast scherzo describing a grown-up Kikimora, clattering from morning till evening, whistling and hissing from evening till midnight. The commotion in the music seems to represent Kikimora's slyness, thundering bursts of laughter and clowning. It is not an emotional composition, but rather music whose timbre intonations suggest Kikimora's pranks to the listener.

The Enchanted Lake

"I know such a lake," Lyadov used to tell, "a simple Russian lake in a forest, beautiful in its peaceful surroundings. One had to feel the changes that take place in color, light, shadows and air, in the constantly changing silence, and in the apparent immobility. I began to look for a description of such a lake in Russian fairy tales. But Russian fairy tales do not stop the story in order to describe natural phenomena which I needed for the music. I wanted a description where everything came to a standstill, then suddenly something rustles, a breeze glides over. . . ."

Lyadov called *Enchanted Lake* "a fairy tale picture." It is not a sketch of a lake. It is an abstract, mysterious enchanted lake in which Lyadov's imagination sensed or perceived unusual visions. It is not a fairy tale narrative because the program contains neither plot nor action. It seems to represent a conception favorable to the birth of a fairy tale.

The score of the music is one of the most peaceful musical representations in Russian musical literature. It does not contain onomatopoeia. Lyadov expressed in music what he heard and saw in his imagination. In the orchestration and harmonic texture, Lyadov created a musical perception of light and shade in the air as well as the mirrorlike surface of a lake, characteristic of such a fairy tale picture as *Enchanted Lake*.

The composition's melodic structure consists of short, fleeting melodic intonations and unstable harmonies. A sudden breeze has stirred the mirrorlike surface of the lake, which breaks up in a series of ripples. Fleeting clouds suddenly obscure the sun and colorful lights and shadows pass over the lake. Such occurrences are represented by an undulating theme played by the violoncellos or by skipping melodies in the woodwinds. The music seems to vibrate. The flutters, trills, and tremolos of strings, kettledrums, and other instruments evoke an image of the rippling surface of a lake or of something spiritual and insubstantial.

Lyadov's intention was to represent nature alone in *Enchanted Lake*. "How pictorial it is, clean, with stars and mystery in its depth! And what is more important, without people with their wishes and complaints—only dead nature, cold, evil, fabulous, as in a fairy tale." What he created, however, is a representation of living nature perceived by human feelings and emotions.

The orchestration of *Enchanted Lake* is reminiscent, at times, of devices Rimsky-Korsakov used to describe the sea in *Scheherazade* and *Sadko* or the lake in *The Invisible City of Kitezh*. Among these devices is the oscillating movement of harmonies in the strings played against sustained tones in the brass and woodwinds. To increase the effect of orchestral transparency, Lyadov often uses muted strings alone. Strings accompanied by a harp, by the individual timbres of woodwinds and by a celesta, create a sensation of airiness and vagueness of outline, color and shade. Thus, one senses the misty appearance of the lake seen in Lyadov's contemplation.

Although Lyadov becomes impressionistic in the *Enchanted Lake,* the national character and feeling of the music make Lyadov's impressionism a unique Russian phenomenon. In Lyadov's words:

"Russian in Russian music is something that makes it Russian for the ear, and that cannot be expressed in words. It is something that can be transmitted only by the means of music, and that represents the soul of the music."

Eight Russian Folk Songs

The *Eight Russian Folk Songs* are an arrangement of Russian folk songs in the form of a symphonic suite. The songs represent the most popular genres in Russian folklore. The variety of orchestral arrangements is programmatically and esthetically justified. For example, the pizzicato effects, in the arrangement of the "Dance Song," imitate a Russian balalaika; the arrangement of the "Drawling Song" has a pattern of supporting melodies reminiscent of improvised peasant choral polyphony. Every song has its distinct orchestration, setting it off from the other songs.

The cycle can be divided into three groups, each containing one slow and one or two fast songs. Contrasts of slow and fast songs are common in Russian folklore. Glinka contrasted a fast and slow song in *Kamarinskaya*. The three groups in Lyadov's cycle are as follows: (1) A "Spiritual Song" (moderato) and a "Christmas Carol" (allegretto); (2) a "Drawling Song" (andante), a "Comic Song" (allegretto) and a "Bylina About Birds" (allegretto); (3) a "Lullaby" (moderato), a "Dance Song" (allegro) and a "Khorovod Song" (vivo). Lyadov's variational development of the songs is characteristic of Russian national music.

Spiritual Song

The "Spiritual Song," narrative in character, is a musical picture of wandering blind singers. Their mournful lamentation, represented by the nasal timbre of an English horn, resembles tunes in Russian church music. Spiritual songs in Russian folklore also resemble *bylinas* and other lyrical epical songs. Their content is often a mixture of Russian Christian orthodoxy and pagan antiquity.

Wandering blind singers appear in Mussorgsky's *Boris Godunov* and Rimsky-Korsakov's *Sadko*. Lyadov varies his instrumentation in the "Spiritual Song." The melody is picked up, successively, by different instrumental groups and is enriched by imitative devices.

"Kolyada" (*Christmas Carol*)

Celebrations of the Christmas season included fortune-telling, mummery, dancing, and singing. The season's celebration would be climaxed by mummers, who would visit villagers, sing carols, honor the host with songs, congratulate his family and wish him prosperity, a good harvest, and an increase of cattle. Villagers would thank the singers with presents of food and sweetmeats.

There were two types of Russian carols: the serious and the comic. Lyadov chose a comic carol. His symphonic miniature stresses the conversational, question and answer character of the song by contrasting orchestral groups.

Drawling Song

A Russian drawling song is rich in spiritual clothing. It is a slow, smoothly flowing melody whose intonations and rhythms express Russian nature, life, and feelings. Drawling songs are usually sung by a chorus. The musical texture is polyphonically enriched by means of interwoven melodies, improvised by the singers. In Lyadov's arrangement, the melody is played by violoncellos whose timbre is ideally suited to the song's emotional quality. Various instrumental groups play the interwoven melodic strands. The lyrical melody expresses thoughtful moods, wistfulness, and sorrow.

Comic Song

I Danced with a Mosquito.

This song describes a hot summer evening and the open-hearted gaiety and humor of villagers. The dance character of the song is enhanced by a musical imitation of the incessant drone of a mosquito. Clear harmonies on first beats also accent the song's dance style. The gradually accelerated movement of a supporting melody played by violins is transformed into a continuous drone by the entire string group. The orchestration does not include double basses and violoncellos. The main theme, played by a piccolo or flute, is accompanied by the staccato of woodwinds joined by tremolos of violins and altos.

Bylinas About Birds

Bylinas are Russian epic songs about national heroes, animals, and birds. The melodic structure of a *bylina* corresponds to the smooth narrative exposition of the words. Bylinas usually begin with a prologue initiated by a singer and sung in the style of a declamatory recitative. The main tune of the "Bylina About Birds" consists of three tones, A, B flat and G. The phrase is repeated variationally and the final tone of the phrase is the beginning of the next repetition.

Orchestral instruments imitate the twitter and chirp of birds. The orchestration, including unstable harmonies and chromatically interwoven tunes, evokes an imagery of far-away fairyland. The symphonic picture ends on a dominant tone, as if the narrative has suddenly ended with a question on one of the epic aspects of the story.

Lullaby

The "Lullaby" is a simple melody which evokes the imagery of a peaceful twilight and a mother singing her baby to sleep. The song is played by strings (con sordini). The violins incessantly repeat a simple two-measured phrase accompanied by "swaying" altos. Passing chromatic tones lend an intense emotionality to the musical texture. The melody becomes slow towards the end and dissolves into a pianissimo: the child has fallen asleep.

Dance Song

The "Dance Song" is a lively and graceful peasant dance. The playful melody is repeated with different figurations which give the song a purely instrumental character. While a flute plays these figurations, the pizzicato on the strings imitates balalaika effects. A small drum (tamburino) supplies the rhythmic accentuation of the dance.

Khorovode

Russian *khorovodes* (round dances) are danced at mass celebrations. The *khorovode* is an antiphonal dance, consisting of a dialogue of two parts. The participants are divided into male and female groups. The melody in Lyadov's arrangement consists of two unequal contrasting parts. The first part, played by the full orchestra, is performed by the men who invite the participants to dance. The second part, a lively melody played by pizzicato strings and staccato woodwinds, is danced by the girls who dash with light steps over the grass and show off the finery of their holiday dresses.

CHAPTER 17

Taneyev

TANEYEV, THE FOUNDER of the Russian school of music theory, was a pianist, conductor, teacher, and composer. As a composer, Taneyev continued the traditions of realism of Russian classical music. As a teacher, he sought to formulate objective rules and laws of composition and to develop scientific foundations of musical disciplines. His contribution to music theory is a study of imitative counterpoint.

Taneyev studied with Tchaikovsky at the Moscow Conservatory. Although he admired Tchaikovsky's music, he developed his own creative principles which he maintained throughout his life. Taneyev regarded music as a means of expressing philosophical ideas. He rejected modern music and its esthetics.

Sergei Taneyev was born on November 13, 1856, in Vladimir, a city in central Russia. His parents were cultured people devoted to music.

At the age of five, Taneyev began to take piano lessons with a private teacher. In 1865, his family moved to Moscow. In 1866, he enrolled in the Moscow Conservatory, where his piano teacher was Edward Langer. In 1871, Taneyev studied piano with Nicholas Rubinstein and theory of music with Tchaikovsky. In 1875, Taneyev was graduated with a gold medal from the schools of piano and composition. In 1878, when Tchaikovsky left the Conservatory, Taneyev was appointed in his place to teach harmony. Later he also taught piano and composition.

As a pianist, Taneyev was known for his interpretations of Bach, Mozart, and Beethoven. He introduced Tchaikovsky's piano compositions to the Russian public.

Taneyev attended Moscow University for a short time and was acquainted with outstanding Russian writers, including Turgenev and Saltykov-Shchedrin. During his travels in Western Europe in 1876 and 1877, he met Zola, Saint-Saëns, and Franck.

Taneyev was considered the leader of the Moscow school of composition, and exercised a strong influence on Russian musical culture in the latter part of the nineteenth century. He died on June 6, 1915.

Taneyev's views on music were summarized in the introduction to his book, *Podvizhnoy kontrapunkt strogavo pisma* [Imitative Counterpoint]. "Our tonal system is being transformed into a new system which destroys tonality, and substitutes chromatic harmony for diatonic. Destruction of tonality results in a decline of musical forms. The stability of a single tonality gives way to quickly changing modulations. Contrasting harmonies, a gradual or sudden transition to a new tonality, and a prepared return to the main tonality disclose salient characteristics of a composition. These elements, which help a listener understand musical form, are gradually disappearing from contemporary music. The result is the fragmentation of musical form and the decadence of the entire composition. A firmly cohesive composition has become rare. Large compositions are chaotic masses of mechanically connected parts which could be rearranged at will." [1]

As a pianist and conductor, Taneyev preferred Russian and Western classical music. Under his direction, students of the Moscow Conservatory gave the first performance of Tchaikovsky's opera *Eugene Onegin*. His productions of Beethoven's *Fidelio* and of Mozart's *Don Juan* and *Magic Flute* were outstanding events in Moscow.

As a teacher of music theory, Taneyev influenced his pupils Rachmaninov, Scriabin, and Metner. The polyphonic interweaves in the music of Rachmaninov and Metner are a direct result of Taneyev's teaching. Scriabin, however, broke away from Taneyev's influence.

Taneyev and Tchaikovsky had different views on the function of music theory in composition. Tchaikovsky attached importance to spontaneity in musical creativity. Taneyev, on the other hand, believed that musical creativity should be based on preliminary theoretical analysis and preparation of thematic materials. He thought that Russian composers should master the accumulated experience of Western musical culture and technique and adapt it to the needs of Russian music.

The implementation of these ideas occupied the greater part of Taneyev's life. He not only analyzed the achievements of great Western composers, but also applied the results of his research in the composition of his music.

In a letter to Tchaikovsky (June 21, 1891), Taneyev wrote about his method of composing the dramatic trilogy *Oresteia* (Agamemnon, Choephorai, and Euminides): "I spend a great deal of time on preparatory work, and less time on final composition. Some items I have not finished within the last few years. Important themes which are repeated in the opera, are used by me objectively, without any reference to a particular situation, for studies in counterpoint. Gradually, from this chaos of thoughts and sketches something orderly and definite begins to emerge. Everything extraneous is discarded. That which is unquestionably suitable remains." [2]

Taneyev's rationalism was the result of his conviction that the truth and moral integrity of music were synonymous with its objectivity and purpose. He looked upon classical concepts of composition as perfect examples of a technique of composition divorced from everything casual and extraneous.

Taneyev's compositions reveal his mastery of the classical technique of composition. However, it is interesting to note that Taneyev's intellectual approach to composition deprived his music of the emotionalism which characterizes the music of his teacher, Tchaikovsky. Taneyev's music did not reflect social problems of his time. His preoccupation with moral, spiritual, and philosophical ideas separated him from actual Russian social realities.

Taneyev composed symphonies, string quartets and quintets, a piano quintet, songs, choral compositions, and an opera. The opera is the musical trilogy *Oresteia* (1887–1894) based on Aeschylus' tragedy. Taneyev shifts the stress from human passions to the abstract idea of reason and justice opposing fate. In the end reason and justice triumph.

In the cantata *Johannes Damascenus* (1885), Tanayev reflects on human life, fate, and grief of parting with life. The cantata *After Reading the Psalm* (1914) embodies Taneyev's ethical and philosophical ideas. The concluding words of the cantata express Taneyev's credo:

> I want a heart purer than gold
> And a will strong in labor,
> I want a brother who loves his brother,
> I desire the truth of justice.

CHAPTER 18

Glazunov

ALEXANDER GLAZUNOV continued the national musical traditions of his teachers Balakirev and Rimsky-Korsakov and became an accomplished composer of classical examples of Russian symphonic music. The main elements of Glazunov's style were derived from Glinka's nationalism, Borodin's epic heroism, Rimsky-Korsakov's descriptive tone painting, and Tchaikovsky's lyricism. Glazunov's music reflects Russian life, nature, folklore, and history. Elements of Russian national melodies, rhythms, and polymelody of folk songs make his music unmistakably Russian. Although Glazunov often used authentic Russian themes in his compositions, he usually transformed them into original thematic constructions.

Glazunov was born on July 29, 1865, in Petersburg. His father was a bookdealer; his mother was musically inclined and played the piano.

At the age of ten, Glazunov started to take piano lessons with a private teacher. His favorite composers were Glinka and Chopin. In 1878, Glazunov enrolled in the Real School and discontinued his piano lessons. In 1879, he became acquainted with Balakirev, and the friendship with Balakirev influenced Glazunov to devote himself to music.

Under the guidance of Balakirev, Glazunov composed music and studied classical musical literature. Balakirev advised Glazunov to study music theory with Rimsky-Korsakov. During the two years that he studied with Rimsky-Korsakov, Glazunov composed a string quartet and a symphony.

In 1882, the orchestra of the Free Music School under the direction of Balakirev performed Glazunov's symphony in E flat major. The symphony of the sixteen-year-old Glazunov met with success. In his review of the symphony, Cui greeted it as a work of a remarkably talented composer. During these years Glazunov became acquainted with Tchaikovsky, Stasov, and the composers of the New Russian School. When the Balakirev circle was dissolved, Glazunov joined Belayev's group.

Glazunov's compositions were published by Belayev and became known in Western Europe. In 1899, he was appointed professor of instrumentation at the Petersburg Conservatory; and in 1905, he was elected by the faculty as director of the Conservatory. Glazunov died in Paris on March 21, 1936.

Glazunov's music is optimistic. He preferred simple imageries and avoided psychological representations. His music seems to lack spontaneity of expressive power which characterizes the music of Borodin, Mussorgsky, and Tchaikovsky. Glazunov was aloof from contemporary social problems. Hence, his preference in his music for serenity and objective contemplation "from a distance."

"The main characteristic of Glazunov's compositions," wrote Stasov, "is the incredibly large sweep, power, inspiration, cheerful mood, marvelous beauty, rich imagination, sometimes humour, sentimentality, passion, and always the amazing clarity and freedom of form." [1]

Glazunov preferred to compose instrumental music. His principal compositions include eight symphonies, overtures, cantatas, string quartets, suites, piano music, symphonic poems, a violin concerto, two piano concertos, and ballets. He was not interested in opera, and his vocal compositions are few.

Glazunov's symphonies are not musical confessions in the manner of Tchaikovsky. They are objective representations of reality in well-constructed and balanced musical forms. His musical themes lack tense, dramatic, and dynamic elements. His themes are usually characterized by well-defined melodic turns and intonations which Glazunov subjects to variations and transformations.

Glazunov often uses polyphonic devices, including imitations and various combinations of thematic elements. He uses polyphony as a means of thematic development and continuity of tonal flow, and of structural unity. In his instrumentation, Glazunov avoids sharp orchestral contrasts. He prefers smooth changes of timbres and sonorities. Thereby he achieves a variety of color effects and subtle nuances of dynamics.

Glazunov's preference for rational musical forms could be traced to Taneyev's influence. The epic characteristics, smoothness, and unhurried development of Glazunov's musical conceptions are similar to Borodin's. Although the philosophical conceptions of Tchaikovsky's symphonic style were foreign to Glazunov's world outlook, the dramatic elements of Tchaikovsky's thematic developments influenced his mature style.

As a ballet composer, Glazunov ranks next to Tchaikovsky as one of the foremost Russian ballet composers. Glazunov's most successful ballet, *Raymonda* (1898), is a magnificent spectacle characterized by colorful orchestral effects, appropriateness of music to scenic requirements, and effective dramatic situations. However, despite the grandeur of its symphonic conceptions, *Raymonda* is not as effective emotionally and psychologically as Tchaikovsky's ballets. Glazunov's principles of musical development were different from Tchaikovsky's. Intensity of feeling and action and of dramatic conflicts were foreign to Glazunov's style. *Raymonda* is a series of musical suites of various dances in symphonically developed choreographic scenes. It is a magnificent spectacle of pictures and episodes with colorful music and a variety of orchestral effects.

The libretto of the ballet is a romantic story of true love based on a medieval Provençal story. Raymonda, the young niece of Countess Sybille, awaits the return of her fiancé, de Brienne. In the meantime, Raymonda enjoys the company of her girl friends.

Raymonda becomes tired and falls asleep. She dreams that the statue of the "white lady" who owned the castle previously has come to life and leads her into the garden. There Raymonda sees her fiancé and is ready to embrace him. Suddenly, there appears before her an Arabian chief, Abderahman, who tells Raymonda that he is in love with her. The dream ends.

Next day, a reception is being prepared in the castle for the arrival of de Brienne. Abderahman arrives with a retinue and tries to abduct Raymonda. De Brienne arrives and challenges Abderahman. Abderahman is killed in the duel. Raymonda and De Brienne are married in a magnificent ceremony.

The ballet contains a variety of national dances. There is a beautiful waltz in the first act. In the second act, Abderahman's retinue dances a traditional Spanish dance, a "Dance of Saracens," and a "Dance of Jugglers." Leading motives which seem like musical sketches of the acting persons give unity and continuity to the ballet.

CHAPTER 19

Rachmaninov

SERGEI RACHMANINOV's music reflects Russian culture in the end of the nineteenth and beginning of the twentieth centuries. His work was welcomed by the Russian intelligentsia as an expression of its hopes and aspirations.

Like the short stories of Chekhov, Kuprin, and Bunin, which were protests against Russian social conditions at the turn of the century, Rachmaninov's music expressed feelings and emotions of average Russian men and women who lived in a petty, narrow-minded environment. The desire to free people from slavery and barbarity was turned by Chekhov and Kuprin into a protest against the pitiable and vile reality in which these people lived.[1] Hence, the desire of these writers to be understood by people who suffer from such conditions.

These aspects are peculiar to Rachmaninov's art. His music is characterized by spontaneity and emotional excitement which can captivate and charm music listeners. These factors, the result of Rachmaninov's protest against the drabness and boredom of daily existence, paralleled experiences of Chekhov's heroes, who craved life and love, and for whom any deed, sacrifice, or suffering to attain happiness was not work, but joy.[2]

In lyricism, sincerity of emotions, and in reflections of tragedy of love and life, Rachmaninov's music is similar to Tchaikovsky's. National characteristics of his music reveal influences of Borodin, Mussorgsky and Rimsky-Korsakov. The rhythmic, bell-like chords of the C Sharp Minor Prelude are reminiscent of heroic elements of Borodin's music. Psychological elements of Rachmaninov's melodies with their *podgolosky* (ornamental supporting melodies) are often similar to Mussorgsky's. Rachmaninov's representations of Russian nature continue Rimsky-Korsakov's traditions of these genres. The imagery of Russian antiquity aroused by some of Rachmaninov's *Études Tableaux* (Picture Études) reflects impressions which he experienced in his childhood, when he lived on his mother's estate not far from the ancient City of Novgorod. Rachmaninov's imagery is similar to the imagery of Russian antiquity in Rimsky-Korsakov's operas *Pskovityanka* (The Maid of Pskov) and *Sadko, The Guest From Novgorod.*

Oriental influences, which occur in the music of Glinka, Borodin, Mussorgsky, and Rimsky-Korsakov, also appear in Rachmaninov's music. However, oriental influences in Rachmaninov's music are not revealed in a distinct oriental imagery. Rachmaninov's oriental intonations are merged with his melodies, for example, the lyric second theme in the first movement of the Second Piano Concerto.

Rachmaninov seldom used Russian folk songs. Nevertheless, his music contains typical Russian intonations and elements of Russian national melodies. The smoothness and effortlessness of Rachmaninov's melodies are characteristic of Russian songs. There is a pictorial quality in Rachmaninov's melodies. They often evoke associations or representations of the Russian countryside, forests, rivers, and of the endless steppe.

The lyricism of Rachmaninov's music is enhanced by rhythmic elements, which also augment the dramatic elements of his style. Rachmaninov's rhythms are complex and dramatic. They are revealed in persistent marchlike drives, in rhythmic irregularities, and in clashes of different rhythmic patterns.

Sergei Rachmaninov was born on March 20, 1873, in Oneg, his mother's estate near the City of Novgorod. Here he spent his early childhood. The estate had to be sold because of financial difficulties, and Rachmaninov went to live with his grandmother whose estate was not far from Novgorod.

Rachmaninov's paternal grandfather, Arkadi Alexandrovich, studied piano with John Field, the Irish pianist and composer, who settled in Petersburg in 1804. Rachmaninov's father, Vasili Arkadievich, was musically gifted, but did not pursue musical studies. His mother, Lyubov Petrovna, was her son's first music teacher. At the age of four, Rachmaninov played piano duets with his grandfather.

When Rachmaninov was seven years old, his family moved to

Petersburg. In 1882, he enrolled in the Petersburg Conservatory where he studied piano with V. Demiansky. In 1885, Rachmaninov left for Moscow with his cousin Alexander Ziloti, a pupil of Nicholas Rubinstein and Liszt. Rachmaninov enrolled in the Moscow Conservatory and studied piano with Nicholas Zverev. From 1888, Rachmaninov studied piano with Ziloti. Taneyev was his teacher of counterpoint and Arensky of free composition.

Rachmaninov's musical talent was extraordinary. After hearing a complex composition for the first time, he was able to play it at the piano.

In 1891, Rachmaninov was graduated with a gold medal from the school of piano, and in 1892, from the school of composition. His graduating thesis in composition was the opera *Aleko*.

During the following years, Rachmaninov concertized, conducted, and composed. In 1917, he left for a concert tour of the Scandinavian countries. In 1918, he came to the United States and resided here until his death on March 28, 1943.

Rachmaninov's harmonic style is individual. He avoids complex dissonances. His colorful harmony enhances the national feeling of his melodies. The pictorial quality of his music evokes associations of Russian northern nature. His polyphony is characterized by interweaves of independent melodies and intonational elements. It is national in that it reveals influences of the spontaneous polyphony of Russian folk songs. Rachmaninov rejected modern concepts of music. "Melody is music and the foundation of all music. . . . I do not appreciate composers who abandon melody and harmony for an orgy of noises and dissonances as an end in itself." [3]

The best features of Rachmaninov's style are disclosed in his piano compositions. The texture of his piano music is dense, resonant, but clearly defined.

Many of Rachmaninov's compositions are outstanding for their power to arouse pictorial representations and imageries of nature. "In his music and performance are inherent the breath of Russian spring, the awakening of nature, the vernal rejoicing which captures the soul during the powerful overflow of Russian rivers in flood-time." [4]

In a conversation with Asafiev, Maxim Gorky remarked about Rachmaninov: "How well he hears silence." [5] Asafiev comments on Gorky's remark: "A musician or music critic is 'poor' indeed if he does not 'hear' the forest, field, sea, and even the stars. I often take solitary walks, and I listen. I do not notice anything. I sing and I listen, especially to the steppe. I think that great men in music became great because they created beauty amidst our abomination, and they could hear not music alone, but nature as well. My conversation with Gorky was not about a naturalistic imitation of nature in music, the so-called onomatopoeia. The conversation was about fashionable (at that time) trends in esthetics of music which ignored the listener and the significance of perception." [6]

Rachmaninov's compositions include piano sonatas, piano concertos, a Rhapsody on a Theme by Paganini, play suites, preludes, études, vocal compositions, symphonies, a symphonic poem *The Isle of Death,* operas, and chamber compositions.

Rachmaninov's piano concertos are fascinating compositions for the concert stage. They are dramatic, romantically elated, lyrical, heroic, oratorical, and with extraordinary piano effects. The best known concertos are the Second and the Third.

The Second Concerto in C Minor (1900–1901) is particularly known for the variety of its artistic imagery. Its pathetic lyricism discloses Rachmaninov's talent at its best.

The first movement, moderato, opens with piano chords, which create an impression of muted distant bells. The main theme, a swaying melody played by the orchestra, is accompanied by rhythmic piano arpeggios. Gradually, the emotional intensity of the melody is increased, while the energy of the arpeggio accompaniment subsides.

The expressive subordinate theme is characteristic of Rachmaninov's melodic style. It is a contemplative, languorous melody which rises impetuously in two measures to a culminating tone, and then descends smoothly to the starting tone. The lyric imagery of this theme dominates the movement.

The development, based on an elaboration of a short motive from the subordinate theme, is characterized by rising dynamics. This motive, transformed into a marchlike rhythmic figure, accompanies the main theme in the recapitulation (Maestoso. Alla Marcia). The marchlike episode is of short duration. It is followed by a rhythmically augmented theme played by muted French horns. The slackened tempo of the theme creates a feeling of peace and tranquility. Then the theme is played by the piano, and is slowly dissolved in gentle swayings of the transformed motive which is used in the development section. The emotional tension of the music gradually subsides, and the lyricism of the music seems to fade away in the distance only to come to life in an energetic outburst in the last measures of the movement.

The unhurried contemplative theme of the second movement, adagio sostenuto, continues the lyric mood of the subordinate theme of the first movement. Both themes are intonationally related. An accompaniment of smoothly flowing triplets enhances the feeling of peace and tranquility. It is the characteristic pensive mood of Rachmaninov which Gorky had in mind when he said, "How well he hears silence." The music of the second movement reveals a variety of emotional nuances.

The finale is based on a rhythmic, scherzolike transformation of the main theme of the first movement, and the subordinate lyric theme of the movement. However, the mood of the lyric theme dominates the finale. The concluding section of the finale is built on the lyric theme which becomes optimistic, triumphant, and oratorical. It is played in unison by the orchestra, and is accompanied by powerful passages played by the piano.

The Third Concerto in D Minor (1909) is more dramatic than the Second Concerto. It is characterized by intense, dynamic symphonic developments and piano virtuosity. A quietly flowing pastoral melody is Russian in feeling and imagery. The orchestral accompaniment is firm and resolute. The melody and the accompaniment seem to characterize the lyric and volitional aspects of Rachmaninov's nature.

The second movement is a lyric and rapturous outpouring. It is in the form of a theme and variations. The finale is an exulting, hymnlike apotheosis. It is a triumphant affirmation of the power and beauty of life.

The Rhapsody on a Theme by Paganini (1934), Rachmaninov's last composition for piano and orchestra, is a series of variations. The theme from Paganini's A minor Caprice was transcribed by Liszt and used by Brahms in his Variations on a Theme by Paganini. With the exception of the eighteenth variation, the Rhapsody does not contain the variety of lyric episodes which characterize the Second and Third Concertos. It discloses the rhythmic and dynamic contrasts and impetuous tonal accumulations of his piano style, and the pictorial quality of his music in general.

Rachmaninov's twenty-four preludes (1901, 1910) are composed, like Chopin's preludes, in all tonalities. However, they are more extensive than Chopin's preludes. Rachmaninov's preludes combine emotional and pictorial elements, representations of nature merged with human feelings and reactions, which are found in the works of some Russian painters of the latter part of the nineteenth century; for example, Levitan (1861–1900). Some preludes, in C Minor for example, seem to evoke old Russian ritual tunes. The heroic Prelude in B Flat Major evokes an imagery of a festive occasion. The Prelude in E Minor is a Russian ballad in the style of Mussorgsky and Rimsky-Korsakov.

Rachmaninov's *Études Tableaux* are programmatic compositions. The Étude in A Minor (op. 39 #6) is a musical fairy tale about Red Riding Hood. The imagery of the preludes is more dramatic than the imagery of the études.

The preludes and the études reveal Rachmaninov's piano style at its best, as "a refined interweave of singing decorative patterns, or of smooth melodic lines enwrapping the main melody as young sprouts entwine a tree-branch." [7]

Rachmaninov's three operas, *Aleko* (1892), *The Avaricious Knight* (1904), both based on Pushkin's texts, and *Francesca da Rimini* (1904), based on Dante's text, are dramatic compositions.

Aleko was influenced by Tchaikovsky's lyric operatic style. It is a psychological drama based on Pushkin's poem "The Gypsies." The hero of the opera, Aleko, is a Byronesque character, disappointed, misunderstood, and rejected by everyone. In his poem, Pushkin stresses Aleko's independence, love of freedom, and his realization of human dignity. Rachmaninov, on the other hand, stresses Aleko's sufferings and doom, the tragedy of a lonely, misunderstood person.

An old Gypsy tells how his beloved, Mariula, left him many years ago. Aleko's angry reaction to the story reveals his cruel and revengeful nature. Zemfira's song, "Old husband, stern husband," irritates Aleko and arouses his jealousy. In a fit of jealousy Aleko murders Zemfira and her lover. The Gypsies depart, leaving Aleko a despairing and lonely person.

The Avaricious Knight is unique in operatic literature because it has only one actor, the knight (the baron). The opera, based on Pushkin's play of the same name, develops the declamatory principles of Dargomijsky's *The Stone Guest,* and of Rimsky-Korsakov's *Mozart and Salieri.*

In leading motives and symphonic developments, Rachmaninov discloses the callous feelings of the baron who has become a slave of his treasures that he guards in the basement of his castle. The passion for gold has deprived the baron of compassion, sympathy, and love of his only son. Avarice has destroyed the baron's conscience, and it pitilessly brings him to his death.

In *Francesca da Rimini,* Rachmaninov was inspired by the Fifth Song of Dante's *Divine Comedy.* The prologue and epilogue of the opera represent infernal whirlwinds which carry the souls of sinners. In the prologue, Dante, accompanied by Vergil, descends into purgatory. Dante calls Vergil's attention to two shadows, which are the souls of Francesca and Paolo. Dante asks Francesca to tell her story.

The scene changes, and the spectator sees two representations of the story. In the first representation, Lancello Malatesta, Francesca's husband, is torn by jealousy and suspicion of Francesca's infidelity. Lancello pleads with Francesca to love him, but Francesca does not answer him. In the second representation, Francesca and Paolo, Lancello's brother, read a book about a happy love, and they kiss. Lancello steals up from behind and murders the lovers.

The scene changes again, and represents gloomy purgatory. An infernal whirlwind carries the souls of moaning and wailing sinners, and among them are Francesca and Paolo who had been punished for their intimacy.

The libretto of the opera was written by Tchaikovsky. Rachmaninov uses leading motives to characterize the heroes and symphonic developments to dramatize situations. There is a discrepancy between Tchaikovsky's libretto and facts. Francesca was a daughter of Guido da Palenta, the lord of Ravenna in the second half of the thirteenth century. She was married to Giovanni, son of Malatesta da Rimini. Giovanni was deformed and a detestable person. He discovered the love of Francesca and his brother Paolo, and killed them.

Rachmaninov's First Symphony in D minor (1895) was not a successful composition. Its first performance under Glazunov's direction was a failure. Cui's criticism of the symphony was caustic: "If there had been a conservatory in hell, and if one of the students were given an assignment to compose a programmatic symphony on the theme of 'The Seven Egyptian Plagues,' and if the student had composed a symphony somewhat similar to Rachmaninov's symphony, he would have brilliantly fulfilled the assignment, and thrilled the inhabitants of hell." [8]

An abundance of polyphonic combinations in the symphony makes the texture of music complex and dull. The main theme of the first movement, which is derived from the stern and tragic theme of the introduction, appears in various transformations throughout the symphony. This monothematic principle of construction, makes the music monotonous. The ideological and psychological intentions of Rachmaninov are not clear, and the symphony fails to arouse significant musical associations.

The Second Symphony in E Minor (1907) is a more mature composition. It is lyric and melancholy, and without tense, dramatic conflicts. Although the symphony does not have a program, the pictorial quality of the music evokes imageries of Russian landscapes described by the poetry of Pushkin and Nekrasov.

The Third Symphony in A Minor (1935–1936) is a melancholy composition. It is a series of musical reminiscences of Russia which Rachmaninov carried with him while living abroad. The festive finale is composed in the traditional style of finales of Russian symphonies. However, the appearance of the *Dies Irae* theme seems to clash with the holiday spirit of the music.

The Rock, a Fantasy for Orchestra (1893) was composed by Rachmaninov after he had read Chekhov's story "On the Road." The epigraph of the story, a quotation from Lermontov, became the epigraph of the fantasy:

> A golden cloud spent the night
> On the breast of a giant rock.

The program of the fantasy is the tragedy of loneliness, represented by a sad and pensive melody; and the happy dream, represented by a light and dreamy melody, which seems to suggest a cloud moving away towards the horizon.

The main character of Chekhov's story is a man of advanced years. He is tactful, talented, and with an inquisitive mind, but he cannot find his place in life. He fails because he never thinks of his own welfare, but tries to help others. He never finds out how to achieve his dream.

At a remote road station, the man meets a young girl and starts a conversation with her. The conversation lasts a long time, and the man and the girl feel a mutual attraction. But the words which might have changed their lives are left unspoken. The girl departs, and the man stands motionless and looks at the tracks left by the runners of her sleigh. The snow obliterates the sleigh tracks, and the man, covered with snow, begins to resemble a white rock. But his eyes search for something in the snowclouds.

The meaning of the story is a dream of happiness and a fervent desire to change life. How and by what means to change it is left unanswered.

It is not fortuitous that Rachmaninov chose Chekhov's story. Rachmaninov sympathized with Chekhov's attitude to life and dissatisfaction with Russian social conditions. He shared Chekhov's protest against the somber aspects of life, and he believed in a happier future. *The Rock* was a symbol of a social awakening.

The Isle of Death (1909) is a symphonic poem in which Rachmaninov expressed his feelings about Böcklin's painting of the same name. The steady rhythm of the music arouses a vision of doom and of unchanging "sea of eternity" which surrounds the dismal island. An expressive lyric melody which symbolizes the thirst for life is heard in the middle part of the poem. Mournful and pessimistic tones of *Dies Irae,* the Latin hymn of the Day of Judgment, interrupt the lyric melody. The vision of doom appears again, and the composition ends.

The Bells (1913) is Rachmaninov's setting to music of Poe's poem in the translation of the Russian poet Balmont. The substance of the poem, which is an interpretation of human life, is presented in four musical pictures. Different-sounding bells symbolize the stages of human life, from youth to the grave.

Merry bells of a troika symbolize the dawn of life. Solemn wedding bells call to happiness and love. But happiness is deceptive and short-lived. Alarm bells announce a terrible calamity. Dismal and monotonous funeral bells announce the end of life. Despite the symbolism of the poem, Rachmaninov's setting contains colorful and realistic musical representations.

The *Symphonic Dances* (1940) continue the pessimistic thoughts of *The Isle of Death.* "There is an opinion that Rachmaninov proposed to call the three parts of the composition *Morning, Noon, and Evening.*" [9] In the first part, a sharp and angular melody is contrasted with a mournful melody. The main theme of Rachmaninov's First Symphony, which is heard near the end, seems like a recollection of the distant past. A passionate and anguished waltz in the second part seems to describe troubles of mature life. Distorted intonations of *Dies Irae* in the third part suggest thoughts of death. The music expresses Rachmaninov's skepticism and pessimism in his last years.[10]

Rachmaninov's music is interwoven with Russian life and culture. Herein lies its strength and vitality. "His music tenderly glorifies the beautiful in life. It has static moments of long contemplations, when it seems as if the tonal flow has come to a standstill or hardly moves. At times, the music storms and roars in passionate and exciting scales of anger or indignation. Then follows a holiday celebration of a 'ringing' of joy or of gloomy chimes. This is how Rachmaninov's music uplifts, lets down, and lulls the emotions of a listener [11] . . . who is not interested in rationalistic refinements of polyphony and harmony. On the contrary, he experiences in the music the presence of human breathing, a vital flow of sociable living speech which goes from heart to heart." [12]

CHAPTER 20

Scriabin

SCRIABIN'S COMPOSITIONS of his early and middle periods resurrected romantic elements of the music of Chopin and Schumann. Unlike Chopin, who was influenced by Polish national intonations and rhythms, Scriabin seldom used melodies and rhythms of Russian folk songs.

Stylistic resemblances in Scriabin's and Chopin's music are in prolonged melodic constructions; in the mobility of the bass voice; in devices of piano textures; in contrasts between states of rest and passionate impulses; in poetic moods and complete merging of creative intentions with the piano timbres. Scriabin's music does not possess the pictorial quality of Chopin's large forms. Chopin's music is more objective. Scriabin makes greater use of changes in the values of notes. He prefers diatonic successions in which the leading tone is often absent and there is greater stress on subdominant functions. Schumann's influences are reflected in the impetuosity of Scriabin's lyricism, in restless imagery, capricious rhythms, and tragic elements of his music.

Scriabin's early style, intonations, rhythms, and representations of nature sometimes resemble similar elements in the music of Rimsky-Korsakov. Scriabin was a disciple of the New Russian School, and he acknowledged the succession of his early style from the styles of Rimsky-Korsakov and Mussorgsky.[1]

In his mature period, Scriabin developed new musical means to express his mystical ideas. The abstract character of these ideas required musical idioms which would not arouse familiar associations or representations. The style of Scriabin's nature period is unique in Russian music.

Alexander Scriabin was born on December 25, 1871. His father,

Nicholas Alexandrovich, was connected with the Russian diplomatic service and lived mostly abroad. His mother, Lyubov Petrovna, was graduated from the Petersburg Conservatory, where she studied piano with Leschetizki. She died while Scriabin was very young. Scriabin was brought up by his paternal grandmother and aunt.

In 1883 and 1884, while a student in the Cadet Corps, Scriabin took private piano lessons with G. Konus, a student at the Moscow Conservatory. His teacher of piano was Safonov, and of counterpoint, Tanayev. After graduation from the Cadet Corps, Scriabin decided to abandon the military career for music. In 1892, he was graduated from the school of piano.

During the 1890's, Scriabin formulated his philosophical ideas which influenced the evolution of his musical style. A partial paralysis of the right hand changed Scriabin's world outlook and brought on thoughts about life, religion, God, and the meaning and purpose of music. The funeral march of his First Piano Sonata in F Minor (1893) reflects Scriabin's depression during these years.

At first Scriabin sought a solution of his dilemmas in the idea of a pantheistic merging with nature. Later he rejected pantheism, as well as Christian dogmas, and formulated the ideas of an unlimited subjectivism, faith in an unknown God, and assertion of his (Scriabin's) Messianic role as a composer. Next, Scriabin asserted his "boundless omnipotence," "boundless power," "invincibility," and his "I." He wished to announce his triumph through music to all the people, and give them confidence to rid themselves of sufferings brought on by ignorance and weakness. Scriabin actually reached a state of self-deification by regarding himself as the creator of the universe.

Scriabin's philosophy was essentially based on the theory of solipsism which holds that the "self" is the only reality. In an entry in his philosophical writing book Scriabin wrote: "The external world is the result of my subjective spiritual activity. The world is nothing else than an antithesis created by my personal consciousness. The 'not I' which is opposed at will by the 'I' is necessary only so that the 'I' in the 'I' could create." [2]

Scriabin became preoccupied with the idea of the emancipation of individual consciousness, "the spirit," and with the creative activity of a powerful self-affirming personality. "I am the apotheosis of creation; I am the aim of all aims; I am the end of all ends." [3]

The program of Scriabin's large compositions of his mature period,

The Divine Poem (1904), *The Poem of Ecstasy* (1905–1907), *Prometheus: The Poem of Fire* (1909–1910), and the last five piano sonatas (1911–1913), is the abstract mystical idea of the spontaneous development of individual consciousness through successive stages, and the attainment of absolute self-knowledge and omnipotence.

The content of Scriabin's music does not always correspond to his philosophy. The paradox of Scriabin is that, while he dreamed of Universal Brotherhood and emancipation of all the people from suffering, he invented musical formulas which expressed subtle, subjective emotions. His ideas about the emancipation of intellect through the power of music from sensuality were, probably, the result of Russian social conditions at the turn of the century, and of the hopes for freedom which encouraged the Russian intelligentsia at that time. It is also probable that Scriabin was influenced by the ideas of Russian symbolist poets in the early 1900's. Scriabin's music with its dramatic pathos, languor, excitement, and ecstasy was a call to a new life and unattainable ideals. Scriabin died on April 14, 1915.

Scriabin's compositions of the early and middle periods were collections of piano miniatures, including mazurkas, preludes, études, impromptus in the form of a mazurka, and piano sonatas.

The twenty-four preludes (op. 11) are musical minatures which describe momentary emotional states or feelings. Their content varies from quiet contemplation and melancholy reflection to impetuous and dramatic flights of fancy. The preludes anticipate the piano poems of Scriabin's mature style.

The twelve études (op. 8) continue the traditions of Chopin and Liszt. The études are brilliant piano compositions which express a variety of moods and feelings, including the dramatic Étude in G Sharp Minor, the elated and passionate Étude in D Sharp Minor, and the fragile Étude in B Minor.

The ten mazurkas (op. 3) exemplify the dance rhythms which Scriabin loved very much. The impromptus in the form of a mazurka (op. 7) are subjective in their reflections of various capricious moods and elusive imageries.

Scriabin's first five piano sonatas are programmatic compositions based on his philosophical ideas. The sonatas reveal emotional characteristics similiar to those of his musical miniatures, but in a more sustained and logical process. The best known is the Third Piano Sonata in F Sharp Minor. The program represents various "states of the soul." The first movement, allegro drammatico, represents "the free and wild soul which plunges passionately into the abyss of misery and struggle." In the second movement, allegretto, "the soul takes an imaginary, momentary, deceptive rest . . . and desires to become oblivious of everything." The third movement, andante, represents "tender and melancholy sensations . . . vague desires, inexpressible thoughts." In the fourth movement, presto, "the soul struggles in the maelstrom of emancipated passions." [4]

The main characteristic of Scriabin's early and middle styles is the predominance of subdominant elements whose successions and turns evoke an atmosphere of contemplation and reverie, and of emotional tension.

In the compositions of his mature period, Scriabin wished to suggest symbolic meanings of what lies beyond sensory perceptions which could not be successfully conveyed in romantic imageries and representations.

Scriabin's concern with the irrational reduced his musical imagery to vague allusions or hints. His musical idioms became enigmatic and whimsical. He attempted to describe emotional experiences divorced from reality. His music expressed purposeless, ecstatic intoxication, and emotional energy without emotion.

Stylistically, the music of Scriabin's mature period is a succession of symbolic motives and chords, including motives of the will, dream, alarm, creation, self-assertion, longing, fear, flight, and protest. Unlike Wagner's motives, Scriabin's motives do not express passions, do not describe natural phenomena, and do not characterize people. Scriabin's motives transmit various stages of spiritual states and experiences. Their transformations are in accordance with the philosophical program of the music. The motives are short and are not developed. They are symbolic carriers of secret meanings within the mystical atmosphere of the music.

The harmonic background of the motives is a mystical six-tone chord derived from the upper partials of the harmonic series (8, 9, 10, 11, 12, 13, and 14: C, D, E, F sharp, G, A, and B flat) arranged in intervals of fourths (C-F sharp-B flat-E-A-D), and which appear in various alterations. Mystical whiffs, puffs, calls, and distant sonorities attempt to conjure the world beyond, the mysterious primordial world without sensory imagery.

Attempts to arouse unusual sensations, which reside beyond the normal psychic life, compelled Scriabin to resort to specific combinations of tones which arouse in a listener an acute and abnormal reaction. The main role in the combination of tones is assumed by harmony which becomes very complex and chromatic. However, this extraordinary complexity results in a disintegration of tonalities and isolation of constituent tone groups. The result is that expressive possibilities of harmonies are diminished and impoverished.

The music of the short piano compositions of Scriabin's mature period is whimsical and capricious. Sudden or unusual tonal changes, contrasts of tone registers, and outbursts of dynamics produce peculiar and subtle changes of color effects. Impetuously rising passages seem to create a fleeting imagery of storming primordial forces. Unstable endings on harsh dissonances create an impression of incompleteness, as if everything has suddenly been interrupted without completion or conclusion. The whimsical "play of sensations" seems to represent symbolical reflections of secret and indefinite spiritual processes experienced by Scriabin.

Through various combinations and nuances, the mystical chord assumes a variety of meanings or suggestions. It is a mystical call, a delicate rustle, a vertiginous whirl, or an angry outburst.

Scriabin's "Poems" composed in his mature period are short and compact compositions which express a momentary emotional state, a sudden feeling of anxiety. The titles of the poems are interesting: "Poem of Languor" (op. 52), "The Mask, Oddity" (op. 63), "Fragility" (op. 51), "Enigma" (op. 52), "Irony" (op. 56), and "Wish" (op. 57).

The "dance" became for Scriabin a symbol of a soaring spirit. Piano miniatures symbolize this idea: "Dance of Languor" (op. 51), "A Caress while Dancing" (op. 57), "Gloomy Flame, Garlands" (op. 73).

The "Poem Nocturne" (op. 61) describes "drowsy sweet bliss." The music is a play of tone colors which seems to suggest hardly perceptible, changing sensations. It is a musical representation of the "twilight zone." Although the poem is in sonata form, it lacks contrasts. Short, evanescent themes are interwoven with a figurated texture. There are illusive accumulations of indefinable feelings which are suddenly broken off to be followed by a sensation of sinking into will-less contemplation and a deep somnolence. Then there seems to emerge a vague onomatopoeia. All these arouse an impression of mystical sensations.

The music of Scriabin's last composition, Five Preludes (op. 74), is nervous, enigmatical, and mystical. There is an abundance of peculiar sound effects. The second prelude, which is played slowly and contemplatively, expresses complete emotional prostration. The music seems to become an indistinct mumble.

Scriabin's philosophy of mystical activism determined the musical forms of the large compositions of his mature period: *The Divine Poem, The Poem of Ecstasy, Prometheus,* and the last five piano sonatas. The essential aspect of this philosophy is the overcoming of the sensuous world. Scriabin regarded himself as a being invested with superior power to lead people on the road to happiness and bliss.

The content of art is sensation. Consciousness without sensation which it creates is empty. In itself, the "I" deprived of creativity, that is, the subject without an object, is nothing. The creative spirit, by overcoming sensuousness in an apotheosis of ecstasy, attains the triumph of happiness as an end in itself.

"The world is the activity of my consciousness." [5] This activity does not bring about changes of consciousness. Consciousness, when deprived of activity, is nothing. Consciousness includes many states or elements. A state of consciousness is a creative moment. A state of consciousness is unchangeable and can only be superseded by another state.[6] There is no emergence or development of new states or elements of consciousness. By itself, every state of consciousness is inert and negates all other states.

Time and space are created by the discriminating activity of consciousness. Differentiation between consciousness and the object of creativity determines space. Differentiation of sensations determines time. In distinguishing sensations, consciousness derives notions of *before* and *after*. The past and the future are part of the present.

Activity of consciousness takes place when states of consciousness negate each other, including the final state of consciousness.[7] The "creative spirit" understands these negations as the struggle of the spirit with its own created obstacles. The climax of the struggle is the "dance" of states of consciousness resulting in the loss of the distinguishability of the world, and which is then followed by the merging of the self with the mystical unity in a state of bliss. This is ecstasy, the absolute differentiation and, at the same time, absolute unity of all states of consciousness, followed by complete dissolution of all elements of consciousness, obliviousness of the world, and the revelation of the substance of existence as the affirmation of human happiness.

The musical forms of Scriabin's large compositions are generally series of episodes whose order is determined by his mystical ideas. All elements of musical form are predetermined. They are not developed, and they do not produce new tonal elements. Thematic development in the classic-romantic meanings does not exist in Scriabin's musical forms.

For Scriabin, the composer-philosopher of mysticism, all states of time exist simultaneously and are revealed to consciousness in a single moment. However, for some subjective consciousness the world disintegrates into numberless states of time. Scriabin's objective was to overcome these numberless states by means of a *Universal Mystery* in a single moment of ecstasy which would be followed, as he imagined it, by a total merging of the subjective spirit with the mystical whole.

Empirical time for Scriabin the composer was indispensable only as far as it was necessary to distinguish the musical symbols of the various sensations and of the origins or sources of the world. These symbols are represented by musical motives or themes whose development in time is unnecessary. Scriabin thought that it would be sufficient to give a musical hint which would point out a path to ecstasy.

Scriabin's sonata form is simple in its design. The exposition is a statement of motives or symbols. Instead of a development, there is an arbitrary repetition, variation, abridgment, and expansion of motives. The recapitulation is a representation of the universe by means of tonal displacements. The end of the movement is frequently a vertiginous whirl of motivic elements which seems to represent the apotheosis of ecstasy and joy. It is a musical representation in a "dance" of the dissolution of the self in a state of bliss.

The absence of a logical succession of thematic elements and of a definite plan of modulations makes Scriabin's musical form an arbitrary succession of motives. Scriabin's sonata form demonstrates his solipsism in that the motives-symbols which represent states of consciousness could not be developed. The unifying principle of the musical form is the excited reaction of Scriabin overwhelmed by intoxicating sensations.

There is a contradiction between the classic-romantic sonata principles and the use of these principles by Scriabin in his last compositions. Scriabin uses sonata schemes to embody and to transmit his philosophy of objective idealism, that is, the self-development of the spirit, the decline of the sensuous world, the dependence of art on cosmic power, and the role of the last artistic act, *The Mystery,* in the cosmic revolution. However, the sonata schemes which in the time of Haydn and Mozart, and then during the nineteenth century, served as vehicles for generalized reflections or representations of social and cultural realities, with their struggles, feeling, and passions, are least adaptable to Scriabin's abstract conceptions of objective idealism. Scriabin was partial to sonata schemes at a time when musical impressionism denied further possibilities of such schemes. Nevertheless, sonata schemes helped Scriabin achieve an outward unity in his musical forms regardless of his philosophic conceptions.

While seemingly preserving aspects of sonata style processes, Scriabin excluded from them social, cultural, and esthetic factors and substituted instead various impulses. This is true despite the extensive emotional exaltations, developments of thoughts, and the magnitude of experiences in his last symphonic and piano compositions. This is even true in his early piano sonatas. As a solipsist, Scriabin became an objective idealist who, while trying to express in music the objective reality of the spirit, succeeded only in substituting for the supposed objectivism the psychological content of his subject. The more Scriabin became preoccupied with aspects of his *Universal Mystery* which would be the last act of dematerialization, the less significant became the subjective content of his music.

Scriabin appreciated the importance of formal unity in a musical work and he tried, by means of various rational schemes and formulas, to construct synthetic musical forms which would correspond to his mystical conceptions. He was opposed to the sensuousness and the esthetics of impressionism and to the indefiniteness of its musical forms. Nevertheless, Scriabin should be regarded as a musical impressionist because his last compositions evoke the haziness, the mistiness of impressionism and the indefiniteness of its forms and moods. Scriabin often favored the distant sonorities used by Debussy in order to reproduce the imagery of the mystical world of his philosophy. At the same time, Scriabin's denial of nature and his affirmation of the self-sufficing spiritual energy of "expression," classifies him as a musical expressionist.

The program of *The Divine Poem* is the emancipation of the human spirit. The three movements, "Struggle," "Delight," and "Divine Play," describe the three stages of the spirit. According to Scriabin, *The Divine Poem* represents the evolution of human consciousness freed from old beliefs and secrets. Consciousness sweeps away these beliefs and secrets, and attains through pantheism the happy intoxicating affirmation of its freedom and of the unity of the universe.

The most important theme of *The Divine Poem* is the introductory theme of self-assertion. The motives of the first movement, which is in sonata form, represent struggle, gloom, and revolt.

The theme of the second movement represents languor. The finale, which is an expression of joy, is a "dance" of the liberated human spirit. The theme of self-assertion concludes the composition.

The Poem of Ecstasy expresses joy of creative activity. "I call you to life, hidden strivings." It is a symphonic movement in sonata form which includes polyphonic interweaves of the motives of languor, flight, will, self-assertion, creative dream, daring, fear, protest, suffering, and other themes. The motives become links of a continuous melodic chain.

The idea of *The Poem of Ecstasy* is the passivity of the spirit, the awakening of the will, clashes and struggles with threatening forces, and, finally, the triumphant assertion of the will.

The ecstasy which concludes the movement is hardly an overcoming by the spirit of the sensory world. Scriabin's evocation of the state of ecstasy is not an abstraction. It is a sumptuous state of sensations of love and bliss. Scriabin, the mystic, advocates the overcoming of the sensory world. However, in the instant of overcoming, the sensory remains very real and triumphant.

Prometheus: The Poem of Fire is the symbol of energy of the universe. It is the creative principle, fire, light, life, struggle, effort and thought. *The Poem of Ecstasy* represents the creative "I"; in *Prometheus,* the creative "I" is in the background, while the objective origin is in the foreground.

Prometheus is a combination of a symphonic poem, piano concerto, and cantata in which a chorus sings without words. The score calls for a keyboard of light which illuminates the concert hall with various colors. The music is based on Scriabin's six-tone mystical chord.

The exposition begins with the theme of reason. The piano answers with the themes of will and reason. Motives of storm, struggle, appeal, dance, and triumph follow each other. The subordinate theme is a dance-like motive. The exposition ends with a lyrical section.

The exposition is followed by polyphonic interweaves of motives and themes, including the theme of Prometheus, the dance-like subordinate theme, and an accumulation of intervals of a fourth.

The recapitulation is not as forceful as the exposition. However, in the coda, the chorus accompanied by the whirling dance music brings the symphony to a stunning conclusion. The meaning of the coda seems to be that the creative spirit overcomes the sensory world by the power of art.

Scriabin's final composition was supposed to be a *Mystery*, a grandiose religious-artistic act whose performance, as Scriabin imagined it, would bring about a "world cataclysm." The cataclysm would be followed by the disappearance of the human race and the emancipation of the spirit held captive by material and physical sensuality.

The *Mystery* was supposed to be introduced by a *Preliminary Act,* a combination of elements of an oratorio, dance, and scenic play. Scriabin wrote the text of the "Preliminary Act." The idea of the *Act* is that death is the supreme bliss because it releases the spirit from captivity by earthly sensuality. Neither the *Mystery* nor the *Preliminary Act* was completed by Scriabin.

Scriabin's idea might have been influenced by the symbolist movement in Russian poetry. At the turn of the century there developed in Russian philosophy the idea of the coming end of the world. The idea was spread by V. Solovyov, who was a mystic and an idealist. Solovyov's ideas, which were based on the prophecies of the Apocalypse, influenced Russian symbolist poets. The poet Andrei Bely wrote, in 1905, of the "approaching end of world history" and of the prophetic importance of Russian poetry, which predicted "the transformation of Heaven and Earth into a new City of Jerusalem." The symbolist poet

Alexander Blok wrote in his diary after the October Revolution: "What is being destroyed is not the world but a system." The imagination of the symbolists conjured a vision of world catastrophe. Scriabin was acquainted with Russian symbolist poetry.[8]

Scriabin's music was a reaction and protest against Russian social conditions of his time. In his desire to free human personality and help it attain joy and happiness, Scriabin reflected similar ideas in Russian literature of his time. In this sense, one could understand his utopian philosophy and his attempts to express it in his music.

Scriabin's manipulation of motives or symbols never equals the dramatic developments of Tchaikovsky's symphonies.[9] Moreover, the strength and meaning of musical forms are in the qualities of intonations of a particular era. Such intonations might overcome the inertia of musical elements. Scriabin's music ignored intonations which express Russian life and social realities.

Scriabin's philosophy is an anachronism in Russian culture. His Messianic idea, extreme individualism, intoxication with instinct, with struggle as an end in itself, parallel Nietzsche's philosophy. Scriabin's idea of "ecstasy," the divine dance, recalls Nietzsche's Dionysian ecstasy and the consequent loss of individuality in the reunion with nature.

In his music, Scriabin attempted to express not only moods and emotions, but also a world outlook. He believed that music could express ideas. He was convinced that the expressive potentialities of music were more accurate than logical deductions.[10] Scriabin's music, when separated from its philosophical bases, is the creation of a refined, ecstatic Russian intellectual. It is destined to remain an expression of a lonely Promethean enthusiast whose visionary schemes of objective development of the spirit are filled with remarkable subjective and lyrical content. When one disregards Scriabin's fantastic ideas, there is left in the balance art whose heroic strivings represent a unique phenomenon in Russian music.

Part Two

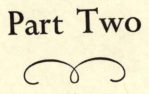

CHAPTER 21

⌒◦⌒

Marxist-Leninist Philosophy
and Esthetics of Art

SOVIET ART is a means of appreciating and reorganizing the world by man. The content of this art is reality reflected by Soviet artists in the light of dialectical and historical materialism (the materiality of the world and the dialectical character of its development), and Communist social-ethical ideals.

The foundations of Soviet philosophy and esthetics of art were formulated by Lenin:

Every artist, everyone who considers himself an artist, has the right to create freely according to his ideal, independently of everything. However, we are Communists and we must not stand with folded hands and let chaos develop as it pleases. We must systemically guide this process and form its result.[1]

The Soviet government grants freedom of creative expression. However, it is not freedom in the Western sense. In the Soviet state, the freedom of an artist is inseparably linked with the Communist party spirit. This was Lenin's interpretation of the Communist meaning of artistic creativity and freedom of expression. Lenin emphasized that true freedom in a Communist society is inimical to, what he called, bourgeois anarchy and individualism. Soviet freedom of artistic creativity represents conscious service by an artist to revolution and Communism. Soviet art is predicated upon the Marxist principle of the class struggle of the proletariat and it must, therefore, serve as a weapon in the struggle for the building of Communism.

The boundaries of an artist's freedom are determined by the conflict or conformity of his art with the Soviet state and the sociopolitical objectives of the proletariat. So long as the artist's creativity does not oppose the interests of the state and agrees with necessities determined by the Communist party, his artistic freedom is not limited. The Soviet government encourages any art which reflects Marxist-Leninist ideology and objectives which the party demands of art. Artistic freedom is creative participation in the dialectics of Communist necessity.

The Communist party does not reject art of the past. Lenin emphasized the importance of a comprehensive assimilation and mastery of the heritage of the past as a necessary prerequisite for the building of a new Communist culture. The Soviet interpretation of Pushkin, Lermontov, Rimsky-Korsakov, or Mussorgsky, invariably tries to present an evaluation favorable to the Communist principle of class struggle and unfavorable to pre-Soviet Russian political, social, and cultural realities. Lenin's ideas represent the basis of Communist party policy in carrying out a cultural revolution. They have profoundly influenced Soviet study of art and art criticism, and the struggle against what the Communist party calls formalistic art, that is, art characterized by attention to personal peculiarities in structural and compositional factors.

Lenin was not an art expert. He was an authority on Marxist theory and the practice of revolutionary struggle. His writings show evidence of a keen insight into art problems from the Marxist point of view stressing historical materialism in which all human phenomena, historical, social, and psychological, are viewed and interpreted in terms of social and economic causes. In Communist theory, historical materialism formulates the laws of social development, of socioeconomic patterns and of transition from one social pattern to another. Communist theory maintains that art and literature invariably reveal social patterns and class struggle, that artistic creativity is always subordinated to the principles of historical materialism.

The theoretical content of Soviet statements, documents, and published materials dealing with art are imbued with the ideas of Marx and Lenin. The problems under constant scrutiny are: Communist party ideology and the ideological content of art and literature; national character of Socialist art works; vitality and fidelity to life in Communist realistic art and its capacity to afford easy understanding for masses of the people; capacity of art and literature to solve important historical problems presented by building a Communist society, and ideological education of the masses. The decisions of the Communist party substantiate the succession of Soviet art to the art of the past and the necessity of continuing the development of classic traditions.

The Communist party does not reject art and literature created in non-Communist cultures. The party accepts such artistic productions with the explanation that in a non-Communist class society, the vitality and lifelike imagery in art and literature can often overcome false ideological and political ideas. This also applies to the great Russian writers and composers of the past such as Pushkin, Gogol, Lermontov, Tolstoy, Goncharov, Rimsky-Korsakov, Mussorgsky, Tchaikovsky, Rachmaninov, and others. The Communist party believes that Soviet art and literature are progressive because Communist ideas are true representations of reality. The question of accepting or rejecting works of art representing non-Communist class reality is not new in Communist ideology. It interested Engels in his evaluation of Balzac, and Lenin in his evaluation of Tolstoy. The argument has been revived and settled in a comparison of Chernishevsky and Tolstoy.

Chernishevsky's fame is based on his master's dissertation, "Esthetic Relations of Art to Reality," which he wrote as a graduate student at Petersburg University (1853–1855). In his search for the meaning of "the beautiful," Chernishevsky reached the conclusion that the beautiful is life itself in its natural manifestations. Art, according to Chernishevsky, should be a representation of reality: a novel, a drama, a comedy, or a poem must represent people, characters, actions, and feelings as they are in reality. Communist philosophy and esthetics have adopted Chernishevsky's esthetics because it agrees with the principles of Soviet realism in art.

Communist esthetics regards Chernishevsky as more advanced and progressive than Tolstoy, but agrees that the artistic level of Tolstoy's writings is superior to Chernishevsky's. Soviet criticism admits that life, in all its manifestations and psychological aspects, is realized by Tolstoy more deeply and with greater versatility. The same criticism maintains that Tolstoy does not reveal the progressive thinking of Chernishevsky and that Chernishevsky's writing does not possess the descriptive power of Tolstoy's imagery. Soviet criticism also maintains that the works of Dostoyevsky are tinted with reactionary ideas, but that these works are appreciated because of their descriptive power and truthful representation of isolated aspects of life. In general, Dostoyevsky has been criticized in Soviet Russia because the psychological aspects in his novels, such as *Crime and Punishment* and *Brothers*

Karamazov, are, in the opinion of most Communist critics, contrary to Communist ideas of Soviet life and environment.

Communist estheticians admit that if the content of a work of art were exhausted by its political ideas, such art could only satisfy the artistic needs of people holding identical political ideas or opinions. It is a fact, and Communist philosophy concurs, that great works of art constantly afford enjoyment to people whose political convictions differ and vary. The music of Beethoven, Chopin, Brahms, Tchaikovsky, Rachmaninov, and others can attract and emotionally move a worker, a bourgeois, and an aristocrat. But, according to Communist esthetics, only the art of a progressive culture, that is, Communist culture, all things being equal, will be understood fully and comprehensively. Communist esthetics admits that the music of great masters, the paintings of great painters, and the novels of great writers can be enjoyed not only in a Communist society, but by backward, conservative, and reactionary people as well. The reason for this, according to Communist esthetics, lies in the human significance of art, in its unifying humanistic qualities calling for the Brotherhood of Man.

Survival of Art Forms

Communist philosophy has its own theory explaining why art forms survive or die. This theory is based on Marx's theory of absolute and relative social and political truths. Marx defined a classless Communist society as an example of absolute social and political truth and a class society as an example of relative social and political truth. Marx assumed that through class struggle mankind will gradually advance toward absolute truth, that is, a classless Communist society.

In Marx's philosophy, art, namely sculpture, painting, and music, has a lasting quality only if it can overcome class limitations. The more art overcomes class limitations, the more it becomes an artistic truth which reflects the thinking and emotional life of free men, "the everlasting in reality itself." But, according to Marx, contradictory conditions favor relative artistic truths which have no unity with life and progressive political ideas.

Marx's philosophy is the core of Soviet art realism: art can achieve unity with life and with progressive political ideas only in a Communist society in which Communist reality becomes the object of art. The art of this Communist realism is a product, and like any other product, it serves a public which, Communist estheticians claim, can understand it and enjoy its beauty. In Communist phraseology, art production creates the object for the subject and also the subject for the object.

In Communist esthetics, art expressing only political views is useful and valuable at a particular historic moment. The most valuable works of art are those in which Communist political ideas are merged with a wealth of realistic imagery of life and with perspectives of Communist life in the future.

The Individual and the People in Art

Communist philosophy accepts Marx's idea that exceptional concentration of artistic talent in separate individuals and the suppression of talent in the vast mass of people is the result of division of labor in a class society. Therefore, in a class society, the artistic endowment of the people finds its genuine expression in the creativity of a great artist who, through tremendous efforts, overcomes social obstacles, but often perishes in the struggle. To prove this point, Soviet musicologists allude to the struggles of Haydn, Mozart, and Beethoven to achieve recognition.

Soviet philosophy accepts the Marxist position that universal development of artistic talent is a practical possibility. Marx stated that if, under certain conditions, each individual were an excellent painter, it would not exclude the possibility of each individual revealing originality in painting. In line with Marx's ideas, the Communist party believes that under suitable social conditions, any individual can develop creative originality in art, and that inequality of talent is a result of social inequality in a class society.

Beauty, Truth, and Culture

The problem of beauty, truth, and culture is an old one in Western civilization. Communism believes the solution is in dialectic materialism. Dialectics is a method of arriving at the truth by disclosing and overcoming contradictions. Materialism assumes that matter is primary, consciousness is secondary. Dialectic materialism is a world outlook and a philosophical theory whose method of study of thinking, of what is set in motion, passes, shifts, and is logically connected in society and in nature, is scientific and dialectic. Thus, beauty is Communist life in all of its manifestations; truth is Communist social reality; culture is a form of active social existence in a Communist society.

From the materialistic point of view, the problem of beauty, truth, and culture never was, and never could be, a purely esthetic concern. In Communist thinking, the perception of beauty and truth as unique and independent concepts in Western civilization is due to the practical contradictions in class societies and to the division of labor in a capitalist society where consistent unity of beauty and truth could never be attained.

Communism teaches that beauty was never part of, and never could enter the life of oppressed classes, and that the truth of life was unattractive and ugly in class societies. According to Marxian Socialism, because of the division of labor in a capitalist society, bourgeois culture is mainly interested in man's spiritual development. Artistic activity, the content of culture, is interpreted in spiritual terms. Therefore, artistic activity in a capitalist society is contrasted with labor whose function is directed only towards the satisfaction of physical and utilitarian wants. According to Socialist thinking, this is inevitable because man's spontaneous activity in a capitalist society and his existence as a free creative individual are separated from the production of material needs of life. Labor, whose single objective is directed towards the satisfaction of these needs, becomes a negative form of independent action.

In Communist philosophy the essence of culture in a Socialist society emerges from man's spontaneous production of material needs of life. Labor, while concerned with the production of needs to satisfy physical existence, is no longer a drudgery, but a means of vital activity, a definite way of life in which man creates not only as a mere physical being but also as a perceptive individual. Thereby labor becomes more than a means of satisfying man's physical requirements and achieving self-preservation and survival. Labor is for everyone a vital requirement and a realized necessity where everyone's ability is best used for the common good. As an artistic activity labor becomes a means of man's versatile development emerging in the mastery and remaking of nature. Culture in Marxian Socialism is a form of active social existence corresponding to man's nature, unfolding as a process of gradual historical development of human abilities and capacities in the course of labor activities, and spontaneously revealing itself in a wealth and variety of created objective reality.

Communist philosophy identifies the beautiful with what it regards as morality for people living in a classless Communist society. In the words of Maxim Gorky, "by beauty is understood a combination of various materials, including sounds, colors, and words, which imparts to the created work a form acting on feeling and mind of men as a force that excites wonder, pride, and joy in their ability to create." [2] The beautiful in art is an artistic re-creation and reflection of the beautiful in nature and social life. Beauty in art is beauty of form and of socialist ideas. The Soviet esthetic ideal of beauty and truth stems from Hegel's ideal of a free, harmonious development of man in suitable social conditions. According to Communist philosophy, only a Communist society affords the best conditions for the development of man's physical and mental power, and of truth and beauty in art.

The concepts "moral" and "morale" are synonymous in Communist philosophy because Communist ethics discloses the social substance of Communist morale and, therefore, of Soviet art. Thus, Soviet art realism must disclose the ethical values of Communist reality. Nineteenth century Russian esthetics partly supported this ethical view of art and saw in art a tool for the moral education of man. Tolstoy's *What Is Art?* (1898) is an example. Soviet esthetics accepts the principle of moral education through art, but rejects the premises of Christian morality in Tolstoy's esthetics and ethics.

Communist morale is partly an adaptation of the idealism which characterizes nineteenth-century Russian literature: service and devotion to the common people, self-abnegation, brotherly friendship, fraternity of comradeship, self-searching, self-criticism, repentance, the submergence of the personal "I" in the "we" and, in general, the idealism of Russian intelligentsia and revolutionists who favored impersonal self-sacrifice for the benefit of the common people. This adaptation is evidenced by the Communist party's advice to art organizations to notice and correct the ideological shortcomings or mistakes of individual artists.

The Communist party looks upon art as a means of building up Communist morale. The concept of morale should be understood realistically. Its aim is the unification of the working-class movement with scientific Socialism. The objective is, in the words of Lenin, to transform the working class from *a class in itself* into *a class for itself*. Communist morale is the interpretation of Communism by itself. The Communist party tells the Soviet citizen "thou shalt" do and think so-and-so, and the artist, painter, sculptor, composer, or writer follows the dictum of the party. This is substantiated by the directives and statements of the Communist party. The only common ground in Western and Communist morale is that both claim permanent validity.

Soviet Esthetics and Formalistic Art: Soviet Realism

Much Soviet criticism of formalistic art is based on "Formal Independence of Individual Peculiarities" in Hegel's *Esthetics* in which Hegel states that the distinctive features of bourgeois art are rooted in the formalistic independence of individual artists. According to Hegel, formalistic art is different from art in previous historical eras when personality was united with social aspects and stable conditions of life and morality.

The Communist party does not approve independence of individual artists. Yet this independence is a historical peculiarity that determines the nature of art in non-Communist countries. The Communist party will not agree to freedom of social connections between the independent artist and the objective world. Artistic freedom in the Western sense means free interaction between individual actions and the objective course of events. This is precisely what the Communist party condemns.[3] Soviet philosophy and esthetics claim that freedom in social or world outlook results in outward adventurism as a new type of relation between the artist and the objective world expressed by the artist in extremely contradictory forms which have nothing to do with life or reality as it actually is.[4] Soviet philosophy and esthetics regard "pure art" or "art for art's sake" as humbug which does not even deserve the name of art. It maintains that there cannot be a "pure esthetic content" in art divorced from political, moral, and scientific ideas and values which are essential in reality.

Opposed to formalistic art is Soviet realism.

Soviet realism is an artistic method that demands from an artist a truthful, historically concrete, representation of reality in its revolutionary development.

Intrinsically there is nothing esthetic in this requirement. The concepts of Socialist realism can be successfully applied not only in the arts, but in social sciences and propaganda as well.

A truthful reflection of reality in Soviet realism does not mean a representation of outward manifestations. It means a revelation of all that is essential in reality, and of all that is still in an embryonic stage, but will eventually develop in accordance with the laws of historical materialism.[5]

Art as a Political and Economic Force

Soviet philosophy and esthetics regard art as a powerful force in politics and economics.[6] The idea was originally stated by Marx and Engels.[7] Art in Soviet Russia has become a field of human activity, practical and theoretical, which furthers and promotes knowledge, cognition, and mastery of the world, and helps bring about changes in the world's political and economic conditions. Art in Soviet Russia is a social phenomenon, a form of social consciousness that will, according to the Soviet philosophy of art, eventually receive international importance and recognition, and will assimilate international experience in all branches of human activity.

The function of art as a political and economic force is implied in Lenin's *Theory of Reflection*. The *Theory of Reflection* is a dialectic-materialistic theory of knowledge developed by Lenin on the assumption that matter and nature exist independently of human consciousness, thinking, and perception. The substance of the theory is that man's consciousness dialectically reflects the external world; esthetic consciousness is a form of social consciousness, that is, a specific reflection of the world; feelings, tastes, ideals, and theories are different forms of esthetic perception of the world; art is a form of esthetic consciousness reflecting the external world in which an artist finds ideas, plots, conflicts, characters, and imageries.

It follows from Lenin's theory that esthetic consciousness reflects the social needs of a group, and clashing esthetic views reflect the struggles within society. Reflections of contradictions in the external world intensify the content of art works, give representations of life of the people, of mass movements, protests, revolts, and show the people as the fighting and impelling force in history.

Reflection of revolutionary contradictions is a criterion of Soviet realism. A composer becomes a progressive innovator and creator of advanced contemporary music when he joins popular liberation movements, defends the interests of the masses, accepts the ideas of Socialism, and spurns indifference to politics. Applying the *Theory of Reflection* to music from Mozart to Debussy, Soviet esthetics would regard it, with some exceptions, as music of doubtful truth, of limited ideas, of constrained and narrow-minded objectives. Though beautiful and affording artistic enjoyment, this music would be regarded as incapable of becoming a tool in the reconstruction of society along political lines.

CHAPTER 22

Music and Soviet Realism

SOCIALIST REALISM portrays Communist truth, party spirit, and nationality as an expression of the interests of the proletariat. The development of the arts is guided by the Communist party. The esthetic qualities of revolutionary socialist reality are the vital bases of art. The working class (the people who have mastered socialist consciousness) is the hero of art. Communist ideas are the bases of art. Art, assuming a historical meaning and perspective of development, becomes closely connected with forms of social consciousness, such as ethics, philosophy, and politics.

However, the representation of reality in its revolutionary development is difficult to put in practice in music. It is difficult to give a programmatic explanation of every symphonic composition, to describe its meaning, and to translate these into a concretely palpable imagery. It is easier to understand the ideological and emotional content and the feelings which a symphony narrates and seeks to develop in the listener. This brought about a modification of socialist realism. "Socialist realism is a method, type, or form of figurative emotional thinking which corresponds to the objective esthetic wealth of (Soviet) reality, to the practice of revolutionary struggle of the proletariat, and to the building of Socialism. Socialist realism is a means of true reflection of (Soviet) reality from the position of Socialist esthetic ideals." [1]

Soviet realism stresses social bases of ideological and imaginative content in the historical development of the art of music. A means of achieving ideological content in music is the Soviet theory of musical intonations which rejects the metaphysical understanding of musical form and suggests instead the process of intonations in a musical composition. The idea of intonations has been formulated by the Soviet

285

composer and music critic Asafiev who, basing his ideas on Marxist-Leninist dialectics, developed a theory of musical intonations as a function of social consciousness.[2] Asafiev related the development of the means of musical expression to fundamental aspects of human intoning in speech as a manifestation of thought.

Speech intonations denote the character and temperament of a person. Kindness, harshness, manifestations of the will, purposefulness, passivity, intensity, and emotional weakness affect the intonational structure of an individual's speech in fluctuations of pitch, timbre, pauses, dynamics, and tempo. Every language has its own peculiar intonations. Folk songs often embody generalized characteristic intonations of national speech.

An understanding of the essence and quality of speech intonations often gives an idea what is meant by the intonational nature of musical expression. Just as intonational changes in speech bring out nuances of emotional stresses and the meaning of occurrences in reality, so, in music, melody and all tonal means disclose the musical image that reflects feelings and thoughts, objective logic of events, and processes in the external world. Music, like speech intonations, possesses expressive, meaningful, individual, characteristic functions revealed in similarities of tonal components such as pitch, meter, rhythm, timbre, and dynamics. According to Asafiev, there is no musical art as a process of revelation of musical creative conceptions outside of musical intonations. The process of intoning is interwoven with human thinking. Thought, to become expressive in sounds, is intoned and thereby becomes an intonation.

Soviet realism demands that Soviet composers write music based on musical intonations, that is, intoned meanings which are supposed to be the carriers of the ideological significances of Russian nationalism and of Soviet reality.

Each historical epoch possesses its own inherent system of intonations, not in a static state, but in a constant state of evolution and mutation, in living practice, in historical forms of musical creativity. Each historical epoch has its own "dictionary of intonations," and is subject to "intonational crises," that is, transvaluations of intonations.

Thus music becomes an art of intoned meaning, a sound image that reflects reality. According to materialistic dialectics, this cognized intoned meaning is an apprehension, through imagery, of activity of human consciousness inseparable from the development of social consciousness.

Intonation unifies into a single process the various aspects of musical creativity: performance, perception, style, form, and expressive elements. Intonation is "humanized" sound expression reflected in music by the social consciousness of the composer. In its narrow meaning, intonation is the meaningful element in melody, rhythm, harmony, and timbre.

The concept of an "intonational dictionary of an epoch" means the selection of particular intonations of an era. It is the totality of music assimilated in public consciousness, in thoughts and emotions of people. The ideological and emotional worth of music is recognized, welcomed, and appreciated by listeners. Gradually the exciting, appealing, and meaningful moments in music become set in the consciousness of listeners who begin to regard the composition as a generalized expression of an epoch, a source of achieved artistic enjoyment. This, for example, is the reason why Beethoven's symphonies, beginning with the Third, became individualized symphonies, not generalized symphonies.

Musical recollections, impressions, and fragments become interwoven with life experiences, feelings, and aspirations, penetrating the artistic life and traditions of people. These tonal aspects come to mind not as abstract representations, but as living intonations. The listener separates them from the composition. They become "words" of music, a "dictionary" of meaningful tonal combinations of a musical era.

As "words," these intonations penetrate new compositions and undergo metamorphoses. The intonations become norms of taste and habit, a collection of musical thoughts that are constantly present in the consciousness of a social group. When a new composition is heard, it creates a listening acquaintanceship; does it contain the usual intonations, how are they transformed, and how do they compare with the previous intonations?

In the penetration of characteristic intonations into social consciousness, in their stability as listening links, is the feeling of close ties of music and reality, and the understanding of the meaning of the composer's musical conceptions.

The background of great compositions is a world of music as an activity of public consciousness: musical interjections, rhythmic intonations, popular motivic fragments, harmonic turns, and extracts of musical impressions of an epoch. This represents the aural dictionary of intonations which is constantly being enriched with new contributions.

The best pages in Beethoven's music were slow in attaining popularity, but their intonational content was deeply imbedded in social reality. When Beethoven's music overcame antiquated social obstacles, it became the musical beacon of social reality, a position it presently occupies.

The sources and roots of realistic aspects in music are in the intonational contacts of people and in the recognition of generalized musical elements in compositions of the past and of the present. The problem of Soviet musical realism is the continuous process of mastery, evaluation, recognition, and rejection of intonations by the social environment.

An intonational crisis is a transvaluation of the worth of a composition. A composition lives as long as its intonations are active and living. Such is the real life of musical styles, schools, trends, and genres. Some intonations live through generations. The average listener, despite his limitations, is often more sensitive to intonational qualities than a professional musician and critic.

In Beethoven's music there are intonations of humanity and of nature. They are intonations that reconstruct social reality. In the Third, Fifth, Seventh, and Ninth Symphonies one hears reality expressed intonationally. There is a quotation by Schindler of Beethoven's explanation of the poetical idea of the *Appassionata Sonata* op. 57 and of the sonata op. 31 #2: *Lesen sie nur Shakespeare's Sturm.* [Read Shakespeare's *Tempest*.] The *Appassionata,* according to Soviet estheticians, reveals intonations of nature in its cosmic aspect, that is, the poetical idea of nature. Beethoven's world of lofty contemplations, his meditations, his lyrical and dramatic monologues and dialogues, his inner conflicts of grief and joy, of daily life—these are expressed through intonations that are the treasure of mankind. Beethoven, according to Soviet estheticians, intonationally created in his art a cosmos, nature, humanity, and himself, for the perception of present and future generations.

The means and methods of achieving Soviet musical realism occupy the attention of Soviet estheticians and musicians. The solution of the problem is in the education of a compositional ear for music, that is, (1) in the selection and cultivation of musical intonations reflecting or embodying aspects, features, and emotional states in a Communist sociey, and (2) in the elaboration of a Soviet musical logic and of specific musical forms, where form is not an academic arrangement of tonal and rhythmical media, but an indissoluble union of design with content brought about by development of musical themes reflecting Soviet life and society.[3]

From the Soviet point of view, theoretically and abstractly, the problem is simple. The basis of the Communist world outlook is dialectic materialism which, as Communism teaches, is the most complete, perfect, reliable, and profound system of social development. Music is capable of communicating in artistic imagery the factors and aspects of social development. The result is Soviet musical realism.

The mission of Soviet composers is to compose music that will possess maximum qualities of development and procedure of tonal elements. This means a music embodied in the most interesting forms that reveal thematic development of musical ideas.

Theoretically it looks simple. But the development of a musical theme is the result of psychic processes that do not lend themselves to Communist dictation and control. Therefore, the practical solution of esthetic form in Soviet musical realism becomes very complex. It is complicated by relationships of musical logic and form to aspects of world outlooks, ideologies, and all the manifestations of human emotions.

Communist esthetics asserts that there is a close connection between the musical thinking of a composer and the philosophic views, ideas, and achievements of a culture era. Soviet musical realism is based on this assumption. For example, Soviet estheticians claim that the logic and forms of Beethoven's music can be understood only on the basis of the teaching of dialectics which was developed during the Beethovenian era by Kant and Hegel.

Thus, in Soviet thinking, without a dialectic understanding of development of musical processes, one cannot understand the characteristics and traits of Beethoven's music.

Beethoven probably was the greatest master of thematic development in Western music. His music is imbued with the idea of thematic development, from the smallest details to the broadest generalizations.

Beethoven's musical thinking was influenced by Western European idealistic ideas. At the same time, the creative instinct and consciousness of Beethoven were constantly attracted to the realistic world and to the incarnation of realistic imagery in music by means of salient intonational themes and motives, such as the motives of fate, tragedy, and of onomatopoeic effects.

Thus, in Soviet thinking, if Beethoven could create music of an emotional appeal that transcends national and cultural boundaries, why could not Soviet composers reflect Soviet reality for the benefit of the entire world?

The fact is that Beethoven's musical thinking did not attain materialist dialectics as Communism understands it socially and economically. His method of acceptance, rejection, and analysis of motivic developments and rhythmic manifestations may have been dialectic, that is, a critical examination of contrasting themes, a so-called musical thesis and antithesis, resulting in a spontaneous imaginative reflection of reality and spirituality.

What Beethoven attained was a mastery of intonational abstraction of music. Only through utmost abstraction of expressive and imaginative elements was Beethoven able to develop abstract factors and concepts in a manner that was never achieved by any other composer, for example, in the Third, Fifth, Sixth, Seventh, and Ninth Symphonies; in the *Coriolan, Egmont, and Leonora No. 3 Overtures*. This argument is accepted by Soviet estheticians who regard this abstract dialectic logic of Beethoven as the greatest musical achievement and example for study, understanding, and creative imitation by Soviet composers.

According to Communist thinking, the growth of empirical factors and qualities in romantic music coincided with the evolution of decadent philosophic thoughts and world outlooks in the nineteenth century societies. Romantic music "broke" with dialectics and the concept of the world as a struggle of social and economic contradictions. Thus, during the nineteenth century, Beethoven was revealed as a colossal genius who stood above all composers because of his marvellously consummated developments of musical ideas.

We only have specific conceptions of world outlooks and feelings of nineteenth-century composers: Berlioz's hero dissatisfied with life, submerged in fantastic dreams, unable to cope with life, and seeking forgetfulness in death; Liszt's pessimistic reflections on the fate of a composer in a world of contradictions, and on the struggle between spirituality and sin (*Faust*); Franck's concern with the mystic idea of deliverance and salvation; Brahms' feeling of retrospect, regret, and resignation; Wagner's concern with social and economic problems (*Ring of the Nibelungs*), love as a psychological aspect (*Tristan and Isolde*), and, finally, religious mysticism (*Parsifal*).

Soviet musical realism attempts the development of thematic materials, tonality, and rhythm, where rhythm is the all-inclusive concept of anticipations, fulfillments, consummations, and intensities in the tonal flow. Soviet esthetics regards Beethoven's treatment of these elements as a revelation of active musical development embodying abstract ethical and esthetical drives.

Post-Beethovenian romanticism is characterized by weakening and fragmentation of musical forms. This loosening process was determined by the varieties of emotional and imaginative content in the forms. This weakening resulted in predominance of independent lyric sections and varieties of musical episodes. This was the problem not only of symphonic music but of program music as well. It represented a new type of musical thinking and development of musical ideas.

Soviet esthetics sees an interesting example of this in the symphonic works of Tchaikovsky. Tchaikovsky's emotional elements are more pithy and concise than Beethoven's. There is of course a profusion of concrete developmental elements in Tchaikovsky's symphonic works. But, according to Soviet estheticians, Tschaikovsky does not achieve the continuity of dialectic development in Beethoven's symphonic works.

The problem of Soviet musical realism is how to produce a new type of realistic rhythmic symphonic development. Soviet esthetics bases its conclusions on Marxist-Leninist principles of struggle, development, and onward march of social aspects. Rest and conciliation of opposite social aspects are inherent in the struggle of opposed elements and are relative. Soviet musical realism is called upon to create compositions not only with dynamic developments, but also music of a contemplative, peaceful character expressing emotions and impressions of Soviet reality. Laconism in Soviet music is viewed as a characteristic trait of contemporary Soviet art. This means the fixation of that which is essential, and the curtailment of casual aspects. This enables Soviet composers to express a lot in a short time. As an example Soviet estheticians refer to Tchaikovsky's Sixth Symphony in which the music represents a psychological saturation which is impossible in real life. No one can experience in one hour that which was experienced by the hero in the Sixth Symphony.

If a composer wishes to embody a significant thought, or to re-create a picture of life, he must aim at conciseness. An example of this conciseness is the system of leading motives. The degree of musical laconism is its intonational concreteness. The greater the intonational concreteness, the more laconic the image. The less significant a musical theme, the more diffuse is the manner of musical exposition presented by the composer.

Musical conciseness as found in the style of Beethoven is a result of intonational concreteness. A skillful employment of musical conciseness does not mean a preponderance of harmonic or timbre aspects but a preponderance of a definite image. The result is direct and purposeful thematic development.

In classical dramatic sonata form the intensity of development of the active image excludes lyrical subordinate themes. In contemporary Soviet music the influx of images calls for mastery of thematic development. Contrasting dynamic changes of motivic fragments, which in classical music momentarily interrupt action in the tonal flow, become indispensable in Soviet music as a means for establishing victory of vital life-asserting aspects of Soviet reality.

Soviet musical realism attempts: (1) the crystallization of vivid, graphic thematic materials embodying living, pulsating musical intonations of Soviet reality; and (2) new types of thematic development based primarily on the principle of struggle of "two worlds" —the new socialist world and the old capitalist world.

Soviet esthetics does not brush aside old forms, especially the sonata style employed by the great composers. But it condemns slavish adherence to schematic designs, passive submission to musical logic and stereotyped conventionality, and, above all, to formalistic forms.

In Beethoven's music the quality of themes and their dialectic development reveal social and emotional factors in powerful musical forms. According to Communist thinking, Soviet themes embodying intonations of progressive ideas and emotions in a Communist society will produce the new music of the future.

CHAPTER 23

Myaskovsky

NICHOLAS MYASKOVSKY belonged to the Russian prerevolutionary intelligentsia and, after the October Revolution in 1917, he joined the Soviet intellectuals sympathetic to socialist ideology. His music had been influenced by the traditions of Russian classical music and Russian literature.

Myaskovsky's sympathy for people and responsiveness to social problems made him a successor to Tchaikovsky in musical psychorealism. However, Myaskovsky's music shows emotional restraint. Despite its spontaneity of lyricism, his music is often intellectual and professionally disciplined.

Myaskovsky was born on April 20, 1887, in Modlin, near Warsaw. His father was a military engineer whose assignments took him to various cities in Russia. He finally settled in Petersburg, where Nicholas enrolled in the Military Academy.

After graduating from the Academy in 1903, Myaskovsky served as a military engineer in Moscow. He wrote a letter to Rimsky-Korsakov asking him to recommend a teacher with whom he could study music theory. Korsakov recommended Reinhold Glière, a pupil of Taneyev. In 1904, Myaskovsky was transferred to Petersburg. He resigned from the army in 1907 to devote himself to music. He enrolled in the Petersburg Conservatory, where he studied with Korsakov and Lyadov, and from which he was graduated in 1911.

Myaskovsky composed his first symphony while a student at the conservatory. In 1912, he made his debut as a music critic. In 1921, he was appointed professor of composition at the Moscow Conservatory, where he taught for almost thirty years. As a teacher of composition, Myaskovsky was regarded as a successor of Taneyev. Among his

293

pupils were Kabalevsky and Khachaturyan. He participated in Soviet musical organizations and was one of the editors of the magazine *Soviet Music*. Myaskovsky died August 8, 1950.

Myaskovsky's compositions include twenty-seven symphonies, three sinphoniettas, overtures, symphonic poems, a concerto for violin and orchestra, a concerto for violoncello and orchestra, thirteen string quartets, two sonatas for violoncello and piano, a sonata for violin and piano, songs, and piano compositions.

In his early compositions, Myaskovsky carried on the national traditions of nineteenth century Russian composers, including Glinka, "The Powerful *Kuchka,*" and Tchaikovsky. These influences are revealed in Myaskovsky's love of Russian folk songs and in his desire to reflect Russian realities in music. His prerevolutionary compositions reflect his pessimism and dissatisfaction with Russian social conditions.

The First World War was a turning point in Myaskovsky's musical creativity. As a field engineer in the army, he learned the feelings and psychology of Russian peasant soldiers. He wrote down many of their folk songs, which he used as thematic material in his Fifth Symphony (1918). This symphony established Myaskovsky as an important composer of Russian national music.

In his symphonies composed after the October Revolution, Myaskovsky attempted to reflect in musical imageries the socialist ideology of the new Russian society. The Sixth Symphony (1922–1923) is supposed to represent the sufferings and sacrifices endured during the Civil War, which followed the October Revolution. In the Eighth Symphony (1922–1924), Myaskovsky tried to bare the struggle of peasantry against the oppression of landlords. The Twelfth Symphony, composed for the fifteenth anniversary of the October Revolution, tried to compare a picture of collective farm construction with the stagnation prevailing in old villages. The Sixteenth Symphony (1935–1936) was composed under the influence of the loss of the airplane *Maxim Gorky*. The funeral march of the symphony is contrasted with what to Mysaskovsky is an expression of the power and courage of the Soviet people.

In the Twenty-third Symphony (1941), composed during his sojourn in the Caucasus, Myaskovsky used ten contrasting Caucasian melodies. The symphony, which is suitelike in form, continues the interest in Caucasian folklore, in Russian classical literature of Pushkin and Lermontov, and in the music of Glinka and Balakirev.

The Twenty-second and Twenty-fourth Symphonies, and the poem-cantata *Kirov Is With Us,* composed during the Second World War, reflect Myaskovsky's patriotism.

Myaskovsky did not approve of modern trends in Western music. In his criticism of modern music, Myaskovsky made his evaluations on the basis of his knowledge of Russian classical music and his skepticism of modern methods of composition.[1]

During the 1940's, Myaskovsky revised some of his early compositions, which he thought did not adequately reflect contemporary feelings and aspirations of Soviet society.

Myaskovsky's symphonies bridge prerevolutionary Russian symphony and Soviet symphony. The finales of his Sixth, Eighth, Sixteenth, and Twenty-first Symphonies are constructed on different intonations from the finales of former Russian symphonies. The finales of Russian symphonies assert joy, happiness, courage, enthusiasm of victory, and the holiday revelry of Russian crowds. There is no ordinary crowd in Myaskovsky's symphonic finales. It is an angry, indignant wave of people, whose collective character is a tremendous primordial force bent on revenge. . . . The music of the finales of Soviet symphonies reveals the characteristic purposive principle: it is not the people, not humanity in general, but *our* people in their joy of living; not human action in general, but the revelation of feelings (joy, grief) prompted on streets and squares by rhythms and intonations of exciting and cherished action of the masses . . . The finales of Myaskovsky's symphonies, like the finales of Tchaikovsky's symphonies, are stimuli to escape from the world of personal thoughts and reflections, the release, so to speak, of Faust from his laboratory into the world of men.[2]

Myaskovsky's symphonic style is intellectual. It is characterized by logical and rational principles of composition. His contributions to the Soviet symphony are significant. For example, the slow movements of his symphonies with their lyrical introspective melodies evoke moods of meditation, reflection, and contemplation of Russian nature. In these movements, Myaskovsky's music is reminiscent of the music of the slow movements of Borodin's and Tchaikovsky's symphonies.

Myaskovsky's and Shostakovich's "war" symphonies, composed

during the 1940's, have similar ideological backgrounds; but stylistically, they are different. Shostakovich's artistic generalizations are based on active representational themes; for example, the invasion theme in the Seventh Symphony. Myaskovsky's symphonies are further characterized by his reflection and meditation on current events.[3]

CHAPTER 24

☙ ❧

Prokofiev

PROKOFIEV'S STYLE is not based on contemporary abstract concepts representing subconscious activities of the mind. Prokofiev created an individual musical language which expresses life and human experiences. Many of his stylistic features have become identified with Soviet music.

Prokofiev respected Russian classical traditions of music. His music reveals influences of Glinka and composers of the "Powerful *Kuchka*," especially in representations of Russian nature and Russian life, in march-like characteristics of his music, and in his preference for happy themes in major tonalities. He developed Russian national intonations by integrating elements of his melodic style with elements of Russian folklore.

Prokofiev's music is linked to the classical sonata style in which he developed individual expressive means. His melodies, harmonies, rhythms, and orchestration are unique. Beginning with the Classical Symphony in D Major (1917), Prokofiev's music reveals stylistic features which characterize his entire creative life. The musical characteristics of his youthful period (1907–1918) were adapted to new ideas in the music of his mature period (1933–1953).

Sergei Prokofiev was born on April 23, 1891, in Sontsovka, a village in the Ekaterinoslav Province in the Ukraine. His father, Sergei Alexeyevich, managed the estate of a wealthy landowner, Sontsev. His mother, Maria Grigoryevna, was a talented pianist, who cultivated in her son a love for classical music.

Prokofiev began to compose at the age of five and a half. His first compositions were a waltz, a march, and a rondo.

In the spring of 1900, the Prokofiev family visited Moscow. They attended several operatic performances, including Gounod's *Faust* and Borodin's *Prince Igor*. The operas made a deep impression on Prokofiev. Upon returning to Sontsovka, he composed an opera *Velikan* (The Giant) for piano without vocal parts. The libretto, written by Prokofiev, is a fairy tale with autobiographical details. Some of the descriptive elements of the music anticipate *Peter and the Wolf*.

In 1901, Prokofiev composed an opera *Na pustinikh ostrovakh* (On Deserted Islands). The libretto, written by Prokofiev, is a story of a sea storm, shipwreck, and landing of passengers on a deserted island.

In 1902, Maria Grigoryevna took her son to Moscow. Prokofiev was introduced to Taneyev who advised him to study music theory. In the winter of 1902, on the recommendation of Taneyev, Prokofiev studied harmony with J. N. Pomerantsev. Prokofiev was indifferent to the routine of exercises in harmony. He was more interested in composing, and Pomerantsev's method of teaching harmony bored him.

Prokofiev gained more from the teaching of Glière, who visited with the Prokofievs in Sontsovka during the summers of 1902 and 1903. Under the guidance of Glière, Prokofiev composed short sonatas and miniatures for piano, which he called "ditties." From 1902 to 1906, he composed sixty ditties, which reveal the rhythmic peculiarities in his later style.

In the late summer of 1904, Prokofiev went to Petersburg to enroll in the Conservatory. In September, he passed the entrance examinations and enrolled in the Conservatory. His teachers were Lyadov in harmony, Rimsky-Korsakov in orchestration, and Esipova in piano. In 1909, Prokofiev was graduated from the class of composition. He remained at the conservatory to study piano and conducting. In 1914, he was graduated from the classes of piano and conducting.

During the prerevolutionary period (1907–1917), Prokofiev composed over thirty compositions in various genres. In 1918, he left Russia. His travels took him to Japan, Hawaii, and the United States. In 1923, he settled in Paris. In 1933, Prokofiev returned to Russia, and this was the beginning of his mature creative period during which he composed some of his best compositions. He died on March 5, 1953.

Prokofiev's melody and harmony are based on the seven-tone diatonic major or minor scale with a single tonic center. Prokofiev alters tones of the scale by means of sharps and flats. For example, in the C

Major scale the C may be changed to C Sharp or C Flat, the D may be changed to D Sharp or D Flat, and so on. The altered tones may become fundamental tones of the scale. Thus the diatonic scale may be expanded from the original seven tones to eight, nine, ten, eleven, or twelve tones. The scale Prokofiev uses is actually a combination of the diatonic and chromatic scales.

In a diatonic scale, generally the important tones are the tonic (the first tone), the dominant (the fifth tone), the subdominant (the fourth tone) and the leading tone (the seventh tone). Through modulation (change of tonality), the altered tones in Prokofiev's scale may temporarily assume functions of the above-mentioned tones.

In Prokofiev's system, each tone of the seven-tone diatonic scale may become a temporary tonic tone of a new scale. The altered "subtonic" tone of a temporary tonic thus becomes the leading tone of this tonic tone.

The new subtonic (leading) tones enrich Prokofiev's melodies with chromatic ornamentations and colors. A raised fourth step (subdominant) of the scale, which acts as a leading tone into the fifth step (dominant) of the scale, is often used by Prokofiev. The result is movement by intervals of an augmented fourth (the Lydian fourth), which frequently characterizes Prokofiev's melodies.

A major or minor triad is a consonance (a chord characterized by repose) which may act as a tonic triad. Prokofiev frequently transforms a consonance into a dissonance (a chord characterized by tension) by simultaneous sounding of a consonance and a chord built on a new subtonic (leading) tone. This is characteristic of Prokofiev's system of harmony.

Prokofiev frequently uses a tonic chord with a raised fourth step of the scale (F Sharp in the C Major scale, or C Sharp in the G Major scale, and so on). For example, in a C Major triad (C, E, G), the "Lydian Fourth" may appear as a G Flat, F Sharp (F Sharp is enharmonic with G Flat), or as E Double Sharp (E Double Sharp is enharmonic with F Sharp or G Flat). Different spellings (C-G Flat, C-F Sharp, or C-E Double Sharp) depend on the function of the altered tone.

Altered tones and their harmonizations are used by Prokofiev to describe in music situations and characters. For example, the depressed mood of Cinderella in the *Cinderella Ballet,* the love of Romeo and Juliet in the *Romeo and Juliet Ballet,* and the authoritative theme of the Lady of the Copper Mountain in *The Stone Flower Ballet*.

Prokofiev's progressions of harmonies frequently result in a polyphony of layers.[1] This polyphony is not an interweave of melodies, but an interweave of groups or combinations of harmonies. The polyphonic texture results from doubling, tripling, or "thickening" (many-voiced parallelism) of basic melodic lines in the progressions of harmonies.[2] The harmonic parallelisms in Prokofiev's music resemble Russian folk song polyphony.

Prokofiev's harmonic style is an expansion of harmonic elements in the music of Schubert, Chopin, Liszt, Schumann, and Wagner. The music of these romantics is based on diatonic major and minor scales, with altered tones and chromaticisms. Alterations and chromatic elements in the music of these romantics accomplish modulations by assuming an alteration or a chromatic tone as a leading tone (the seventh tone) of a new tonality. They also enrich a tonality. "Prokofiev used to speak of the kindred nature of Schubert's music. He had in mind Schubert's favorite device of 'explosive' tonal digressions." [3]

Although altered tones introduce new dominant and subdominant functions in romantic music, the feeling of the original tonality is seldom obscured. The music of Wagner's *Tristan and Isolde* demonstrates temporary digressions from the tonic, or evasions of the tonic. Wagner's alterations and chromaticisms result in contrasts in functional relationships of harmonies. The basic tonality is sometimes obscured.

Altered tones in Chopin's *Polonaise Fantaisie,* the *F Minor Fantasia,* and the *F Minor Ballade* never obscure the fundamental tonalities of the compositions.

In Prokofiev's music the tonic is supreme. "The tonic is impulsive, exciting, and moving. This contradicts 'Tristanian' precepts and ideas that evasion of the tonic will produce continuity of melodic tension. On the contrary, the supremacy of the tonic will produce a healthy, natural perception of dynamics and mobility, without any suggestion of stagnation or setting." [4]

Altered tones which are used as fundamental tones of a tonality occur in Russian folk songs. A lowered second and seventh steps of a scale are common in Russian folk songs. Alterations within diatonic major and minor tonalities are basic in Prokofiev's style, and the altered tones are as important as the seven tones of the scale.

Prokofiev altered any number of tones in a tonality. In the march in *The Love for Three Oranges,* he lowered the third step of the scale. In the Fifth and Sixth Piano Sonatas, he altered all tones of the scale. Thus, Prokofiev used the chromatic scale not as a system of tone rows, but as a system of diatonic major and minor tonalities enriched with altered tones equal in importance to the basic tones of the scale.

Chords built on altered tones are regarded by Prokofiev as belonging to the tonality, and are used independently or in conjunction with other chords of the tonality. Although Prokofiev retained the functions of the tonic tone of a tonality, his use of intervals of thirds, fourths, fifths, and sixths made up of altered tones expanded chord relationships within a tonality. In cadences, Prokofiev often stresses "authenticity" (tonic chord immediately preceded by the dominant chord) and the function of the leading tone. Prokofiev evolved an expanded diatonic scale which became a chromatic series different from the traditional chromatic scale. This chromatic series includes all diatonic formations and a complex of various tonal series unified into a single chromatic tonality. An innovation in Prokofiev's chromatic series is a complicated tonic chord which includes dissonant intervals of seconds, tritones, and sevenths. In his music, Prokofiev demonstrates that dissonant combinations are independent chords which do not require resolutions into consonances.

Prokofiev demonstrated that perception of consonances and dissonances depends on the meaningful aspects and the convincing realism of the music, and on the development of social listening perception, rather than on rules of preparation and resolution of dissonances as taught in harmony books.

In the expanded diatonic scale, Prokofiev found all harmonic functions he needed for his musical imagery. His use of the expanded scale opened new opportunities for composers reluctant to use abstract atonal speculations of Schönberg's tone rows.

Prokofiev's system of modulation is based on the principle that any triad in the expanded diatonic scale may be regarded as a leading tone triad or a fundamental triad, regardless of its previous function. There is no such thing as an "unrelated" tonality in Prokofiev's style. Prokofiev frequently modulates by shifting the tonic center a tone or semitone up or down the scale. In this respect, his system of modulation resembles that of Rimsky-Korsakov. "As our moods change, so do the expressive and intonational qualities of our speech. Modulations of large parallel layers of music by intervallic steps are colorfully justified, and, at the same time, they produce a melodic movement from tonality to tonality." [5]

Prokofiev's music is energetic, assertive, and with a characteristic harshness of outlines. It is clear, rhythmic, and often dancelike. The variety, flexibility, and dynamic quality of his rhythms reflect contemporary feelings and experiences. With the exception of the waltz, Prokofiev's rhythms have no specific dance characteristics. He uses old and contemporary rhythms with national or traditional elements. He introduces dance elements in his symphonies, sonatas, and operas, but he frequently lessens the flexibility of dance rhythms in his ballets, which are, therefore, difficult for choreographic interpretation.

Prokofiev's melodies are clear and precise. They are usually built on tones of major or minor triads, which represent the essence of Prokofiev's "neo-classicism." Sudden "displacements" of tones, angularities of melodic outlines, and leaps immediately reveal Prokofiev's individual style. Distortions and exaggerations of melodic outlines seem to suggest ridicule, caricature, and excitement. Certain intervals are used by Prokofiev for intonational expression. For example, the interval of a ninth is used as an intonational expression of grief in the death scene of the ballet *Romeo and Juliet* and in the funeral of Semyon Kotko in the opera of the same name.

Prokofiev's melodic style gradually changed from his youthful period to his Soviet period. The changes paralleled the development of Prokofiev's conceptions of Russian past and present, and of problems of contemporary life. Instrumental characteristics and scattered, declamatory features of his early melodies gave place to singing epic heroic and lyric romantic themes which express intonations of emotional states. The emotional tensions and colors of such themes are enhanced by the displacement of the musical texture a semitone up or down the scale, and by intervals of augmented fourths or minor thirds.

Another characteristic of Prokofiev's mature period is the wide range of his melodies. From low or middle registers, a melody rises upward into high registers; for example, the subordinate theme of the Second Violin Concerto. The acoustical effects of such melodies enhance the imageries evoked by the music.

Prokofiev's themes are often played in unison by orchestral groups or by instrumental solos, and almost without chordal support. Such treatment of melodies evokes a feeling of loneliness, especially when the melody is accompanied by another melody, or by light tremolos. An example of this is the first theme of Cinderella in the *Cinderella Ballet.*

In his mature period, Prokofiev composed melodies which evoke feelings of contemplation and meditation. These melodies, built on tones of major and minor triads, are characterized by even rhythms, unisons, parallel octaves, and low registers.

Influences of Russian intonations are prominent in Prokofiev's mature compositions, including the Fifth, Sixth, and Seventh Symphonies, and *The Stone Flower* ballet. His epic heroic compositions, the cantatas *Alexander Nevsky* and *Zdravitsa* (The Toast), contain melodic recitatives, lyric melodies, and marches. They also include intonations which resemble Russian folk songs and urban melodies. Prokofiev frequently used free rhythmic accentuations found in Russian songs. By combining melodic and declamatory elements, he carried on the traditions of Dargomijsky and Mussorgsky.

The descriptive characteristics of Prokofiev's melodies are remarkable. With a few tones, Prokofiev delineates an image, or the essence of an idea or representation. This is especially prominent in his ballets and operas.[6]

In his opera *War and Peace,* Prokofiev achieved the "symphonization" of the music, that is, the construction of large, complete, dramatic operatic forms. In his ballets, an important function is given to lyric symphonic music, rather than to specific dance genres. The thematic developments of melodic elements in his ballet music are intermixed with irregular rhythms and expanded cadences. These developments are similar to the developments in Prokofiev's symphonic cycles.

The waltz with its graceful rhythms is Prokofiev's favorite dance in which he carried on the waltz traditions of Glinka and Tchaikovsky. Russian waltzes are different from waltzes of Viennese composers, including Johann Strauss. Viennese waltzes have strong, accented rhythms, short melodic phrases, and instrumental characteristics. Russian waltzes are lyric and symphonic. Their melodies have a singing quality, the floating rhythms are softer and unified.

"Prokofiev reveals without complications and philosophizing perceptions of reality in musical statements of facts of life. His musical themes are not abstract generalizations, and they are not carriers of emotional tension. They are emotion itself revealed as music, and concentrated in musicalized thoughts, intonations." [7]

What could be more commonplace than the story of *Peter and the Wolf?* The music is simple, natural, and without profound analyses of reality. This does not mean that Prokofiev was indifferent to occurrences in life, or immersed in the pursuit of selfish pleasure.

Prokofiev reveals a characteristic of the Russian common man, the peasant, noticed by Levin in *Anna Karenina*. The Russian peasant understands the facts of life and does not need the profound philosophy of Kant and Hegel. Prokofiev feels reality and understands the joy of life—for example, in the *Classical Symphony* and in his piano compositions. One hardly needs explanations of the reality and imagery in *Peter and the Wolf.* One does not need a historical discourse about the Teutonic invasion in *Alexander Nevsky.* The music is self-explanatory, just as is the "invasion" music in Shostakovich's Seventh Symphony.

Prokofiev contributed a unique approach to contemporary styles of music. His music is not an abstract manipulation of tone elements and designs. His music is a continuous development and representation of life as it is lived and experienced. His musical themes are thoughts and emotions which reveal life with its joys, problems, and tensions in meaningful musical intonations.

CHAPTER 25

◅◅◦▻▻

Shostakovich

THE MELODIC and harmonic idioms of Shostakovich's style are different from classic-romantic idioms, and his music does not lend itself to immediate appreciation and popular appeal. The dissonantal quality of his music and the absence of sensuous, emotional ardor in his style are not designed for easy, relaxed enjoyment; however, his works contain many pages of affable lyricism and of friendly, humorous, sparkling music. In representations of stormy periods of contemporary Russian history, in dramatic tensions, and in philosophical and ethical conceptions, the imagery of some of Shostakovich's symphonies attains the summit of Soviet realism in music.

Shostakovich's compositions include piano preludes, fugues, sonatas, songs, cantatas, chamber music, concertos, operas, ballets, music for films, and symphonies. His outstanding contribution has been in symphonic forms in which he projected musical and esthetical problems based on aspects of Russian history and on imagery of Soviet reality.

Dmitri Shostakovich was born in Petersburg on September 25, 1906. His father, Dmitry Boleslavovich, was a chemical engineer. His mother, Sofya Vasilyevna, studied piano at the Petersburg Conservatory.

At the age of nine, Shostakovich began to study piano, first with his mother, then at the music school of I. Glasser. At the age of eleven, Shostakovich began to compose.

In the fall of 1919, Shostakovich enrolled at the Petrograd Conservatory. He studied piano with L. Nikolayev, one of the foremost piano teachers, and composition with N. A. Sokolov and M. O. Steinberg.

305

In 1923, Shostakovich was graduated from the School of Piano, and two years later from the School of Composition. In 1927, he participated in the first Chopin Piano Competition in Warsaw and was awarded an honorary diploma. However, a career of a piano virtuoso did not appeal to Shostakovich, and he decided to devote himself to composition. At present, he is considered as the dean of Soviet composers.

In 1958, Oxford University conferred upon Shostakovich the title of Doctor Honoris Causa. Thus, Shostakovich became the third Russian composer after Tchaikovsky and Glazunov to receive this honor.

Shostakovich's melodic style does not appeal at first hearing to one accustomed to usual classic or romantic melodies. His melodies are predominantly diatonic, with intervals of fourths and fifths, scalelike progressions, and are embellished with alterations which are tone digressions or modulations, transitions from one key to another. Altered tones are scale degrees raised a semitone by a sharp or lowered a semitone by a flat. These alterations do not change the functional importance of scale degrees but endow Shostakovitch's themes with an expressive quality, impetuosity, drama, grotesqueness, and, in general, with a variety of realistic imageries.

Altered tones are important in classic and romantic music. Shostakovich's melodic alterations differ from classic patterns. His alterations are usually downward, especially in minor tonalities. For example, in the natural A minor scale,—a, b, c, d, e, f, g, a, Shostakovich lowers the second, fourth, fifth, seventh, and eighth degrees: a, b flat, c, d flat, e flat, f, g flat, a flat. The lowered second degree, known as the *Neapolitan* degree, has been used since the seventeenth century. A lowered fourth degree is uncommon. Lowered fifth, seventh, and eighth degrees (the eighth degree is the tonic tone and the lowering generally occurs in upper ranges of a melody) are seldom found in nineteenth century music but are used in Shostakovich's melodic style. Shostakovich's simultaneous use of regular and altered scale degrees often results in the twelve-tone chromatic scale.

In classic harmony, alterations and modulational deviations are independent of each other. Shostakovich's alterations and modulational deviations are synthesized; that is, they are simultaneously alterations and modulational deviations. He retains fixed scale patterns; but altered tones, anchored by melodic accented cadences, represent either modulations where the regular tonic of the scale is substituted by other tones or just tone digressions. Shostakovich's alterations result in tonal instabilities, emerging and disappearing tonal vacillations. For example, a lowered fourth degree, F flat in the C major scale, is actually the third tone E in the C major triad, C-E-G. The melodic movement will show that the F flat is an unstable tone, not the E in the C major triad. The apparent unity of alterations and sudden deviations into remote tonalities is characteristic of Shostakovich's harmonic style.

The alterations of the fifth and eighth degrees introduces altered fifth and tonic tones into the tonic triad. For example, the C major triad may include two fifths, a G natural and a G flat, and two tonics, C natural and C flat. Shostakovich expands the classic use of a major and minor third in a tonic triad, C-E flat -G and C-E-G. In a cadence, Shostakovich sometimes uses the dominant fifth tone of the scale lowered by a semitone, and the tonic tone also lowered by a semitone. Using the chromatic series, Shostakovich creates modulational deviations into remote tonalities which are unrelated in the classic harmonic system but become related in his system.

The tonal characteristics in Shostakovich's music are at first disturbing to one accustomed to classic-romantic idioms. A listener who has heard a composition of Shostakovich will hardly fail to recognize his pungent, angular melodies with their altered tones, sudden bends, and turns.

Shostakovich's melodies are vividly descriptive. Shostakovich seldom writes melodies without imaginative or representative aspects, particularly in his mature style beginning with the Fifth Symphony. Short, melodic outlines embodying various feelings become zigzags of melodic links in which tonal and rhythmical nuclei emerge and disintegrate, evoking a bustling and emotionally chaotic imagery.

Despite its originality, Shostakovich's melodic style is rooted in Russian intonations and in Russian classical music. Influences of Russian revolutionary songs, heroic intonations, and rhythms which are indicated in the Fifth Symphony become prominent in the Eleventh Symphony.

Shostakovich prefers short musical themes whose boundaries are often indefinite. Some of his themes, especially in finales and symphonies, are often constructed of short intonational links which seem to obliterate cadences and instead, enhance dynamic effects.

Shostakovich is a master of thematic development. He exhausts every motivic and rhythmic element of a theme with a convincing, inexorable logic. His musical developments contain devices of fragmentation of thematic materials, and variations of thematic fragments. He often repeats the same theme in different ways, for example, in the first movement of the Seventh Symphony. He avoids regular sequences and prefers not to repeat exactly what was said before. He often uses genres of marches and dances. His marches are mournful, grotesque, and sometimes festive. He uses dance patterns to stress an idea, thought, or a specific imagery. Motives are often subjected to transformations and modifications which bring out unexpected suggestions in the tonal flow. This enables him to produce a continuity of tonal flow which holds a listener's attention. Shostakovich's instrumental style has been influenced by Russian and Western traditions of music. He does not imitate, but re-creates these influences. His symphonic music is the most significant example of his style. The clarity and exactness of his orchestral writing stem from the school of Rimsky-Korsakov to which he belongs through his studies with Steinberg, a pupil of Rimsky-Korsakov. Shostakovich's orchestral writing is rational, the dynamic and timbre effects are excellent, and the orchestral texture is clear. One will have little difficulty in recognizing the reflective soliloquies, sudden harmonic alterations, and timbre polyphony of his orchestral style.

Musical recitatives and oratorical characteristics occur in Shostakovich's symphonic and chamber compositions. In such cases, instrumental timbres are frequently likened to a human voice. He sometimes uses (in the Seventh Symphony) metrical patterns with seven, eight, ten, twelve, and even thirteen pulsations, which enhance the narrative or oratorical features of the music.

Shostakovich uses traditional classical symphonic forms as constantly developing musical processes. In his later symphonies, forms of the sonata-symphonic style are means of communicating and associating with audiences, and of merging personal, national, and social elements in music. Therefore, Shostakovich often disregards rules of the sonata form and of the sonata cycle. He usually prefers extended three-part forms (ABA), occasionally with sonata form elements, and the passacaglia, which is an old Italian-Spanish dance form.

Contemporary Soviet music criticism makes a distinction between "symphonism" and "symphonic" (orchestral) music. Not every composition for a symphony orchestra is symphonic in its substance. Not all music which contains aspects of "symphonism" is necessarily orchestral music:

The essential aspect of symphonism is the progressive growth and dialectic development of musical imagery organically combined with psychological saturation and utmost concentration . . . In our times, the sonata-symphonic cycle has proven its vitality as a convenient rational scheme. It retains its dramatic significance in such compositions as Shostakovich's Fifth Symphony and in Myaskovsky's Twenty-seventh Symphony. The great symphonists of the past, headed by Beethoven and Tchaikovsky, never thought of the sonata form as serene and unchangeable. The creators of contemporary symphonies regard the sonata form as a point of departure in a struggle for a new word in music.[1]

Although Shostakovich's style is intellectual, it reveals a dignified, restrained emotional complex. In his symphonic music, he seems to be interested more in an idea than in possibilities of orchestral color. Hence the peculiarities of his melody, harmony, and orchestration:

The unquestionable victory of the rights of the national Soviet system of music without emphasized references to tunes from bygone stages of Russian life, a music perceived as the emotional language of Soviet reality, is represented by the summits of Shostakovich's symphonism. In them, the intense pulse of the Soviet epoch is felt with incontestable authority and power of emotional suggestion.[2]

The variety of human feelings and emotions expressed by Shostakovich's music makes his art a documentation of Soviet reality. The appeal of his music depends largely on the listener's emotional and intellectual associations and reflections comparable to those expressed by the music.

First Creative Efforts

Shostakovich's First Symphony in F minor was his graduation thesis at the Conservatory. The symphony was performed on May 12, 1926, and met with great success. The music is joyous, sparkling, and optimistic. The festive finale is an appropriate summary of the emotional content of the symphony.

At first, the symphony was regarded as a juvenile expression of a gifted youth. The music critic Asafiev wrote that "the symphony belongs to those compositions with which one sympathizes for what they promise, rather than for what they give." [3] Compared to Shostakovich's later symphonies, the First Symphony reveals traces of tragic emotion and lyric outpourings of his mature style.[4]

The first four measures of the introduction of the symphony (Allegretto) contain the basic thematic elements of the first movement, which is in sonata form. Shostakovich's early symphonic style does not contain extensive emotional and dynamic structures. Instead, he uses variations and transformations of themes which evoke a varied imagery. In the first movement of the symphony, this method of composition results in dramatically contrasting thematic formations.

The introduction of the symphony seems to suggest uneasiness and anxiety, and the searching for a positive idea. This idea is expressed by an angular marchlike first theme played by a bassoon. A graceful, waltzlike subordinate theme, played by a flute, contrasts sharply with the severity of the first theme.

The beginning of the development section presents fragments of previously heard themes. The feeling is of tense expectation, which is ended by the appearance of the main theme. The dynamics gradually rises from piano to fortissimo and is climaxed by a transformed subordinate theme which is no longer graceful, but coarse and harsh. The musical revelry is held in check by the march-like first theme played by four French horns and then by three trumpets.

In the recapitulation, the march-like main theme rushes through the orchestra and fades away in the distance. The waltz-like subordinate theme, played by a flute, relieves the tension.

The music of the coda is a dramatic surge of short duration. The themes of the introduction are heard against thundering kettledrums. The feeling is of curious expectation of what is to come next in the scherzo.

The scherzo, composed in sonatina form (a sonata form without a development section), is a sparkling gallop reminiscent of Prokofiev's sharp rhythms. "The music evokes an imagery of happy crowds of people and glimpses of happy faces." [5] The scherzo anticipates Shostakovich's later compositions in this genre.

An energetic first theme played in four pulsations is contrasted with a lyrical chromatic theme played in three pulsations. The rhythmic contrast of the two themes is changed in the recapitulation. The lyrical theme, which is now played in four pulsations, loses its charm and refinement, and, accompanied by the bustling first theme, is sternly announced by French horns and trumpets.

The third movement (Lento) consists of three parts. The first part opens with a succession of chromatic chords. Against this background emerges an expressive chromatic melody played by an oboe. This melody is derived from thematic elements of the introduction and the step-by-step descending progressions in the main theme of the first movement. The music evokes a feeling of languor and "a premonition of something evil." [6] Motivic fragments are detached from the oboe melody and developed into new thematic groups played, in turn, by a solo violoncello and trumpets.

The second part of the movement opens with a variant of the oboe melody. Slow dissonantal chord progressions evoke an imagery of a funeral procession and of dramatic tension. [7]

In the third part of the movement, the trumpet fanfares of the first part, and the mourning rhythms of the second part, give way to a feeling of unrest. The lyrical oboe theme of the beginning of the movement is broken into separate phrases and disappears. Fragments of this lyrical theme appear in the coda. The tension of the music reaches a climax, which is broken by the explosive finale.

The finale is a prototype of Shostakovich's finales of later symphonies. It is energetic, optimistic, and evokes a feeling of determination and action.

The agitated, impetuous main theme is intonationally related to the main theme of the first movement, and is developed in three rising tonal waves characterized by strong, whimsical rhythms. A second theme, which is a variant of the lyrical oboe theme of the third movement, unifies thematically the finale with the preceding movements.

The music of the finale expresses the ebullient enthusiasm of a youthful composer. However, in the light of Shostakovich's later finales, one can sense in the finale of the First Symphony an emotional pathos and energy which became so characteristic of his mature style.

The First Symphony was followed by a crisis in Shostakovich's musical creativity. Trying to break away from conservative academic trends, Shostakovich began to experiment with modern musical tendencies. At that time there were two music groups in Russia: The Association of Contemporary Music and The Association of Russian Proletarian Musicians. The first group was sympathetic to modern trends in music; the second group was not distinguished in ideas and aims. Music critics in Leningrad were sympathetic to Schönberg's atonal serial music resulting from using the chromatic scale as a system of tone rows.

Shostakovich succumbed to modern tendencies. His first sonata and piano pieces are mechanical and dissonantal. In 1928, he composed an opera, *The Nose*, whose plot based on Gogol's story bares the narrow-minded thinking and customs of the Russian middle class. The style of the opera is devoid of singing and real characters. It is an abstract musical caricature which overwhelms an audience with musical eccentricities and distortions.

The Nose was followed by three ballets, *The Golden Age* (1930), *The Bolt* (1931), and *The Bright Stream* (1934). *The Golden Age* is a musical revue which deals with a Russian football team abroad. *The Bolt* ridicules moribund middle class ideas. *The Bright Stream* represents the adventures of a group of artists on a collective farm in the Kuban region. The music of the ballet is not distinguished, and the libretto is contrived and not convincing.

In 1927, Shostakovich composed the Second Symphony for chorus and orchestra in which he attempted to reflect revolutionary subjects and contemporary Soviet ideas. The symphony was unsuccessful because "the immature world outlook (of Shostakovich) and his narrow creative efforts doomed the solution of such a complex, ideationally innovatory assignment." [8] "The music of the symphony and its poetic text of abstract slogans are devoid of vivid imagery and emotional expression." [9] The symphony was Shostakovich's first attempt to reflect in music ideas and imagery of Soviet reality.

Shostakovich's style from 1927 to 1934 was a combination of a scathing musical journalism and "a magnificent, empty, rigid ceremonial of gestures and motions of a peculiar musical pantomime." [10]

In 1932, Shostakovich composed an opera *Katerina Izmailova* (*Lady Macbeth of Mtsensk District*), based on a story by the Russian writer Nicholas Leskov. In composing the opera, Shostakovich might have been influenced by the expressionism of Alban Berg's opera *Wozzeck*, whose plot consists of murders and nightmares.

The heroine of Shostakovich's opera, Katerina Izmailova, is a strong, passionate merchant woman motivated by love and cupidity. She is ruined by the crude, backward environment of provincial life. Katerina murders her husband and father-in-law who had hindered her love affair with the shop assistant, Sergei. The crime is discovered. Katerina and Sergei are condemned to penal servitude in Siberia. On the way to Siberia, Sergei is unfaithful to Katerina. Katerina grapples with her rival, Sonetka, and jumps into a river dragging her rival with her.

In the opera, Shostakovich attempts to vindicate Katerina and portray her as a victim of the stifling atmosphere of nineteenth century middle class existence. The exciting, entreating intonations which describe the emotional states of Katerina are contrasted with grotesque, merciless characterizations of the other actors. The naturalism of the libretto is shocking.

The *première* of the opera took place at the Maly Opera Theater in Leningrad on January 22, 1934. It was produced at the Bolshoi Theater in Moscow in January, 1936. The newspaper *Pravda* condemned the opera in an editorial entitled "Confusion Instead of Music," and referred to the "beastly cast of mind" of the character and the naturalism of the libretto.[11]

During Stalin's cult of personality the opera was buried in oblivion. In 1962, a new version of the opera was presented. Shostakovich revised the score and the libretto, rewrote the music of two interludes between the first and second, and seventh and eighth scenes, and narrowed the range of some vocal parts.

The revised opera is a social drama, described by Shostakovich as a "tragic satire," whose characters are delineated with relentless musical realism. The plot unfolds a picture of life in the chief town of a provincial district in prerevolutionary Russia ruled by police officers and petty government clerks and thugs. The story exposes the drab and sinister existence in the home of a miller, Izmailov. The patriarchal tenor of life in the Izmailov household harbors savagery, lust, petty tyranny, and malice.

In the opera, Katerina Izmailova, a gifted woman, is a victim of dark, backward social conditions. She is oppressed by a despotic father-in-law and a degenerate husband. The drama which takes place in the Izmailov household is a poignant social tragedy rather than a casual episode in a provincial criminal chronicle.

Shostakovich's music does not hint at everyday conditions of life which prevailed in old Russia. The score is acerbic in its characterizations and descriptions, for example, in the music of the fugue accompanying the marriage ceremony, in the sudden outcries of the drunken priest, in the farcical waltz accompanying the drunken father-in-law,

Boris Timofeyevich, who is driven by senile voluptuousness, and in the servile intonations of the hero, the cowardly, vulgar Sergei. However, the music of Katerina is tragically humanized beginning with her lyric romance in the first act and ending with her delirious monologue about a "black lake in the forest" in the last scene showing the halting place for transported convicts in Siberia.

From 1929 to 1932, Shostakovich composed music for the films *New Babylon, Alone, Golden Mountains,* and *The Encountered.* While a student at the Leningrad Conservatory, Shostakovich played the piano in movie theaters. This helped him develop a technique of musical representations of caricatures, psychological suggestions, and dramatic contrasts. It was an assignment which required appealing melodies and motives for terse, vivid musical sketches of movie imagery.

In 1929, Shostakovich composed the *May First Symphony* for chorus and orchestra. It is modern in its melodic and harmonic idioms, sketchy in its abstract construction, and related in conceptions to the Second Symphony. However, the symphony was an advance in Shostakovich's attempts to embody in music a content on the basis of Communist ideology.[12] The music of the symphony integrates in intonations of revolutionary oratory pastoral representations of the awakening of nature in spring, and ideological concepts of the May First celebration.[13]

In 1933, Shostakovich composed twenty-four preludes for piano. In 1934, he composed a piano concerto and a sonata for violoncello and piano. The music of these compositions breaks with modern speculative experiments. The preludes are reminiscent of Bachian polyphony. The piano concerto shows influences of Bach, Haydn, Beethoven, Chopin, and Mahler. The melodic style of the sonata for violoncello and piano is Russian in its song intonations and lyricism.

Shostakovich's Fourth Symphony (1935–1936) concluded his experimental creative period. The symphony reflects Shostakovich's enthusiasm for Mahler's symphonies with their long movements, emotional contrasts, nervous excitement, urban dance genres, and extended structural patterns.[14]

The symphony is characterized by juxtaposition of contrasting themes rather than by their development. This creates an impression of monotony and conglomeration of tonal layers.

Shostakovich's problem before composing the Fourth Symphony

was the elaboration of a new musical language. His problem after completing the Fourth Symphony was a careful selection and synthesis of what he had accomplished.[15]

The Fourth Symphony with its subjectivity and emotional elements seems to have been a reaction against the Second and Third Symphonies in which abstract concepts and revolutionary oratory favored the "masses" over personal elements. The merging of personal elements with public and social concepts was first achieved by Shostakovich in his Fifth Symphony, which began his mature creative period in the late 1930's.

Mature Creative Period

In his Fifth Symphony in D Minor (1937), Shostakovich broke with naturalism and formalistic experiments. The symphony revealed the main characteristics of Shostakovich's mature style:

Skill to penetrate into the essence of reflected vital phenomena; ability to perceive contradictions of reality; and virile force of feelings. . . . The new content and the newly discovered imagery brought to life new characteristics and devices of his musical language, a new approach to basic forms of instrumental music—*the sonata cycle in the symphony.* . . . Shostakovich leaned more on broader intonational foundations. His harmonic language, devices of polyphonic development, orchestration, and manner of constructing musical form, became more vivid and striking. Musical images became the means of artistic generalizations. Shostakovich's compositions created during these years were accepted by listeners as artistic reflections of important facets of Soviet life. Among these compositions, the first place belongs to the Fifth Symphony.[16]

"The theme of my composition," wrote Shostakovich, "is the formation of personality. It is precisely man with all of his experiences whom I saw in the center of the conception of this composition, which from beginning to end is lyrical in its cast. The finale of the symphony resolves the tense, tragic moments of the first parts in an optimistic, cheerful vein." [17]

The apparent subjective slant of the symphony aroused controversial discussions among Soviet music critics. A personal expression is not a criterion of Soviet realism. Soviet criticism evaluated the symphony as a composition whose meaning transcends subjectivity:

It is a well-known fact that objective results of creativity often do not coincide with subjective intentions of a composer. And if pretentious conceptions often produce insignificant results, in more rare cases a modest autobiographical theme might grow to dimensions of broad, vital generalizations. Such is the autobiographical character of Rembrandt's creativity, some of Beethoven's and Tchaikovsky's works, Tolstoy's and Gorky's, which not only did not interfere with, but actually helped them gain universal significance. In any case, a correct evaluation may be reached solely by an analysis of the work, whose objective meaning sometimes turns out to be surprising even to the artist himself.[18]

The "formation of personality" in Shostakovich's statement is symptomatic of subjective trends in Soviet art of the period. The main theme in Dzherzhinsky's opera *Quiet Don,* in Khrennikov's *In Storm,* and in Prokofiev's *Semyon Kotko* is the emergence of a new consciousness among many Russians who, after many self-searchings, embraced the revolution.

However, the Fifth Symphony is not a tale of isolated facts. It is an impression of ideas, feelings, conflicts, and hopes of an epoch in artistic generalizations. The dramatic concept of the symphony, the wealth of its imagery which evokes varied associations, and the aspects of objective narration leave the bounds of autobiography. Shostakovich is not a passive observer narrating about life. Only in this sense is he a subjective artist:

The music of the Fifth Symphony sounds like an excited, deeply felt account of life—varied, gay, and difficult, saturated with indomitable energy, tension of struggle, and drama of universal social-historical conflicts.[19]

As an original reflection of Soviet realism, the symphony represents man's active participation in life with all of its contradictions, clashes, and struggles. It anticipates features of Shostakovich's later symphonies. All of these elements Shostakovich expressed within the forms of the sonata-symphonic cycle, which he adapted to the specific needs of his musical and dramatic concepts.

The first movement of the Fifth Symphony is in sonata form. A short introductory theme, played by violoncellos and double basses, is energetic, angular, and discontinuous. Rising intonations of minor sixths and fifths seem to question. They are answered by resolute, affirmative intonations of descending minor sixths and thirds which seem to portend the coming struggle. Canonic imitation of the theme by violins enhances the sharpness of the imagery.

Two main themes follow the introduction. The first theme is a wistful, pensive, wandering melody. In this theme, in contrast to the questions and answers of the introduction, the composer seems to be absorbed in recollections. The second theme is in a similar emotional mood. It consists of short rhythmical figures and pauses which interrupt the melodic flow. The subordinate theme is a soaring melancholy theme played by violins against a chordal accompaniment of harps. The lyricism of the theme is different from the lyricism of subordinate themes in Tchaikovsky's symphonies:

Tchaikovsky's pensive lyrical themes evoke a reverie which has no place in a desperate struggle with fate. In Shostakovich's Fifth Symphony, the image created by the subordinate theme breaks imperiously into the midst of the combat . . . to help man in his struggle, giving him firmness, resolution, and ability to resist and overcome dark, destructive forces.[20]

The peaceful character of the subordinate theme is stressed later by pastoral motives played by a flute against sustained chords played by violoncellos and double basses. The exposition ends with an expressive dialogue of altos and violoncellos, and answered by flutes and clarinets.

The development begins with the first main theme played by French horns against the sustained pastoral motive played on a piano. Several tonal waves swell the development. Fragments of the introduction and other themes are polyphonically interwoven. Each tonal wave is introduced by martial rhythms of trumpets, which become the carriers of the "leit-timbre" of the development,[21] creating a feeling of tension and anxiety. There follows an episode in which the first main theme, played by flutes, is canonically imitated by violas, violoncellos, and double basses against a chordal accompaniment played by trumpets. This is followed by another episode, poco sostenuto, in which the first main theme is rhythmically transformed into a grim, relentless march, which is interrupted by resolute intonations of the introduction. It is "a sinister procession which sweeps away everything in its path." [22] The march anticipates the imagery of the "invasion" variations in Shostakovich's Seventh Symphony. The succession of culminating tonal waves is reminiscent of tonal waves in the developments of Tchaikovsky's symphonies. Shostakovich's culminating waves stress heroism, resolution, and power. Tchaikovsky's culminating waves represent emotional climaxes.

The recapitulation continues the resolute, tense feeling of the development. The coda is a return to the contemplation of stern reality. The forces opposing man are strong and relentless. The struggle will demand great efforts, suffering, and sacrifices.[23]

The second movement, the scherzo, overflows with happiness and joy. A succession of witty, contrasting musical sketches evokes an imagery of life with its daily pursuits. Displaced rhythmical accents and changing orchestral colors are reminiscent of Mahler's orchestral *ländlers,* Austrian dances in triple time, precursors of the modern waltz.[24] Expressive qualities of the timbre of French horns, and the high register of a bassoon, are used by Shostakovich to portray good-natured humor.

The hilarious first section of the scherzo is followed by another section which is characterized by a cheerful, dance-like melody played by a solo violin accompanied by harp chords and pizzicato of violoncellos. Unexpected changes of harmonies seem like casual reminiscences of Shostakovich's youthful, ironic, grotesque parodies of middle class "folklore," but without deliberate affectation and exaggeration.

The introspective third movement, Largo, "speaks of the suffering, sorrow, and agonizing experiences of a struggling man." [25] The main theme is in the style of a slow, mournful Russian song. It evokes "an image of a mournful soliloquy of the composer with himself." [26]

The movement consists of three sections, each characterized by a development or variation of the main theme. The lyricism of the music "is without expressionist excitability, moribund refinement, and a desire to arouse in a listener indefinable longings; on the contrary, spiritual clarity, warm affection, clear, noble human emotions, make the music a significant expression of strong simple feelings." [27]

The first section develops a recitative-like melody played by violins to the accompaniment of sustained chords by the entire string group.

The second section begins with a mournful flute melody which briefly recalls the dramatic imagery of the main theme of the first movement of the symphony. Subtle tonal changes which result from the lowered second and fourth steps of the natural minor scale enhance the sincere feeling of the music. Motivic fragments played by an oboe produce the effect of musicalized speech intonations.[28]

In the third section, the main theme assumes the character of passionate supplication and pathetic speech. The coda brings a feeling of peace.

"In its nature and expression, the emotional unity of the Largo is related to the restrained coloring of Rembrandt's later portraits. The prevailing mood is incarnated with a variety of truthful, psychologically sensitive inflections, which leave an impression of significant events experienced in life." [29] "Not in many pages of his music does Shostakovich come closer to Tchaikovsky's lyrical contemplation, as he does in this movement, in spontaneous, straightforward lyrical utterances. Separate episodes are stylistically reminiscent of Tchaikovsky. For example, the culmination of the movement, with the excited theme heard in the high register of the violoncellos, has very much in common with the recapitulation in the first part of Tchaikovsky's *Manfred Symphony*." [30]

Soviet music critics suggested the comparison of the Largo to the style of J. S. Bach. The influence of Bach's art in Shostakovich's Largo is neither in the outward similarity of certain compositional and polyphonic devices, nor in the relationship of musical intonations. In the compositional devices and intonational means of Shostakovich's music there is nothing specifically Bachian. However, the name of Bach is not mentioned fortuitously. The comparison with Bach is suggested by the resolute unity of Shostakovich's lyricism; by its severe intellectualism, inwardly passionate, but devoid of romantic amorousness; and by its faculty for prolonged concentration on a single emotion which reveals stable, impersonal aspects.[31]

The concept of the finale of the symphony is the victory of the will. The finale resolves the tense, emotional elements of the preceding movements in an optimistic vein. This has been pointed out by Shostakovich: "It has been said that the finale of the Fifth Symphony is different from the preceding movements. I disagree with this. In conformity with the basic theme of the symphony, the finale answers all questions which have been proposed in the other movements." [32]

The music of the finale is cheerful. After the energetic intonations and lyrical moods of the first movement, the witty musical sketches of the scherzo, and the mournful soliloquy of the Largo, the strong, hopeful music of the finale evokes an optimistic imagery. The finale synthesizes the emotional elements of the symphony in a confident and affirmative vein.

"The idea of the finale is the assertion and victory of the will, and the call to activity. This is expressed in the general plan of the development of the music of the finale, and in the dynamic, assertive character of the main and subordinate themes." [33]

The finale is in sonata-allegro form. The exalted mood of the music is established in the very beginning. A powerful musical trill played by the entire orchestra introduces the impetuous main theme. The opening motive of an interval of a fourth, imitated by the steady accompaniment of the kettledrums, evokes a momentary reminiscence of "The Marseillaise." The subordinate theme, constructed mainly of uniform eighth tones, further intensifies the inexorable rhythmic momentum of the music.

Imageries of popular celebrations occur in Mussorgsky's *Boris Godunov*, and in the finales of Tchaikovsky's Fourth and Fifth Symphonies. The imagery of Shostakovich's finale suggests a purposeful procession of people in a festive holiday spirit. The coda seems like a dramatic reassertion of hope in life and man.

The Sixth Symphony in B Minor (1939) is unusual in its form and conception. It consists of three movements. The first movement is a complex polyphonic improvisation. Thus, the symphony lacks a traditional first sonata-allegro movement. This makes the sonata-symphonic cycle incomplete.

The scherzo-like second movement is an effective piece of orchestral writing, odd rhythms, and thematic contrasts.

A dance-like finale, reminiscent of Rossini's sparkling overtures, is lively entertainment music. In its dance-like rhythms and orchestral effects, the finale seems like a succession of musical representations of daily life in a Soviet city, or of the holiday spirit of celebrations and popular entertainments.

In the Sixth Symphony, "Shostakovich makes his debut as a 'Soviet Rossini' who resurrected on a new foundation the remarkable, but unfortunately forgotten, tradition of entertaining, colorful, effective, and contagiously optimistic music." [34]

The symphony reveals another facet of Shostakovich's symphonic style. "In its representations of contrasting genres of daily life, the symphony could be compared to frescoes and triptychs of early Renaissance painters, Giotto, Christus, and Orcagna. These painters painted simultaneous, contrasting representations of heavenly bliss, purgatory, pious hermits, mundane love scenes, and Death followed by a retinue of devilish characters. Such contrasting representations make the paintings dramatic and effective." [35] Similar devices of artistic expression, based of course on different ideas, are used by Shostakovich in the Sixth Symphony. "Not the shady side of existence, but a sunny, optimistic picture of life represents the dramatic conception of the Sixth Symphony. The composer seems to say in his music that life is beautiful, but, while enjoying life, one should not forget its complexity, contradictions, and stunning contrasts." [36]

The Seventh Symphony in C Major (1941) is a musical memorial of the struggle of the Russian people against the German invasion in the Second World War. The ideological background of the symphony has been explained by Shostakovich: "Life has posed a question of the role of workers of culture in those days. We defend the liberty, honor, and independence of our motherland. We struggle for the best ideas in human history. We fight for our culture, science, and art, for everything that we created and built. A Soviet artist will never stand aside from historical combat which now goes on between enlightenment and obscurantism, culture and barbarism, light and darkness." [37]

Soviet music criticism regards the Seventh Symphony as a musical monument to the war years. "Inspired by patriotic feeling, the symphony is not a narrow-minded composition. Glorifying heroic deeds of the Soviet people, and replete with love for the common man, the symphony has acquired world-wide significance. Its humanism is stern and courageous. The music is imbued with the ethical pathos and spiritual power of fighters who defended the world in mortal combat with Fascism." [38]

The first sonata-allegro movement is a musical panorama of war and peace. Although there are no program notes, the programmatic conception of the symphony is clear. The march-like main theme in C major, built mainly on intervals of fourths and fifths, is energetic and confident. A chromatic alteration of an F sharp in the third measure adds a feeling of tension to the theme. The esthetic effect of this chromatic alteration should not be compared to the effect of the chromatic alteration in the main theme of Beethoven's *Eroica*. The alteration in Beethoven's symphony breaks up the main theme into two parts, one active, the other passive, which Beethoven contrasts in the development of the first movement. The alteration in Shostakovich's theme is peculiar to his melodic style.

The transition to the subordinate theme is a lyrical theme played by violins against a regularly swaying accompaniment of violas and violoncellos. The subordinate theme, a peaceful and unhurried melody, appears in a rondo-like section A-B-A-C-B-A, where A is the subordinate theme, while B and C are alternating episodes.

The peaceful character of the transition and subordinate themes is reminiscent of peaceful landscape representations in classical symphonies. Such representations have attained utmost expression in Beethoven's *Pastoral Symphony*. Similar representations in Shostakovich's symphony seem to be symbolic of peaceful life. The concluding section of the exposition is a nocturne which seems to represent the last moments of peace that is about to be swept away by war.[39]

Instead of a development section, Shostakovich introduces eleven variations on a new theme. The main characteristics of this section (280 measures in length) is a persistent, uniform rhythm, and an accumulation of tonal masses in the key of E flat major, a tonality far removed from the C major tonality of the symphony. The theme is dull, pedantic, and march-like. It evokes a staggering musical representation of the Fascist invasion. The section is reminiscent of Shostakovich's youthful musical parodies of middle class "folklore." Now, the musical parody has become a symbolic image of evil forces, a realistic ghastly image of enemies of mankind, murderers, and destroyers of culture.[40]

Each variation paints a different picture of the monstrous invaders. The music of the contrasting orchestral timbres evoke representations of a ruthless enemy and ravages of war, of destruction and sufferings, and of death marching over mountains of corpses.[41]

The musical episode which follows the variations includes a distorted invasion theme and abrupt changes of tonal and rhythmical elements. The ruthless enemy war machine has been finally halted and it begins to break up, becoming a disorderly jumble.[42]

In the recapitulation, the main C major theme is heard in the key of C minor. The theme is no longer march-like and optimistic. It is tense and pathetic, "a musical sketch of a wounded fighter, with a face distorted by pain and suffering, who rises amidst the ruins, roar, and smoky flames of the gigantic battle." [43]

A mournful, march-like episode follows. It is a requiem in memory of the heroes. In the words of Shostakovich: "Ordinary people honor the memeory of heroes. At first I wanted to have words here. In fact, I almost began writing them. Then, I managed without a text, and I am glad I did. Music expresses everything more strongly." [44]

The pastoral scene painted in the exposition is now absent. Instead, there are visions of a depopulated, burned desert. The subordinate theme, in a minor key, is played by a bassoon and is accompanied by unsteady, dull, steplike pizzicato chords of strings. The theme seems like a human voice narrating the sufferings and disasters of war. In the words of Shostakovich, "After universal mourning, it is, perhaps, the personal grief of a mother. This is the grief when there are no more tears remaining." [45]

The coda of the exposition is a second recapitulation. The main and subordinate themes, played in C major, are bright and clear. In the end of the coda are heard a distant roll of a drum and echoes of the invasion theme. In the words of Shostakovich: "The end of the movement is bright and lyrical. Human love. Enough words about those who perished. Conversation, walks. And only in the last measure of the movement, a distant roar is heard, the war has not yet ended." [46]

The second movement, the scherzo, is in three-part form. It is not a witty, hilarious scherzo. The gracious, refined melody of the first section, reminiscent of Russian song intonations, is in a four-pulsational pattern instead of the customary three-pulsational pattern of a scherzo. The music is subdued, but tense. "It seems as if the glow of the conflagrations which raged in the first movement fell upon the second movement." [47]

The middle section is in the key of C sharp minor. It is a short melody with an accompaniment of measured triplets of a C sharp minor triad. It sounds like a distorted reminiscence of the Adagio of Beethoven's *Moonlight Sonata*. "The music sounds like a poignant question which many people asked during the war: how could the German people who gave the world great thinkers, and artists and humanists like Beethoven, beget such an evil, man-hating power as Fascism? . . . This unusual scherzo, despite the absence of program notes, together with the historical fresco of the first movement, is a true account of innermost thoughts and feelings of a Soviet man in wartime." [48]

The third movement, Adagio, expresses, according to Shostakovich, "rapture with life and admiration of nature, impressions of the unforgettable view of Leningrad, the steady flow of the Neva River, its granite banks, the well-proportioned buildings of the Admiralty and the Winter Palace, and of the avenues receding into the distance." [49] The idea of the adagio could also be described as "the motherland in the year of military trials." [50]

Soviet music criticism interpreted the Adagio as an expression of the tension of a heroic struggle, a representation of the motherland enveloped by storms of war, and of a will to victory.

The meaning of the Adagio has been summarized by Asafiev: "Every detail of the Seventh Symphony reflects tragic conflicts which seem to grow before our consciousness, and which we experience as trials that have involved everyone. One contemplates them, and one reasons them out with one's heart and intellect. The slow movement of the symphony absorbs one. One breathes the air with the music and suddenly catches himself. Indeed, this is how life was in those tragic days. This is precisely how, under pressure of real physical danger, influxes of emotional anxieties and tensions of the will have succeeded each other in your heart, when the organism gathered every ounce of energy to repel death. Here music speaks not only with the language of Shostakovich, but also with the feelings of all people going out to defend the city." [51]

The finale opens with a rumble of kettledrums and a theme played by muted violins. They are answered by an energetic phrase played by double basses. Exclamations of strings, oboe, and French horn are heard in the distance. As in the exposition of the first movement, the music creates a feeling of open spaces. The music becomes animated as if the boundless spaces are filled with multitudes of people moving in from every direction. However, the music is not associated with a pastoral summer scene, but with a stern winter landscape covered with a blizzardly haze. This was the composer's intention. When Shostakovich began to compose the finale, he described it as a gradually swelling festive ode which sounds from every corner of the earth.[52]

The thematic fragments merge with the main theme whose short intonational links lessen cadential elements, and thereby enhance accumulations of dynamics. The exposition and development of the finale merge into a single section. Figurations and rushing passages intensify the tonal flow which seems to sweep away all obstacles in its path.

There follows a slow, mournful middle section, a solemn saraband. It is an expression of grief calling for vengeance and heroic deeds. The composer's thoughts seem to travel into the distant future to gaze from there on our days. This is how Shostakovich explained his intention.[53]

Changing colorful harmonies seem to uncover new bright vistas.

"The end of the finale evokes an imagery of victory illuminated by bloody glares of the conflagration of war." [54]

The Eighth Symphony in C Minor (1943) is a sequel to the Seventh Symphony. Its tragic character incurred diverse criticisms by Soviet music critics who felt in the music influences of the war. "The Eighth Symphony reflects 'night' more than 'day.' " [55] "A truthful, dramatically powerful reflection of ghastly sights of the war." [56] Shostakovich himself described the idea of the symphony as "man and a brutal force which destroys everything in its path; the grief brought on by war; catharsis and a look into the future." [57] The symphony "reflects the traumatized consciousness of a humane artist deeply shocked by human sufferings, but who does not see a clear road to victory ahead of him." [58] The Seventh and Eighth Symphonies are successive stages in the development of a chain of ideas and images." [59]

The Ninth Symphony in E Flat (1945) lacks tragic aspects and heroic imagery. It is characterized by a superficial brilliance and witticisms. After the Fifth, Seventh, and Eighth Symphonies, the Ninth puzzled Soviet critics, and it was evaluated negatively. "A tragical satirical pamphlet aimed against the benign complacency and rosy illusions which supposedly spread after the war." [60] "Shostakovich, the profound thinker-humanist has not yet mastered within himself the ironic sceptic and stylist." [61] "The carefree joy of the Ninth Symphony is not burdened with deep thoughts. However, the mournful Largo, in contrast with the rest of the symphony, serves as a stern warning." [62]

On February 10, 1948, the Central Committee of the Communist Party adopted a resolution which condemned antinational [63] and formalist [64] tendencies in Soviet music, and called upon Soviet composers to compose realistic, ideologic music based on classical traditions of Russian music. In line with this resolution, Shostakovich turned away from solely representing dramatic conflicts toward affirmation of bright, positive aspects of Soviet reality within readily understood musical genres of vocal, programmatic, and concert music. Such compositions were the oratorio *The Song About Forests* (1949), in which Shostakovich integrated simple melodies and genres with symphonic devices: *Ten Poems for a Mixed Chorus* on texts of revolutionary poets (1951), and a cantata *The Sun Shines on Our Native Land* for a children's chorus, mixed chorus, and orchestra (1952). Interestingly, *The Song About Forests* broke with the "cult of personality," that is, the customary ending of oratorios and cantatas with a glorification of Stalin.

The Tenth Symphony in E Minor (1953) has no program. According to Shostakovich, he wanted to express in the symphony experiences and thoughts of his contemporaries, people who ardently love peace and struggle against the threat of war.[65] However, among Soviet critics, the symphony aroused controversial discussions. They questioned the stylistic trends in Soviet symphonic music and the harm of transforming Socialist realism into a dogmatic scheme.[66]

The symphony was characterized as "gloomy and pessimistic; the tragedy of a lonely personality which sees no end to sufferings and doubts; nonresistant acceptance of an evil, reactionary origin; a sensation of pain and suffering verging on hysteria." [67] Whether these criticisms are justified or not, the fact is that the symphony reflects contradictions in contemporary Soviet reality.

Despite the resolution of the Central Committee, the psychological depressions and affectations of the symphony "mirror the suppression of natural, simple, joyous feelings, emotional brightness, and harmony. . . . it is now more evident how irrational is any unification of Soviet art, even in a demand of a thorough inclusion by each composer of all aspects of life in every composition." [68]

The musical realism of Shostakovich is not always a perception of a harmonious, peaceful reality. It would be a plausible conclusion that Shostakovich's best symphonies are those in which he represents dramatic conflicts of social significance.

The Eleventh Symphony in G Minor (1957) is programmatic. Based on events of the Russian revolution in 1905, the symphony evokes associations of those events. The first movement is entitled "The Palace Square" (in Petersburg); the second movement is called "January 9" (the "Bloody Sunday" in Russian history, when Tsarist troops fired on marching workers); the third movement is "Eternal Memory," a funeral march based on the song "You Fell, Victims," a revolutionary song which became popular after 1905. The finale, "The Tocsin," is based on several revolutionary songs, "Rage, Tyrants," "Varshavyanka," "March Bravely in Step, Comrades," and "Uncover Your Head."

The program of the symphony and the popularity of thematic materials are significant and vivid for Russian audiences. For a Western listener, who has only an objective acquaintance with revolutionary events in 1905, and with Russian revolutionary songs, the realistic representations and the emotional appeal of the music will probably remain academic considerations.

Other significant compositions by Shostakovich are the first piano concerto (1933, 1934), the violin concerto in A minor (1947, 1956) and chamber compositions. The piano cycle of twenty-four preludes and fugues is unique in Russian-Soviet musical literature. The rhythmic precision, percussive technique, soundings of many equal-timed notes in rapid movement, clear outlines, and emotional restraint of Shostakovich's piano style reveal the influence of Prokofiev's pianism. Shostakovich does not favor ostentatious virtuosity. He sometimes indulges two-part polyphonic discourses in which the two parts tend to be far apart thereby evoking a feeling of loneliness or emptiness, an effect used by Prokofiev. His harmonic figurations are simple, structural aspects rational and intellectual. In many features Shostakovich's piano style represents a transvaluation of classical pianism requiring exactness and clarity of execution, rather than of exuberant romantic pianism and of spicy impressionistic soundings. He shuns deliberate, refined color effects preferring instead contrasting piano registers to disclose dramatic effects of various piano timbres. He favors transparent piano textures adapting them to specific requirements of a composition. For example, in the piano quintet (1940) the piano becomes a single-voiced instrument similar to a string instrument which, in this case, is also single-voiced; in the finale of the first piano concerto, the percussive piano part and a triumpet solo evoke characteristic jazz effects.

Soviet music critics found common elements in the violin concerto and Tenth Symphony. The first movement of the concerto, the "Nocturne," is a protest against injustice and oppression. The scherzi of the two compositions are variants of Shostakovich's gloomy, grotesque imagery. The passacaglia of the concerto and several episodes in the symphony seem to recall the misfortunes and the destruction of innocent people. The finales of both compositions are gay and optimistic. The imageries of the two compositions are related, but expressed differently.[69] It is of course questionable whether a Western listener will "read" similar interpretations into Shostakovich's music.

Generalizations about the ethics and esthetics of Shostakovich's symphonies are debatable. Even Soviet music critics have changed their opinions about Shostakovich's music. For example, the second movement of the Eighth Symphony was described in 1946 as "a musical eccentricity with a lot of invention and ingenuity . . . there is something artificial and importunate in the humorous episodes of the second movement." [70] In 1958, the same critic described the second movement as "a coarse, grotesque march whose episodes communicate a drunken, devil-may-care gaiety . . . a procession of insolent, unbridled conquerors intoxicated by victory." [71]

There is no doubt, however, that the Fifth, Seventh, Eighth, and Eleventh Symphonies reflect in dynamics of clashes and struggles events in Russian-Soviet history and the formation of the intellectual Soviet man. But, as a composer, Shostakovich is worthy to take his place among the great Russian composers, including Glinka, Mussorgsky, Borodin, and Tchaikovsky.

Even with dogmatic Soviet criticism, Shostakovich's music makes a strong impression. There were composers who used music and the theater to address ideas to the world. Wagner, for example, used music and the theater to lecture the world on social ideas, love, and religion. Many might hardly care for Wagner's philosophy, but might admire much of his music. Shostakovich addresses himself to Russian-Soviet audiences who can feel the pulse of Russian events in his music.

Life has its disappointments, frustrations, happiness, and joy. Shostakovich is a composer of "musical poems" of Russian-Soviet life. He is optimistic and confident; but he is also in some of his music introspective and full of agonizing doubts.

Critical realism in music does not depend on classic-romantic criteria of "beautiful" music. A critical musical realist is not concerned with composing beautiful music. He is interested in communicating an idea, thought, or an image. It is not conceivable that Shostakovich could describe the Fascist invasion in the first movement of the Seventh Symphony in charming, graceful melodies and harmonies.

A great composer can penetrate the innermost meanings of life. This is the essence of realism. Shostakovich is a critical realist related to Mussorgsky. His music comments on important events in contemporary life. It is not a peaceful objective contemplation. His "symphonism" integrates spontaneous passionate outbursts, emotional outpourings, and profound meditation.

Shostakovich's music will undoubtedly outlive changing Soviet dogmas. His symphonies will always be regarded as musical panoramas of events, clashes, and conflicts in an important era of Russian history.

CHAPTER 26

Kabalevsky

KABALEVSKY'S Socialist Realism is his attempt to represent in music the patriotism and moral integrity of Soviet people. In his operas *The Taras Family* and *Nikita Vershinin,* the patriotism and humane qualities of Soviet men and women are contrasted with the cruelty of German invaders (in *The Taras Family*), and with the corruption of White Guards counterrevolutionaries (in *Nikita Vershinin*).

Kabalevsky's music evokes representations of Soviet people of various social strata and generations. He is a national composer because his music seems to express feelings and aspirations of the Russian proletariat. The national character of Russian socialist songs is reflected in his vocal and choral compositions, including vocal monologues (compositions with alternating vocal sections and symphonic developments), *An Order For The Son* and *We Shall Not Be Conquered* (1941); the ballade for voice and piano, *In The Dark Thick Grove* (1941); the suite for chorus and orchestra, *National Avengers* (1942); and the cantata for two vocal soloists, chorus, and orchestra, *The Great Motherland* (1942).

Folk song influences permeate Kabalevsky's cycle of twenty-four preludes for piano (1943). The thematic material of each prelude includes a Russian song. The influence of Russian folk songs in the preludes is stressed in the epigraph of the cycle, a quotation from Lermontov,

> Should I wish to delve into national poetry,
> I shall look no further than in Russian songs.

Kabalevsky uses folk song materials quite freely. He develops them, adds his own themes, and creates a variety of characteristic preludes: a dramatic prelude in D minor, a dance-like prelude in E major, a pastoral prelude in F minor, and a prelude in E flat minor representing a winter scene. Some preludes are musical representations of everyday life. Others evoke associations of Soviet life during the Second World War (military signals, a funeral march, and a song of victory). His piano style and complex harmonic texture enhance the national character of the preludes.

Dmitri Kabalevsky was born in Petersburg on December 30, 1904. His father, a graduate in mathematics from Petersburg University, was a specialist in state insurance.

As a child, Kabalevsky loved to improvise on the piano. He received his first musical education at the Scriabin Music School in Moscow (1919–1925), where he studied piano with the director of the school, V. Selivanov. Kabalevsky began to compose in 1922. His first compositions were published in 1927 and 1928. In 1927, he made his debut as a music critic.

In 1925, Kabalevsky enrolled in the Moscow Conservatory. His teachers of composition were Katuar and Myaskovsky. His teacher of piano was Goldenveiser. He was graduated from the class of composition in 1929, and his name was inscribed on the board of honor at the conservatory. In 1930, he was graduated from the class of piano. At present, Kabalevsky makes his home in Moscow.

Kabalevsky's style reveals several stages of artistic growth. His early works composed during the 1930's are lyrical and refined, without tragic and dramatic elements. During this period, Kabalevsky was influenced by impressionist and modernist trends, and the romanticism of Scriabin's middle period. However, these influences were temporary. As Kabalevsky's style matured, lyricism remained an important characteristic of his music which was gaining in sincerity of feeling and in dramatic qualities.

Significant developments in Kabalevsky's style were his Piano Concerto in A Minor (op. 9) and String Quartet in A Minor (op. 8). In these compositions, there is a change from modernist influences toward Russian classical traditions of Tchaikovsky and Mussorgsky. "Russian songs, which are represented in the concerto episodically, overflow the string quartet." [1] The two compositions use authentic Russian songs. The finale of the concerto is based on a Russian *bylina* tune. The introduction of the quartet develops intonations of ancient Russian lamentations. "Intonationally and harmonically, the andante of the quartet is reminiscent of Yurodivy's (God's fool) lamentations in Mussorgsky's *Boris Godunov*." [2]

The influence of Russian folk music in Kabalevsky's style is revealed by his use of alternations of major tonalities and their related minor tonalities; for example, C major and A minor.

Kabalevsky's themes are often constructed of gradual variations and intonational enrichment of thematic motives. A motive is succeeded by its variation, and then by another viariation, and so on. The main themes of Kabalevsky's three symphonies are constructed in this manner.

In his harmonic style, Kabalevsky favors the introduction of major subdominant harmonies into a minor tonality and the use of major seventh chords. A succession of minor thirds used by Kabalevsky results in a scale constructed of alternations of tones and semitones. This scale was used by Rimsky-Korsakov.[3] Kabalevsky favors continuity of metrical elements in thematic materials. This results in a better integration of content and design in his musical forms.

Despite the variational structure of a theme, Kabalevsky seldom uses variational principles in thematic developments. He does not follow the variational symphonic principles of Glinka, Balakirev, and Rimsky-Korsakov. He prefers the methods of Beethoven and Tchaikovsky, who broke up a theme into smaller units and developed individual melodic fragments and motives. Kabalevsky breaks up a theme into intonational units, which he develops into new figurations and patterns, often with new emotional significances. Correspondingly, the melodic patterns of harmony and rhythmic elements also change.

In his piano compositions, Kabalevsky avoids brilliant bravura passages. He prefers harmonic and melodic figurations, polyphonic interweaves of several melodic lines, and light decorative runs and arpeggios. Piano virtuosity is always subordinated to thematic considerations and developments.

Kabalevsky's early compositions are not characterized by dramatic, emotional, and dynamic contrasts. His style gradually evolved from subjectivity of expression toward direct reflections of Soviet life. Among these compositions are the Second Symphony in C Minor (1934), and the *Poem of Struggle* for chorus and orchestra (1930). In the *Poem of Struggle*, Kabalevsky for the first time used intonations of revolutionary songs. However, it is not a significant composition because it suffers from predominance of structural considerations which, according to Kabalevsky, are the result of "theories of a dialectic method of composing music." [4]

Kabalevsky's First Symphony in C Sharp Minor was completed in 1932. It is a programmatic composition in two movements. The first movement, andante molto sostenuto, entitled "The Crown and the Lash," describes the Russia of the Tsar and his gendarmerie. Intonations of grief, anger, and protest run through the entire movement. The second movement, allegro molto agitato, describes the struggle for freedom and a better life. The musical themes are peremptory calls to revolt. The festive conclusion of the movement, which echoes with songs and dances, seems to proclaim victory and joy of living.

Kabalevsky's Third Symphony in B Minor (The Requiem) (1933), for chorus and orchestra, was composed before the Second Symphony. While working on the Second Symphony, Kabalevsky was commissioned to compose for radio performance in the memory of Lenin a symphonic composition, which became the Third Symphony. It is in two movements performed without interruption. The first movement, which is an emotional introduction to the second choral movement, seems to be a representation of a struggle for a better life expressed in declamatory and impetuous intonations. The music is tense and dramatic. The second movement, andante marciale, represents a funeral procession. The music is a development of thematic elements of the first movement. The finale is heroic and optimistic.

In the Third Symphony, Kabalevsky revealed himself as a master of dramatic symphonic conceptions based on intonations of heroic imagery. One of the themes of the symphony contains elements of the leading motive of heroism in the opera *The Taras Family* (1947–1950). The motive is an upward forceful rhythmic movement of intervals of a fourth and a sixth.

The Second Symphony in C Minor (1934), is probably Kabalevsky's best symphony. Although it has no program, its optimistic spirit seems to reflect Kabalevsky's faith in Soviet reality. The first movement is dramatic and agitated. The main theme is forceful, and the lyrical subordinate theme seems to suggest hope in a better life.

The development is based on a polyphonic interweave of the two themes. The music is energetic, dynamic, and oratorical. The recapitulation is similar to the exposition. An impetuous coda ends the movement.

The second movement is a lyrical andante which evokes imageries and feelings of Russian nature. The third movement, prestissimo, is a combination of a rondo and a sonata form. The exposition and development section are an impetuous scherzo. The recapitulation represents the finale of the symphony. It is a festive movement whose holiday spirit evokes imageries of similar finales of the symphonies of Borodin and Tchaikovsky.

Kabalevsky's Fourth Symphony (1956) is a generalization of his artistic experiences. "It is a concentration of moods and images which are found in many of Kabalevsky's compositions. Lyrical and elegiac episodes alternate with heroic and tragic sections. The symphony is a musical narration about Soviet people willing to fight and, if necessary, to die 'for truth and for a future,' and who will be followed by thousands of Soviet young people ready for similar deeds. The festive and optimistic finale of the symphony is similar in spirit to the finale of Kabalevsky's Second Symphony." [5]

Kabalevsky is interested in music for children and young people. His compositions in this genre include songs, children's choral ensembles, and piano pieces. The contemporary subject matter of the compositions appeals to Soviet children, and is presented in simple musical forms. For example, the cycle of piano compositions "From the Life of Pioneers" includes such titles as "The Drummer," "The Game," and "The Pioneer Song." A children's sonatina in C major evokes an atmosphere of games, gaiety, and lightheartedness.

Kabalevsky composed music for films and incidental music for radio plays based on Schiller's *William Tell* and Shakespeare's *As You Like It*. His contribution to Soviet operatic genres is significant. His operas *Colas Breugnon, In Flames, The Taras Family,* and *Nikita Vershinin* are discussed in the chapter on Soviet opera. The social and political implications of his operatic librettos are significant for Soviet audiences. For American audiences, only the music of the operas might be interesting. The overture to *Colas Breugnon* has been performed in the United States.

Kabalevsky is a composer dedicated to the advancement of Communist principles of musical creativity and of music education. Soviet composers are not expected to be nonpolitical and cosmopolitan but to be nationalists. Soviet nationalism in music is a combination of the epic traditions of Glinka and the composers of the Balakirev circle, of

the lyric dramatic traditions of Tchaikovsky, and of Soviet nationality
as an expression of the interests of the Russian proletariat. A Soviet
composer is expected to create representations of heroic Soviet men
and women, and reflect the Messianic tendency of the party and the
ethics and philosophy of a Communist society. Kabalevsky is dedicated
to these principles.

CHAPTER 27

Khachaturyan

KHACHATURYAN'S music is characterized by spontaneity, brilliance, and charm. The splendor and pictorial quality of its Armenian national elements are historically related to the Caucasian impressions, color, and virtuosity of Balakirev's style, and to the oriental elements in the music of Glinka, Borodin, and Mussorgsky.

The exotic lyrical patterns and improvisatory characteristics of Khachaturyan's music are the result of national Armenian intonations. The content of Khachaturyan's orientalisms is different from that of nineteenth century Russian orientalisms in that his orientalisms are reflected as perceptions of Soviet realism.

The blending of national Armenian vocal and instrumental intonations with contemporary orchestral techniques make Khachaturyan unique among Soviet composers. His music reflects the phase of Soviet musical culture which seeks to develop cultural and spiritual aspirations of Soviet nationalities. "At the same time, Khachaturyan is closely associated with Russian music as an outstanding school of artistic craftsmanship, and with its humane lyricism." [1]

Aram Khachaturyan was born in Tbilisi, in the Caucasus, on June 6, 1903. His father, Ilya, was a bookbinder. There was an old piano at home, and one of Khachaturyan's early musical experiences was learning to play by ear popular tunes and dances.

At the age of ten, Khachaturyan was enrolled in the Commercial School of Tbilisi. He was not an enthusiastic student because he was mainly interested in music. Khachaturyan joined an amateur ensemble of wind instruments in school, playing the brass tenor and baritone. In the eighth year, he left school without graduating.

In the fall of 1921, Khachaturyan's brother, Suren, who was a producer at the Second Moscow Art Theater, invited Khachaturyan to go to Moscow and pursue his studies.

In Moscow, Khachaturyan passed the entrance examination at Moscow University, and enrolled in the section of biology of the faculty of mathematics. He attended the university for two years.

In the fall of 1922, Khachaturyan passed the entrance examination at the Gnessin Musical Technical School. In 1925, at the suggestion of Mikhail Gnessin, Khachaturyan began to study composition. In 1926 and 1927, he composed a "Dance" in B major for violin and piano, and a "Poem" for piano in C sharp.

In the fall of 1929, Khachaturyan enrolled in the Moscow Conservatory. Gnessin and Myaskovsky were his teachers of composition; Vasilenko and Ivanov-Radkevich were his teachers of instrumentation. Khachaturyan was graduated in 1934, and his name was inscribed on the board of honor at the Conservatory.

Khachaturyan's realism was the result of his use of national and popular musical elements. He stated his ideas about the role of music in national culture in an article *"Kak ya ponimayu narodnost' v muzike"* (How I Understand Folk Characteristics in Music). Music is a language created by the people. The people create intonational musical forms which reveal at once the national elements of an art work. Melodies created by the people express feelings and thoughts of many generations, and determine forms, genres, and characteristics of style of national music. A composer is a rightful heir of the incalculable wealth of national music. He should draw from it and create his own artistic imagery and values. The individuality of a composer's creativity is the result of its connection with national and popular arts. The outcome is the inspired use of national musical elements, and the creation of new melodies imbued with the spirit, character, and style of national music.[2]

The most important influence in Khachaturyan's music is the art of the Ashugs and Khanendes. The Ashugs are wandering Caucasian folk poets and singers. Khachaturyan was early captivated by their ingenious and colorful improvisations and bewitching rhythms. In their melodies he discovered an inexhaustible source of musical impressions which have influenced his musical style.

Ashugs are poets and musicians, fascinating storytellers of bygone days, and commentators on contemporary events. Constant wander-

ings developed in Ashugs courage, cheerfulness, and optimism, qualities reflected in their music and poetry.

By adopting elements of various folklores, Ashugs developed a
characteristic style of musical performance which combines speech,
recitative, melody, and instrumental accompaniment. By improvising
verses and stories in various Eastern languages, Ashugs leave the
boundaries of a particular nationality. They are regarded as friends
and teachers of the people.

Khanandes are wandering minstrels whose rhapsodic style of performance is distinct from the excited and lively performance of
Ashugs. Khanandes sing to the accompaniment of a tambourine, a
daf; an oriental lute, a *tar;* and a bow instrument, a *kemanja.*

The art of Ashugs and Khanandes is not only a source of Khachaturyan's music, but also a basis of the folk character of his style.
Khachaturyan did not copy the style and music of Ashugs and
Khanandes, but he freely adapted their improvisations and traditions
to his style.

Khachaturyan was also influenced by the music of Sazandars, who,
like Ashugs and Khanandes, are professional performers and interpre-
ters of the Eastern art of *mugams.* A *mugam* is a vocal-instrumental
poem whose various episodes are unified by a musical mode (scale)
which is also called *mugam.*

There are seven basic *mugam* scales, each based on a repeated
tetrachord (a diatonic series of four notes): G, A, B, C, called *rast;*
A, B, C, D, *shur;* B, C, D, E, *seyga;* B, C, D, E, flat, *shushter;* G, A
flat, B, C, *chargya;* D, E, F sharp, G, *bayate shiraz;* and G, A flat, B, C,
khumayun.

The scale is completed by repeating the tetrachord, for example:

rast;   G, A, B, C,   C, D, E, F,   F, G, A, B flat;   tonic C
shur;   A, B, C, D,   D, E, F, G,   G, A, B flat, C;   tonic D
seyga;   B, C, D, E,   E, F, G, A,   A, B flat, C, D;   tonic E
shushter;   B, C, D, E flat,   F sharp G, A, B flat;   tonic G
chargya;   G, A flat, B, C,   C, D flat, E, F,   G, A flat, B, C;   tonic C
bayati shiraz: D, E, F sharp, G,   (A) B flat, C, D, E flat;   tonic G
khumayun: G, A flat, B, C,   (D) E, F, G sharp, A;   tonic C and A

The last tone of each tetrachord is the tonic of the scale. The exceptions are the *mugan shushter* whose tonic is G; and the *mugam
khumayun* whose tonic is C and A. Besides these seven basic *mugams,*
there are about seventy subordinate *mugam* modes.

The names of the seven basic *mugams* indicate their esthetic qualities. *Rast* is courageous; *shur* is lyrical; *seyga* evokes a feeling of love; *shushter* is sorrowful; *chargya* is passionate; *bayati shiraz* is somber; *khumayun* expresses grief.[3]

Thus, the tonal structure of Khachaturyan's music includes not only the diatonic scale system, but also the *mugam* modes.

The style of Khachaturyan's music is a synthesis of the improvisatory styles of the Ashugs and Khanandes, and of the symphonic traditions of Russian music. The synthesis is already evident in his early compositions which he composed during his student years at the Moscow Conservatory (1929–1934); a sonata for violin and piano; a trio for clarinet, violin, and piano; a symphony; and an orchestral dance suite in five parts. The parts of the suite are an Armenian-Azerbaijan dance; an Armenian round dance; an Uzbek dance; an Uzbek march; and a Lezghinka.

Khachaturyan seldom uses folklore themes. However, he retains the intonational and rhythmic characteristics of Armenian, Azerbaijan, and Georgian music. He re-creates in his music the melodies and improvisations of Ashugs, and the colorful combinations of their instruments which are based on characteristic scales and overtones. The *mugam,* as a vocal instrumental poem performed by Khanandes, includes instrumental interludes with melodic and dance-like characteristics. Similar characteristics occur in Khachaturyan's style.

The colorful harmonic style of the French impressionists Debussy and Ravel left its imprint on Khachaturyan's music. The dynamics and rhythmic features of Prokofiev's music helped Khachaturyan enhance expressive elements of his orchestral themes.

Khachaturyan's compositions include symphonies, symphonic poems, ballets, chamber compositions, music for films and the theater, piano compositions, songs, choral compositions, and concertos for piano, violin, and violoncello.

The three concertos, especially the piano concerto, and the music from the *Gayne* ballet, are probably Khachaturyan's best-known compositions. The piano concerto is an excellent example of his style. It is characterized by colorful harmonies, capitivating rhythms, virtuosity, improvisations, and sensuous melodies. Its optimistic holiday spirit seems to proclaim the beauty of life and nature, and the joy of living.

Pianistically, the concerto is a synthesis of the piano styles of Liszt, Tchaikovsky, and Prokofiev.

The first movement, allegro ma non troppo e maestoso, is in classical sonata form combined with improvisational elements. The main theme, in D flat major, is strong and courageous. The subordinate theme is a lyrical Armenian melody with dance-like characteristics. The orchestral accompaniment of the subordinate theme reproduces the sounds of national Caucasian instruments used by Ashugs and Khanandes.

The development section is dance-like and swift, without dramatic contrasts and clashes. The development is in complete accord with the joyful spirit of the exposition.

The recapitulation, which is dominated by the main opening theme, is followed by a virtuoso cadenza based on a motivic development of the lyrical subordinate theme. A coda based on the main theme concludes the movement.

The second movement, andante con anima, is a song for orchestra and piano. A dreamy, contemplative melody in the improvisatory style of Ashugs, is an example of Khachaturyan's treatment of Armenian folk lyricism.

The third movement, allegro brillante, is effective virtuoso music in the form of a rondo-toccata. Intonationally, the theme of the movement is related to the main theme of the first movement. The rhythmic momentum of the finale is interrupted by lyrical episodes which gradually prepare the appearance of the main theme of the first movement. The momentum of the tonal flow increases, and the movement comes to an end with a majestic statement of the opening theme of the concerto.

The tonal elements and forms of Khachaturyan's music have a unique quality. They are national, but, at the same time, they seem to expand beyond the geographic boundaries of his native Caucasus. The simplicity, clarity, and folk character of his music often leave a listener feeling the universality, rather than the specific national aspect, of his art. The emotional quality of his music proves that folk idioms have characteristics which appeal to people of many countries. Khachaturyan's music may not be profound or philosophical, but it speaks of the joy and happiness of life.

CHAPTER 28

Soviet Ballet

DURING THE years following the October Revolution, Soviet artists and composers realized that new trends and ideas which would reflect Soviet ideology should be introduced into the Russian ballet. In the early 1920's, new ballets were produced which were skillful acrobatic presentations. In these ballets, composers and choreographers tried to present images of the revolutionary proletariat. These exhibitions had no effect on the popularity of Russian classical ballets. Eventually, through the introduction of a new choreographic style and of a Soviet ideological content, the structural and esthetic principles of Tchaikovsky's ballets became the bases of the Soviet ballet. Tchaikovsky's reforms of the ballet included logical arrangement and interdependence of scenes; subordination of scenic representations to dramatic action; continuity of symphonic developments which preclude rearrangement of scenes and new interpretations of scenic action; emphasis of psychological elements of musical representations; a comprehensive denouement of the finale, followed by a thematic recapitulation and a coda.

Tchaikovsky was the greatest Russian ballet composer. His ballets are superb examples of a musical-choreographic art. It was logical for Soviet composers to develop a Soviet ballet style in which the principles of Tchaikovsky's ballets would be adapted to contemporary needs and problems.

Tchaikovsky changed the content and character of the ballet as a choreographic spectacle. Instead of being purely entertaining, Tchaikovsky's ballets are realistic narrations of human fortunes, happiness, true love, and passionate feelings of loving hearts.

Despite the legendary subjects and fantasy of the scenarios of his ballets, Tchaikovsky does not romanticize contrasts of real life with fantasies of an unreal world or of a dream. Siegfried and Odette in *Swan Lake,* Aurora and Desiré in *Sleeping Beauty,* Masha and the prince in *Nutcracker* are pictured by the music as real people endowed with real feelings, hopes, wishes, and with the best features of a human character.

Tchaikovsky describes the emotional and the spiritual worlds of his ballet characters with musical means similar to those which he used in his other musical genres. As a great symphonic and operatic composer, Tchaikovsky did not find it difficult to develop the artistic possibilities of choreography. In his ballets, he created musical characterizations and representations of persons. The music and choreography of his ballets express the drama of scenic action.

The fantasy of Tchaikovsky's ballets is often a replica of the poetry and fantasy of Russian folklore. The story of Odette, who is transformed into a beautiful swan by the magician Rorbart, is similar to the story of Tsarevna-Lebed (Tsarevna-Swan) and the wicked magician in Pushkin's *Tale About Tsar Saltan.* The theme of the triumph of love in *Sleeping Beauty* is found in Russian fairy tales. The music of *Sleeping Beauty,* despite the French scenario,[1] is Russian in style and in representations of the happiness and beauty of life. Cinderella and her prince, Red Riding Hood and the wolf, Hop-o'-my-thumb and his brothers are characters found in Russian fairy tales. To Tchaikovsky, such stories represented a striving for happiness, and a struggle with forces of evil and darkness.

Tchaikovsky's *Nutcracker Ballet* has deeply human and realistic feelings. It is a poem of childhood's dreams and hopes in which one can understand the meaning of Tchaikovsky's thoughts about love and happiness. The "Waltz of the Snowflakes" seems like a representation of the Russian winter which Tchaikovsky loved and which he described in his *Winter Dreams Symphony.*

The realistic, expressive means of Tchaikovsky's ballets, his characterizations of persons and situations, the ability of his themes and melodies to express emotional experiences and feelings, drama and conflicts, and the integration of symphonic music and choreography —all these features were indispensable for the development of a Soviet ballet which would create an imagery of popular heroic spectacles, epic tales, and of social and psychological dramas. The aim of Soviet ballet composers and choreographers was to create a spectacle in which dances, enriched with expressive pantomime, would present a continuous dramatic development, while the music would describe or express the characters, emotions, and experiences of persons.

The scenarios of Soviet ballets called for further changes in the music, choreography, and traditional forms of the ballet. The adagio of the Soviet ballet, the choreographic duet which reveals characterizations or descriptions of the characters, has been enriched with a variety of new functions. Some adagios, characterized as *duets of agreement,* reveal their joy, happiness, love, and emotions. Examples of such adagios are the love duets in Prokofiev's *Romeo and Juliet* and *Cinderella,* and in Khachaturyan's *Gayne.* Duets of agreement occur in Tchaikovsky's ballets; however, Soviet ballets broadened their scope and concept.

Other adagios reveal a variety of dramatic situations or circumstances which affect or influence the heroes, for example, the love duet of Spartacus and Phrygia in Khachaturyan's *Spartacus.* Musical themes which represent tragedy and heroism are interwoven in the duet with the theme of love.

An innovation in the Soviet ballet is a *duet of disagreement* in which are represented clashes of antagonistic elements. Examples of such duets are the adagio of Maria and Zarema in Asafiev's *The Fountain of Bakhchisarai,* which discloses Zarema's despair and her jealousy of Maria, and the duet of Danilo and the Mistress of the Copper Mountain in Prokofiev's *The Tale of the Stone Flower.* The dance of Danilo and the Mistress is a choreographic representation of the defeat of the Mistress by the lofty ideals of a human heart. The Soviet ballet discloses through a variety of adagios a diversity of conflicting situations, characters, and psychological clashes of the plot.

Another innovation of the Soviet ballet is a duet of *illusory agreement:* for example, the adagio of Aegina and Harmodius in *Spartacus.* The tension and the oriental atmosphere of the scene and the colorful harmonies of the music describe the seduction of Harmodius by Aegina. The illusion is broken by the arrival of Roman soldiers who seize Harmodius. The sensuous music is interrupted, and the theme of oppression and slavery is heard in the orchestra.

The Soviet ballet expanded the functions of the *monologue dance,* which has become a solo dance that reflects a dramatic situation and describes emotional reactions of the dancer. For example, the lullaby dance of Gayne in the *Gayne* ballet, and the lament of Phrygia in the final scene of *Spartacus*.

The monologue dance is frequently a solo "address" by the dancer to the people who are represented by the corps de ballet. The address of the solo dancer is meant to arouse the people to heroic deeds.

The Soviet ballet has developed new intonational elements for entire ensemble dancing. The lyric waltz of a Tchaikovsky ballet usually describes the individuality of the hero or heroine. The Soviet ballet has developed instead rhythmic and heroic intonations which express contemporary life and events.

The Soviet ballet changed the functions of incidental musical episodes. Incidental musical episodes of a Soviet ballet are meant to enhance the action and the drama of the occasion, rather than to afford entertainment and relaxation for an audience. For example, the music which accompanies the feast of Crassus in *Spartacus* evokes a variety of dramatic representations. The musical theme which describes the comfort and voluptuousness of the guests is contrasted with the powerful theme of the rebels. The dancing of the slaves during the feast ends with a glorification of the victorious Spartacus.

The variety of musical forms of Soviet ballets has influenced expressive elements of the choreography. Both the music and the choreography embody aspects of life and realistically describe persons and dramatic situations.

The scenarios of Soviet ballets include representations of stories and accounts of past and present heroic struggles, of psychological dramas of classical literature, and of tragic situations.

Soviet composers have rejected the idea that the music of the ballet should be subordinated to the choreography. The Soviet ballet requires the collaboration of choreography and music brought about by the identity of the dramatic plot and the artistic conception of the scenario.

The scenario of a Soviet ballet does not usually provide an occasion for an exhibition of dancing, but for the creation of a spectacle in which dances and expressive pantomime present a continuous dramatic action which describes or expresses characters, actions, and emotional experiences of persons. A Soviet ballet aims to present a dramatic spectacle of ideas and feelings based on ideological content, folk characteristics, and realism.

The first important contribution to the Soviet ballet was Glière's *Krasni Mak* (Red Poppy), which was produced at the Bolshoi Theater in 1927. The story of the ballet is the love of Tao Hua, a dancer in a bar in a Chinese port, and the captain of a Russian ship anchored there.

Chinese coolies unload the ship. The work is backbreaking. The Russian captain suggests to his crew to help the coolies unload the ship. Tao Hua looks on and her admiration of the Russian sailors is noticed by her "fiancé," the adventurer Li Shen Fu.

The chief of the port assigns Li Shen Fu to assassinate the Russian captain. The plan involves Tao Hua, who, during a ball, is supposed to offer the captain a cup of poisoned tea. But Tao Hua drops the cup. The enraged Li Shen Fu shoots Tao Hua. The Russian ship sails for home. The dying Tao Hua gives the Chinese partisans a red poppy, the symbol of freedom which had been given to her by the captain.

In 1957, the ballet was presented in a new version called *Krasni Tsvetok* (Red Flower), which propagandized the Chinese Communist Revolution. The new scenario was a representation of clashes of "Communist" and "Imperialist" forces, and of the friendship of the Russian and Chinese peoples.

Tao Hua's two musical themes are heard in the first scene. The first theme is a graceful dance melody in the pentatonic (five-tone) scale played against a background of two sustained harmonies. This harmonization signifies the quiet and passive character of a dancer in Old China. The second theme is passionate and romantic. It is heard against an accompaniment of chromatic chords which seem to express dissatisfaction and a desire for happiness. In the development of the ballet, the second theme is used to describe emotional and dramatic situations.

The first scene presents a picture of the hard life of Chinese coolies. A ponderous pentatonic theme describes the monotonous rhythm of their work. The coolies perform a dance of "forced labor" and a dance of "victorious labor." The joyless life of the coolies is contrasted with the carefree life of rich European settlers who drink and dance in an exclusive restaurant.

Soviet sailors are characterized by the opening motive of "The Internationale." The motive is used throughout the ballet as the symbol of fraternity of Russian and Chinese workers. The first act ends with the sailors dancing the popular Soviet dance, "*Yablochko*" (The Apple).

The second act describes the conspiracy to assassinate the Russian captain. The chief of the port and the conspirators are characterized by chromatic melodic fragments and excited rhythms. The sudden appearance of Soviet sailors is accompanied by the theme of "*Yablochko*." The music which describes the conspiracy is contrasted with the passionate musical theme of Tao Hua.

The next scene shows Tao Hua smoking opium. In two adagio dances, Tao Hua describes the images and thoughts induced by the opium. The scene ends with the simultaneous playing of the motive of "The Internationale" and of Tao Hua's romantic theme. The music seems to symbolize Tao Hua's desire to learn the truth about Communist life.

The third act opens with a representation of a ball given by the chief of the port. The guests dance modern Western European and American dances, including the Charleston. The dance music is followed by symphonic episodes which describe the attempt on the captain's life and the revolt of the Chinese people. The concluding scene shows the shooting and death of Tao Hua. The music of the death scene is based on the theme of "The Internationale" and of Tao Hua.[2]

Glière composed the ballets *Medniy Vsadnik* (The Bronze Horseman, 1949), based on Pushkin's poem; *Taras Bulba* (1952), based on Gogol's story; and *Doch Kastilii* (The Daughter of Castile, 1955), based on Lope de Vega's (1562–1635) drama *Fuenta Ovejuna* (Spring of Sheep).

Asafiev composed twenty-seven ballets of which the most successful were *Plamya Parizha* (The Flame of Paris, 1932), *Bakhchisaraiskiy Fontan* (The Fountain of Bakhchisarai, 1934), and *Kavkazskiy Plennik* (The Captive in the Caucasus, 1938). The three ballets inaugurated the lyrical and psychological trend in the Soviet ballet.

The Flame of Paris was the first Soviet heroic ballet. It was presented at the Mariinsky Theater in Leningrad on November 7, 1932. The scenario described events of the French Revolution from 1789 to 1792, including the march of the Marseilles Battalion and the popular uprising which resulted in the taking of the Tuilleries on August 10, 1792.

The music of the ballet is an arrangement of songs which were popular during the French Revolution, including the "Carmagnole," "Marseillaise," and Ça Ira; of selections from the music of Lully, Gluck, Grétry, Gossec, Méhul, Lesueur, and Cherubini; and of Asafiev's original music composed in the style prevalent during the Revolution. Music of French court dances and selections from the music of Lully were used by Asafiev for characterizations of the royal court. The music is gloomy and tragic to show the doom of the old regime.

The music of the ballet attempted to recall the music which filled the streets and squares of Paris during the Revolution. "I was interested," wrote Asafiev, "in the musical wealth and content of a great epoch as a historical document and as a living, passionate and emotional speech which recalled for us the heroic pathos, grandeur, grief, and wild joy of popular rejoicing. . . . I compared the musical material and orchestrated it in a manner which would reveal the content of the ballet in a continuous symphonic development and in an accurate imagery." [3]

The Fountain of Bakhchisarai is based on Pushkin's poem. The story takes place in the palace of the Crimean Khan Girey. Girey loves Maria, a Polish princess who has been kidnapped during a Tatar raid on Poland, and placed in Girey's harem. Maria declines Girey's advances. Zarema, a Georgian girl whom Girey gave up for Maria, loves Girey. Maria dies, and Girey orders Zarema thrown into the sea. In memory of Maria, Girey built in his palace a marble fountain, which is now remembered as the Fountain of Tears.

The ballet recalls the spirit of Pushkin's times. Asafiev tried to penetrate the poetic atmosphere in which Pushkin's imagery originated and to show how the poetic atmosphere had changed and affected the poem's imagery since Pushkin's time.

Asafiev's ballet is a social and psychological drama. "I did not stylize Polish music of the 1820's, but I tried to convey musically the passionate and fervent pathos of Poland struggling desperately for its independence and national culture in the ardor of Kosziuszko, in the lyricism of Mickiewicz, and in the tragic intonations of Chopin's Poland. The image of Maria is a musical and poetical transformation of the romantic aspect of a Polish girl, and, at the same time, a reflection of a girl in Pushkin's drama. This image, like other images in *The Fountain of Bakhchisarai*, is real in our contemporary, tense atmosphere. The romanticism of Pushkin's poem is a passionate struggle to liberate the poet's world-feeling and creative consciousness from survivals of feudalism and serfdom. Pushkin's romanticism shows the emergence of a new individual consciousness through a 'regeneration' of the emotion of love in a poetically transformed repudiation of a despotic and proprietary view of women. This does not diminish the significance of the struggle of conscience, which finds itself on the borderline of two social formations, with survivals of the past which had held it captive. . . . After the Napoleonic wars, and until the destruction of the Decembrists, young and progressive Russian nobility tried to get rid of 'khan conscience.' Russia was full of Gireys, as it was full of harems. Love was becoming an individual, creative emotion which overcame the lustful egoism of a serf conscience." [4]

The Captive in the Caucasus was presented in Moscow and Leningrad in 1938. The story of Pushkin's poem is as follows. A Circassian mountaineer brings to his native village in the mountains a wounded Russian prisoner. As the prisoner lies chained in the *sakla* (a Caucasian dwelling), a young Circassian girl, who feels sorry for the prisoner, brings him food. The prisoner's wounds heal soon, and he is allowed to walk in the village street. His chains will not let him escape through the rugged mountains. The girl loves the prisoner, and she tells him that her father wants to sell her to a rich suitor from another village. The prisoner listens to her story, but his thoughts are with the girl he left at home. One night, the Circassian girl brings a dagger and breaks the prisoner's chains. She tells him that he is now free to escape. The prisoner asks her to go with him. The girl refuses to escape with him because she knows that he loves another girl in Russia. They come to a river. The prisoner walks into the water and swims to reach the other bank. When he steps ashore, he hears a distant moan. He looks behind him and sees the body of the girl carried away by the river's current.

The scenario of Asafiev's ballet introduced new elements into Pushkin's story. The scenario contrasts the wild and rugged Caucasus with the aristocratic Petersburg of Pushkin's time. The love of the prisoner and the Circassian girl is represented in the first and last scenes. The second scene is the prisoner's dream. The dream is the romance of Vladimir and Polina, the heroes of a Petersburg short story popular in

Pushkin's time. The ballet is unified by three interludes: the prisoner, in chains, spends the day with the herd in the mountains; a storm scene; and an intermezzo.

The idea of the ballet is devotion to the motherland. The historical elements are exemplified vividly by lyric intonations and parlour music popular in Pushkin's time. The wild and rugged Caucasus is described by native melodies and dances.

Some of Asafiev's ballet scenarios are stories of national liberation; for example, in *Partizanskiye Dni* (Partisan Days); or of heroic exploits in *Ivan Bolotnikov* and in *Stepan Razin*.

The story of *Partisan Days* describes events during the Russian Civil War. Some of the Cossacks in a Cossack village in Northern Caucasus have joined the Bolsheviks; others have joined the White Guards. Nastya, a poor Cossack girl, is forced to marry a rich Cossack, Andrei. During the marriage celebration, drunken kulaks jeer at a poverty-stricken peasant, Fedor. The indignant Nastya breaks with her husband and throws away the marriage ring and bridal veil. Fedor and Nastya leave the village and join a group of Cossack partisans.

The scene shifts to a small resort town where drunken White Guards interrogate the captured Fedor, and then they shoot him. Partisans arrive, and after defeating the White Guards, join the Red Army.

Meanwhile, Nastya, her lover, the mountaineer Kerim, and a sailor are held captive by White Guards, and, with other imprisoned partisans, expect to be shot. However, Bolshevist Cossacks occupy the village and save their comrades. Vanguards of the Red Army arrive in the village and are joyously greeted by partisans and villagers.

Stepan (Stenka) Razin was a seventeenth century Cossack pirate on the Volga River. He sailed the Caspian Sea and ravaged the Persian coast. He rebelled against the Moscow government and established a Cossack republic in the City of Astrakhan situated where the Volga flows into the Caspian Sea. According to a popular legend, Razin kidnapped a beautiful Persian princess during the raid on Persia. While he was sailing with the princess up the Volga River, he noticed the jealous looks of his crew and threw the princess into the river. Razin was captured by troops of the Moscow government and brought to Moscow, where he was quartered alive on June 6, 1671.

In *Partisan Days* and in *Ivan Bolotnikov,* Asafiev used songs which were popular during the Russian Civil War. *Stepan Razin* is an epic ballet-*bylina* with choral episodes which describe the Russian people and Razin's exploits. The music of the finale of the third act is a development of the famous Russian song "Down the River Mother-Volga." In the music which characterizes the Russian people, Asafiev used melodic elements of Russian folk songs, free metrical and rhythmical patterns, and polyphonic interweaves typical of Russian folk songs. *Ivan Bolotnikov* and *Stepan Razin* were the first Soviet ballets which showed peasant insurrections and their leaders.

As a music critic and musicologist, Asafiev understood the problems and traditions of ballet genres. Thorough delineation of actors, and clarity and appropriateness of music are characteristic of his ballet style. His collaboration with librettists and choreographers helped Asafiev develop ideas which have influenced Soviet ballet composers.

Alexander Krein's ballet *Laurencia,* presented in Leningrad in 1939, is one of the most popular ballets in the Soviet repertoire. The scenario of the ballet is based on Lope de Vega's drama *Fuenta Ovejuna* (Spring of Sheep). The drama describes the struggle of the Spanish people against feudal power; the love of Frondoso and Laurencia; and the struggle of the King of Castile with Spanish grandees.

The story of Krein's ballet is a social drama based solely on the struggle of the inhabitants of Fuenta Ovejuna against their feudal lord. The first scene shows the villagers, Frondoso and Laurencia, the Comendador (who is the feudal lord), and the Comendador's guard. The second scene depicts the intensification of the social conflict and the development of the drama of Laurencia and Frondoso. The villagers celebrate the marriage of Laurencia and Frondoso. The Comendador arrives with his guard and orders the guard to separate the newlyweds. The third scene describes the misery of the villagers and their hatred of the Comendador. The finale represents the struggle of the people with the Comendador's guard and the deliverance from the tyrant.

Krein's music provides opportunities for the creation of choreographic representations by dance, action, and mimicry. "Dance action is one of the positive contributions of *Laurencia.* This is important because in ballets of the 1930's musical descriptions of actors, even of the main heroes, did not have adequate dance action. Khan Girey in *The Fountain of Bakhchisarai* and the prisoner in *The Captive in the Caucasus* are described by music which is suitable for dancing, but not for mimic action." [5]

The most important motive of the ballet describes the main idea of the ballet, the conflict between the people of Fuenta Ovejuna and feudal power. Frondoso's heroic theme is based on a folk tune. This theme also represents popular indignation and struggle with the Comendador. The motive of the Comendador and of feudal power is based on rhythmic elements of a march, chorale, and polonaise. In the end of the first scene is heard a festive and gallant theme. It represents the Comendador, who has ordered his guard to bring the village girls to his castle where he dissembles the role of a hospitable host. There is a love motive of Frondoso and Laurencia in the second scene. When the Comendador orders the newlyweds separated, the love theme is transformed into an expression of grief and despair.

The struggle of the villagers is revealed in a variety of solo and mass dances in which Krein used Spanish folk tunes. Spanish dances alternate with "scenes of action," which are developed on the themes of the main characters.

The image of Laurencia, the heroic woman who leads the villagers to storm the Comendador's castle, is unique in ballet literature. The image of a heroic woman does not appear in classical ballets. Tao Hua in *Red Poppy* is a lyrical character. Nastya in *Partisan Days* and the women in *The Flame of Paris* are not even described individually by the music, but are revealed choreographically.

The supreme achievement of the Soviet ballet is Prokofiev's *Romeo and Juliet* composed in 1935 and 1936. The music of the ballet was first heard in the form of an orchestral suite on the concert stage, and then as piano music.

As a ballet, *Romeo and Juliet* was first presented at the Kirov Theater in Leningrad in 1940. It was not Prokofiev's first ballet. Before *Romeo and Juliet,* Prokofiev composed five ballets: *Ala and Lolliy* (1914), *Skazka o Shute, Semerikh Shutov Pereshutivshem* (The Buffoon, 1917), *Stalnoy Skok* (The Age of Steel, 1925), *Bludniy Syn* (The Prodigal Son, 1928), and *Na Dniepre* (On the Dnieper, 1930). However, these ballets are not significant because they contain many features of Prokofiev's early style, including grotesqueness and expressionist elements. In *Romeo and Juliet,* Prokofiev's mature style is at its best. It is lyric and dynamic, and it reveals Prokofiev's ability to depict with a few short musical sketches characters and situations.

The music of *Romeo and Juliet* is a psychological description of Shakespeare's characters. Through thematic transformations, Prokofiev reveals the experiences and emotions of the characters. Short and pungent leading motives describe Friar Laurence, the nurse, and Mercutio. Romeo is described by two themes. A lyrical theme represents Romeo the romantic dreamer; an impetuous theme represents Romeo the lover. Juliet's theme, which consists of three leading motives, undergoes several transformations during the course of the ballet. One leading motive describes Juliet as a carefree girl; the second motive represents her spiritual world; the third motive, which is meditative and peaceful, describes Juliet dreaming of love. At the end of the ballet, the third motive becomes sorrowful and even tragic. In the death scene, the theme is transformed into hymn-like glorification which seems to express the triumph of love over death.

Other themes describe the realism of Shakespeare's drama. A dissonantal theme describes the feud of the Montagues and the Capulets. Lively genre scenes enhance the realism of the ballet. The harmonic texture of the music brings out the dramatic situations of the ballet. Happiness and joy are represented by simple and clear harmonic structures. Conflicts and emotional clashes are revealed by acerbic and complex harmonic progressions. The orchestration helps to disclose dramatic elements. In the first act, Juliet is described by clear timbres of a flute, clarinet, celesta, and a harp. Juliet and Romeo in love are described by violins, violoncellos, and French horns.

Prokofiev's next ballet, *Zolushka* (Cinderella), based on Charles Perrault's fairy tale, was presented at the Bolshoi Theater in 1945. *Cinderella* did not achieve the success of *Romeo and Juliet.* Its musical characterizations are vivid and emotional. However, the fairy tale plot is not as challenging as Shakespeare's drama is, and it leaves the spectator with a sensation of pleasure rather than with a feeling of a deep emotional experience.

Prokofiev's last ballet was *Skaz o Kamennom Tsvetke* (The Tale of the Stone Flower). It was presented at the Bolshoi Theater in 1954. It is the only ballet of Prokofiev's Soviet period of creativity which is based on a Russian subject. The libretto is a story of the miner Danilo, and the courage and loyalty of his bride Katerina.

The hero of the ballet is Danilo, who is an apprentice to a stone carver, Prokopyich. Danilo personifies a national artist, who seeks perfection in art and who would like to create a malachite bowl of unsurpassed beauty. Danilo departs to the realm of the Mistress of the Copper Mountain to see a magic stone flower which, according to a story told by old-timers, contains the essence of beauty.

A long time passes, and there is no news from Danilo. He has disappeared in the palace of the Mistress. His bride, Katerina, patiently waits for him. She is the personification of honesty, courage, and loyalty. With fortitude Katerina overcomes loneliness and need, and rejects the insolent advances of the shopkeeper Severyan. In the end, the Mistress of the Copper Mountain rescues Katerina from Severyan's persecution by putting the hated shopkeeper to death. With the help of a girl who knows magic, Katerina penetrates the realm of the Mistress and rescues Danilo from captivity.

The drama of the ballet is based on two contrasting representations. On one side are the workers engaged in fruitful labor for the good of the people; on the other side are the cruel proprietors and their underlings who try to hinder free and inspired creativity.

The musical characterizations of personages in *The Tale of the Stone Flower* continue Prokofiev's realistic representations in *Romeo and Juliet*. The coarseness and inhumanity of Severyan are musically described by acerbic timbres, accented dissonances, and clattering basses. Severyan's leading motives, intonations, and the dances in which he participates characterize his boldness and bravery. Severyan appears as a national heroic type, rather than as a personification of evil power. The proprietor is characterized by deliberately grotesque and dissonantal devices which seem to accentuate his cruelty. The Mistress of the Copper Mountain personifies the power of nature. She is a friend of workers, helps honest people, and punishes evil, covetous people. At the same time, her feminine charm is irresistible, and one must possess exceptional will power to resist her seductive charms. Danilo successfully resists the Mistress' charms and, as a reward, she gives him his freedom and many presents. The melodious leading motive of the Mistress represents the power of nature which inspires man to constructive labor and creativity.

Katerina's themes are delicate and emotionally expressive. Compared to Juliet and Cinderella, Katerina is distinctly Russian, and her music is intonationally Russian in its expression. Danilo's simple and melodic theme reflects the purity and nobility of his intentions.

Khachaturyan's ballets occupy an important place in the Soviet ballet repertoire. His first ballet, *Schastye* (Happiness), presented at the Bolshoi Theater in 1939, was a national musical and choreographic spectacle which portrayed the life of people in Soviet Armenia. The idea of the scenario was that true happiness could be attained by devoted service to one's country and people. The music was a symphonic adaptation of Armenian folk songs, melodies, and dances. The ballet was not very successful. Khachaturyan did not compose a ballet, but music for a ballet. His symphonic conceptions did not always conform to choreographic requirements.

In 1941, Khachaturyan adapted much of the music of *Happiness* to a new ballet, *Gayne,* which was first produced on December 3, 1942, in Perm, a city in northeastern European Russia, where the Kirov Theater was evacuated from Leningrad.

The story of *Gayne* takes place at an Armenian collective farm not far from the Turkish border. The ballet shows scenes of life on the farm, cotton picking, and carpet embroidering. The action takes place during the war in June, 1941, and the ballet shows the patriotism of workers on the collective farm. Gayne's personal tragedy is caused by her husband's treacherous activities. Festivities and dances follow the ending of the strife.

The ballet is a musical and choreographic drama of human characters and emotions. The idea of the story is the identity of personal and national happiness. Khachaturyan develops this idea in the music, scenic action, and pantomime.

When the curtain rises, the scene shows peasants picking cotton. While girls dance the "cotton dance," Gayne sits under a poplar tree deep in thought. Her husband, Giko, who has returned from the city, does not want to work on the farm. He is cruel and coarse. When Giko insults Gayne, her brother, Armen, stands up for her. This is the beginning of the drama. At this moment, Kazakov, the commanding officer of the border patrol, arrives on the scene with two soldiers; Giko hides.

After greeting the soldiers, the farmers renew the interrupted celebration. Gayne joins in the dancing. Her encounter with Kazakov has produced a deep impression upon her.

In the evening, Gayne and her girl friends weave a carpet. Ovanes, Gayne's father, and her brother Armen come to the house. Ovanes dances with the girls. Gayne's daughter, Ripsimeli, whose sleep has been interrupted by the dancing, is lulled back to sleep by Gayne's "lullaby dance."

During the night, Giko and three strangers come to the house. Gayne overhears their conspiracy to burn the storehouse in which the cotton has been stored. The angry and furious Gayne rushes after the strangers, but Giko bars her way. After a short struggle, the exhausted Gayne falls to the ground.

The next scene shows a Kurdish camp at daybreak in the mountains of Armenia. Aysha, the daughter of the old shepherd Djamal, and a group of Kurds are sitting near the campfire. With the rising of the sun, Aysha begins to dance. One by one, the Kurds join her in the dance.

Armen arrives on the scene. The musical motives of Aysha and Armen are heard in the dance music. Ishmael, a young Kurd who is jealous of Armen, insists that Aysha leave Armen. Aysha is infuriated by Ishmael's request. Ishmael draws a knife. Aysha throws herself between Armen and Ishmael. Djamal stops the quarrel. He takes the knife away from Ishmael and gives it to Armen to punish Ishmael for violating the sacred law of hospitality. Armen throws away the knife because he wants to be friendly with Ishmael.

The warlike dance of the mountaineers is interrupted by the arrival of three suspicious looking strangers. Armen decides to detain them. The dancing stops. Giko's theme is heard in the orchestra. While Djamal offers food to the strangers, Armen sends two Kurds to alert the border patrol.

The strangers hasten to leave. They were lost in the mountains and they ask Djamal for guides to show them the way. Armen volunteers to guide them. The careful Djamal sends along Ishmael and two shepherds. The suspicious strangers fall upon Armen. During the melee, the border patrol, which has arrived on the scene, recognizes the strangers as saboteurs and arrests them.

The alarm bell is heard and the glow of a fire lights the sky. The storehouse in which the cotton is stored is burning. The patrol and the shepherds rush to help the farmers to put out the fire. Giko, who has managed to elude the patrol, is seen near the burning building. He rushes to the bell to sound the alarm and call for help. Gayne, holding her daughter in her arms, exposes Giko to the crowd. Giko seizes the child and, threatening to kill it, tries to escape. Armen and the patrol arrive on the scene and seize Giko. Giko draws a knife and wounds Gayne.

The finale shows the farmers resting on the shores of Lake Sevan. The collective farm has been rebuilt. Gayne and Kazakov are together again. There follows a series of dances, including the "sword dance," which is probably the best-known dance in the repertoire of the Soviet ballet.

Khachaturyan's music is Caucasian in its melodies, rhythms, and intonations. The musical characterizations of the actors are effective and the dramatic elements are successfully developed. The colorful national scenes are faithful representations of Caucasian scenery.

Khachaturyan's ballet *Spartacus* is a heroic, choreographic drama. The libretto is based on Plutarch's and Appian's accounts of Spartacus.

The revolt of Roman slaves led by Spartacus took place from 73 to 71 B.C. Spartacus was a Thracian captured by Romans and sold into slavery. He was placed in a school for the training of gladiators. Spartacus persuaded other gladiators that it would be better to risk life for freedom rather than to die for the entertainment of Roman spectators. Spartacus and seventy-eight gladiators escaped and took refuge on Mount Vesuvius.

Spartacus and his men were joined by runaway slaves and dissatisfied people. After a few successful clashes with Roman troops, Spartacus' army grew to almost seventy thousand. The insurgents occupied the whole of southern Italy.

Spartacus decided to press towards the Alps and the freedom beyond. The Romans, led by Gaius Cassius, governor of Cisalpine Gaul, and the praetor Gnaeus Manlius were defeated by Spartacus. Instead of attacking Rome, the rebels went to Lucania in southern Italy.

Marcus Licinius Crassus assumed command of Roman troops. He defeated Spartacus in a battle, and Spartacus withdrew towards the straits of Messina, intending to cross into Sicily. Dissension broke out among the insurgents. The Germans and the Gauls left Spartacus and were defeated by the Romans. Spartacus and his army retreated to Calabria. In a battle with the Romans, Spartacus' army was annihilated, and Spartacus died sword in hand. Some of the insurgents who escaped towards the Alps were destroyed by Pompey the Great.

The story of Spartacus represented material for propagandist elements in the Soviet ballet. Marx characterized Spartacus as a "great general, a noble character, a free representative of the proletariat of antiquity." [6] According to Lenin, "Spartacus stirred up a war to defend the enslaved class. Similar wars have been fought in the era of colonial domination whose oppressions still exist." [7]

The scenario of the ballet is propagandistic in its conception. The result is a dramatic ballet which re-creates the heroic image of Spartacus, the emancipatory idea of his revolt, and the spirit of his time. Khachaturyan is "a contemporary artist and humanist who has raised the image of legendary Spartacus as a banner of struggle against colonial oppression." [8]

The ballet is a series of several scenes: (1) the introduction which represents the triumph of Rome, the slave market, and the circus; (2) the gladiators' barracks, the Appian Way, and Crassus' banquet; (3) the tent of Spartacus, and the tent of Crassus; (4) the epilogue, the death of Spartacus.

The acting persons are Spartacus and his wife Phrygia; Crassus and the courtesan, Aegina; slaves and the trainer of gladiators, Batiat; and armed gladiators.

"The music brings a ray of sunshine into this dark kingdom of blood, sweat, corpses, and frenzied crowds. Khachaturyan has introduced the *Dies Irae* into the music of the battle of the *andabatae* (gladiators who fought blindfolded by a helmet). The motive makes the gloom of the battle more convincing." [9] The symphonic bacchanal which accompanies the orgy of Crassus' banquet is a musical representation of Crassus' animal instincts, the depravity of Aegina, and the seduction of the slave Harmodius by Aegina. Then follows a Gaditanian dance (Gaditanus, at present the city of Cadiz in southern Spain, was founded by Phoenicians) of Phoenician priestesses of love.

The music of the gladiators' combat is a realistic description of the fight. The theme of Spartacus is heroic. Musical episodes supply the continuity of the ballet. Despite excessive naturalistic representations of erotic elements, Khachaturyan's music effectively interprets historical scenes of Roman life and the heroic idea of Spartacus' revolt.

On April 4, 1962, the Bolshoi Theater presented a revised version of *Spartacus*. The new version consisted of two acts: (1) the Roman triumph, the slave market, the circus, night in Rome, and the barracks of the gladiators; (2) festival at Crassus' villa, and the death of Spartacus.

Other significant Soviet ballets are Kara Karayev's *Sem Krasavits* (Seven Beauties, 1952), and *Tropoyu Groma* (The Path of Thunder, 1957). Karayev is an Azerbaijan composer. The libretto of *Seven Beauties* is based on a poem by the Azerbaijan-Iranian poet, Nizami Ganjevi. The story describes the life of the Azerbaijan people. Karayev has used Azerbaijan folk songs, rhythms, and dance genres. The main characters are Ayesha, a gentle girl in love with the young Shah Bahram, whose power makes him a tyrant; a villainous Vizier and his entourage.

The pleasure-seeking Bahram is entertained by dances of the seven beauties (Indian, Byzantine, Khwarezm, Slav, Maghrib, Chinese, and Iranian), including the "Adagio of the Most Beautiful," the "Dance of the Maghrib Beauty," and "The Dance of the Courtesans."

Other dances describe scenes from popular life; for example, the "Dance-Game of Ayesha and Menzer," the "Dance with the Horn," and the "Dance-Wrestling Match of Menzer and Bahram." In a "Sorrow Dance," the women express their grief for the ruined harvest.

The Path of Thunder, based on a novel by Peter Abrahams, describes racial problems in South Africa. It is a story of the tragic love of a colored youth, Lanny, for a white girl, Sarie. Sarie, who is a village school teacher, meets Lanny and they fall in love. White South Africans, who are Lanny's enemies, try to separate the lovers.

The ballet is propagandistic. The South Africans are characterized by acerbic harmonies and grotesque intonations. The dramatic and lyrical dances reveal the love of Lanny and Sarie. The music of the ballet contains elements of South African folklore.

Alexei Machavariani, a Georgian composer, composed a ballet *Othello* based on Shakespeare's drama. The scenario is interesting because it interprets Othello's character in accordance with Pushkin's statement that "Othello is not jealous by nature; on the contrary, he is trustful."

The scenario of the ballet pictures Othello not as a jealous man, but as a person who has lost faith in truth and justice. Some of the events which are only mentioned in Shakespeare's drama are shown in the ballet as motivations for future actions—for example, Othello's appointment of Cassio as his lieutenant, which arouses Iago's resentment, and Othello's account of his meeting with Desdemona during which he tells her the story of his life are described choreographically in the ballet.

The ballet emphasizes the love of Othello and Desdemona. Othello's happiness is interpreted in a Moorish dance. Machavariani's music reveals elements of Georgian melodies and rhythms. In the development of dramatic elements and of individual characterizations, Machavariani continued Prokofiev's methods of thematic transformations combined with symphonic episodes in order to reveal experiences and emotions of acting persons.

The Soviet ballet has developed along lines different from Western and American ballets. The scenarios of Soviet ballets are dominated by national, heroic, social, and psychological elements, and have a propagandist slant which identifies them with the aims and objectives of Soviet realism.

The evolution of the Soviet ballet will probably continue to stress national and historical characterizations and genres of Soviet life. The propagandist idea of the struggle of "two worlds" will also dominate the Soviet ballet. The music of the ballets will continue to develop musical and intonational elements appropriate to the imagery of Soviet realism.

CHAPTER 29

Soviet Opera

OPERA HAS ALWAYS been popular in Russia. Tchaikovsky believed that the opera gave a composer an opportunity to influence masses of the people. Mussorgsky created in his operas generalized images of masses of the people representing a powerful force in Russian life. Rimsky-Korsakov imbued the Russian fairy tale opera with political allegory.

Soviet composers have recognized the power of operatic forms to influence masses of the people and to portray aspects of Soviet life. Soviet composers aim to develop the ideological content of operas, and thereby convey to the Russian masses Soviet social ideas. However, it is difficult to combine the dynamics of Soviet life and events with traditional schemes of melodic operas. The aim of Soviet composers is to find convincing operatic forms which vividly represent Soviet reality.

During the early 1920's, Soviet operas were adaptations of revolutionary plots to classical operas. For example, Puccini's opera *Tosca* became *Struggle for the Commune;* Meyerbeer's opera *Les Huguenots* became *The Decembrists*. These adaptations had little artistic value, and did not remain long in the operatic repertoire.

New Soviet operas based on revolutionary themes first appeared in the middle 1920's. The first opera based on Soviet ideas was *Za Krasny Petrograd* (For Red Petrograd, 1925), composed by A. Gladkovsky and E. Prussak. The opera, which described the defense of Petrograd against the troops of General Yudenich, lacked dramatic unity and a definite plot, and was soon removed from the operatic repertoire. A more successful opera was *Orliny Bunt* (The Revolt of the Eagle, 1925), composed by A. Pashchenko. The plot of the opera described the revolt of the peasants under the leadership of Emelyan Pugachov in 1773.

During the late 1920's appeared two unsuccessful operas—*Dekabristi* (Decembrists) by V. Zolotaryov, and *Tupeiny Khudozhnik* (The Narrow-Minded Painter) by I. Shishov. Zolotaryov's attempt to present an event from Russian revolutionary past in classical operatic forms failed to arouse the interest of Soviet audiences because classical operatic forms were not suitable for Russian revolutionary music.

Some Soviet composers adopted modern musical idioms used by Western composers. About 1930, V. Deshevov composed an opera *Lyod i Stal* (Ice and Steel), and L. Knipper composed an opera *Severny Veter* (The North Wind). Both dispensed with traditional melodic elements, arias, ensembles, and choruses. This operatic trend was climaxed by Shostakovich's opera *Nos* (The Nose), based on Gogol's story.

The Nose was presented in 1930 at the Maly Opera Theater in Leningrad and met with little success. The part of "the nose" was sung with the singer holding his nose to produce a nasal effect. The orchestra played all kinds of noises; for example, the sound of tramping horses was imitated by kettledrums and a celesta, and the sound of shaving with a razor was imitated by harmonics of double basses. Shostakovich's second opera, *Katerina Izmailova* (Lady Macbeth of Mtsensk District), was severely criticized in an editorial entitled "Confusion Instead of Music" in the newspaper *Pravda* on January 28, 1936.

Some Soviet operas were successful. Their plots, which were not based on purely propagandistic ideas, made it possible for a composer to use classical operatic traditions; for example, Glière's opera *Shakh-Senem* (1924). This opera, composed by Glière for the State Theater in Baku (in the Caucasus), was based on national Azerbaijan melodies and dances. The opera is about the beautiful Shakh-Senem, who is in love with the penniless singer Kerib. Shakh-Senem's father, the rich and cruel Bakhrambek, would have nothing to do with a pauper like Kerib who composes songs about freedom, and would not permit Kerib to marry his daughter. To escape Bakhrambek's anger, Kerib has traveled to distant countries.

Seven years have passed. Kerib hears that Shakh-Senem is being forced to marry the rich Shakh-Veled against her will. Kerib hurries to his beloved on a magic horse. Their love is victorious, and not even the threat of death can prevent their happiness.

The music of *Shakh-Senem* revealed some influences of Balakirev's *Tamara,* of Rimsky-Korsakov's *Scheherazade,* and of Borodin's *Polovetsian Dances.*[1]

Other successful Soviet operas were *Absalom i Eteri* (Absalom and Eteri, 1919), and *Daisi*[2] (Dusk, 1923), composed by the Georgian composer Paliashvili; *Almast* (about 1930), composed by the Armenian composer Spendiarov; and *Ker-Ogli* (1937), composed by the Azerbaijan composer Gadjibekov. *Ker-Ogli* was based on a story about the Ashug (a singer of national melodies) Ker-Ogli, who was the leader of a popular uprising.

Paliashvili's operas are lyrical and emotional, rather than dramatic. The scenarios of *Absalom and Eteri* and of *Daisi* are based on moral and ethical ideas. The operas consist of arias, ensembles, and choruses. The music develops Georgian folk song materials.

While hunting, Absalom, the son of King Abio, meets the beautiful Eteri and falls in love with her. Eteri, a poor orphan maltreated by her stepmother, becomes Absalom's wife.

Eteri's beauty attracts the attention of the courtier, Murman. The jealous Murman poisons Eteri, and the sick girl is carried to his castle. Absalom pines for Eteri, and the separation undermines his health. Eteri returns to her husband, but it is too late. Absalom dies. The despairing Eteri stabs herself with a dagger which Absalom gave her, and dies.

The story of *Daisi* takes place in Georgia in the second half of the eighteenth century. Maro, a beautiful Georgian girl, is being forced to marry the unpopular general Kiazo whom she does not like. Malkhaz, a Georgian youth, loves Maro. Because of their rivalry, Kiazo and Malkhaz hate each other.

Georgia is invaded by cruel enemies, and Georgian soldiers rush to defend the country. Kiazo must leave to join in the fight. However, jealousy and hurt pride overcome Kiazo's sense of duty. He challenges Malkhaz and kills him in a duel. Maro, who has loved Malkhaz, is driven to despair. Dusk has fallen on her life. The remorseful Kiazi joins his countrymen in the defense of the country. He wants to expiate his guilt.

In the 1930's, Soviet composers thought that a new Soviet "song" opera should integrate traditional operatic forms with popular songs and melodies.

The idea was adopted by Tikhon Khrennikov, Ivan Dzerzhinsky, Leon Khoja-Einatov, and later by other composers including Dmitry Kabalevsky, Yuri Shaporin, and Sergei Prokofiev. The stories of the "song" operas dealt with Soviet life and Russian revolutionary past.

Dzerzhinsky's "song" opera *Tikhii Don* (And Quiet Flows the Don), based on Sholokhov's novel, exemplified the new trend. The realism of the opera, combined with popular songs and melodies, set a pattern for the style of a Soviet opera.

The shortcomings of the "song" operas were pointed out by Asafiev.

The healthy trend which we are discussing, though it vigorously champions truth and directness, has proved itself incapable to accomplish the task set before it, and resulted in an oversimplification of the Soviet operatic style. The importance of recitative and its use have been misunderstood. Recitative has become a kind of measured speech common to all characters, or a dry naturalistic report in a matter-of-fact prose characterized by various intervals. The constant use of the march step of popular songs has become the unavoidable scheme of "they said, then marched on singing" of the rousing finales of active scenes. The repetition of this device has turned into a cliché the choral mass expression of heroic emotions, the most valuable contribution of living song to Soviet opera. The art of composing musical ensembles which would represent the peaks of dramatic collisions has been completely lost. Melody, the powerful means of emotional expression and characterization, has been substituted by strophic and fragmentary modern street ditties reminiscent of limericks and sentimental romances. Although this is necessary for a realistic atmosphere, it has led to the degeneration of the aria as an expression of passionate feeling.[3]

Dzerzhinsky's other operas include *Virgin Soil Upturned* (1937), based on Sholokhov's novel; *Thunderstorm* (1940), based on Ostrovsky's drama; *The Volochayevsk Days* (1941); *The Blood of the People* (1941); *Nadezhda Svetlova* (1942); *Prince Lake* (1946); the comic opera *Snowstorm* (1946), based on Pushkin's story; *Far From Moscow* (1954), based on a story by B. Azhayev; and *The Fate of a Man* (1960), based on Sholokhov's story. The operas did not achieve great success because they suffered from fragmentary plots, a scarcity of dramatic situations, and from scanty musical characterizations.

One of the popular Soviet "song" operas is Khrennikov's *V Buryu* (In the Storm), based on N. Virta's novel *Odinochestvo* (Loneliness). The opera was first staged at the Stanislavsky and Nemirovich-Danchenko Theater in 1939, and still remains in the Soviet operatic repertoire. The plot of the opera is a story of class struggle in a village in the Tambov Region during the Russian Civil War (1920–1921) and the counterrevolutionary rebellion headed by Ataman Antonov. The opera is a good example of Soviet realism.

The main characters are Ataman Antonov; Natasha, the daughter of Frol Bayev; Frol Bayev, a peasant who is a "seeker of truth"; Lyonka and Listrat, the sons of a poor peasant woman, Aksinya; the kulak Storozhev; Andrei, a friend of Bayev. The action takes place in the village of Dvoriki in the Tambov Region.

The essence of the story is the regeneration of Frol Bayev who realizes his mistake in supporting Antonov. Bayev reaches the conclusion that "the truth" can be found only in Soviet ideals.

The story begins as Antonov's bands approach the village of Dvoriki. Communist partisans, led by Listrat, assemble near the village council. Chirikin, a partisan, brings to Listrat instructions from the regional party headquarters to defend an important railroad station through which trains pass with grain for Moscow and Petrograd. Listrat sees Natasha, who seems to be worried. He knows that she is in love with Lyonka, whom she has not seen for a long time. Listrat consoles Natasha.

The villagers are divided in their loyalties. Frol declares that the villagers should find out from Antonov his reasons for fighting. Listrat tries to convince Frol that the Bolsheviks are right, but Frol does not believe him. Lyonka, who works for Storozhev, comes to say good-bye to Listrat. Storozhev gloats over the departure of the partisans from the village.

Lyonka asks Frol's permission to marry Natasha. Frol rebukes Lyonka and tells him that he will not have him for a son-in-law. Natasha meets Lyonka and tells him that although she loves him she cannot reconcile herself to the thought of marrying a poor laborer who works for Storozhev.

Meanwhile, someone has sounded the alarm. Antonov and his soldiers have entered the village. Frol presents Antonov with an offering of bread and salt.

The scene changes to Aksinya's cottage. She is worried because her sons are fighting on opposite sides. Lyonka has joined Antonov's band. Suddenly Listrat enters the cottage. He had come to the village on a reconnaissance mission and decided to visit his mother. During the happy reunion of Listrat and Aksinya, Lyonka arrives on the scene and points his revolver at Listrat. Listrat, who has retained his composure, tells Lyonka to put away the gun. Aksinya tries to make peace between her sons. Listrat understands that Storozhev deceived Lyonka into joining Antonov's band. He tries to point out to Lyonka his mistake, but Lyonka refuses to listen. The conversation changes and Lyonka tells Aksinya that he came to ask her advice: he is going to get married. Aksinya embraces Lyonka. The brothers are friends again, and Listrat tells Lyonka: "Get married, get married, perhaps the war will end soon and we shall build life again."

The tramping of horses is heard. Aksinya opens the door and recognizes Storozhev leading a mounted band of rebels. Storozhev enters the cottage and looks for Listrat. He fails to find Listrat, who had hidden himself in a haystack. Lyonka's insulting remarks infuriate Storozhev and he whips Lyonka. Storozhev's lashing has changed Lyonka's feelings; and, after Storozhev's departure, he leaves with Listrat to rejoin the partisans.

Antonov's arbitrary rule antagonizes the villagers. Frol, accompanied by the villagers, comes to complain to Antonov. When Antonov orders Frol flogged, Natasha seizes a rifle and threatens Antonov. Surprised by Natasha's action, Antonov releases Frol.

Frol is shocked by the turn of events. He begins to realize his mistake, and he understands that he was deceived by Antonov and Storozhev. The bodies of dead partisans are brought into the village. The peasants curse Antonov for the bloodshed. Frol, accompanied by his friend Andrei, departs for Moscow "to seek the truth," to see Lenin.

Frol and Andrei arrive in the Kremlin. In Lenin's reception room they meet Listrat, who has arrived with a delegation of Tambov Bolsheviks to attend the tenth party congress. Listrat puts Frol and Andrei at ease, and tells them of the victories of the Red Army. After a conference with Lenin, Frol and Andrei return to Dvoriki.

Upon arrival Frol tells the villagers of his visit to Lenin. The villagers listen with rapt attention. Among them is Natasha with her baby in her arms. Frol shows the villagers the message he brought from Moscow. The message bears Lenin's signature.

Frol and Andrei are going to visit other villages and show Lenin's message. On the edge of the forest they are seized by Antonov's men. Storozhev demands from Frol the "Kremlin papers." Frol refuses to part with it. He is beaten unmercifully, but he tells his tormentors: "You may kill me, but you will not kill the truth." Storozhev kills Frol.

Antonov and his bands are defeated. Storozhev is captured and put under guard in a shed. Listrat and Chirikin arrive to interrogate Storozhev, but he refuses to answer their questions. Chirikin casually mentions that Antonov's sweetheart, Kosova, has confessed. Listrat leaves a lantern and a paper and suggests to Storozhev that he write a confession. Everyone leaves, with the exception of Lyonka and Natasha.

Storozhev knocks on the door of the shed and asks Lyonka to light the lantern. Lyonka unlocks the door and enters the shed. While Lyonka bends over the lantern to light it, Storozhev throws himself upon Lyonka. In the ensuing struggle, Storozhev seizes Lyonka's knife and plunges it in Lyonka's back. Storozhev escapes in the darkness.

Natasha enters the shed and sees Lyonka lying wounded on the floor. Lyonka tells her to sound the alarm, but Natasha takes Lyonka's rifle and rushes after Storozhev. It is dawn. Suddenly two rifle shots are heard from the direction of the ravine. The alarm is sounded, and Listrat with a mounted detachment rush to block the roads to the forest. Natasha returns and runs to Lyonka. Chirikin announces that Natasha has killed Storozhev. A chorus of thanks concludes the opera.

The ideological content of the opera and the popular song elements of the music satisfy the demands of Soviet realism. However, the lyrical scenes between Lyonka and Natasha are melodramatic, especially in the fourth scene of the third act in which Natasha's hysterical fit is reminiscent of the Mad Scene in Donizetti's *Lucia di Lammermoor*. Frol, as a peasant patriot fearless in the face of death, is reminiscent of Glinka's Ivan Susanin.

Khrennikov's "song" opera *Mat* (Mother) based on Maxim Gorky's novel, was composed for the fortieth anniversary of the October Revolution (1957). The melodies of the opera are derived from popular urban songs. Khrennikov uses extensively revolutionary songs; for example, in a demonstration scene workers sing the "Marseillaise," "Varshavyanka," and "Comrades, The Bugles Are Calling." The characterizations of the heroes and their monologues are in line with the propagandistic concepts of Soviet realism.

In the late 1930's, Prokofiev became interested in Soviet opera and in the next few years composed several operas: *Semyon Kotko* (1939), based on V. Katayev's story "I am the Son of Working People"; *The Duenna* (1940), based on Richard Sheridan's play; *War and Peace* (1946, 1952), based on Tolstoy's novel; and *The Story of a Real Man* (1948), based on B. Polevoy's story.

Prokofiev rejected traditional operatic forms because he believed that contemporary opera should portray the heroes as they are in life. According to Prokofiev, songs, not arias and polyphonic ensembles are practiced in daily life. Therefore, traditional arias and polyphonic ensembles have no place in contemporary operas.

Prokofiev realized the difficulties of composing a Soviet opera. "It is one thing to sing operatic arias about heroes of past centuries, people who wore wigs, velvet breeches, and pumps with buckles. In this case, operatic conventions do not present particular difficulties for a composer. However, when a composer wishes to describe in an opera a contemporary hero, a man who speaks the contemporary language and who might use a telephone, it is very easy to slip in the representation of an operatic scene and to err against artistic truth." [4]

Prokofiev found a subject for a Soviet opera in V. Katayev's story "I am the Son of Working People," which was published in 1937. The romantic story of Semyon Kotko, the hero of the story, appealed to Prokofiev.

However, Prokofiev and Katayev disagreed about the operatic plot. Katayev wanted a Ukrainian popular opera with arias, songs, and dances. Prokofiev rejected the plan and proposed a declamatory opera based on spoken prose and with a minimum of arias. Prokofiev's plan prevailed, and Katayev wrote the libretto.

The plot of the opera is the theme of "two worlds." Semyon Kotko, a young Ukrainian peasant, returns to his village after the First World War. He is in love with Sofya Tkachenko, the daughter of a rich peasant, and wants to marry her and settle down to a peasant's life. The chairman of the village council, Remenyuk, and a sailor, Tsaryov, are willing to act as matchmakers.

However, German soldiers are still roaming the countryside. A detachment of German soldiers comes to the village. The Germans kill Tsarov. Tkachenko instigates the Germans to burn Semyon Kotko's cottage. Semyon and Remenyuk escape and join the partisans. They return to the village and, after saving Sofya, who is being forced by her father to marry a rich landlord, Klembovsky, they rejoin the partisans to fight for a better life.

Prokofiev's music characterizes the heroes and the situations. Prokofiev was unconcerned whether his music would sound strange and unfamiliar to an opera audience. His declamatory methods, while complicating the scenic aspects of the opera, enhanced their esthetic values.

"In *Semyon Kotko,* Prokofiev, with the power of conviction inherent in his great talent, followed his favorite path of 'esthetic influxes' in vocalizations and instrumentally exalted textures. He achieved, if not victory, an expressionistically stunning success." [5]

Prokofiev's method of recitatives and symphonic developments influenced other Soviet operatic composers who dealt with similar subjects; for example, Kabalevsky in his operas *In Flames* and *The Taras Family*.

Prokofiev's opera *Betrothal in a Nunnery* was based on a play by the English playwright Richard Sheridan (1751–1816). Because of the war, the opera was first produced on November 3, 1946, by the Kirov Opera and Ballet Theater in Leningrad.

Fascinated by the lively plot of Sheridan's *The Duenna,* Prokofiev tried to express in music the lyrical elements of the heroes, disregarding sarcastic and comic aspects. "I thought I shall not make a mistake by stressing the lyricism of *The Duenna,* rather than exaggerating the comic elements." [6]

Prokofiev's *Duenna* has turned out a successful opera buffa with its traditional characters: a querulous father; an old man fooled by a clever soubrette; an old maid looking for a rich fiancé; and two young couples who get married after overcoming many obstacles. The comic elements of Sheridan's play blended perfectly with Prokofiev's optimistic and effervescent musical style.

The plot of the opera brings to mind the buffa operas of the eighteenth century. A Sevillian nobleman, Don Jerome, wants his daughter, Louise, to marry a rich fishmonger, Mendoza. Louise, who is in love with Antonio, refuses to marry Mendoza.

Louise's nurse upsets the plans of Jerome and Mendoza. By clever intrigues, the nurse brings about the marriage of Mendoza to an elderly duenna whom Mendoza has mistaken for Louise. Louise, having falsely obtained her father's consent, marries Antonio. Her brother, Ferdinand, marries the beautiful Clara d'Almanza.

Humorous scenes in the opera alternate with lyrical and romantic episodes. As a musical satire, the opera ridicules the voluptuous Mendoza and the greedy Jerome. Jerome's vocal part in the opera is mainly declamatory, with a somewhat derisive and grotesque orchestral accompaniment.

Jerome is not as repulsive as Mendoza. He is ridiculous in his constant grumbling and senile irritability. Louise resembles the pretty coquettish heroines of Mozart's and Rossini's operas.

The declamatory elements of the music have probably been influenced by the styles of Dargomijsky and Mussorgsky. The declamations reveal a variety of intonational aspects of human speech: passionate outpourings, emotional exclamations, excitement, gibes, and irony. Each character is delineated by individual intonational characteristics: the trickery and courage of Louise; the modesty of Clara; the mockery of Ferdinand; and the ardor of Antonio.

Declamatory episodes are alternated with vocal episodes; for example, Antonio's serenade in the first scene, the arioso of Clara and Jerome, and the lyrical quartet in the finale of the fifth scene. Orchestral accompaniments with their rhythmical dance genres lend spontaneity to the appeal of the opera.

While rejecting classical operatic forms, Prokofiev also disapproved of traditional methods of writing operatic librettos. His Soviet operatic librettos were written in prose adopted from literary sources. This principle Prokofiev followed in his first operatic version of *War and Peace* (1941–1942). The libretto meticulously followed Tolstoy's text. The opera avoided complete vocal forms. Dialogues and recitatives, accompanied by symphonic music, predominated.

It took Prokofiev ten years to perfect the opera. He limited the function of "musicalized prose," and stressed instead the expressive elements of melodies. The result was an original realistic opera.

Tolstoy's novel does not lend itself easily to operatic forms. It is a psychological drama and an epic heroic narrative. Prokofiev's opera consists of two parts. The first part contains six lyrical scenes which describe Natasha Rostova's love for Andrei Bolkonsky, and her growing interest in Anatole Kuragin; Natasha's clash with Bolkonsky's father, who opposes his son's marriage to Natasha; the ball given by Ellen Bezukhova, and Natasha's passion for Anatole; Anatole's and Dolokhov's plot to abduct Natasha, the failure of the plot, and Natasha's despair.

The first scene of the second part represents the field at Borodino on the eve of the battle with Napoleon's troops; the song of soldiers and volunteers; Andrei's reflections on Natasha's faithlessness; and Kutuzov's review of his troops. The second scene shows Napoleon's headquarters during the battle. The third scene is the Russian military council at Fili during which Kutuzov decides to evacuate Moscow. The fourth scene represents the cottage in Mitishchi where Andrei Bolkonsky lies mortally wounded, and his meeting and reconciliation with Natasha. The epilogue of the opera is a celebration of the Russian victory and a glorification of Kutuzov's wisdom.

The magnitude of Tolstoy's novel precludes a unified operatic presentation. The opera demands a knowledge by a listener of all developments in Tolstoy's novel. Otherwise the impression is of a series of separate musical illustrations of some features of Tolstoy's novel.

Prokofiev's *War and Peace* lacks a central musical-dramatic idea. It seems like an opera of Natasha's fate, a "chronicle of events," and a representation of popular and patriotic enthusiasms during the war with Napoleon. Love and war follow each other. This is due to the magnitude of Tolstoy's novel in which "war" and "peace" represent a unity. Prokofiev selects aspects of "war" and "peace." He is successful in lyric representations of Andrei and Natasha, but not in representations of Kutuzov and the people. Prokofiev does not portray life in Moscow, on country estates, and in the Rostov-Bolkonsky families. Tolstoy's characters are not mannequins, and interaction between city and country seats described in the novel is not fortuitous, but the essence of life during the period. The opera creates the impression that the action takes place somewhere, but it is not in Moscow, not in a forest, and not at a country estate. The opera is a fanciful expressionist arrangement. . . . Kutuzov does not attain the status of a national leader and hero. Prokofiev did not benefit from the drama. The music describes objective episodes and emotional states in colorful lyricism and in contemporary tense, expressive, laconic dynamics. Occasionally, popular epic scenes of masses of people serve as footnotes for action. The crux of the matter is not the success or failure of representations, but the lack of unified dramatic action, and the absence of a central idea in the opera.[7]

The opera, despite its scenic and dramatic imperfections, successfully reveals psychological and historical aspects of Tolstoy's novel. The scene of Andrei dying in a peasant cottage in Mitishchi and his reconciliation with Natasha is probably Prokofiev's greatest operatic achievement.

Prokofiev's adaptation of Dargomijsky's and Mussorgsky's ideas of intonational, musicalized speech, and his symphonic methods are reminiscent of Wagner's methods. The symphonic accompaniment continuously "comments" on the imagery of vocal declamations and enhances the emotional significance of the action on the stage. Prokofiev uses leading motives which, in various transformations and combinations, unify the dramatic and musical elements of the opera and the emotional experiences of the heroes.

A variety of dance genres, including a polonaise, march, waltzes, and mazurkas, and choral episodes (the singing of people's guardsmen and the people's chorus in the finale) enhance the realism of the opera.

Prokofiev's last opera, *Povest o Nastoyashchem Cheloveke* (The Story of a Real Man, 1947–1948), was performed at a preview by the Kirov Opera and Ballet Theater in Leningrad on December 3, 1948. Its first official presentation took place at the Bolshoi Theater in Moscow in October, 1960. The opera met with adverse criticism by Soviet critics.

The opera is based on a story by the Soviet writer B. Polevoy. It describes the life of plain Soviet people during the Second World War. Although the music of the opera uses authentic Russian songs, folk songs, and simple tonal textures, it was criticized for its naturalistic details and conventional descriptions of morals and manners.[8]

Kabalevsky's opera, *Kola Bryunyon, Master iz Klamsi* (Colas Breugnon, Master of Clameci, 1937) is based on Romain Rolland's story. It portrays an artist who asserts his right to create without interference of the feudal lord. The opera is a series of lyrical episodes with charming folk song reminiscences.

The first act shows the inhabitants of Clameci enjoying a happy, joyous existence. The arrival of the duke brings misfortune and destruction. The interlude which precedes the second scene describes a national holiday accompanied by dances and revelry of the inhabitants. The second half of the second act shows the disaster which has overwhelmed the inhabitants of Clameci. The plague brought by the duke's soldiers has decimated the population, and fire has consumed the city. The interlude before the fourth scene describes the calamity which leads to a popular uprising. The interlude to the sixth scene is a call to insurrection.

The overture of the opera is one of Kabalevsky's best symphonic compositions. The colorful and impetuous music evokes an image of Colas as a good-natured, mocking Gaul, characterized by Romain Rolland as "active, heroic, intoxicated with reason."

In the introduction to the first edition of *Colas Breugnon*, Romain Rolland called the novel a book "without politics and without metaphysics." However, the words of Colas belie the political neutrality of Romain Roland: "Who will explain to me the need for existence of all these brutes, aristocrats, politicians, feudal lords, and gnawers of our France? While singing her praises, they rob her in every corner, and, encroaching upon our silver, they cast their eyes on neighbors' property . . . and are ready to swallow half of the land, but they do not even know how to plant a cabbage! Enough, my friend, calm down, it does not pay to become excited. All is well as it is . . . until we shall improve it (and this we shall do at the first opportunity)."

Kabalevsky's second opera, *Pod Moskvoy* or *V Ogne* (In Flames, 1942), is composed in a heroic and patriotic style. The opera describes popular enthusiasm and selflessness of partisans during the defense of Moscow in the Second World War. However, "the listener's perception of the opera is complicated by the composer's attempt to give a detailed account of every episode in accordance with the rules of musical form as taught at schools. The flexibility of musical dramaturgy is not in a succession of fast and slow tempos and in planned modulations, but in the use of any form and musical element in order to hold and guide the listener's attention. Kabalevsky, afraid to lose the status of a professional musician, tires the audience, which looks rather than listens, with the knowledge of a serious, learned musician. This should not be construed as a criticism of profound school teaching, but as a thrust at a master of dynamics of a musical-dramatic style.[9]

The Taras Family (1947–1950) is based on B. Gorbatov's story, "Nepokoryonniye" (The Unvanquished), published in *Pravda* in 1942. Gorbatov describes the struggle of workers in the Donets Basin with German invaders. However, the libretto of the opera transferred the action to central Russia because Kabalevsky wanted to compose a Russian, not a Ukrainian, opera.[10] The opera is a good example of Soviet realism.

Fascist bands are approaching the workmen's settlement in which lives the family of Taras Yatsenko. Taras' oldest son, Stepan, leaves to direct a group of partisans. The youngest son, Andrei, leaves with the Soviet Army. Only Taras, his wife Yefrosinya, Andrei's wife Antonina, and Taras' daughter, Natasha, remain in the family cottage.

The sky is lit by glows of fires. The thunder of artillery is heard in the distance. Consumed with hatred of the enemy, Taras seeks shelter in his home. He is worried about his daughter, who has joined the partisans. Contempt and pity fill Taras when he learns of the faintheartedness of Andrei who has surrendered to the enemy and then escaped. Taras condemns his son: "You did not have the conscience to die? You have struck yourself out of your life, and I have cut you out of my heart."

The factory in which Taras has worked for twenty years has been destroyed by the workers. The invaders drive the old workers to the ruins of the factory and order them to repair damaged tanks. The threats of the Fascists fail to compel the workers to work for them. Taras tells the Fascists: "You threaten us with death? Your words are meaningless. Those who are moved by intense anger will never be afraid. Should we die, our sons shall remain. Alive you shall not leave our country!"

The culmination of the opera is the scene in which the captured Natasha is threatened by the Fascists. To their threats, Natasha replies: "I'll tell you nothing. We are not afraid. There is no death. It is all up with cowards, but for heroes there is immortality." Natasha, who gave her life for the motherland, is the heroine of the opera. The images of Taras and Stepan are less active.

In *The Taras Family*, Kabalevsky uses intonational elements of a recitative-declamatory style, and a system of leading motives which symbolize the ideological concepts of the opera. The motive of Taras consists of ascending intonations. It is declamatory and oratorical, and it seems to express Taras' determination not to submit to the invaders. The Komsomol members of the underground are characterized by a lyrical melody. The Fascist invaders are described by a dull, descending orchestral melody. Throughout the opera, the themes are transformed to describe changing situations of the plot.

Nikita Vershinin, produced at the Bolshoi Theater in Moscow in 1955, is a less significant opera than *The Taras Family.* The plot of the opera, based on V. Ivanov's play *Armoured Train 14-69* (1955), deals with events of the Russian Civil War. The music includes peasant and revolutionary songs. Choruses and melodies of the opera are composed in the style of Russian folk songs.

Kabalevsky's operas *In Flames, The Taras Family, Nikita Vershinin,* and Khrennikov's opera *In the Storm* represent a "common sense" trend in Soviet opera. These operas embody ethical concepts, simple feelings, and experiences of common people, rather than intellectual refinements, musical abstractions, and symbolisms. Russian opera at the turn of the century, for example Rimsky-Korsakov's *Le Coq d'Or,* embodied a world of fantasy which emotionally was a psychorealistic representation.

The lust of Dodon, the Tsar of a fantastic realm, and the Shemakhanskaya Tsarina represented corrupt Tsarist Russia. Both Dodon and the Shemahanskaya Tsarina are unreal characters, and their feelings are illusions. Soviet opera had to overcome symbolic operatic trends and develop instead representations of the Soviet era. This led Khrennikov and Kabalevsky to revive in Soviet opera ethical concepts, heroic deeds, and sincerity of feelings of Soviet people.[11]

Yuri Shaporin's opera, *Dekabristi* (The Decembrists) is based on a play by Alexei Tolstoy. It deals with the revolutionary uprising against the regime of Tsar Nicholas the First on December 14, 1825. The opera was first performed by the Bolshoi Theater in 1953. Shaporin spent thirty years writing the opera. The style of the opera continues the Russian classical traditions of Borodin and Mussorgsky. Shaporin's music evokes the atmosphere of the period. Despite its adherence to nineteenth century Russian operatic traditions, the opera is an outstanding contribution to Soviet opera.

A Soviet opera which has achieved success is Konstantin Dankevich's opera *Bogdan Chmielnicki* (1951). Chmielnicki (1593–1657) was hetman of the Cossacks in the Ukraine. The persecution of a neighboring Polish nobleman who robbed Chmielnicki's estate and flogged his son to death led Chmielnicki to lead a Cossack revolt against the Poles. In Dankevich's opera, Chmielnicki is portrayed as a national hero who effected in 1654 the union of the Ukraine with Russia.

Other Soviet operas are Alexander Kasyanov's *Stepan Razin* and *Yermak;* Vissarion Shebalin's *Taming of the Shrew,* based on Shakespeare's play and produced in 1957; and Yuli Meitus' *Molodaya Gvardia* (The Young Guards), produced in 1950.

Razin was a sixteenth century adventurer. Some of his exploits have been perpetuated in Russian folk songs. Yermak was a leader of Razin's followers who settled on Stroganov's estate in Perm, in northeastern Russia. In 1580, Yermak and his followers crossed the Ural Mountains into Siberia and subdued the Mongol khans. The scenario of *Young Guards* is based on a novel by A. Fadeyev. It deals with the fight of an underground Young Communist organization in the town of Krasnodon during the Second World War.

Soviet operatic composers subordinate their music to the needs of the Soviet State. A Soviet composer may develop an individual style. However, artistic freedom of Soviet composers is merely creative participation in the dialectics of Communist necessity, and not the freedom of expression of personal ideas and emotions.

A controversial development of Soviet opera was Vano Muradeli's opera *Velikaya Druzhba* (Great Friendship), which was produced at the Bolshoi Theater in 1947.

The formalist elements of Muradeli's opera were criticized in a resolution adopted on February 10, 1948, by the Central Committee of the Communist Party. The resolution, which was entitled "About Muradeli's opera *Great Friendship,*" censured formalist tendencies in Soviet music to enjoy the artistic form alone, independently of its content, and called upon Soviet composers to master the principles of Soviet realism and "to become imbued with a realization of the lofty aims of musical creativity which the Soviet people demand; to reject all that enervates our music and impedes its development; to ensure enthusiasm about creative activity and the rapid growth of Soviet musical culture; and to stimulate the creation in every phase of musical composition of works worthy of the Soviet people." [12]

On May 28, 1958, the Central Committee adopted a resolution "which corrected the mistakes in the evaluation of the operas *Great*

Friendship, Bogdan Chmielnicki, and *Out of the Fullness of the Heart*
(G. Zhukovsky's opera *Ot Vsevo Serdtza*), in the resolution passed in
1948; the 1958 resolution restored justice and liquidated the abnormal situation which prevailed during the period of the cult of Stalin's
personality; conditions became more favorable for creative experi-
mentation and the search of expressive means which would enhance
realistic music." [13]

The first edition of Dankevich's opera *Bogdan Chmielnicki* (1951)
was criticized by Soviet music critics for the inadequate representation
of "the basic social-historical conflict" between the Ukraine and
Poland; the insufficient development of leading motives; the excess of
climaxes; and the poor description of the enemies. The revised edition
of the opera included a prologue and scenes which represented
Chmielnicki's troops capturing the Polish nobleman's castle; the
suffering of the Ukrainians oppressed by the Polish invaders; and the
struggle of the Ukrainians against the invaders. [14]

The dogmatic idea of a single style and creative manner of Soviet
operas has been discarded by the Communist party. [15] The party has
recognized that Soviet realism admits the existence of various musical
styles which are determined by the creative individualities of Soviet
composers. However, the party demands "a relentless struggle against
revisionist theories because they mean the repudiation of Communist
ideology and a change-over to reactionary modern esthetics." [16]

The Communist party will not tolerate divisive national trends in
Soviet culture. According to Communist philosophy, national trends
represent the idealization of the "reactionary past," and the attempt to
exaggerate the importance of national traditions which are incompatible with the common interests of Soviet peoples. Although the party
does not deny the significance of national elements in Soviet artistic
culture (national peculiarities of music, for example, of Russian
themes or of oriental melodies), the ideological and esthetic principles of Soviet realism are regarded by the party as being more important. It is safe to predict that the opposition of the musical and esthetic
principles of Soviet realism to the "cosmopolitanism" of modern
Western music will continue unchanged. Exotic "barbaric" rhythms,
acerbic polytonal harmonies, garish timbres, archaic melodies, and
objective atonal constructions will be kept out of Soviet opera and
music.

In contemporary Soviet opera, historical themes of struggle against feudal oppression and of emancipation movements still engage the attention of Soviet composers. Scenarios which deal with postwar Soviet life also interest Soviet composers. It is difficult to compose Soviet realistic operas because operas based on scenarios which describe the peaceful life and labor of Soviet workers do not contain the exciting elements and dramatic conflicts of war scenarios.

The absence of social and political conflicts in scenarios of Soviet operas is regarded as a serious defect by the Communist party. Moreover, the absence of these conflicts in operatic plots might result in systematic arrangements of operatic forms. In his operas, *In the Storm* and *Mother,* which set an example of propagandistic ideas of Soviet realism, Khrennikov sought to overcome systematic arrangements of elements of operatic form by the introduction and development of lyrical peasant elements and of speech and song intonations which expressed feelings, dramatic conflicts, and heroism. Khrennikov tried to accomplish this "without troublesome displays of clumsy technicalities." [17]

Soviet composers try to create new operatic forms which will be compatible with the ideological content of Soviet scenarios. The experiments aim to invent operatic forms which will control and guide the attention of an audience to the ideological meaning of the plot. The search is for musical form as dynamic expression of patterns of Soviet social, ethical, and political ideas, and of the life and psychological experiences of Soviet workers. It is not an easy problem to solve.[18] Musical form is not amenable to dialectics of Communist necessity. However, whatever new operatic forms will be developed by Soviet composers, their main purpose will be to carry out the ideological and educational objectives of the Communist party.

Notes

CHAPTER 1

1. J. Keldysh, *Istoriya Russkoy Muziki* (History of Russian Music). Moscow, 1948, p. 41.
The *Gusli* was an ancient Slavic string instrument played by plucking metal strings stretched between pegs across a wooden board. The organ was used in Byzantium. Historical sources do not mention the existence of organs at the Kiev court. *Zamra* probably was an Oriental instrument.

2. The word *kalika* is derived from *caliga,* a heavy-soled Roman shoe or sandal worn by the Russian religious wanderers.

3. *Stoglavy* means *sto glav,* that is, one hundred chapters. The rules of the Council were included in one hundred chapters.

4. At present the Leningrad Academic Chorus.

5. Keldysh, *op. cit.,* p. 85.

6. Quoted in *ibid.,* p. 86.

7. "Rus, Rus . . . Why does one aways hear thy sad song which sweeps over thy length and breadth, and from sea to sea? What is in this song? What is it that calls, sobs, and breaks my heart? What are these sounds which kiss so painfully, rush into the soul, and entwine my heart?" Gogol (1809–1852), *Myortviye Dushi* (Dead Souls). Moscow, 1960, p. 316.

8. "Suddenly a score of young peasants burst forth with song. They sang about Mother Volga, valor, and a maiden's beauty. The plaintive melody floated in the air, like a field of rye swaying gently in the wind, and the wanderers were saddened. The song brought tears to a young woman who cried: 'My life is without sunshine; my life is as dark as night; and I am like a tethered swift steed, like a swallow without wings.' " Nekrasov (1821–1878), *Komu Na Rusy Zhit Khorosho?* (Who Lives Well in Russia?). Moscow, 1962, Vol. 2, pp. 309–310.

9. "The first tone was followed by tremulous, drawling tones sounding like a plucked string which vibrates and then comes to rest with a final dying quaver. Gradually, there began to flow a plaintive song, 'There is more than one path across the field.' As he sang, the audience was pervaded by a feeling of tranquility and wonder. I must confess that I have rarely heard a voice so full of passion, power, and sweetness. It sounded like a true, ardent Russian soul and

it aroused my deepest emotions. Turgenev (1818–1883). *Zapiski Okhotnika* (A Huntsman's Diary). Leningrad, 1958, Vol. 2, p. 182.

CHAPTER 2

1. J. Kremlev, *Russkaya Mysl o Muzike* (Russian Thought on Music), Leningrad, 1954, Vol. I, p. 8.
2. T. Livanova, M. Pekelis and T. Popava, *Istoriya Russkoy Musiki* (History of Russian Music), Moscow, 1940, p. 126.

CHAPTER 3

1. J. Kremlev, *Russkaya Mysl o Muzike* (Russian Thought on Music). Leningrad, 1954, p. 8.
2. *Ibid.*

CHAPTER 4

1. "The roots of Tchaikovsky's intonations were in the lyrics of Russian household romances and songs." B. V. Asafiev, *Pamyati, Petra Ilyicha Tchaikovskovo. Izbraniye Trudi.* Moscow, 1954, Vol. 2, p. 32. [In Memory of Peter Ilyich Tchaikovsky. Selected Works.]
2. Nikolai Ogarev (1813–1877), was one of the outstanding political leaders of the Russian emancipation movement, and collaborator of Herzen. Ogarev was an amateur musician who composed several romances based on texts by Lermontov. Three romances, *Clouds, Song of a Goldfish,* and *Speeches with Sense,* were published by Muzgiz, Moscow, in 1943. (V. A. Kiselev. N. P. Ogarev, *Musikant. Voprosy Musikalnovo Znaniya.* Moscow, 1956. Vol. 2, pp. 361–386.)
3. Nekrasov's famous poem *Komu Na Rusy Zhit Khorosho?* (Who Lives Well in Russia?) is a panorama of social, cultural, and political conditions in nineteenth century Russia.
4. Elegiac romances were developed later by Glinka, Borodin, and Tchaikovsky. (Asafiev, *op. cit.,* Vol. 2, p. 84.)
5. *Ibid.,* p. 82.
6. *Ibid.,* p. 43.
7. J. Keldysh. *Istoriya Russkoy Muziki* (History of Russian Music), Moscow, 1948, p. 344.

CHAPTER 5

1. B. V. Asafiev, *Izbraniye Raboti o M. I. Glinke. Ruslan i Ludmila. Izbraniye Trudi.* Moscow, 1952, Vol. 2, p. 190. (M. I. Glinka's Ruslan and Ludmila. Selected Works.)

2. E. Kann-Novikova, *Malenkaya Povest o Mikhaile Glinke*. Moscow, 1964, p. 48. (A Short Story About Mikhail Glinka.)

3. The Cossack Republic of *Zaporozhye* inspired the *Peredvizhnink* Repin to paint his famous painting *Zaporozhye Cossacks Writing Their Reply to the Turkish Sultan* (1891). The *Peredvizhniky* were Russian democratic painters-realists of the second half of the nineteenth century, whose paintings were exhibited in mobile (*peredvizhniye*) art galleries. "Repin carried into the past that which he wished to see in the present. This beautiful, free past he glorifies poetically. The Homeric representations of the Zaporozhye Cossacks in the painting are close to the romantic subject of Gogol's *Taras Bulba*. Repin knew this well, and, probably, was inspired by Gogol." (A. A. Fedorov-Davidov, *Ilya Yefimovich Repin*, Moscow, 1961, p. 124.)

4. Gogol, *Myortviye Dushi* (Dead Souls). Primechaniya (Annotations). Moscow, 1960, p. 551.

CHAPTER 6

1. V. Bogdanov-Berezovsky, *Problemi Estetiki v Musike* [Problems of Esthetics in Music], Leningrad, 1960, pp. 181–182.

2. *Ibid.*, p. 182.

3. A. Solovtzov, *Kniga o Russkoy Opere* [Book on Russian Opera], Moscow, 1960, p. 67.

4. *Ibid.*

5. M. Tchaikovsky, *Zhizn P. I. Tchaikovskovo* [Life of P. I. Tchaikovsky], Moscow, 1962, Vol. 3, p. 284.

6. V. Bogdanov-Berezovsky, *Statyi o Muzike i Sovetskikh Kompozitorakh* [Articles on Music and Soviet Composers], Leningrad, 1960, p. 182.

7. In his *Dvadtsat Pyat Let Russkogo Iskusstva* (*Twenty-Five Years of Russian Art*), Stasov hailed *The Stone Guest* as a great work of art, superior to Wagner's music dramas. "The realism of *The Stone Guest* is 'a new era in music,' the basis of the development of European 'Zukunftmusik.' 'The music of the future' is represented not by Wagner's operas, but by Dargomijsky's *The Stone Guest*" (p. 534).

J. Kremlev, *Russkaya Mysl o Musike*, Leningrad, 1960, Vol. 3, p. 28.

CHAPTER 7

1. A. Groman, D. Zhitomirsky, J. Keldish, M. Pekelis, *Istoriya Russkoy Muziki*. Moscow, 1940. Vol. 2, p. 45. (History of Russian Music.)

2. *Ibid.* p. 45.

3. *Ibid.*, p. 46.

4. *Ibid.*, p. 46.

5. *Ibid.*, p. 47.

6. *Ibid.*, p. 49.

7. Stasov maintained that national aspects are not compatible with musical

lyricism and psychology. J. Kremlev, *Russkaya Mysl o Muzike* (Russian Thought on Music.), Leningrad, 1960, Vol. 3, p. 44).

8. *Ibid.*, p. 28. "Wagner is less an artist, and more a reflecting, inventing, and reasoning head." *Ibid.*, p. 55. "I hate and I cannot stand all these Parsifals, Tannhäusers, Lohengrins and Flying Dutchmen. It is the same stuff and non-sense as Byron's Lara, Corsair, and Zuleika. . . . What was pardonable in his time, is inexcusable in our time. No one understands now the nonsense of Byron's poems, and it is a hundred thousand times more foolish to listen to Wagner's silly nonsense."

9. N. Rimsky-Korsakov, *Letopis Moyei Muzikalnoy Zhizni*, Moscow, 1926, pp. 388–389. (Chronicles of My Musical Life.)

CHAPTER 8

1. V. M. Bogdanov-Berezovsky, *Tvorcheski Oblik S. V. Rachmaninova.* Moscow, 1949, p. 138.

CHAPTER 10

1. A. Groman, D. Zhitomorski, J. Keldysh, M. Pekelis, *Istoriya Russkoy Muziki.* Moscow, 1940. Vol. 2, p. 236. (History of Russian Music.)

CHAPTER 11

1. Stasov's article on Mussorgsky. J. Kremlev. *Russakaya Mysl o Muzike.* Leningrad, 1960, Vol. 3, pp. 33–36.

2. "Love lyrics" did not interest Mussorgsky. *Ibid.*, p. 35.

3. B. V. Asafiev. *Izbraniye Trudi. Intonatsionnaya Kultura Glinki.* Moscow, 1952. Vol. 1, pp. 299–303. (Selected Works. The Intonational Culture of Glinka.)

4. The similarity of Mussorgsky's and Perov's esthetics was analyzed by Stasov in an article published in *Russkaya Starina* (1883, No. 5). J. Kremlev, *Russkaya Mysl o Muzike,* Leningrad, 1960, Vol. 3, pp. 38–40.

5. M. Mussorgsky, *Pisma i Dokumenti* [Letters and Documents], Moscow, 1932, p. 223.

6. *Ibid.*, p. 233.

7. *Ibid.*, pp. 125–126.

8. *Ibid.*, pp. 138–139.

9. *Ibid.*, p. 142.

10. *Ibid.*, p. 145.

11. *Ibid.*, p. 235.

12. V. G. Belinsky, *Works.* Moscow, 1948, Vol. 3, p. 217; J. Kremlev. *Russkaya Mysl o Muzike.* Leningrad, 1954, Vol. 1, p. 12.

CHAPTER 12

1. A. Groman, D. Zhitomirsky, J. Keldysh, M. Pekelis, *Istoriya Russkoy Muziki,* Moscow, 1940, Vol. 2, p. 274. (History of Russian Music.)

2. A comparison of Korsakov's orchestral writing and of Repin's famous painting *Ivan Grozny and His Son Ivan on November 15, 1581* is given by A. A. Fedorov-Davidov in *Ilya Yefimovich Repin.* Moscow, 1961, p. 107: "Repin is a painter, not a philosopher or a sociologist. For Repin, 'philosophizing' in painting was not a development of concepts or abstractions, but an expression of the emotional life of people, and of the feelings they arouse. In this original emotional-representational 'philosophizing,' Repin was helped by the spontaneous emotional quality of music, and by the reflections which it evokes. Such emotional meditations are in Rimsky-Korsakov's poem *Antar* with its themes of love, power, and revenge. The influence of Rimsky-Korsakov's music is in the 'musicality' of the structure of Repin's painting, and in its luxurious colors. The silvery glitter, resembling sparkling fishscales, in the rose tunic of the Tsarevich, the blood on the gaily colored rugs, the red and pink colors, ringing and singing against the dark brown and red background of the interior and of Grozny's garments, make a symphony of colors."

CHAPTER 13

1. N. Rimsky-Korsakov, *Letopis Moyei Muzikalnoy Zhizni,* Moscow, 1926, pp. 119–121. (Chronicle of My Musical Life.)
2. *Ibid.,* p. 139.
3. *Ibid.,* p. 40.
4. Cui's criticism of Rakhmaninov's Symphony in D minor: "If there is a conservatory in hell, the music is especially fit for it." *Molodiye Godi, Sergeya Vasilyevicha Rachmaninova.* Leningrad, 1949, p. 163. This is a good example of Cui's style of criticism. Quoted in J. Kremlev, *Russkaya Mysl o Muzike,* Leningrad, 1960. Vol. 3, p. 128.
5. N. Rimsky-Korsakov, *Letopis Moyei Muzikalnoy Zhizni.* Moscow, 1926, p. 228. (Chronicle of My Musical Life). "Cui belittled Tchaikovsky." Kremlev, pp. 93–102.
6. *Ibid.,* p. 40.
7. *Ibid.,* pp. 110–111.
8. *Ibid.,* pp. 116–117.
9. *Ibid.,* p. 115.

CHAPTER 14

1. Asafiev, *A. G. Rubinstein,* Vol. 2, pp. 201–207.

CHAPTER 15

1. In the newspaper, *Russkiye Vedomosti,* 1872, No. 267.
2. Hanslick's statement was: "The truthfulness of musical expression is a preposterous dream. . . . A musical Idea requires only beauty without any concern for meaning."

3. P. I. Tchaikovsky, *Vospominaniya i Pisma* (Memoirs and Letters), Moscow, 1924, p. 78.

4. J. Kremlev, *Russkaya Mysl o Muzike.* Leningrad, 1960, Vol. 3, p. 221. Tchaikovsky's letter to Madame Von Meck, December 11, 1883.

5. B. V. Asafiev, *Selected Works. Kompositor-Dramaturg Pyotr Ilyich Tchaikovsky,* Moscow, 1954, Vol. 2, pp. 59–62. (Composer-Dramatist Peter Ilyich Tchaikovsky.)

6. J. Kremlev, p. 237. "Tchaikovsky was careful to avoid the boundary where realism would destroy beauty. Hence his admiration for Mozart's music."

7. *Ibid.,* p. 223.

8. J. Kremlev, *Simfonii P. I. Tchaikovskovo,* Moscow, 1955, p. 162.

9. *Ibid.,* 230–232. Tchaikovsky admired Wagner's symphonic technique, but rejected his operas and music dramas.

10. J. Keldysh, *Istoriya Russkoy Muziki* [History of Russian Music]. Moscow, 1954. Vol. 3, p. 271. Article by Myaskowsky: "Tchaikovsky and Beethoven," 1912. Myaskowsky considered Tchaikovsky as the greatest symphonist of the post-Beethovenian era, the equal of Beethoven in influencing masses of people by his music.

11. B. V. Asafiev, *Izbraniye Trudi. Simfonia.* Moscow, 1957. Vol. 5, p. 79. (Selected Works. The Symphony.)

CHAPTER 16

1. Belayev played the viola with the orchestra of the "Petersburg Circle of Music Lovers." N. Zaporozhetz, *A. K. Lyadov.* Moscow, 1954, p. 24.

2. J. Kremlev, *Istoriya Russkoy Muziki.* Moscow, 1954, Vol. 3, p. 109. (History of Russian Music.)

3. M. Gorky, *O Skazkakh* [About Skazkas]. *O Literature* [*On Literature*]. Moscow, 1937, p. 174.

4. D. I. Pokhitonov, *Iz Proshlovo Russkoy Operi.* [From the Past of Russian Opera]. Moscow, 1949, p. 53.

CHAPTER 17

1. S. I. Taneyev, *Podvizhnoy Kontrapunkt Strogavo Pisma* [Imitative Counterpoint], Moscow, 1909, Introduction.

2. P. I. Tchaikovsky, S. I. Taneyev, *Pisma* [Letters], Moscow, 1951, p. 173.

CHAPTER 18

1. V. Stasov, *25 Let Russkovo Iskustva* (Twenty Years of Russian Art), Petersburg, 1894, Vol. 1, p. 696.

CHAPTER 19

1. J. Keldysh, *Istoriya Russkoy Musiki.* Moscow, 1954, Vol. 3, p. 352. (History of Russian Music.)

2. *Ibid.*

3. J. Keldysh, Vol. 3, p. 351.

4. B. V. Asafiev, *Izbraniye Trudi. Rachmaninov.* Moscow, 1954. Vol. 2, p. 311. (Selected Works. Rachmaninov.)

5. J. Keldysh, Vol. 3, p. 350.

6. Asafiev, *Muzikalnaya Forma Kak Protzes* (Musical Form as a Process), Vol. 5, p. 220.

7. Asafiev, Vol. 2, p. 311.

8. A. Solovtzov, *S. V. Rachmaninov.* Moscow, 1955, p. 13.

9. J. Keldysh, Vol. 3, p. 405.

10. *Ibid.*, p. 405.

11. Asafiev, *Rachmaninov*, Vol. 2, p. 306.

12. *Ibid.*, p. 310.

Chapter 20

1. J. Kremlev, *Estetika Prirodi v Tvorchestve N. A. Rimskovo-Korsakova* (The Esthetics of Nature in N. A. Rimsky-Korsakov's Creativity). Moscow, 1962, pp. 46–47.

2. J. Keldysh, *Istoria Russkoy Muziki* (History of Russian Music). Moscow, 1954, Vol. 3, pp. 417–418.

3. A. Alshvang, *Izbraniye Statyi. O Filosofskoy Sisteme A. N. Scriabina*, Moscow, 1959, p. 245. (Selected Articles. About A. N. Scriabin's Philosophy.)

4. J. Keldysh, p. 428. The program notes were authorized by Scriabin.

5. Alshvang, p. 250. Scriabin's notes in *Russkiye Propileyi*, 1919, Vol. 6, p. 177.

6. *Ibid.*, p. 250. Scriabin's notes, p. 178.

7. Alshvang, p. 250. Scriabin's notes, p. 180.

8. J. Keldysh, p. 421.

9. Asafiev, Vol. 5, p. 257.

10. Alshvang, p. 220.

Chapter 21

1. Lenin, *O Kulture i Iskusstve* (About Culture and Art), Moscow, 1957, pp. 519–520.

2. M. Gorky, *O Literature* (About Literature), Moscow, 1955, p. 35.

3. "All-forgiving liberalism of rotten sentimental complacency." (Editorial in *Pravda*, Dec. 3, 1962. Reported in *The New York Times*, Dec. 4, 1962.)

4. "Our people resolutely reject abstractionism which has suddenly begun to be imitated by a few persons who do not care to notice its frankly reactionary and antipopular essence." *Ibid.*

5. J. B. Borev, *Osnovi Kategorii Estetik* (Fundamental Categories of Esthetics). Moscow, 1960, pp. 385–386.

6. "A front-page editorial in *Pravda* demanded that organizations of the party, professional unions, the press, and the public join in fighting uncompro-

misingly against any deviation from the Soviet concept of art as a propaganda vehicle for the Communist party and state." (*The New York Times,* Dec. 4, 1962.)

7. K. Marx and F. Engels, *Ob Iskusstve* (About Art), Moscow, 1937, p. 19.

CHAPTER 22

1. J. B. Borev, *Osnovi Kategorii Estetik* (Fundamental Categories of Esthetics), Moscow, 1960, p. 385.

2. B. Asafiev, *Muzikalnaya Forma Kak Protzess* (Musical Form as a Process), *Izbranniye Trudi* (Selected Works), Moscow, 1957, pp. 153–276.

3. "Socialist art resolvedly and firmly rejects the unjustified imitation by a few of our musicians of low-quality bourgeois musical composers who are ready to make the whole of Soviet music sound like thundering jazz." (Editorial in *Pravda,* Dec. 3, 1962, *The New York Times,* Dec. 4, 1962).

CHAPTER 23

1. B. Asafiev, *Izbranniye Trudi* [Selected Works]. Moscow, 1957, Vol. 5, p. 126.

2. *Ibid.,* pp. 79–81.

3. *Istoriya Sovetskoy Muziki* [History of Soviet Music], Moscow, 1959, Vol. 3, p. 362.

CHAPTER 24

1. T. Bogdanova, *Natsionalno-Russkiye Traditsii v Muzike Prokofieva.* [National Russian Traditions in Prokofiev's Music]. *Sovetsky Kompozitor* [Soviet Composer]. Moscow, 1961, p. 80.

2. *Ibid.,* pp. 80–81.

3. V. Berkov, *Kizucheniyu Sovremyonoi Garmonii.* [Study of Contemporary Harmony]. *Sovetskaya Muzika* (Soviet Music), 1962. No. 4, p. 42.

4. B. Asafiev, *Izbranniye Trudi* [Selected Works]. Moscow, 1957, Vol. 5, p. 110.

5. B. Asafiev, "Nikolai Andreyevich Rimsky-Korsakov," *ibid.,* Vol. 3, 1954, p. 213.

6. I. Nestiev, *Prokofiev.* Moscow, 1957, pp. 496–502.

7. Asafiev, *op. cit.,* Vol. 5, p. 87.

CHAPTER 25

1. A. Alshvang, *Izbranniye Statyi* [Selected Articles]. "Symphonism Bethovena" (Beethoven's Symphonism), Moscow, 1959, pp. 5, 7.

2. B. Asafiev, *Izbranniye Trudi* [Selected Works]. *Symphoniya* [The Symphony], Vol. 5, Moscow, 1957, p. 92.

3. G. Orlov, *Symbonii Shostakovicha* [Symphonies of Shostakovich]. Leningrad, 1961, p. 12. Asafiev's article *Russkaya Symfonicheskaya Muzika* [Russian Symphonic Music].

4. *Ibid. Za 10 Let* in *Muzika i Revolutzia* (Ten Years of Russian Symphonic Music). Published in *Music and Revolution*, 1927, No. 11, p. 28.

5. Orlov, *op. cit.*, p. 10.

6. *Ibid.*, p. 22.

7. *Ibid.*

8. *Ibid.*, p. 44.

9. *Ibid.*, p. 46.

10. *Ibid.*, p. 42.

11. *Pravda*, Editorial, January 28, 1936.

12. Orlov, *op. cit.*, p. 50.

13. *Ibid.*, pp. 52–53.

14. *Ibid.*, pp. 59–60.

15. *Ibid.*, p. 61.

16. *Istoria Russkoy Sovetskoy Muziki 1935–1941* (History of Russian Soviet Music), Moscow, 1951, Vol. 2, p. 389.

17. B. Asafiev, *op. cit.*, Vol. 5, pp. 83–84.

18. *Istoria Russkoy Sovetskoy Muziki*, Vol. 2, p. 416.

19. D. Shostakovich, *Moy Tvorcheski Otvet. Vechernaya Moskva.* [My Creative Answer. Published in *The Moscow Evening* newspaper] January 25, 1938.

20. G. Orlov, *op. cit.*, p. 82.

21. *Ibid.*, p. 78.

22. L. Danilevich, *D. Shostakovich. Sovetsky Kompozitor*, Moscow, 1958, p. 61.

23. Orlov, *op. cit.*, p. 83.

24. The *ländler*, often called the "peasant waltz," originated in Landl, a region on the border of Southern Germany and Austria. The *ländler*, a peasant waltz is danced by Leporello and Masetto in the ball scene in Mozart's opera *Don Juan*.

25. *Istoria Russkoy Sovetskoy Muziki*, Vol. 2, p. 423.

26. *Ibid.*

27. Orlov, *op. cit.*, p. 89.

28. Orlov, *op. cit.*, p. 92.

29. *Ibid.*, p. 93.

30. *Ibid.*, p. 89.

31. *Ibid.*, p. 94.

32. *Istoria Russkoy Sovetskoy Muziki*, Vol. 2, p. 426.

33. *Ibid.*

34. Orlov, *op. cit.*, p. 133.

35. *Ibid.*, p. 137.

36. *Ibid.*, p. 138.

37. Orlov, *op. cit.*, p. 139. Shostakovich's statement in *Pravda*, March 29, 1942.

38. *Ibid.*, p. 182.

39. Danilevich, *op. cit.*, p. 85.

40. Orlov, *op. cit.*, p. 154. Quoted from I. Nestyev's *Put Iskaniy* (The Path of Quest). *"Ob Evoliutszii Tvorchestva D. Shostakovich"* (About the Evolution of Shostakovich's Creativity). *Sovetskaya Muzika,* 1956, No. 11, p. 11.

41. *Ibid.,* p. 156.

42. *Ibid.,* p. 159.

43. *Ibid.,* p. 160.

44. *Ibid.,* p. 161.

45. *Ibid.,* p. 162.

46. *Ibid.,* p. 164.

47. Danilevich, *op. cit.,* p. 90.

48. Orlov, *op. cit.,* p. 171.

49. Danilevich, *op. cit.,* p. 91.

50. Orlov, *op. cit.,* p. 172.

51. Asafiev, *op. cit.,* Vol. 5, p. 80.

52. Orlov, *op. cit.,* p. 177.

53. *Ibid.,* p. 180.

54. I. Martinov, *D. D. Shostakovich.* Moscow, 1946, p. 78.

55. L. Danilevich, *Vosmaya Symfonia D. Shostakovicha* [Shostakovich's Eighth Symphony]. *Sovetskaya Muzika,* 1946, No. 12, p. 64.

56. Orlov, *op. cit.,* p. 187.

57. D. Shostakovich, *Dumi o Proydenom Puti* [Thoughts About the Traversed Path]. *Sovetskaya Muzika,* 1956, No. 9, p. 14.

58. J. Keldysh, *RSFSR. Part Three. Russkaya Sovetskaya Muzika* [Russian Soviet Music]. Moscow, 1958, p. 145.

59. D. Rabinovich, *Dmitry Shostakovich—Composer.* Moscow, 1959, pp. 96–99.

60. Orlov, *op. cit.,* p. 240.

61. I. Nestyev, *Zametki o Tvorchestve D. Shostakovicha* (Neskolko mysley vizvanikh Devyatoy symfoniey. [Remarks about Shostakovich's Creativity. A Few Thoughts Aroused by the *Ninth Symphony*] *Kultura i Zhizn* [Culture and Life], September 30, 1946.

62. Orlov, *op. cit.,* p. 240.

63. Scanty use of Russian national themes and melodies.

64. "Formalist tendencies" in music denote the mechanics of music and musical artisanship, and the dexterity of musical construction independent of content. A "formalist composer" believes that one should only enjoy the variety and complexity of musical constructions, not the content of music. (L. Kulakovsky, *Muzika Kak Iskusstvo* [Music as an Art]. *Sovetsky Kompositor* [Soviet Composer], Moscow, 1960, p. 84.

65. Danilevich, *op. cit.,* p. 116.

66. *Ibid.,* p. 129.

67. Orlov, *op. cit.,* pp. 249–250.

68. J. Kremlev, *O Desyatoy Symfonii D. Shostakovicha* (About Shostakovich's Tenth Symphony). *Sovetskaya Muzika* [Soviet Music], 1957, No. 4, pp. 83–84.

69. L. Danilevich, *op. cit.,* pp. 129–130.

70. L. Danilevich, *Vosmaya Symfonia D. Shostakovicha,* p. 61.
71. Orlov, *op. cit.,* pp. 100, 202.

CHAPTER 26

1. L. Danilevich, *Dmitri Kabalevsky.* Moscow, 1954, p. 21.
2. *Ibid.,* p. 42.
3. *Ibid.*
4. *Ibid.,* p. 29.
5. L. Danilevich, *Kniga o Sovetskoy Muzike* [Book about Soviet Music]. Moscow, 1962, pp. 402–403. Also, see J. Keldysh, *RSFSR. Part Three. Russkaya Sovetskaya Muzika* [Russian Soviet Music]. Moscow, 1958, p. 190.

CHAPTER 27

1. B. Asafiev, *Izbranniye Trudi. Tri Imeni* [Selected Works. Three Names]. Moscow, 1957, Vol. 5, p. 131.
2. Georgi Khubov, *Arama Khachaturyan. Sovetski Kompozitor* [Soviet Composer]. Moscow, 1962, pp. 319–320.
The word *narodnost* has no adequate equivalent in the English language. It is an all-inclusive term of all characteristics of a people's art. The word *narodni* means more than national or popular. The title *narodni artist* conferred on Soviet artists implies that the artist's creativity and work represent the best characteristics of Russian art and culture.
3. Khubov, *op. cit.,* pp. 9–22.

CHAPTER 28

1. French influences in Tchaikovsky's music have been mentioned by Laroche in an article *"Recollections about P. I. Tchaikovsky,"* which was published in the newspaper *Novosti* [The News], No. 323, 1893, and republished in a book *Recollections about P. I. Tchaikovsky,* Moscow, 1962, pp. 17–18. "It has always seemed to me that he (Tchaikovsky) was influenced not so much by snatchy reading of Byron, as by French writers of the 1830's, especially by Alfred de Musset whom he enthusiastically loved. From these Frenchmen, Tchaikovsky adopted the refined mental anguish which was so alien to him in life, but which is so often revealed in his music (*Fatum, Francesca da Rimini, Manfred, Mazeppa, Hamlet, Sixth Symphony*). I always attributed to these influences, and to his love of Lermontov, the reason why he did not like the latest naturalists, especially Zola, whose talent he recognized, but for which he felt a deep aversion. One day, while reading Zola's *L'Assommoir,* Tchaikovsky came across a detail which aroused his indignation, and he tore the book into shreds. Compare this with his love of Mérimée's stories, and of Stendhal's *La Chartreuse de Parme,* and you will get an impression of a romantic who, in the 1870's and 1880's, has retained the tastes of the times of Louis Philippe."

2. L. Danilevich, *Kniga o Sovetskoy Muzike* [Book about Soviet Music]. Moscow, 1962, pp. 94–99.

3. B. Asafiev, *Izbranniye Trudi. Muzika 'Tretievo Sosloviya'* [Selected Works. Music of the 'Third estate']. Moscow, 1957, Vol. 5, pp. 138–140.

4. *Ibid.*, pp. 141–143.

5. *Istoriya Russkoy Sovetskoy Muziki* [History of Russian Soviet Music]. Moscow, 1959, Vol. 2, p. 335.

6. Georgi Khubov, *Aram Khachaturyan. Sovetsky Kompositor* (Soviet Composer), Moscow, 1962, p. 337.

7. *Ibid.*, p. 341.

8. *Ibid.*, p. 342.

9. *Ibid.*, p. 355.

CHAPTER 29

1. L. Danilevich, *Kniga o Sovetskoy Muzike* [Book about Soviet Music]. *Opera Gliera Shakh-Senem* (Glière's Opera *Shakh-Senem*). Moscow, 1962, p. 71.

2. "Sumerki."

3. B. Asafiev, *Izabranniye Trudi. Opera* (Selected Works). Moscow, 1957, Vol. 5, p. 71.

4. I. Nestiev, *Prokofiev*. Moscow, 1957, pp. 323–324. Quoted from *Literaturnaya Gazeta* [Literary Gazette], September 20, 1938.

5. B. Asafiev, *Puti Razvitiya Sovetskoy Muziki* [Paths of Development of Soviet Music]. Moscow, 1957, Vol. 5, p. 55.

6. Nestiev, *op. cit.*, p. 409.

7. Asafiev, *op. cit.*, p. 75.

8. Nestiev, *op. cit.*, p. 424.

9. Asafiev, *op. cit.*, p. 69.

10. Danilevich, *op. cit.*, p. 103.

11. Asafiev, *op. cit.*, pp. 70–71.

12. J. Keldysh, *RSFSR. Part three. Russkaya Sovetskaya Muzika* [Russian Soviet Music]. Moscow, 1958, pp. 151–152.

13. L. Danilevich, *Kniga o Sovetskoy Muzike* [A Book about Soviet Music]. Moscow, 1962, p. 358.

14. *Ibid.*, pp. 289–290.

15. *Ibid.*, p. 318.

16. *Ibid.*, p. 358.

17. Asafiev, *op. cit.*, p. 72.

18. "The search of a musical language in keeping with the era of socialism is a noble, but not an easy, task set for a composer." Prokofiev, *Rastzvet Iskusstva* [The Flowering of Art], pp. 97–98. Quoted by T. Bogdanova in *Natsionalno-russkiye Traditsii v Muzike S. S. Prokofiev* [National-Russian Traditions in the Music of S. S. Prokofiev]. *Sovetsky Kompositor* (Soviet Composer). Moscow, 1961, p. 5.

Bibliography

Alshvang, A. *Selected Articles*. Soviet Composer. Moscow, 1959.

Alshvang, A. *Selected Works in Two Volumes*. Volume 1. Publishing House "Music." Moscow, 1964.

Asafiev, B. *Selected Works*. Volume 1, 1952; 2, 1954; 3, 1954; 4, 1955; 5, 1957. Edition of the Academy of Science USSR. Moscow.

Balabanovich, E. B. *Chekhov and Tchaikovsky*. State Publishing House of Music (Muzgiz). Moscow, 1962.

Barenboim, L. *Anton Grigoryevich Rubinstein*. Volume 1, 1957; 2, 1962. Muzgiz. Leningrad.

Berkov, V. *A Study of Contemporary Harmony*. Soviet Music, 1962.

Bobrovsky, V. *Instrumental Chamber Ensembles of D. Shostakovich*. Soviet Composer. Moscow, 1961.

Bogdanova, T. *National Russian Traditions in Prokofiev's Music*. Russian Composer. Moscow, 1961.

Bogdanov-Berezovsky, V. (Editor), *The Young Years of Rachmaninov*. Muzgiz. Leningrad-Moscow, 1949.

Bogdanov-Berezovsky, V. *Articles About Music and Soviet Composers*. Leningrad, 1960.

Borev, J. B. *Foundations of Categories of Esthetics*, State Publishing House, 1960.

Danilevich, L. *D. Shostakovich*. Soviet Composer. Moscow, 1958.

Danilevich, L. *Dmitri Kabalevsky*. Muzgiz. Moscow, 1962.

Danilevich, L. *A Book About Soviet Music*. Muzgiz. Moscow, 1962.

Fedorov-Davidov, A. *Ilya Yefimovich Repin*. Moscow, 1961.

Gogol, N. V. *Dead Souls*. Academy of Science USSR. Volume 5. Moscow, 1960.

Gogol, N. V. *Short Stories*. Volume 3. State Publishing House of Bélles-Léttres. Moscow, 1952.

History of Russian Soviet Music, 1935–1941. Muzgiz. Volume 2. Moscow, 1959.

History of Russian Soviet Music. Muzgiz. Volume 3. Moscow, 1959.

Kabalevsky, D. *Selected Articles About Music*. Soviet Composer. Moscow, 1963.

Kashkin, N. D. *Selected Articles About P. I. Tchaikovsky*. Muzgiz. Moscow, 1954.

Keldysh, J. *RSFSR (3)*. *Russian Soviet Music*. Moscow, 1958.

Keldysh, J. *History of Russian Music*. Volume 3. Muzgiz. Moscow, 1954.

Khubov, Georgi. *Aram Khachaturyan.* Soviet Composer. Moscow, 1962.

Kremlev, J. *Symphonies of P. I. Tchaikovsky.* Muzgiz. Moscow, 1955.

Kremlev, J. *Russian Thought About Music.* Volume 1, 1954; 2, 1958; 3, 1960. Leningrad.

Kremlev, J. *The Esthetics of Nature in the Art of N. A. Rimsky-Korsakov.* Muzgiz, 1962.

Kulakovsky, D. *Music as an Art.* Soviet Composer. Moscow, 1960.

Lermontov, M. Y. *Complete Works.* Academy. Moscow-Leningrad, 1935–1937.

Livanova, T. *Educational Activities of Russian Classical Composers.* Muzgiz. Moscow-Leningrad, 1951.

Livanova, T; Pekelis, M; Popava, T. *History of Russian Music.* Moscow, 1940.

Lunacharsky, A. V. *In the World of Music. Articles and Speeches.* Moscow, 1958.

Martinov, I. *D. D. Shostakovich.* Muzgiz. Moscow, 1946.

Marx and Engels. *About Art.* Moscow, 1937.

Mnazankova, E. *Prokofiev's Opera Betrothal in a Monastery (Duenna).*

"Music of the Soviet Ballet." *Collected Articles.* Muzgiz, 1962.

Nedoshivin, G. *Essays About Esthetics.* Moscow, 1958.

Nekrasov, N. *Selected Works.* State Publishing House of Belles-Lettres. Volume 2. Moscow, 1962.

Nestyev, I. *Prokofiev.* Muzgiz, 1957.

Orlov, G. *Symphonies of Shostakovich.* Muzgiz. Leningrad, 1961.

Ossovsky, A. *Selected Articles. Recollections.* Soviet Composer. Leningrad, 1961.

Pokhitonov, D. *From the Past of Russian Opera.* Moscow, 1949.

Pushkin, A. S. *Complete Works.* Published by the Academy of Science. Moscow, 1956–1958.

Questions of Musical Knowledge. Volume 2. Moscow, 1956.

Questions of Philosophy. Academy of Science USSR. Institute of Philosophy. 1959, no. 2; 1960, no. 7, no. 10.

Questions of the Theory and Esthetics of Music. Issue no. 3. Publishing House "Music." Moscow-Leningrad, 1964.

Rabinovich, D. *Dmitri Shostakovich—Composer.* Foreign Language Publishing House. Moscow, 1959.

Rimsky-Korsakov, N. *Chronicles of My Musical Life.* Moscow, 1926.

Rizhkin, I. *The Purpose of Music and Its Possibilities.* Muzgiz. Moscow, 1962.

Shakespeare and Music. Publishing House "Music." Leningrad, 1964.

A Short Dictionary of Esthetics. Publishing House of Political Literature. Moscow, 1964.

A Short Dictionary of Philosophy. State Publishing House of Political Literature. Moscow, 1955.

Solertinsky, I. *Historical Studies.* Muzgiz. Leningrad, 1963.

Solertinsky, I. *Critical Essays.* Muzgiz. Leningrad, 1963.

Solovtzov, A. *A Book About Russian Opera.* Publishing House ZK VLKSM Young Guards, 1950.

Stasov, V. *Selected Essays About Music.* Muzgiz. Leningrad-Moscow, 1949.

Taneyev, S. *Imitative Strict Counterpoint.* Moscow, 1909.

Tchaikovsky, P. Taneyev S. *Letters*. State Publishing House of Cultural Education. Moscow, 1951.

Turgenev, I. *Selected Works*. Volume I. Leningrad, 1958. Selected from complete works in twelve volumes, State Publishing House, 1953–1958.

Zaporoxhetz, N. *A. K. Lyadov*. Muzgiz. Moscow, 1954.

Index

Note: The page numbers of the principal reference to a composer are in *italics*.

395